# Too Afraid to Cry

# TOO AFRAID TO CRY

Maryland Civilians in the Antietam Campaign

Kathleen A. Ernst

STACKPOLE
BOOKS

Copyright© 1999 by Stackpole Books

Published by
STACKPOLE BOOKS
5067 Ritter Road
Mechanicsburg PA 17055
www.stackpolebooks.com

*Acknowledgment is made for permission to quote from the following copyrighted works:* Three Years with Company K, *by Austin Stearns, ed. Arthur A. Kent (Cranbury, N.J.: Fairleigh Dickinson University Press, 1976), used by permission of Associated University Presses;* I Rode with Stonewall, *by Henry Kyd Douglas, ed. Fletcher M. Green (Chapel Hill: University of North Carolina Press, 1940), used by permission of the publisher;* The Diary of Jacob Engelbrecht, *ed. William R. Quynn (Frederick, Md.: The Historical Society of Frederick County, Inc., 1976), used by permission of the publisher;* History of the Brethren in Maryland, *by J. Maurice Henry (Elgin, Ill.: Brethren Publishing House, 1936), used by permission of the publisher;* Medical Recollections of the Army of the Potomac; *and* Memoir of Jonathan Letterman, *M.D. by Jonathan Letterman, M.D., (reprint ed. Knoxville: Bohemian Brigade Publishers, 1994), used by permission of the publisher.*

Printed in the United States of America

10 9 8 7 6 5 4 3 2 1

FIRST EDITION

**Library of Congress Cataloging-in-Publication Data**
Ernst, Kathleen, 1959-
    Too afraid to cry: Maryland civilians in the Antietam Campaign/
    Kathleen A. Ernst: foreword by Ted Alexander.—1st ed.
        p.    cm.
    Includes bibliographical references and index.
    ISBN 0-8117-1602-3
    1.Maryland Campaign, 1862.  2. Maryland—History—Civil War, 1861-1865—Socila aspects.  3. United States—History—Civil War, 1861-1865—Social aspects.  4. Sharpsburg Region (Md.)—History, Military-Sharpsburg Region—History—19th century.  I. Title.
E474.61.E76  1999
973.7'336—dc21                                                    99-36994
                                                                              CIP

For my husband, partner, and companion, Scott.

# CONTENTS

# FOREWORD

Western Maryland, particularly the counties of Washington and Frederick, was a hotbed of turmoil during the Civil War. Indeed, along with Pennsylvania's neighboring Cumberland Valley and Adams County, of which Gettysburg is the county seat, this was an area that from 1861 to 1865 saw more sustained military activity than any other region north of the Potomac. Esteemed Civil War historian Dennis Frye has likened life in Harpers Ferry at that time to living on the Arab-Israeli border in the late twentieth century. He might just as well have been talking about that thin strip of western Maryland bordered by Pennsylvania on the north and Virginia and West Virginia on the south. Through this corridor passed approximately three-quarters of a million Union and Confederate soldiers.

Of this number, most were from the armies that traversed the region in three major campaigns, the Maryland campaign of 1862, the Gettysburg campaign of 1863, and Jubal Early's raid of 1864. In addition, thousands of Union soldiers were garrisoned in the area—at Frederick, at Hagerstown, and at lesser populated towns and villages and in smaller detachments at key points along the Potomac and Mason-Dixon line. To be sure, a less measurable portion of the troop numbers can be attributed to the hundreds of small unit-mounted incursions led by commanders such as Jeb Stuart and John McCausland or partisan leaders such as John S. Mosby and Harry Gilmor. While these latter movements may have been brief, sometimes shorter than a day, their impact could be long lasting.

The battles of Antietam and Monocacy lasted one day. Gettysburg was a three-day round of carnage. Yet for the civilians living in the wake of these man-made disasters, the effects of these battles lasted for weeks, months, and even years. A case in point is the community of Sharpsburg, Maryland. Although much has been written about the bloody day of fighting along

Antietam Creek, most people do not realize that this was the first organized community in the United States to suffer widespread damage from both combat and the sheer presence of two opposing armies. A wide body of anecdotal evidence from both soldiers and civilians, via letters, diaries, and postwar reminiscences, leads us to believe that nearly every house in the town of Sharpsburg was damaged in some way by stray artillery rounds as well as small-arms fire. Further, a number of buildings caught fire and were destroyed, and some of the town's churches had to be rebuilt because of structural damage.

Besides the immediate impact of combat, the residue of military activity also left its mark during the period following the battle of Antietam. The presence of more than 120,000 Rebels and Yankees along with some 50,000 horses and mules generated tons of waste—a tremendous health hazard in and of itself. The threat of disease was further exacerbated by thousands of dead men and animals rotting in the warm September sun, and many more wounded left to care for in field hospitals. Evidence shows that scores of citizens got sick, and many of them died.

Combat and disease were not the only threats posed by a large battle. Economic devastation loomed as an all-too-real possibility. At Sharpsburg soldiers from both sides raided farms and homes, carrying off valuables, destroying property, and confiscating livestock and crops as provender of the armies. In some cases refugees who fled the Sharpsburg area prior to the battle returned to find themselves in economic ruin—a scenario that was repeated hundreds of times throughout this corridor of war. This, then, is the story of Antietam and beyond, looking through the prism of war as it affected the civilian population.

Despite the compelling story of a citizenry's efforts to cope with the impact of war on their region, comparatively little scholarly work has been done on this subject. John Schildt's groundbreaking 1970 study, *Drums Along the Antietam,* was the first serious effort to chronicle the story of the people of the Antietam Valley—mostly in the immediate vicinity of Sharpsburg and Keedysville—and the war's impact on them. One of its major strengths is its examination of the colonial antecedents of the area.

In 1982 this writer's coauthorship of a book called *When War Passed This Way* provided a microcosmic view of the war through the eyes of the people of the southern Cumberland Valley town of Greencastle. Although the emphasis was on events in Pennsylvania, the town's proximity to the Maryland state line ensured that discussion be made of events in nearby Washington County, Maryland.

In 1995 Roger Keller's *Events of the Civil War in Washington County, Maryland* came out. This was the first single volume that attempted to examine the entire war in the county. Keller's study is a broad chronological narrative of events with the focus on the numerous military actions that took place in the county and events that took place in the county seat of Hagerstown.

Nothing similar in scope has been written on Frederick County's role in the war. Paul and Rita Gordon's *A Playground of the Civil War,* published in 1994, provides an interesting collection of stories and an overview of Frederick County during the war. Glenn Worthington's 1932 book *Fighting for Time* was the first detailed study of the battle of Monocacy and remained the standard source on that subject for more than sixty years. Worthington grew up on the Monocacy battlefield and as a boy actually witnessed part of the battle. His narrative primarily sticks to the story of the battle but does include some material on the war's impact on Frederick and the surrounding area.

Now with the publication of Kathleen Ernst's *Too Afraid to Cry,* which could be subtitled "A Study of Life in the Invasion Corridor," we have the most complete and scholarly study of Washington and Frederick Counties during the war. Ernst has spent years delving deeply into previously unpublished material to weave this story of how tragedy and hardship touched the lives of the citizens of this part of western Maryland. Among the rare sources used are the civilian collections at the Antietam National Battlefield Library. These holdings include many previously unpublished accounts of the aftermath of Antietam, some of which were done for an oral history project conducted for the battle site in the early part of the twentieth century. The author also made contact with a number of local families, who graciously allowed her the use of private collections of letters and other accounts.

*Too Afraid to Cry* will leave students of the war with a better understanding of events such as South Mountain and Antietam after the smoke had cleared. It will also give readers a clearer picture of life in general north of the Potomac along the Maryland border during the decisive years of 1861-1865. Kathleen Ernst has done a masterful job at joining together military and social history into a superbly readable story that will stand as the premier work on the subject for a long time.

Ted Alexander
Historian
Antietam National Battlefield

# PREFACE

This book is about untold stories.

I grew up in Maryland and spent a lot of time in Frederick and Washington Counties. I visited Antietam National Battlefield often, hiked the Appalachian Trail, climbed Maryland Heights, biked the Chesapeake and Ohio Canal towpath, canoed Antietam Creek and the Potomac and Monocacy Rivers. It is a beautiful area, where even the casual wanderer constantly bumps into reminders of the horrific battles that exploded there in 1862. I heard a lot of moving stories about the generals who orchestrated those campaigns and the soldiers that they commanded. And all the time I found myself wondering, *But what happened to the people who lived here?*

Several people told me that if I tried to figure that out, I "wouldn't find much." That was before social history was popular, before many people were looking beyond the military aspects of battlefields. The question followed me, though, when I moved to West Virginia and ultimately to Wisconsin. It didn't let go, and I finally gave in and spent twelve years digging for answers. Along the way I wrote several articles, three novels, and my master's thesis on the subject. And still the question haunted me. The more I learned, the more I felt compelled to keep going.

There was much evidence to find and piece together, more than I had imagined. The stories existed; many simply had not been widely told. In time, a sense of the whole emerged. Although countless stories have been lost forever, and any historian faces the danger of overlooking largely silent populations such as slaves and the illiterate poor, I believe the end result is a fair portrait of everyday people—like you and me—in a border state, suffering through civil war.

Today, civilian interpretation is an important part of the Antietam National Battlefield programming, where historian Al Fiedler Jr. did groundbreaking work as he created the "Hardship and Tragedy: The Story of Antietam Civilians" program. Visitors are often encouraged to imagine the impact of the battles on local farm folks and villages even as they trace the footsteps of the soldiers they came to honor. More recently, Cathy Beeler and colleagues helped create an innovative educational program that encourages children to reflect on the experiences of all participants in the battle of Monocacy, military and civilian. Students in the Maryland school system, and visitors to other historic sites and battlefields, are now much more likely to be exposed to the notion that the Civil War was about more than campaigns and generals. It's a welcome change.

The soldiers who participated in the 1862 Maryland campaign did so because, for one reason or another, they had chosen to march to war. The Maryland inhabitants who met them had not made that choice. Their experiences are just as essential to our full understanding of this tormented time. This book was written in memory of those civilians, who endured what we can never fully imagine.

# ACKNOWLEDGMENTS

The voices of those who lived in Frederick and Washington Counties during the Civil War have grown faint, and I'm indebted to many people who helped me find the diaries, letters, stories, and reminiscences that breathed life into this project:

First and foremost, thanks go to Al Fiedler Jr., who spent years finding and interpreting civilian stories at Antietam National Battlefield. Al helped introduce me into the community, generously shared many sources with me, and always had answers to my questions. My research trips to Maryland were not complete without a convivial dinner with Al and his wife, Georgeann, and I'm grateful for their encouragement.

I'm also grateful for the help that Paul Chiles and Ted Alexander, also of the National Battlefield staff, have provided over the years. Paul ferreted out a number of sources, and Ted eliminated a number of errors from the manuscript. Keith Snyder provided additional assistance with photographs. The Antietam National Battlefield staff have been excellent tour guides, helped with photocopying, pointed me toward resources, and generally provided whatever assistance was needed.

I also owe a heartfelt thanks to several local historians who opened their private libraries or shared a wealth of knowledge with me. Doug Bast, of the Boonsborough Museum of History, once rearranged his schedule in the middle of an ice storm to accommodate one of my visits, and his knowledge of Boonsboro history contributed greatly to my understanding of nineteenth-century life there. Kathleen Rudesill opened the Middletown Historical Society for me. George Brigham allowed me to forage through his extensive files and borrow what I needed. Tim Reese let me interrupt his own writing time to ask questions about Crampton's Gap and volunteered to take me on a driving tour that enabled me to understand the landscape. David Wiles of the Clear Spring Historical Society also arranged his schedule to accommodate my visit, provided a tour of Plumb Grove, and provided several photographs. Tom Clemens helped pin down several elusive details and always had a quick response to my questions. Steve Stotelmyer generously shared his information about South Mountain and the Wise family.

One of the real joys of this project was meeting residents in the Sharpsburg area, many of whom shared their family stories, photographs, and/or old homes with me and became friends. Thanks to you all: Maxine Campbell, Lou and Regina Clark, Marian Gale, Linda Irvin-Craig, Missy Kretzer, Wilmer Mumma, Mary Anna Munch and family, Earl and Annabelle Roulette, Denise Troxell, and Ernie and Jan Wetterer.

Galen Hahn, now of North Carolina, shared his stories in letters. Floyd Piper allowed me to use the Piper photos. Frank Wood of The Picture Bank in Alexandria, Virginia, helped identify appropriate period images. Nancy Whitmore and Dennis Murphy assisted with Frederick photos. Todd R. Livesey helped sort out the intricacies of the Library of Congress photo collections.

Volunteers at the Frederick County Historical Society Library identified sources I might have overlooked. John Frye, of the Western Maryland Room of the Washington County Free Library in Hagerstown, answered a wealth of questions and brought a number of sources to my attention. Marsha Fuller's work in compiling local records provided valuable resources. Carl Brown, in the local history room at the C. Burr Artz Library in Frederick, shared his knowledge and stories one quiet afternoon when I thought I'd be learning only from dusty old books.

Linda Zieghan of Antioch University gave her blessing to the project and provided a learning environment that supported a nontraditional approach to history, writing, and education. Richard Haney of the University of Wisconsin-Whitewater offered encouragement and mentoring when the nucleus of this manuscript was written as my master's thesis. Dave Eicher took time from his own overwhelming schedule to comment on the manuscript. Renee Radeuchel volunteered her services as proofreader. Members of the Antietam Discussion Group gave me a variety of new insights into the 1862 campaign. I'm also grateful for the help of my editors at Stackpole Books, Michelle M. Simmons and William C. Davis.

My good friends Dave, Laurie, Matthew, and Daniel Adamiak of Walkersville often provided hospitality on my trips to Maryland. My other frequent hosts were Barbara Ernst and Michael MacGeorge, who made many trips to the airport, shipped countless boxes of books and research materials, kept me fed, and accompanied me on photo excursions. The rest of my family has been equally supportive during the many years this was a work-in-progress: Priscilla Angotti, who tramped the battlefield and did some of the preliminary fact-finding in Frederick; Henry Ernst, who drove me to many used bookstores in search of hidden treasures; and Stephanie Ernst, who never had any doubt I could accomplish whatever I set out to do.

I'm also grateful to Meghan Meeker, who cheerfully tolerated my long hours at the computer. And finally, this book would not have been possible without the support and encouragement of my husband, Scott Meeker. On a cold Wisconsin January day, as we debated whether I should sacrifice my regular income so I could complete this book, he said, "Go for it." And so I did.

CHAPTER 1

# "This Conflict of Opinions and Sympathies"

In 1920 an elderly veteran named John Ware made the long trip from his home in Sewanee, Tennessee, to a tiny village in Washington County, Maryland. It was his second visit; fifty-eight years had passed since his first in 1862. He described the place with charming prose: "Sharpsburg pulls out its shoe string length along the Hagerstown-Shepherdstown Pike, a drowsy little one-street town, a Brer Rabbit sort of a place . . . no reason for going back, certainly no incentive for going forward, just a somnolent little lizard perpetually sunning itself. . . . It is like a painting, this serene landscape."[1]

But Ware hadn't come to admire the scenery. He, and thousands of others who made the pilgrimage, came instead to commemorate a time when the landscape was *not* serene. They came to relive a battle called Antietam Creek by the North and Sharpsburg by the South. Historians identify that battle, which unfolded on September 17, 1862, as "the bloodiest day in American history." No other single day, before or since, ended with so many casualties. By best counts more than *twenty-three thousand* men were dead, wounded, or missing by nightfall.

Ware and the other veterans who visited over the years came and went, just as in 1862 they had come and gone. But left behind, as always, were the local residents. They couldn't face down their memories on rare visits, then return to the anonymous safety of a distant home. They lived every day with reminders of the unimaginable.

In 1862 advancing technology gave the rest of the country a tiny glimpse of their experience. Photographer Alexander Gardner and his assistant, James F. Gibson, had hauled their glass plates and other cumbersome equipment to Sharpsburg and were on the field by September 18. A month after the battle Mathew Brady, the owner of a photography gallery in New

1

York, mounted an exhibit of the Gardner/Gibson images called "The Dead of Antietam." Field photography was in its infancy, and the show was a sensation. These were no carefully posed studio portraits or scenes of jaunty recruits poised for the front. The photos depicted bloated corpses, stiff and pathetic, robbed of shoes and other valuables by scavengers, awaiting burial. A *New York Times* reporter who visited the show wrote:

> The living that throng Broadway care little perhaps for the Dead at Antietam, but we fancy they would jostle less carelessly down the great thoroughfare, saunter less at their ease, were a few dripping bodies, fresh from the field, laid along the pavement. . . . Mr. Brady has done something to bring home to us the terrible reality and earnestness of war. If he has not brought bodies and laid them in our door-yards and along streets, he has done something very like it.[2]

New Yorkers like the reporter were far removed from the battlefields. The Civil War was a year and a half old in the autumn of 1862. The call to arms, the flood of naive patriotism, and boasts of quick victories were in the past. The papers had too often been filled with endless lists of battlefield casualties, and too many doors had been swathed with black crepe. Americans had lost much of their innocence—and yet the woodcuts and engravings published in periodicals had still spared most the blunt horror of fratricide. These photographs pierced the veneer of delicacy. The public perception of war would never be the same.

A thousand miles away, the people who called the battlefield "home" would also never be the same. There, where the Antietam Creek meandered around the little town of Sharpsburg, Maryland, no photographs were needed. There, in the rutted village streets and nearby fertile farm fields, the "dripping bodies" had been all too real.

The military conflict that took place at Sharpsburg is a critical chapter in American history. But Civil War history is more than a schematic of armies and tactics. The women, men, and children who lived in Sharpsburg in Washington County were ordinary people caught in extraordinary circumstances. The war exploded on their thresholds, and the wake from that explosion rippled for miles. Their story is no less important than that of the soldiers, like John Ware, who marched across their cornfields.

>─┤─◆>─○─<◆─┤─◄

Conflict was not new to western Maryland. The area known as Washington County was once a vast forest with bushy undergrowth of hazel and chinquapin, favored hunting ground of the Delaware Indians. Legend tells of a bloody battle between the Delaware and Catawba in the 1730s near the Antietam Creek. When the first white hunters pushed past the ridges of Catoctin and South Mountains, the Delaware turned their attention to the new intruders. When white families followed and established rude farms, women dared milk their cows only with armed guards standing by. But the whites were tenacious. Sharpsburg and Hagerstown, twelve miles away, were both established before America declared independence.

Like the nation, Washington County was formed in 1776, when it was separated from Frederick County to the east. It is nearly triangular in shape, 525 square miles, bounded on the north by Pennsylvania, on the east by the rocky crestline of South Mountain, on the south and southwest by the Potomac River, and on the west by Sideling Hill Creek.

Hagerstown, Washington County's largest city, is situated near the Pennsylvania border. A small town that bore, in the words of a contemporary resident, "the euphonious name of Funkstown"[3] is located a few miles southeast of Hagerstown and in 1860 could boast about one thousand residents. Other communities in South Mountain's shadow include Boonsboro, Keedysville (originally known as Centreville), Rohrersville, and Porterstown.

In 1860 Sharpsburg was simply one more village, laid out in 1763 and named for Horatio Sharpe, the provincial governor of Maryland. The Potomac River rippled only three miles away, with a good crossing spot later known as Blackford's Ford, Boteler's Ford, or Pack Horse Ferry. Intended to serve as seat of Washington County, Sharpsburg lost to Hagerstown by one vote and settled quietly into rural obscurity. In its first century it attracted stolid farmers, most of English and German descent but some from France and Switzerland and a stream of Scottish-Irish who migrated south from Pennsylvania. They applied for land grants and gave their new acreage names like Fellowship, Bachelor's Delight, Love in a Village, Maiden's Choice, Rogue's Harbor, Whiskey Alley, Scott's Grief, and I Am Glad It Is No Worse.

*Many Sharpsburg residents had orchards beside their homes, kept cows and chickens in backlot stables, and tended large garden plots. Fences of stone and pickets were erected to keep animals and buggies out. In this view, looking northwest along Hall Street, the original St. Paul's Episcopal Church, built in 1819, is visible in the background. Photo by Alexander Gardner, 1862.* LIBRARY OF CONGRESS.

By 1800 lessons were being taught in English in one log schoolhouse and in German in another. German churchgoers established Lutheran and Reformed congregations as well as the much smaller Dunker churches. English laborers established an Episcopal church. And when Irish Catholics brought their shovels and axes to the area, attracted by jobs building the National Road and the C&O Canal, they brought a priest along, too.

A few merchants and tavernkeepers made a living in the town proper, and a dyeing and weaving operation nearby employed others. The power of Antietam Creek gave rise to an ironworks in 1764, which employed five hundred people by the 1850s, breaking the valley's serenity with the buzz of sheet-iron, shingle, grist, and saw mills. A blacksmith clanged his trade nearby. Workers browsed for lanterns and tinware and calicos "imported" from the East in the company store. Whiskey made from corn or other grains was one of the best cash crops on the frontier, and despite attempts to impose unpopular taxes on this favored beverage, booze remained a mainstay of the economy. Local bridges over the Antietam and Conocheague Creeks proved inadequate for the growing commerce and transport, and in the 1820s and 1830s a series of stone bridges, with one or more graceful arches, were constructed in the area.

Two miles from Sharpsburg was Belinda Springs. A Sharpsburg physician identified limestone, sulphur, iron, and magnesium in the waters early in the nineteenth century, and soon wealthy families from Baltimore and Washington, jaded with the summer's sultry heat, escaped to the scenic valley to take the water, advertised as "very efficacious in bilious complaints."[4] They stayed in guest cottages, and while the ladies minced over the hills, enjoying the scenery, the men whiled away their time in billiard rooms and ten-pin alleys. With the exception of cockfights, which drew contenders from a wide radius to Sharpsburg's dusty streets, conflict seemed gone from the valley forever.

Still, Sharpsburg was a patriotic village. The community had furnished a company of men during the Revolutionary War and another for the War of 1812. But when that conflict subsided, local residents returned to their own business. Mothers and wives who had watched their men march to war prayed that they wouldn't have to live through that again.

About thirteen hundred people called Sharpsburg home in 1860. They had their own fire company and could relax after dinner with the newly established newspaper. A Masonic lodge had been organized. Farmers were blessed with fertile fields and contentedly hauled wheat, corn, oats, hay, potatoes, wool, rye, butter, honey, and livestock to market each autumn. They were also good orchardmen, raising many varieties that have since faded from existence. Their only enemies were the young boys determined to steal apples on their way to school. "It was my special delight to outwit [the farmer] and fill my pockets with the forbidden fruit," confessed one small boy.[5]

Then suddenly came declarations of war—and with that came new enemies. The notion of civil war was painful to many in both the North and South. But people in the border states of Maryland, Kentucky, and Missouri, where political differences ran deep within families and communities, faced unique schisms. And as residents of those states wrestled with their consciences and convictions, they felt the nation's intense scrutiny. Both the South and the North screamed for their allegiance—with good reason. Had Missouri seceded, the Confederacy would have bordered Iowa, and a Confederate Kentucky would have pushed the South's border to the Ohio River.

Maryland's role was the most complex. The state boasted incredible diversity in economy, agriculture, and politics, partially due to the extremes of its geography. Southern Maryland, with a legacy of large tobacco farms and a dwindling but still present slave-labor force, was culturally most like the South; and the war's first skirmish was fought on Baltimore streets in April 1861, when a mob of pro-Southern civilians attacked the Sixth Massachusetts Regiment as it tried to march through the city. Many Marylanders heartily supported the Union, however, and devoted the next four years of their lives to preserving it. The state of Maryland, the area of western Maryland, the town of Sharpsburg—all these in microcosm reflected the border states' dilemma—the nation's dilemma. And in the 1862 Maryland campaign, western Maryland provided the crucible for testing the faith and tenacity of all Americans, Union or Confederate.

J. Thomas Scharf, Confederate artillerist and naval officer and author of a history of western Maryland published in 1882, believed that Maryland suffered more than most states with the coming of the Civil War:

> Public feeling was, perhaps, even more intense in Maryland than in other states, for the obvious danger to which she was exposed by her geographical position in event of conflict between North and South, and from the very strong counter-currents which existed in popular sentiment. This conflict of opinions and sympathies was nowhere more marked than in Western Maryland.[6]

And nowhere else was the geographic situation more pronounced than in Washington County, where it was possible to have breakfast on the Virginia border and lunch in Pennsylvania.

Most historians have generalized southern and eastern Maryland as predominantly secessionist, concluding that the majority of western Maryland residents supported the Union. Deep and bitter political divisions existed, however. In the hot years of debate prior to the declaration of war, members of many communities and families realized painfully that their definitions of patriotism, of what it meant to be American, differed sharply.

>-⊢-◆>-•-O--<•-⊢-◁

One of the area's prominent extended families was descended from emigrants who had left Hesse Darmstadt, Germany, in 1731. John and Catherine Miller, who came to western Maryland via Pennsylvania and settled in the vicinity of Williamsport, had ten children. The fifth of these, Jacob, was nine when his parents moved to Washington County. Jacob married Catharine Rench in 1811. The couple moved to Sharpsburg and had eleven children.[7] Jacob was an enterprising man who in his lifetime managed several farms, a weaving business, a grist mill, a sawmill, and a flour mill. He also became involved in local politics and served as a frequent jurist, judge of elections, county commissioner, and, for one term, in the state legislature. After Catharine Rench Miller died in 1840, Jacob married a widow named Elizabeth Mumma Houser (Hauser). Elizabeth died in 1858.

By 1859 Jacob was seventy-seven years old. He'd led a full life and was surrounded by an immense extended family. Most of his children had married and begun families of their own. Three of his sons—Andrew Rench, Morgan, and Samuel—were involved in a canal boat operation on the nearby C&O Canal in addition to farming. His youngest daughter, Savilla, had left boarding school in Hagerstown and was evidently living in her father's little house in Sharpsburg. Jacob's letters to an absent older daughter were newsy and affectionate and usually included assurances that her parrot was still safe and well. In 1859 he shared his pride in the local economy:

We are now in the midst of Harvesting and I think Washington County never produced a finer crop of wheat than the present, at all events not to my recollection. —Oats & B[arley] is also verry good. And the corn crop promises verry fair, (so far) as well as the potatoes, and also grass we have an abundant crop. The common clover Hay is all made and the Saplin clover and timethy hay is to make yet. . . . The farmers are using the reaper more and more every year, and I think before many years the wheat rye oats and barly will all be cut with the reapers. [8]

Jacob did not hint of any suspicions that the valley's fertile farm economy might one day bring carnage.

As war clouds gathered on the horizon, Jacob—a vociferous man of strong opinions—and his family cast their lot with the Confederacy. He was involved with establishing a Democratic newspaper in Hagerstown and, because of his sympathies, was "persecuted in various ways by members of the opposite party, who several times drove him from the polls."[9]

The Millers' village home was on what is now known as Main Street.[10] A stone's toss away was the large, substantial home of the John and Susan Kretzer family. Like the Millers, the Kretzers had German roots. Also like the Miller clan, the Kretzers had multiplied in the years since the first member settled in Washington County. Family patriarch Leonard Kretzer arrived during the 1740s and had seven sons, who ultimately established their own homes in Sharpsburg and nearby Keedysville. By 1860 the region was dotted with Kretzer siblings, cousins, and in-laws.

John Kretzer was one of Leonard's many grandsons and, like Jacob Miller, was a prominent man in his community. In 1846 he was commissioned as a captain in the Maryland militia. He was elected county commissioner in 1855 and 1859 and was a founding member of the Sharpsburg International Order of Odd Fellows Lodge. A master blacksmith by trade, he and his family lived in a fine stone house. The 1860 census listed his real estate value at $4,500 and his personal estate value at $1,500—figures well above most of his neighbors. John and Susan had six children: Anna, Theresa, Aaron, Civilla (Savilla), Elizabeth, and Stephen.[11] By 1860 Anna, twenty-two years old, was working at home as a dressmaker; Theresa, twenty-one, was working at home as a milliner; and Aaron, seventeen, was working as a clerk.

Unlike the Millers, however, the family of John and Susan Kretzer were decidedly against secession. His daughter Theresa explained later:

My father, John Kretzer, was a very loyal Union man, and the members of the family all shared his sentiments. We had a large Union flag which, in the early days of the war, we kept strung across the street from our house to a tall pole on the opposite side. There were some Southern sympathizers in town, and on one occasion they cut the halyards which attached the flag to the pole.

After that we ceased to use the pole and attached that end of the rope to the roof of the house opposite ours. [12]

In the limited accounts left by each family after the war, there is no reference to the other. Still, they lived only three doors away from each other. How well had they known each other in the years before the war? How often had they met on the street as the storm clouds of crisis drew near? Those questions will never be answered, but two families—both descended of German immigrants, neighbors in a small town—were beginning to take diverging paths.

Sadly, it was a pattern repeated many times. Angela Davis, a New York native who lived in Funkstown, remembered, "The secession feeling was very strong, and at times bitter, most of the citizens being rebels." When her husband raised a national flag, neighbors destroyed it. "You can imagine how I felt when I realized . . . ," she wrote, "that the national pride of any American could become so blunted or perverted, that he would . . . tear our glorious stars and stripes into fragments and scatter them on the highway to be trampled under foot."

It didn't stop there. Her husband, a storekeeper, received "threats at times of burning his store and house, running his d—d Yankee wife out of town, &c. &c."[13] About the same time John Eckert Knode, considered a Union man, was the victim of arson. When his barn burned, he lost all of his crops, his farming implements, and much of his livestock. His relatives believed it occurred because he had married a woman from a vocal Southern family. "It cost something in those days," wrote the couple's nephew, "to be joined to a Southern woman in wedlock."[14]

>--+->-O--<>-+-<

What caused such painful divisions? In western Maryland, which was neither North nor South, politics were complicated. During the Revolutionary War, local men had eagerly served. Some were Scottish-Irish who had packed bitter resentment toward England in their immigrant trunks. Some had fought Indians for their land and weren't strangers either to warfare or to taking what they wanted. Those who chose to live in the still-wild mountain valleys were independent souls, accustomed to making their own rules, and these were the fathers and grandfathers of the men and women facing civil war eighty years later. In 1861 some believed that their patriot grandparents had fought and died to create the country, and they were willing to do the same to preserve it. And some believed those same patriot grandparents had fought and died to defend the right to declare independence from an unfair ruler, and they—by supporting secession—were willing to do the same.

Slavery was not a subject generally discussed in terms of the looming crisis. That issue was as complicated as any other. Slavery existed even in western Maryland. It was also, generally speaking, tolerated. A Frederick woman, for example, told her daughter that before the war she had borne the odium of being one of only three abolitionists in that town.[15] An early Washington County history referred to an individual as "suspected of being what in those days was considered the most despicable of persons, an *Abolitionist.*"[16]

The German farmers near Sharpsburg, used to working in the fields themselves and generally managing relatively small operations, were far less likely to own slaves than the long-established tobacco farmers in the southeastern counties. Still, local lore whispers of manacles and chains discovered a century later in attics and cellars. Slaves were sold from three locations in Hagerstown.[17] According to legend, the entire economy of a little river community in Frederick County called Licksville—so tough it was hard to walk through town without getting licked—depended on the slave trade. Slaves were brought across the Potomac for Maryland buyers, or Maryland slaves were auctioned to buyers from the Deep South. The town's most prominent features were slave pens and blocks, hotels for the traders, and saloons.[18] "At public sale . . . the unhappy wretches were put upon the auctioneer's block and 'knocked down' to the highest bidder," recalled Jesse Dixon of Urbana, "a father to a South Carolina planter, his wife to a Georgia dealer, and the children scattered among various buyers."[19]

In 1820 Washington County's 3,201 slaves comprised one-eighth of the population—the largest recorded number in the county's history. Later census records show a steady decline. Some slave owners filed legal documents outlining a gradual plan of emancipation for their slaves, spread over a number of years to minimize their financial losses: Simon Long of Washington County, for example, outlined a plan to emancipate twelve slaves over a period of time extending from 1862 to 1885.[20] Some owners allowed slaves, after a certain number of years of service, to hire themselves out—although with the pay split between owner and slave, it was a slow road to purchasing freedom. A woman's or child's price fell somewhere between two hundred and eight hundred dollars in an era when a black laborer might earn one hundred dollars a year. Still, manumission—and Pennsylvania's nullification of fugitive slave laws—combined to decrease the number of human beings kept in bondage. In 1850, more free blacks lived in Maryland than in any other state, although the majority lived in Baltimore and on the Eastern Shore. Ironically, the growing number of free blacks was cause for concern for some white citizens, who resisted situations—such as the

*Washington County slave Nancy Campbell was manumitted in June 1859 by Andrew Miller when she was forty-two years old. She was later employed by the Roulette family.* COURTESY EARL AND ANNABELLE ROULETTE.

independent black church movement of the 1850s—that provided opportunities for slaves and free blacks to mingle.

According to the Eighth Federal Population Census, taken in 1860, Washington County was still home to 398 slave owners and 1,437 slaves. In the Sharpsburg District, 50 slave owners governed 150 slaves, somewhat less than the 203 free blacks in the same area.[21] Of Sharpsburg's free blacks, only nine owned property, with value ranging from $10 to $300. Most free blacks were listed as laborers, servants, or farmhands, although a mason, a quarrier, a lime burner, and a farmer all owned their own property and supported their families with those skills. The same census listed 3,243 slaves and 4,967 free blacks out of a population of 46,591 in Frederick County. A resident of Urbana, southeast of Frederick City, estimated that "a mere majority perhaps of the dwellers held slaves. Of these, from two to twelve were about the range as to numbers."[22]

As for the slaveholders, some of the names on—and missing from—the roster are noticeable. In Frederick, Barbara Fritchie—arguably the town's most famous Unionist citizen—appears on the slaveholders' census for 1860. Tannery owner Gideon Bantz, whose wife Julia became president of the Federal Ladies' Relief Association, is also listed. According to the same census, Frederick lawyer Bradley Tyler Johnson, destined to become a brigadier general in the Confederate army, did not own his one black household servant. In 1861 Otho Nesbitt, a prominent slave owner descended from one of Clear Spring's first white settlers, hired a seamstress to make him a Union flag two yards long, and he hung it from a garret window of Nesbitt Mansion, his large farmhouse just outside of town.[23] In Sharpsburg, respected physician Dr. Augustin Biggs, a "strong Union man," owned three slaves as late as 1860. More than one minister owned slaves.[24]

And so did members of a sect known for their pacifism and opposition to slavery. Among those first white settlers to the fertile valley along Antietam Creek in the 1700s were members of the German Baptist Brethren church (also known as Dunkards, or Dunkers) who had wandered southwest from the original Brethren settlement in Germantown, Pennsylvania. Members of the Dunker church wore plain garb, and the men had long, flowing beards. For many years services were held in the private home of Daniel Miller, Jacob Miller's brother. In 1851 Samuel Mumma, a son-in-law of Daniel Miller, gave a wooded lot on his farm, about one mile north of Sharpsburg on the Hagerstown Turnpike, for a permanent church. This unassuming structure, known at the time as Mumma's Church and now simply as "the" Dunker church, held services for an active community of Brethren. Membership grew after the building was constructed. The Dunker church prohibited such activities as attending Sunday schools, using strong drink, praying without a prayer veil, having photographs taken, and working as a butcher in a market.[25] Church guidelines also stated that "each applicant for baptism, before being immersed in the Antietam had to promise he would own no slaves and would never engage in warfare."

But even the peaceful Brethren could not resolve the issue of slavery that easily. In 1797 the church adopted an official policy declaring that "no brother or sister should have negroes as slaves." The issue was revisited in 1813, and although the church again concluded that trading or owning slaves was "unanimously considered . . . wrong," a further amendment allowed for broader interpretation:

> If there were members having slaves . . . they might hold them in a proper way so long as the church near which they live may deem it necessary for the slaves to earn the money they had cost, and then, with good counsel of the church, they are to be set free, with a good suit of clothing; and if there are any who have not bought, but inherited their negroes, they are to be liberated as soon as the church considers it right and proper. And if members have negro children under their care, or even as slaves, they shall bring them up in an orderly manner, teach them to read, and keep them, if males, to the age of twenty-one years, and if females, to the age of eighteen years, and then, with the counsel of the church, emancipate them, with a good suit of wearing apparel.

Members who persisted in having slaves under other circumstances would be denied communion and other rituals of membership.[26] Some records suggest that members of the church occasionally purchased slaves in order to set them free, while other members "purchased slaves, made them indentured servants on their farms until they worked out their purchase price, then set them free."[27] At least several Brethren were listed in the 1860 census as slave owners.[28] Church records make it clear that slavery was officially condemned by the church, but the debates, over a number of years, also show how pervasive and complex an issue it was. In western Maryland even the pacifist Brethren, it seems, had their own political schisms.

In the years preceding the war, evidence suggests that at least several western Maryland families, white and black, helped runaway slaves escape to freedom via the Underground Railroad; at least one white woman was apprehended.[29] But also at work were "padarolles," bounty hunters who pretended to hide slaves, then turned them in. Professional slave catchers congregated in border towns like Hagerstown and Emmitsburg and were known to illegally haul their captives back from Pennsylvania. Those who openly made their living catching slaves and collecting rewards were known locally as "Georgemen" or "soul drivers." Late in life Allen Sparrow of Middletown recalled:

> I have seen from 20 to 40 Negros hand cuft together one on each side to a long chain, the Georgemen as they cald them then with his whip driving them. They brought them round through the Country same as a man would Horses or Cows. They paid when the Markets were good high prices, from $600 to $1200 per Men and Five to Eight hundred for women, especially if they were young and good looking. There was men that followed it for a living. They took them to Georgia and sold them to work on Cotton Farms. At that time there was very few people but what thought it was all right and I thought if a negro runaway I was in duty bound to catch him as if a horse or anything else had runaway. So mutch for the part of the country I was raised in.[30]

Clagget Fitzhugh was one of the area's most feared slave catchers. Several members of a family named Logan were also active soul drivers along the Maryland–Pennsylvania border, near the base of South Mountain and Antietam Creek. Captives were tied or handcuffed to rings attached to the attic floor of Dan Logan's home, and neighbors sometimes observed black men roped together walking beside his horse. Dan Logan and his wife lived less than two miles from a family named Wentz, who were active in the Underground Railroad.[31] Captured slaves were held until an owner arrived to claim or sell them. Many were manacled in the cellars or attics of tidy farmhouses, but for years the Hagerstown jailer turned a surreptitious profit

*Rachael was a slave on a Clear Spring farm, but little else is known about her life. Historians will always struggle to gain true insight into the experiences of women like Rachael, who left no letters or diaries to illuminate their thoughts and feelings.* COURTESY CLEAR SPRING DISTRICT HISTORICAL ASSOCIATION.

by holding escapees in the city jail while he extorted inflated prices from their owners.[32] Occasionally runaways banded together. Groups of a dozen or more armed men were seen heading north, but it took a greedy—and well-armed—soul driver to attempt the arrest.[33]

It is difficult to explore the dynamics between the intermingled slave and free-black population. It was not uncommon for a free black to marry a slave or for some members of a biological family to be granted freedom while others remained in bondage. There were also a number of residents of mixed blood, perhaps dating back to Maryland's old practice of housing slaves with white "redemptioners"—indentured servants working off their passage from Europe, who were little more than slaves until their years of bondage were served. Redemptioners were advertised for sale in Hagerstown as late as 1818.

It is also difficult to explore the dynamics between the slaves and their masters. Some of the slave owners appearing in census records may have been in the process of allowing the institution to die a natural death by caring for elderly slaves while slowly easing their personal economic system to one of hired labor. By 1860 the youngest of Sharpsburg physician Augustin Biggs's slaves was sixty-five, for example, and he also employed a female domestic and a male farmhand. "So far as I could ever ascertain, very few of [the slaves] had come into their owner's possession through purchase, but in nearly every case by inheritance," noted Jesse Dixon. "This human property coming thus as a heritage was hard to get rid of even by the folks who were not wedded to the institution." Dixon, whose father owned slaves and supported the Union cause, also voiced the myopic, self-serving rationalization on which so many slave owners were raised: "The simple fact is, that those darkies were so simple minded and so reconciled to their condition and withal so satisfied with food and raiment, so utterly dependent on master, that to set them free would have seemed inhumane."[34]

Certainly, some slaves risked severe punishment by trying to escape. Eighteen owned by Elias Chaney—a "thoroughly good" man who was "never known to speak a harsh word" to his slaves—made it to Canada, a two thousand dollar loss for Mr. Chaney.[35] Hagerstown slave George Ross, who had lived "pretty well," chose to run away with his family because he feared his master might sell his wife or children away; this family, too, found safe refuge in Canada.[36]

Another successful escapee was James Pennington, who fled his owner, Frisby Tilghman of Hagerstown, and became a minister in New York. Some years later Pennington received a letter from his brother Stephen Pembroke, begging for the money to purchase his freedom. Pembroke and two sons had run away from Jacob Grove of Sharpsburg, but had been captured and returned to Grove. "[Mr. Grove] told me I might return [to the North] if you would give him his price . . . ," Pembroke wrote. "Act promptly, as I will have to be sold to the South. . . . My two sons were sold to the drivers. . . . I am confined to my room with irons on." The money was raised.[37] In 1847 a dozen slaves ran from their owners, Colonel Hollingsworth and James H. Kennedy of Washington County. They were captured and jailed in Carlisle, Pennsylvania, where a mob of furious blacks helped one runaway woman and a girl escape. Kennedy was injured in the process and died soon after, and his death prompted a flurry of public meetings, resolves, and threats of "border retribution" against the people of Pennsylvania who, it was felt, had allowed the outrage to happen. "Suppose," argued a newspaper editorial, "a hundred of their horses were stolen and brought to Hagerstown, and suppose the owners followed and proved their property and wished to take it away, but a mob arises, in the light of day, in the public streets, strikes them down with bludgeons and stones and wrests from them their property? What would be thought of the mass of our citizens if they made no interference?"[38]

The slaves belonging to Jacob Miller, the politician and businessman living in semiretirement by 1860, also got mired in complex transactions. After his second wife, Elizabeth Mumma Houser Miller, died in 1858, Jacob experienced some financial problems, apparently in connection with settling her estate. The man prosecuting the case against him, one of Elizabeth's Houser relatives, ordered the sheriff to seize any property that could be sold. Jacob Miller bitterly described the scene:

> So the Sheriff came down and took Aaron, John, Nau [illeg.], Jane and her child. Now I would almost as soon he would have taken my life as to have taken them three boys from me, and I believe they would have wrisked their lives for me. So great was their attachment for me that when the Sheriff came down [and] I told them of what was to be done, they submitted at once, and said "Then you will be clear of Hauser." But when the Sheriff came to Harriet, she became enraged and said . . . she hoped the next lea[p] he would make would land him into hell. . . . And if those boys had been bad fellows as some are I would [not] have said a word, but they were not, they ware always ready to do my bidding. Aaron was my teamster [and] took care of the horses, now Hauser has in his un-Christianlike manner deprived me in my old age of having a boy to bring in my horse or take him to the stable when I come home. . . . He has taken these boys and Jane from their mother and from their home of which they were well contented with, and had them sent to the South where they will run the risk of [not] geting a good home.[39]

Jacob Miller's letter suggests a general truth: Slavery in western Maryland was likely to be less physically brutal than slavery in the Deep South, but slave owners still viewed "their people" through lenses tinted by their own ingrained needs. Although individual atrocities were committed by a few owners, the few existing records imply that slaves in Washington County were likely to have been treated better than may have been the case on the large tobacco farms in southeastern Maryland, and certainly on large plantations in the South. Lawbreaking slaves were sometimes sentenced to be sold out of the state—a harsh punishment.[40] Owners also used the spectre of Southern plantations to their advantage, countering unwanted behavior with threats of being sold "to the Cotton States." Stephen Pembroke's master told him, "If you speak about freedom, I will sell you further South."[41] After receiving a similar threat, a young black woman in Boonsboro made herself unmarketable to prospective buyers by chopping her hand off with an ax. Similar acts of self-mutilation were sometimes invoked by fugitive slaves when captured, as a last desperate repudiation of the system.

Years after the war, one former slave said of his owner, Mr. Otto, "He was a good man to his black people." That former slave chose to stay on as a hired man after Emancipation.[42] Henry and Elizabeth Piper's household in 1860 included one free sixteen-year-old black farmhand named Jeremiah and six slaves, male and female, ranging in age from four to thirty-three. The slaves belonging to Henry Piper also chose to stay on as employees after Emancipation.[43] One former slave from Frederick County reported that as a whole owners were kind to blacks there and when crops were good gave the blacks money.[44] Some slaves had Saturdays free and spent them roaming the woods hunting or fishing, sometimes in the company of the masters' children. Diarist Otho Nesbitt of Clear Spring, who was given a slave family by his father, wrote of bringing a doctor daily to his farm to attend a sick little boy, hiring a seamstress to measure the slaves for new clothes, and ordering a new bedstead and sofa from a local carpenter for slaves Eli and Morris. "Morris," he noted, "had always wanted a sofa." When the circus came to town, Nesbitt even gave his slaves money so that they could attend.[45]

Still, nothing could blunt the realities of ownership. Jacob Miller lost his slaves because they were legal property, subject to forfeiture. A woman in Funkstown named Sarah, who received her freedom on the death of her mistress, refused employment with any member of that woman's family, believing that only by leaving them would she truly realize her freedom.[46] And when the war began, A. H. Hager of Hagerstown patriotically equipped his young black "servant," Daniel Fox, and "made a present of his services to Col. W. H. Irwin, of the Seventh Pennsylvania Regiment, for an indefinite period, or as long as the war should last."[47] There is no record of how Mr. Fox felt about that transaction.

>–┼–‹›–O–‹›┼–‹

The simmering political kettle disrupted the comforting cycle of agrarian life. In January 1861, rural schoolteacher and farmer John Koogle noted in his diary, "Ground some hominy this morning, attended a Union meeting this evening."[48] When war was declared, public meetings throughout western Maryland made clear the divided sentiments of area residents. While Union clubs held elaborate flag-raising ceremonies, secessionists published resolutions supporting a state's right to secede.

By May, armies were on both borders of Washington County. Farm families trekked to Hagerstown to behold the unprecedented sight of Union troops marching through; Koogle estimated three thousand soldiers, five hundred baggage wagons, and a battery of cannons passing on June 27. On Sunday afternoons secessionists clattered in their buggies to Harpers Ferry to see the Confederate troops while Unionists clattered in theirs to the Federal encampment at Chambersburg. "This black Republican warfare has thrown everything into confusion," Jacob Miller grumbled. Miller dreaded the "rowdies" in Sharpsburg, who gleefully reported secessionist citizens to nearby Federal troops, hoping for their arrest. "But they were disappointed," he observed. "The offisers said they did not intend to molest any one on account of their political opinion."[49]

Rebel boys slipped across the Potomac to enlist. This was dangerous business, for Federal troops patrolled the river. Some recruits were captured; one Maryland boy was nabbed in 1861 and imprisoned until the end of the war, never having even enlisted. The best fords were closely monitored, and more than one zealous boy drowned trying to sneak past the sentries at more difficult stretches. J. Gabby Duckett of Washington County left home to join the Confederacy with plans to cross the river. Several weeks later his body came ashore near Shepherdstown with a bullet hole in his chest.[50]

Union recruits had equal zeal—and an easier time. They rattled toward Baltimore's training camps in "the cars." A few were caught by surprise. In the flurry of sudden patriotism, Hanson Beachley, the clerk employed by the Davises in their Funkstown store, "paraded around the streets with an old flint-lock musket, boasting that he was ready to go and help defend the Capital from the Rebels." Later, however, when a conscript officer showed up in Funkstown, Beachley quickly got exempted from military service—

*Young men in western Maryland in 1861 had exciting and dangerous choices to make. Some chose to cross the Potomac and enlist in the Confederate army, while friends, schoolmates, and brothers chose to join Federal units. While awaiting their return, their sisters and sweethearts did what they could to support their cause. Few of them could imagine the trials to come. Unidentified young men and women, photographed by E. M. Reicher, Hagerstown, Maryland.* AUTHOR'S COLLECTION.

for having false teeth. That was too prime for the town rhymer, who immortalized Beachley's patriotism:

Where's your Hanson Beachley, the man that was so brave
He swore he'd fight the Rebels, this Union he would save,
But where is he now, in the time he's needed most,
He pulls out his false teeth, and looks like a ghost.[51]

The U.S. government was aware of the area's precarious geography—and fearful of invasion from Virginia. After the Federal garrison at Harpers Ferry, Virginia, was burned and abandoned, Union troops were quickly established in western Maryland. Soon the ladies of Hagerstown were thronging to nearby camps to present flags and watch drills from beneath dainty parasols, and the students at the Female Seminary surrendered their academy to Major General Robert Patterson's headquarters. A young man saw a regiment of Rhode Island troops pass through Funkstown and initially thought "all the men in the United States north of Mason and Dixon's line were in that body of troops."[52] One civilian recalled:

Our town and surrounding neighborhood resemble a vast military camp. Soldiers are seen in every street, and guards [are] on almost every corner. Companies are constantly parading, and the strains of music are wafted to the air on every breeze. On the Sabbath long lines of bristling bayonets glittered in our streets, and the peals of church-bells blended with the stirring notes of the drum and fife, presenting a striking contrast with the order and quietude which usually mark the holy day in our midst.[53]

Events took a nasty turn in June 1861 when vocal secessionist DeWitt Clinton Rench—a "noble, daring fellow"—was killed by a Unionist mob. The twenty-two-year-old law student, member of the prominent Rench clan and related to Jacob Miller by his first marriage, was planning to cross the Potomac and enlist in the company of his college roommate, Henry Kyd Douglas. Before leaving he made a trip to Williamsport on business for his father. As he arrived, words were exchanged with some hot-headed Unionists. A crowd quickly formed, surrounding his horse, and Rench was ordered to leave town. Rench retorted that he would leave when it suited him to do so. One Unionist grabbed the horse's bridle, and others began to throw stones. Rench drew a revolver and fired several warning shots before one or more of his assailants opened fire themselves. One ball caught the boy near his heart, and he died soon after.

Word was sent to Rench's father "that he might take [the body] away provided he would say nothing about it," Jacob Miller related bitterly.[54] Henry Kyd Douglas was equally bitter: "He was shot dead and left upon the ground," he wrote later. "No attempt was made to arrest the murderers. A large body of my regiment were wild for revenge . . . and had it not been for the vigilance of officers, the gun and torch would have visited the town of Williamsport to demand the murderers of Clinton Rench or wreak a cruel vengeance."[55] After Rench's death, townsfolk whispered—without much evidence—that he had been spying for the Confederacy. Williamsport was nonetheless shocked by the public display of brutal sectionalism. The incident "sent a thrill of horror and cast a cloud of gloom over our whole town," wrote a local reporter. "We witnessed the terrible affray and never wish to see another such."[56] One of Jacob Miller's daughters wrote about the impact of their cousin's death in a letter to her sister: "Oh my, I did not know I had so much gall in my nature until this war question was brought up and when one of these Union shirkers murdered our dear cousin. Dear sister, I shudder now at my feelings then. I hated my most intimate friends because they were in favor of the Union, right or wrong."[57]

Tension was rising. "No trust could be placed in a friend, no confidence in a guide, and it was well for a man to keep the doors of his mouth from her that lay on his bosom," wrote the local historian, "for the son rose against the father, the daughter-in-law against the mother-in-law, and a man's enemies were often the men of his own house."[58] In a Funkstown tavern, where Union troops found a cache of weapons assumed hidden by Rebel partisans, soldiers "amused themselves by making the prominent Southern sympathizers hang the American flag from their houses."[59] The postmaster who carried the daily mail by stage from Hagerstown to Frederick was reported to Federal troops by Unionists, who complained that "the Rebel" was likely to destroy their letters instead of mailing them.

The Union troops gradually extended their line along the Potomac River, and as the Southern army felt compelled to threaten attack, nearby residents experienced frequent skirmishes between clashing patrols. In July a call was issued to loyal citizens of the western counties by Francis Thomas, former governor of Maryland, who was charged with organizing a Potomac Home Brigade to protect Maryland's boundaries. On July 25 physician Augustin A. Biggs assured Thomas, "Our citizens are rapidly availing themselves." On August 7, R. Ellsworth Cook wrote Thomas, "Dear Sir, The 'Sharpsburg Rifles' under my command . . . have recruited our ranks to about seventy, all anxious to get into the service immediately." Some of the recruits did want to complete certain farm chores before reporting, which caused Cook considerable anxiety. "The men are considerably scattered," he admitted on August 8, requesting permission to report with the men at hand, with the others to follow when they could. "If this privilege is allowed, I do not doubt my ability to increase the company to over 100 men—and must confess that it would be extremely humiliating if this Congressional District should fail to do her duty."[60] There was some initial confusion regarding such details as pay and equipage, but the brigade members dutifully marched to camp near Frederick, and Cook had the honor of being elected captain of Company A, First Regiment.

Northern soldiers, unaccustomed to Maryland's hot summers and the close quarters of army camp, fell prey to epidemics, and the hospitals quickly filled. In August the military depot and medical facilities were moved to Frederick, taking some of the commotion with them. But the 13th Massachusetts was stationed at Sharpsburg in August 1861, while they guarded Potomac fords. For the residents of Washington County's tiny communities, the soldiers' presence was overwhelming. Couriers on horseback raced through the muddy streets, and sentries patrolled night and day. "At times we were not only surrounded by Union soldiers, but they were right in our midst," Angela Davis recalled, "the stores being crowded with them; most of them wanted crackers and cheese, whiskey and tobacco, cigars and letter paper. . . . Often at midnight we were awakened by the rat-tat-tat of the drum, the shrill notes of the fife and the tramp, tramp of the men, followed by heavy baggage wagons; and would soon find that two or three regiments were passing through town."[61]

Even among Unionists, the initial excitement of the troops faded a bit with time. The economic boon of soldiers ready to buy everything in sight at local stores was offset by the losses that many local farmers experienced. "[The Union soldiers] are committing great depredations . . .," Jacob Miller wrote. "There is a regiment encamped near town in the woods . . . [and] they are thining it out most retchidly cutting all the hickrey. A portion of them are encamped on my land. . . . There they cut down timber to build

*Although many people in
Washington County held strong
political convictions—some
Confederate, some Unionist—
others hoped only that the war
might pass them by altogether.
Unidentified couple,
photographed by E. M. Reicher,
Hagerstown, Maryland.*
AUTHOR'S COLLECTION.

cabbins for their winter quarters, cut down large shingle trees to make clab-
boards to cover them, beside that they cut a great deal of hickrey and ask for
fuel; also burnt over two hundred pannels of fence of mine." A group of
soldiers who crept up behind John Smith's farm wagon managed to uncrate
and release a dozen chickens. "They are up to all kinds of tricks," Miller
concluded. "What one does not know another does."[62]

In December, rumors of a Confederate attack at Williamsport or
Sharpsburg brought the First Maryland Regiment, USA, west to repel the
intruders. Civilians near Hancock endured several brief artillery duels when
a Rebel force unsuccessfully tried to destroy a dam on the C&O Canal and
hamstring area commerce in the process. On December 8 a shelled barn
burned, and the wheat, oats, corn, hay, and straw inside with it. A month
later, Otho Nesbitt wrote, "A flag was sent over to let the women and children [in Hancock] know if the troops did not have the town they would
shell it. Word was sent back to fire away. Then the cannonading commenced." The Union troops who passed through Clear Spring to help

defend Hancock helped themselves to Nesbitt's hay and wood "and went off without paying for anything or even giving certificate of debt."[63]

Invasion seemed imminent once again the following spring, when Confederate major general Thomas "Stonewall" Jackson's force chased Federal major general Nathaniel Banks's troops out of the Shenandoah Valley and back across the Potomac. "[Hagerstown] is filled with refugees and escaped soldiers," wrote a correspondent on May 22, "who give a most horrible account of the sufferings of the Union men."[64] The roads were jammed with citizens scrambling to get out of the way of the advancing army, toting babies and pushing carts and wheelbarrows piled crazily with baskets of food and prized china. Hotels and private homes overflowed with the refugees, and field edges took on a gypsy air as the less fortunate made makeshift camps along the roads. Some shopkeepers in Hagerstown locked their doors and sent merchandise north to Pennsylvania. City officials were among those who fled, trundling public records with them for safekeeping. The Hagerstown Bank collected all bank notes not in circulation and burned them. A new set was issued when the crisis passed, a pattern that would be repeated. Silver and gold coins disappeared almost immediately, hoarded away and kept out of circulation throughout the war.

The threats of impending disaster, although without immediate foundation, exacerbated tensions. Attacks on known Confederate sympathizers became more frequent in Hagerstown. County loyalists also convened there to determine the best way to promote the president's call for more troops. Subcommittees were formed to report on the status of recruits from the various hamlets and villages in Washington County. A contemporary proudly reported, "Washington County has led the state in furnishing troops. . . . Out of a voting population of fifty-five hundred, she has already furnished fourteen companies of one hundred men each. . . . She has four companies that hold the right in as many regiments; she has five companies in the First Regiment Potomac Home Brigade."[65]

The women were also doing their part. Few had silk, but they stitched flags from sturdy cambric, and only a few complained that the red used was too dark. Women in Clear Spring wore aprons of the national colors, with star-studded bibs and striped skirts. Union Relief Associations were organized at several locations within the county; while women sewed shirts and rolled bandages, children were given the tedious task of scraping lint. And in the privacy of obscure cabins or in the noisy crush of Hagerstown's train

*Sharpsburg physician Augustin Biggs (possibly the man in the rear), with his extended family. Augustin had three sons with his first wife (Margaret), Charles, Elward, and William; and a daughter with his second wife (Elizabeth), Stella. The family is posing in front of their home (and Augustin's office) on the Sharpsburg square. Augustin practiced for more than fifty years and delivered at least three thousand babies.* COURTESY MARIAN AND SID GALE.

station came painful good-byes. One woman gave her husband and seven sons to a company.

These things notwithstanding, the war had yet to fully descend on Washington County. When August faded to September 1862, most western Maryland farmers worried as much about their crops as the war news. The weather was hot and unusually dry, and with so many young men off to war, hired harvest hands were hard to come by. Cradlers were needed, plus gleaners to follow in their wake; at the more prosperous farms, men were needed to gather what the mowers felled. Women were baking gingerbread for harvest suppers and hoarding lemons for lemonade. Boys jostled for the honor of hauling jugs of water and whiskey to the fieldhands. Courting couples looked forward to cornhusking bees.

The farmers were good husbands of the soil. They tended their fields with care, kept their reapers and fanning mills in good repair. They eyed the weather and scrutinized their ripening gardens, orchards, and fields. But someone else was interested in their harvest. On September 2 Confederate general Robert E. Lee, commanding the Army of Northern Virginia, wrote Confederate president Jefferson Davis, "The present seems to be the most propitious time since the commencement of the war for the Confederate Army to enter Maryland."[66]

# CHAPTER 2

# "In a Small Commotion"

The Maryland county soon to bear the first brunt of invasion was not Washington but Frederick, to the east. Small agricultural service communities like Middletown and Burkittsville crouched in the lovely valley between South and Catoctin Mountains. The city of Frederick also lay in the shadow of the mountain ridges bisecting Maryland's western panhandle, forty miles from both Baltimore and Washington. By 1860 it was a thriving city of eight thousand people, known for its many high-spired churches. Its location along the National Road and a well-serviced rail line, and its role as county seat, attracted farmers and travelers. Well-to-do residents attended musical concerts, organized Sunday-school fairs, and had their likenesses photographed. The less fortunate tramped to work each day in one of the smelly tanneries near the depot or found employment in one of the town's butcher shops, apothecaries, or brickmaking establishments. Carpenters indulgently gave children wood shavings and odd scraps to play with, and a German clockmaker let them gather every hour to watch a cuckoo clock perform. Most free blacks in Frederick worked as general laborers or 'servants, but some found employment as whitewashers, brickmakers, blacksmiths, chandlers, coachmen, tanners, porters, and barbers.

The town got its first hint of impending conflict in October 1859. When the telegraph tapped a garbled message of insurrection and violence from Harpers Ferry, members of the city fire companies rattled south in "the cars" to offer assistance. In an uneasy and futile attempt to coerce John Brown's surrender, Captain John Sinn was later sent into the engine house where the abolitionist was ensconced with the remnants of his murderous band. The Frederick militia was eventually reinforced by a company of marines commanded by a lieutenant colonel named Robert E. Lee, accompanied by Lieutenant James Ewell Brown "Jeb" Stuart. John Brown was captured, tried, and convicted. On the way to the gallows he handed a guard a prophetic note: "I . . . am now quite certain that the crimes of this guilty land will never be purged away but with blood."[1]

Six months later, John Brown's prophecy came true. *The Examiner,* the local newspaper, trumpeted the heavy news on April 17: "With a sad heart, we record the commencement of Civil War in our once happy, great, and heaven-favored country!" Flags began to appear—the new secessionist flags along with American flags hung everywhere by loyalists. Just as quickly, offending flags were hauled down from windowsills after dark and flagpoles cut. One "sneaking villain" even cut to shreds an American flag in Burucher's Ice Cream Saloon. When four young men cursed the national flag in Libertytown, Unionist citizens forced them to salute it properly and curse secessionism. The painted silk or pieced and appliquéd cotton represented everything each side held dear.[2]

In April, Frederick citizens jammed into a local hall to observe state legislators convening in their own city. Trying to avoid mounting hostility and a secession vote, the governor had ordered the session moved from the statehouse at Annapolis to the quiet western city. That august legislative body was in a dither; it took the Senate from April 26 until June 7 to approve the flying of the national flag over Kemp Hall. It did not bode well for a quick, decisive action that both sides were screaming for. Determined to hold Maryland in the Union, the Lincoln administration eventually ruled against allowing the legislature to decide the critical issue constitutionally. In September 1861, the Third Wisconsin Infantry, which was stationed in Frederick, received special orders. "Guards were stationed on all roads leading out of town," wrote one Wisconsonite, "and detachments of men, accompanied by detectives, proceeded to arrest the members of the Maryland Legislature, who had assembled there for the purpose of passing an ordinance of secession. . . . Her secessionist legislators found themselves, shortly after, assembled at Fort McHenry, with leisure to meditate upon their schemes."[3] All told, fourteen legislators and eight other civilians were arrested. The majority refused to take an oath of allegiance and were shipped east in heavily guarded train cars. The sudden ring of pickets around the city prompted considerable excitement as citizens traveling on ordinary business found their way in or out of the city barred until they could obtain a pass.

Unionist citizens rejoiced at the averted crisis. Outraged secessionists fumed about the suspension of constitutional rights. "It was a trying time,"

*This 1862 sketch made by a soldier in Frederick, Maryland, provides a glimpse of the church spires and distant mountain ridges that delighted so many passersby. Sketch by Charles F. Johnson.* COURTESY CARABELLE BOOKS.

wrote a local historian, "a time when friends and neighbors were compelled to look into each others' faces with feelings of doubt and apprehension; estrangements began in circles that had been closely knit together for years in the quiet activities of a complacent life in a well-ordered community."[4]

Federal troops pitched their tents in pastures around the city, and martial law descended. Soon anyone heard singing "Dixie" was subject to arrest. Civilians were prohibited from crossing the Potomac into Virginia without a pass from military officials. Vocal Confederates were asked to take an oath of loyalty. Nineteen "lewd" women were arrested and carted off to Washington.

The arrests were part of a sweep that ranged from Baltimore to the mountains of western Maryland. Eighteen-year-old Joseph Stonebraker, clerk and son of a well-to-do Funkstown merchant, was one of those taken into custody and asked to give an oath of allegiance. "I told the marshal that I was but a boy, not yet out of my teens," he wrote, "that I could not help being born and raised in the South, that it was only natural that my feelings were in that direction, but at the same time I had never committed any overt act against the Government, and thought it both unfair and unreasonable to be required to take the oath." Unimpressed, the marshal sent the boy to a jail in Hagerstown already overflowing with political prisoners.[5]

Frederick bustled with new activity. Pedestrians jostled each other on crowded sidewalks, crushing women's voluminous skirts. Mothers clutched toddlers' hands to keep from being separated. Blushing girls dared sidelong glances at the frankly admiring young soldiers, made bold by their first excursion far from home. A local reporter described the excitement:

> Our usually quiet inland city is now all life and bustle; business is brisk; throngs of soldiers and citizens crowd the streets, incessantly . . . passing to and fro . . . detachments of troops, enlivened by the notes of the drum and fife, the inspiring bugle, and music from military bands, the brilliant and varied military costumes, and the rush of ladies attracted . . . while the slopes of the Blue Ridge, on the west, glitter in the autumnal sun with the encamped host.[6]

Inspired, loyal men formed Union Clubs and raised liberty poles with appropriate pomp and ceremony. Military officers and their families were honored guests in wealthy homes. On July 4 soldiers stationed in town were feted with a dinner that included, one diarist estimated, two thousand pies.[7] When the First Maryland Infantry, USA, was formed in 1861, Company H was recruited in Frederick. When the Potomac Home Brigade was organized to guard against Confederate raids across the Potomac, the First Regiment was raised in Frederick County as well. The brigade's First Cavalry ("Cole's Cavalry") was also formed in the city. Schoolteachers and carpenters achieved new status as captains and lieutenants. Underage boys ran away to join the army, and their fathers trudged to the camps to haul them home.

Union women organized to give their boys a proper send-off. They stitched silk flags to present, and made countless housewives, or "hussies"— sewing kits with perhaps a bar of soap and packet of medicinal powders—for the men so soon to be without female care. Special requests were made for mittens with an index finger knitted in so the wearer could fire a gun. Sure that their boys would suffer sunstroke in the South, the "patriotic and loyal" ladies of Frederick presented Company H of the First Maryland with one hundred havelocks.[8] The men weren't sure what to do with the muslin caps with protective neck drapes. But they appreciated the sentiment.

The commotion increased in August 1861, when the Federal army established a military hospital in a stone barracks on the outskirts of Frederick that had once housed George Washington's troops during the Revolutionary War and, later, Hessian prisoners of war. In December the Hessian Barracks were named a division hospital for the Army of the Potomac, and three months later it opened as a general hospital for the Union army. A group of Sisters of Charity arrived from Emmitsburg to help with the nursing. That fall the Ladies' Relief Association formed, with Julia Bantz serving as its president. Seven committees were appointed, each assigned the task of collecting and distributing relief goods to the hospital on a designated day of the week. The Frederick ladies collected quilts and blankets, slippers and socks, magazines and backgammon boards for the wounded. When Dorothea Dix asked someone in Philadelphia to send a

*In August 1861, Brigadier General Nathaniel Banks established the United States Hospital on the grounds of the old military barracks near South Market Street in Frederick. Local women immediately organized to provide support to the hospital. During the 1862 campaign, as many as nine hundred sick and wounded soldiers were convalescing there.* COURTESY NANCY WHITMORE.

relief box to Frederick because "they need everything," the Frederick ladies indignantly informed Miss Dix that she was wrongly informed, as the local Ladies Relief Association had provided everything the men could want.[9]

Secessionist women gathered more discreetly. In stifling parlors, behind closed shutters, they stitched shirts and drawers for their boys. Southern-minded men, meanwhile, met quietly and organized their forces. Their commitment was so well-known that in April 1861, when the passage of the Union troops through Baltimore incited a riot, an urgent telegram requesting assistance was sent immediately to Southern organizer Bradley T. Johnson: "Streets red with Maryland blood! Send expresses over the mountains and valleys of Maryland and Virginia for their riflemen to come without delay. Fresh hordes will be down upon us tomorrow. We will fight them and whip them, or die."[10] Johnson acted at once, and his Frederick Mounted Dragoons, most of them boys not out of their teens, eagerly dashed off to the fray.

Frederick native and lawyer Bradley Tyler Johnson was proud of his illustrious Maryland lineage—especially the Revolutionary War hero who graced his family tree. Johnson had represented the Maryland Democratic Party at the 1860 national convention; he also copublished a weekly newspaper, the *Maryland Union*. His militia, which became known as the Frederick Volunteers, followed him across the Potomac when it became apparent that Maryland was not going to secede. Johnson wrote, "[The soldiers] held and believed that their mother State had been betrayed by treachery, and was then bound and manacled, hand and foot." He declined a commission in the Virginia service, determined to organize a distinctive Maryland command instead. His militia became the senior company in the First Maryland Regiment, CSA.[11] His home was seized by the government and became the headquarters for Union major general Nathaniel Banks on his arrival in Frederick later in 1861.

The Confederate First Maryland Regiment was a source of pride for the Frederick secessionists. During these first few months of war, security was still lax, and they often traveled across the Potomac to visit Rebel soldiers—Maryland or otherwise—in camp. One frequent visitor was Catherine Thomas Markell, a young wife and mother from a prominent family. She had married her husband, Charles Frederick Markell (known as Fred) in 1851. They enjoyed a loving relationship, and both were fervently committed to the Southern cause. Fred, a prosperous merchant, was absent from home on most occasions when battles were pending in Maryland or northern Virginia, possibly aiding the Southern troops in some manner. This was no hollow undertaking, even then; more than once Fred was fired on or arrested. Despite their convictions, however, the Markells managed to maintain cordial relations with people on both sides of the political chasm splitting their city.

The Markells were friends with many prominent secessionists in Maryland, including the family of Henry Kyd Douglas, living at Ferry Hill across the Potomac from Shepherdstown. Catherine captured those exciting days in her diary. On one occasion she and a large group of sympathizers pacified Federal pickets in Maryland with cigars and cakes, passing through the lines to visit a camp of Mississippi soldiers at Harpers Ferry. She noted that one of the gentlemen presented Colonel Falkner of the Second Mississippi, "from the Frederick ladies, two immense, handsomely iced poundcakes and a bushel of fine strawberries." The colonel thanked the women prettily before passing the cakes on to his men; the other officers were presented with bouquets and gingersnaps. The visitors were in turn treated to a picnic dinner, drills, and dancing by the black servant of one of the men.[12] As the years went by, Catherine would add notes in the margin of her diary as the men she had met that day were killed.

Frederick's most prolific diarist was Jacob Engelbrecht, a tailor with a keen interest in politics and national affairs. Little in Frederick escaped the notice of this future mayor as he spent his days sitting cross-legged on his counter, stitching, watching events unfold beyond his window, and pausing to jot observations and thoughts in the diaries kept always at hand. He was born in 1797, the son of a Hessian soldier who had been taken prisoner at Yorktown and brought to Frederick. Perhaps in defiance of his father's anti-American roots—or perhaps in celebration of his father's ultimate decision to stay in America—Engelbrecht was an ardent Unionist. Reflecting on the secession threats from Southern states, he wrote, "At this time They are making Wonderful preperation to leave this Glorious Union; for my [part] I say go as quick as you please,—they have been Domone[ering] long enough—the sooner they go the better."[13]

The community was being torn apart. So were some families. One man wrote later, "My grandfather Urner believed the sun rose and set in Abraham Lincoln, and my grandmother Floyd just as stoutly maintained that same astronomical tribute applied to Jefferson Davis."[14] In the Tyson home on East Church Street, the secessionists occupied one floor and the Unionists another; they maintained relative peace by forbidding any discus-

*A contemporary described Jacob Engelbrecht as a "thrifty, jocose individual of German extraction and historical proclivities." Jacob, son of a Hessian soldier, was a keen observer and prolific diarist who kept a careful record of his observations of Frederick life.* COURTESY THE HISTORICAL SOCIETY OF FREDERICK COUNTY.

sion of politics.[15] Heartbroken women dreaded the endless nights, haunted with the knowledge that husbands and sons were in enemy armies.

Even the churches weren't spared. "Church members fell out and would not speak," remembered Allen Sparrow of Middletown.[16] More than one congregation split, and new churches were formed along sectional lines. In Frederick, the rector of the All Saints' Episcopal Church was made so uncomfortable by his secession-minded parishioners that he resigned.

The pastor of the Presbyterian church would soon resign in turn because his Southern politics caused resentment among his mostly Unionist flock.[17]

The war wasn't as much fun as it had been. To curb indiscretions, merchants were ordered not to sell alcohol to soldiers; those who did were raided by the provost guard. (One saloonkeeper, Christian Eckstein, was raided three times.) The military presence was taking a financial toll on men like Jeremiah Cramer, who petitioned the army for help: "The teams are still hauling wood. I am exceedingly sorry that you told the Quarter Master about it. I am apprehensive that he will keep on sending the teams until there won't be a stick left me for winter. I am fearful that you will be the means of losing considerably on that wood. I could have gotten three and a quarter for every cord of that wood."[18] Jacob Engelbrecht noted glumly, "In our town everything is Knocked into pie—Mechanics have no work, Stores, do hardly any thing, Except, Groceries which people must have,—No building going on, in the Brick yards the weeds are growing up."[19] In October 1861, six members of the Third Wisconsin—the regiment detailed to arrest the secessionist legislators—were killed near Harpers Ferry and buried with military honors at Frederick. By the end of 1861, fifteen thousand troops were quartered in Frederick.

A law passed by the Maryland general assembly went into effect in the spring of 1862. This so-called Treason Bill provided a penalty for anyone found to be giving "aid and comfort" to the enemy. The stakes were now higher. Men were arrested for carrying packages of mail for Marylanders in the Confederate army, for spying, for using signal flags to communicate with the enemy. Still, hot-headed Frederick men spoke their minds. In April, when one Sergeant Kelly of the Potomac Home Brigade drank a toast to the Union at a saloon on South Market Street, he was answered by John Sinn, son of Captain John T. Sinn who had confronted John Brown at Harpers Ferry. Sinn the younger then invited a party to the bar and proposed a toast to "the health of Brad Johnson and his followers." Kelly indignantly fetched a squad of soldiers to help empty the saloon. Sinn was arrested, boasting he would never take the oath. Son and father were ultimately incarcerated at Fort McHenry as political prisoners.[20]

In May a young woman whose fiancé was killed announced at his funeral that she wouldn't long survive him; she committed suicide by taking laudanum.[21] Horrified fascination met the news of an engagement at Front Royal, Virginia, in which the two First Maryland Regiments, Federal and Confederate, clashed. And citizens marked each battle with reports from the military hospital at their own Hessian barracks. As the sick and wounded arrived, additional buildings were pressed into service. *The Examiner* published a call for scraped lint, needed for bandages.[22] The Sisters of Charity stationed at the hospital and the Frederick women who worked to keep them provided with relief supplies saw firsthand the toll of war. They could not imagine how much worse it was going to get.

>–•◊►•O•◄•►•◄

By September 1862, Robert E. Lee was eyeing the bounteous western Maryland countryside. Lee had good reason to consider crossing the Potomac. Virginia was stripped bare. The Army of Northern Virginia was starving, and if it stayed in Virginia any longer, the farm families there would starve, too. But across the river the fertile fields of western Maryland had not yet been scarred by war. Apple orchards with fruit-laden branches, endless rows of ripe corn, and well-stocked root cellars beckoned like a siren from the Potomac's north shore.

Politically, such a bold move would allow Lee to harass the enemy on their own soil, feeding the North's growing opposition to the war. A successful venture across the river might nudge England, and perhaps other European countries, to declare support for the Confederacy. Federal troops might also be lured away from Washington to give chase, leaving that prize poorly defended and reducing the threat of a Yankee thrust at the Confederate capital of Richmond. The Southerners also hoped the invasion would "capture" Maryland. After the secession vote had been permanently forestalled, the state was referred to in the South as "the weeping maiden, bound and fettered, seeking relief."[23] Confederate leaders believed their move north would rally support in the bitterly divided state.

And so, with high hopes, the Confederate army began splashing across the Potomac on Thursday, September 4, at several fords near Leesburg, Virginia. The troops had no idea of their destination and speculated about Washington or Philadelphia. A Texan named John Stevens described the chaos:

Imagine a river . . . about 500 yards wide, from two to three feet deep, the water very swift. Now it is just as full of men as it can be for 600 or 700 yards, up and down, yelling and singing all sorts of war and jolly songs, and in this connection you must find room for eight or twelve regimental bands in the river all the time, the

drums beating, the horns a tootin' and the fifes a screaming, possibly every one of them on a different air, some "Dixie" and some
"Maryland, My Maryland," some "The Girl I Left Behind Me"
and some "Yankee Doodle."

Cavalrymen swam their horses. A few musicians lost their drums, much to
the amusement of their comrades, who watched as the instruments floated
downstream toward Washington. Teamsters had no trouble crossing with
their empty supply wagons. Men in the infantry stripped to their bare
essentials, wrapped their ammunition in their trousers and held it above
their heads. Those who had shoes hung them around their necks. Barefoot,
they waded into the current. One soldier, who stumbled on a rock and
went under, wondered if all the good residents of western Maryland had
emptied their icehouses into the river the night before.[24] John Stevens, who
paused on the bank to cook a pumpkin he had found, wondered if he alone
was uneasy. "I could not . . . suppress a feeling of sadness as I beheld this
vast concourse of humanity wading the river, so full of music and apparently never once thinking that their feet (many of them) would never press
the soil on the south side of the Potomac again."[25]

It was a diminished band of cavaliers. Some Confederates balked at the
idea of invading the North; many of these disappeared before the crossing.
Stragglers too hungry or ill shod to keep going were left at Leesburg. Political ideology, hunger, and exhaustion robbed the Southern army of about
fifteen thousand men before they reached the river. But many of those left
were exuberant, dreaming of full bellies and buoyed with the belief that the
Southern army was invincible. Two months earlier, the Union army had
been threatening Richmond; now the Yankees were skulking near their
own fortifications around Washington. The toughened veterans were ready
to finish the job, and reaching the Maryland shore was significant. "There
were few moments, perhaps," wrote a cavalryman, "from the beginning to
the close of the war, of excitement more intense, of exhilaration more
delightful."[26]

The happiest lot were undoubtedly the Marylanders who had joined the
Confederate army, now outlaws in their own home state. "To be a Confederate soldier meant for the Marylander . . . exile from home and kindred,"
wrote Randolph McKim, who served in Lee's army. "It meant to be cut off
from communication with father and mother, brother and sister, and wife. It

meant to have an impenetrable barrier of forts and armies between him and all he loved and cherished best in the world. Oh, the loneliness of the Maryland soldier of the Confederate army!"[27] Jonathan Thomas Scharf of the First Maryland Artillery was among the Marylanders coming home that day. "You could express the joy of all the boys as they trespassed on their sacred soil," he wrote later, "hoping never to leave it again."[28] Captain Lige White, who crossed the river near his home in Poolesville, "threw himself from his horse," remembered Henry Kyd Douglas, "among a group of mothers and daughters, and kissed such a lot of them in five minutes, that I venture to say the record was never broken."[29]

But few had such a reception. The envisioned crowds of cheering civilians waiting on the northern shore were not in sight. One veteran recalled, "The coldness of the water . . . was more than equaled by the frigidity of the welcome extended. Not even the dulcet strains of "Maryland, My Maryland" evoked from the half-submerged instruments of [the] band aroused the enthusiasm of the people; no arms opened to receive, no fires blazed to warm, and no feast waited to feed us, as wet, shivering, and hungry, we stepped out of the water and set our feet on Maryland's soil."[30] Expecting more, some of the men were discouraged. "Instead of an outburst of overflowing joy, at the sight of their deliverers, not one solitary soul had come to the River bank to see us cross or welcome us to the soil," James Steptoe Johnston of the 11th Missouri wrote home to his future wife.[31]

The men shivering on the bank were not an impressive lot. Most had long since shucked their knapsacks, marching hard with light blanket rolls and grimy haversacks and, here and there, a bedraggled toothbrush stuffed into a buttonhole. "We are a miserable looking sight," Franklin Riley of the 16th Mississippi admitted to his diary. "We are dirty, unshaven, tired; our clothes are smelly; toes gap from our shoes. . . . We have not made a very favorable impression on Maryland."[32] Observing his comrades, Edgar Warfield of the 17th Virginia wondered if every Maryland cornfield had been robbed of its scarecrows.[33] The few civilians who ventured to the river to watch the crossing agreed—and yet knowing that the army that had so often bullied the robust Yankees was composed of such gaunt scarecrows demanded at least grudging respect. "They were the dirtiest, lousiest, filthiest, piratical-looking cut-throat men I ever saw," wrote one young man who watched them. "A most ragged, lean and hungry set of wolves. Yet there was a dash about them that the Northern men lacked."[34]

It took four days to get the Southern army onto Maryland soil. Despite the lukewarm reception, the Confederate soldiers liked what they saw. "The lands are in the highest state of cultivation and every farm has a barn almost as large as Noah's ark," one exulted.[35] With bands playing "Maryland, My Maryland" until the song became oppressive, the Confederate army plunged into Maryland.

Some skirmishing took place in tiny communities in the soldiers' path as the Confederate vanguard and Federal rearguard clashed. "Before night our town had changed hands five times," wrote Mollie Hays Jones of Barnesville, in Montgomery County. Mollie, fourteen years old in 1862, spent those September nights sleeping on a carpet in the cellar and her days scraping lint. It was her secessionist family's "happy privilege" to feed and entertain Major General Jeb Stuart, Brigadier General Wade Hampton, and Brigadier General Fitzhugh Lee. Another officer called for his flag and ordered, "Hand the ladies the flag and let them wave it and put their fingers on every star in it." When some Federal cavalry tried to run the Confederates out of the village, Mollie witnessed a "race for life" as some of her guests were pursued. The Southerners might have escaped if a young Unionist girl hadn't waved the Yankees onto the road they had taken.[36]

The news triggered a panicked stampede in Frederick. "This Morning our town is in a Small Commotion," Jacob Engelbrecht wrote in his diary on September 5, 1862. "The report is that Stonewall Jackson has Crossed the Potomack at Nolands Ferry (12 or 14 miles South of this place) with 12,000 Men."[37] Refugees from the southern part of the county trundled into Frederick, looking for asylum, while the city residents headed north.

By evening the Confederate army was reported only a few miles away. Rumors flew like swallows through the city. By one account, the Rebels were taking all cattle, sheep, and horses. "General consternation and a grand stampede of loyal citizens ensued," noted one observer.[38] Civilians jammed local banks to withdraw valuables. Timid Unionists fearful of retribution— public officials among them—fled toward Baltimore or Pennsylvania with food and ancestral silver packed in buggies, wheelbarrows, and saddlebags. Farmers left, too, with strings of horses they intended to hide. "This is a day long to be remembered . . . ," Otho Nesbitt of Clear Spring wrote in his diary on September 10. "About 12 or 1 o'clock everything put for the mountain, and there are scarcely anything left but women and children. . . . Not withstanding the long drought, the day is cloudy and drizzling; probably will be a bad night to sleep in the mountain." Prominent businessmen on horseback "were last seen going toward the mountain with their coattails nearly straight out."[39] Soon the roads were clogged with refugees.

Frederick was serving as a Union supply depot, and Captain William T. Faithful of the First Maryland Regiment, Potomac Home Brigade, received telegraphed orders to drive off all horses and remove or destroy all Federal property. "We succeeded in getting off all the most valuable hospital stores in wagons and ambulances, together with about three hundred convalescents from the hospital, to a place of safety in Pennsylvania," he reported. "After having sent all the most valuable stores by all availing means at hand, we set about destroying by fire the remains."[40] Huge clouds of black smoke boiled into the sky as the provost guard burned government stores of cots, tents, and other supplies. The conflagration only added to the general panic. One witness described the scene as one of terror.[41] Catherine Markell ventured onto her roof to watch the chaos. "Rumors of the approach of the Confederate Army—Federals are burning their stores and 'Skedaddling,'" she wrote. "We stayed on the roof of the house until after midnight. Saw the sick from the Barrick hospital straggling, with bandaged heads, etc., toward Pa."[42] Those who had doubted the rumors of Confederate advance were now convinced.

On Saturday morning, September 6, two Confederate cavalrymen dashed unopposed into town shouting, "Jefferson Davis!" and, "The time of your delivery has come!" They were followed by Colonel Bradley T. Johnson and a hundred and fifty horsemen. By midmorning, pro-Northern citizens cringed to the sound of "Maryland, My Maryland" and "Dixie" being blared in execrable style by a military band as General Stonewall Jackson's advance force of about five thousand men streamed up Market Street and made camp on the north side of town.[43]

The town watched with some apprehension. "We were rather disappointed at our reception, which was decidedly cool," wrote infantryman Alexander Hunter, who arrived later. "This wasn't what we expected. . . . There was positively no enthusiasm, no cheers, no waving handkerchiefs and flags—instead a death-like silence—some houses were closed tight, as if some public calamity had taken place."[44] A South Carolinian noted that although some women did bring out food, "others held their noses and waved the Union flag."[45] William Ellis Jones wrote in his diary, "There was no excitement and the people seemed to be afraid to acknowledge that they had souls."[46]

Dr. Lewis Steiner, a Frederick native, active Unionist, and inspector for the Sanitary Commission, watched Jackson's men with disgust. "A dirtier, filthier, more unsavory set of human beings never strolled through a town— marching it could not be called without doing violence to the word," he wrote.[47] A Union woman described her reaction:

I felt humiliated at the thought that this horde of ragamuffins could set our grand army of the Union at defense. Why, it seems as if a single regiment of our gallant boys in blue could drive that dirty crew in the river without any trouble. And then, too, I wish you could see how they behaved—a crowd of boys on a holiday don't seem happier. . . .Oh! they are so dirty! I don't think the Potomac river could wash them clean; and ragged!—there is not a scarecrow in the corn-fields that would not scorn to exchange clothes with them.[48]

The Confederates, however, were undaunted. A drummer boy with the Fifth Carolina cheerfully explained their state to detractors: "We have a dirty job to do—whipping you Yankees, and you reckon we were going to put on our clean clothes to do it in?"[49] Private Hunter put it differently. "[We] had full haversacks, and therefore light hearts," he wrote, "and in that way we went through the most loyal city in Maryland."[50] With full or aching hearts, the Frederick civilians saw Union flags replaced with the Confederate Stars and Bars.

At the barracks hospital a Union doctor who had stayed with those patients too sick or wounded to flee calmly surrendered the facility to the Confederate army. Union invalids were politely paroled. The Sisters of Charity, who had also stayed, were shocked by the condition of the Con- federate soldiers. More than four hundred exhausted, emaciated, and dehydrated boys were brought to the hospital for medical attention. They informed the nuns that a few handfuls of green corn, picked while on the march, constituted their only food for the past two weeks. The nurses had just begun to minister to the suffering boys when the Union surgeon reminded them that, as employees of the Union government, they were prohibited in providing any aid. "The Union army was daily expected," he added, "and as soon as it would reach the city the Confederate sick

*This column of Confederate troops passed Joseph Rosenstock's Dry Good and Clothing Store at the corner of Patrick and Market Streets, Frederick, in 1862. They were disappointed in their hopes for a strong rally from local men. "A few men ran away from their homes to join them," a Northern journalist noted sarcastically, "but when they saw and smelt the rebel army, they thought better of the enterprise."* Harpers Weekly, *October 4, 1862.* COURTESY THE HISTORICAL SOCIETY OF FREDERICK COUNTY.

would receive the same care and attention as the Union soldiers." For the poor sisters, idleness in the face of such misery was a "trial." The open-hearted citizens of Frederick had no compunction about providing assistance, and thronged to the hospital. The cakes and custards they provided were welcome, but in some cases too rich for the emaciated patients. The sisters watched helplessly as well-intentioned ministrations proved fatal in several cases.[51]

For the next several days, Lee's scarecrow army surged through town. Anxious townspeople soon realized the soldiers were more interested in shopping than causing trouble. "No Commotion or Excitement—but all peaceably & quiet the Soldiers are around the town purchasing Clothing—Shoes boots Caps. & eatables," Jacob Engelbrecht wrote in his diary.[52] Fred Markell was advised to avoid chaos by closing his store and admitting buyers in squads of ten or twelve at a time. Shoes were in desperate demand, for the barefoot soldiers wanted extra pairs to send to their families; they were also looking for other goods for their families in the supply-choked South. "I have in my trunk a quantity of spool cotton and sewing silk for Ma and five pounds of tea for Ma and Grandma which I will endeavor to send home," wrote Greenlee Davidson. "I will also send a few calico dresses and several pair of ladies shoes."[53]

Stores were kept open on Sunday. Those merchants willing—or ordered—to do business were paid in Confederate "shinplasters," which, Steiner noted, "depreciated the paper on which they were printed."[54] Any soldier with money was too dazed by opportunity to entertain business decorum. "Prices are going up rapidly," a Southern correspondent related. "Everything is so cheap that our men frequently lay down a five dollar bill to pay for a three dollar article, and rush out without waiting for the change."[55] Within hours shopkeepers had empty shelves and enough notes to paper their walls. But the town was unable to adequately supply the barefoot army. "I think I am within bounds when I say there were at least ten thousand in town," Engelbrecht wrote on September 9. "A complete Jam, all the Stores & Shops were Sold out, & not one half Supplied."[56]

Some Union homes remained shuttered with dark disapproval, but many Yankee citizens pitied the gaunt boys or relished the opportunity to feed and patronize the Rebels. Confederate civilians, of course, were more gracious. One secessionist farmer, who had been forced to take an oath forbidding him from providing food or even pointing out his spring to the Southern soldiers, sent his wife into town to disperse all the provisions they could spare. Catherine Markell was delighted with her visitors, graciously serving tea and refreshments to a dazzling parade of officers. Somehow she managed to find time for her diary:

Gen. McLaws & staff, Gen. Kershaw and staff, took tea with us. Some 20 officers and many girls here until midnight. Mrs. Hanson sent us a large basket of provisions, as the stores are held by troops, and we could get none. General Barksdale secured a pass & Henry went with Cash & Billy out to Bruner's mill for flour, butter, &c.

Our house was brilliantly illuminated at night, & horses in charge
of orderlies stood 3 deep, the length of the square.[57]

Two days later, more than three hundred soldiers took meals at her house.
She was also hosting Henry Kyd Douglas's parents, who had traveled to
Frederick to see their son, and a number of other Confederate citizens.

In town or camped nearby, there was no shortage of officers for Southerners to admire. For a short, glorious time General Robert E. Lee and
Major Generals James Longstreet, Stonewall Jackson, and Jeb Stuart camped
in a grove near town. Excited sightseers pushed their way out of town even
as hungry soldiers pushed their way in. Some Unionists came out of
curiosity, but the secessionists came to welcome and adore, showering the
officers with bouquets and sugar cakes and asking for autographs or buttons
or horsehairs from their mounts' manes or tails as souvenirs. Meanwhile,
some of the lowly privates watched with longing. "We young ones look on,
and only wish that they would distribute those favors a little more 'per-
miscus,' so to speak," wrote William Owen, an artillery officer.[58]

In the interest of goodwill the heroes persevered—but with some difficulty. Markell and her friends insisted on gingerly shaking Robert E. Lee's
hand, despite a fall that had left both of his hands bandaged to the finger-
tips. "Touch them gently, ladies," he told them.[59] A heel blister had
Longstreet limping around in a carpet slipper. Stonewall Jackson was nursing a wrenched back. Henry Kyd Douglas, one of Jackson's aides, also
noted that the zealous attentions of adoring and animated crowds seemed
to overwhelm Jackson. "He stood for a moment cap in hand, bowing,
speechless, paralyzed. . . . When he got back to his tent, safe, he did not
venture out again until late in the evening." Only lighthearted cavalryman
Jeb Stuart reveled in the attention, ready, as Douglas observed, "to see and
talk to every good-looking woman."[60]

Stuart was, as Markell noted, "a gay, rocking Cavalier & a great favorite
with the girls."[61] Sebastian Graff Cockey, a prosperous storekeeper in
Urbana, had offered his yard for cavalry headquarters. His daughters Martha
and Virginia became great favorites of the Southern men. Anne Cockey, a
cousin visiting from New York, piqued Stuart's fancy; he called her his
"New York Rebel." Major Heros von Borcke recalled an afternoon whiled
away with the Cockeys: "In the agreeable conversation of these ladies, in
mirth and song, the afternoon of our dinner party passed lightly and rapidly

*The caption to this cartoon, "The 'Invasion' of the North," reads, "Old Quaker Lady of Maryland, anticipating the seizure of her House by Lee's Troops, puts out a Washing Stand as a desirable preliminary step thereto. The Rebel Scouts mistake the—to them—Strange Apparatus for an Infurnal Machine, and Skedaddle. Old Lady (to retreating Rebel), 'If thou wants my House, Friend, thou may'st have it; but oh! do wash thyself before entering in.'" Even Confederate sympathizers were shocked by the appearance of the Rebel soldiers.* COURTESY FRANK & MARIE-THERESE WOOD PRINT COLLECTIONS, ALEXANDRIA, VIRGINIA.

away; and then came night with a round moon, whose beams penetrating the windows suggested to our debonair commander a promenade." While on the moonlit stroll, the little group came across a vacant private school. Stuart had an idea: "Major, what a capital place for us to give a ball in honor of our arrival in Maryland!" The delighted ladies promised to attend to the invitations; the cavalrymen would take care of everything else. "A soldier's life is so uncertain . . .," wrote von Borcke, "that in affairs of this sort delays are always to be avoided; and so we determined on our way home, to the great joy of our fair companions, that the ball should come off the following evening."[62]

By the next night, September 7, the musty academy had been swept, aired, and transformed into a grand hall. Candles flickered in the evening breeze. Regimental flags graced the walls. Roses had been gathered to scent the air. The 18th Mississippi Infantry band provided quadrilles and polkas. The troopers gallantly hung their sabers aside before leading blushing ladies, wearing their finest, to the dance floor. "The strange accompaniments of war added zest to the occasion," remembered Captain William Blackford, "and our lovely partners declared that it was perfectly charming." For a short while the war was everything exalted and gallant that the young wished it to be.

But in the midst of gaiety a breathless aide rushed inside and reported that the enemy had engaged the Southern pickets and was driving through the line. Blackford described the scene:

> Just as everything had become well started and the enjoyment of the evening was at its height, there came shivering through the still night air the boom of artillery . . . the lily chased the rose from the cheek of beauty, and every pretty foot was rooted to the floor where music had left it. Then came hasty and tender partings from tearful partners, buckling on of sabers, mounting of impatient steeds, and clattering of hoofs as the gay cavaliers dashed off to the front.[63]

Parents snatched their bewildered children and headed for home. The more romantic ladies stayed, listening uneasily to the sounds of musketry and occasional artillery, waiting. Shortly, however, the Federals who had pushed the Confederate rear guard retired, and Stuart and his men returned. Dancing recommenced. "Many of our pretty fugitives were brought back by young officers who eagerly volunteered for that commendable purpose," von Borcke noted, "and as everybody was determined that the Yankees should not boast of having completely broken up our party, the dancing was resumed in less than half an hour, and kept up till the first glimmer of dawn."[64] The whirling couples tried again to push the war away. But all too soon they were interrupted again—this time by the arrival of bloodied casualties as ambulances filled with wounded rumbled to the only building in Urbana suitable for a hospital. Some of the ladies hurried "like a flock of angels" to help, and their white laces and satins were soon spotted with blood. "I'd get hit any day," one boy told Anne Cockey, "to have such surgeons dress my wounds."[65]

⊱⊶⟨⊹⟩⊷⊙⊶⟨⊹⟩⊶⊰

If Stuart was working to woo the ladies, Lee was working to woo the town. He hoped to gain support from local citizens, not frighten or infuriate them. While in Frederick, he issued an official proclamation addressed: "To the People of Maryland." Although it expressed the offer of assistance, Lee made it clear that he wanted above all else to maintain peace with the civilian population: "It is for you to decide your destiny freely and without constraint. This army will respect your choice whatever it may be."[66]

Strict orders demanded the respect of private property. Native son Bradley Johnson was named provost marshal. Farmers were to be compensated by foraging troops. Lewis Steiner noted melodramatically that the "reign of terror continued," but admitted that "no personal violence was done to any citizen."[67] One of the few overt acts of violence was reportedly committed by secessionist civilians, emboldened by the army's presence. They wrecked the office of *The Examiner* at Market and Church Streets; the editor, Frederick Schley, had prudently skedaddled. A Southern correspondent noted the offense indulgently, referring to the paper as "a Black Republican newspaper of the darkest dye."[68]

Even Stonewall Jackson needed a pass to enter the town on Sunday evening to attend services at the Evangelical Reformed Church. Dr. Daniel Zacharias, who had been pastor of the church since 1835, was much beloved by his congregation. "Dr. Zack" was a staunch Unionist but had two sons in the Confederate army: John Forney, a local physician soon to serve as an assistant surgeon with the Army of Tennessee; and Granville, a private in the Maryland Guerrilla Zouaves.[69] Perhaps because his own family was so painfully divided—or perhaps simply by virtue of his own care and tolerance for all his parishioners—the Evangelical Reformed Church remained the chosen place of worship for both Unionist and secessionist members. Catherine Markell, who was a faithful congregant and relied heavily on her pastor's counsel during difficult times, attended service that evening and noted with excitement that the hero Stonewall Jackson arrived with her friend Henry Kyd Douglas and sat only two pews away. To her astonishment, "Dr. Zach prayed for the President of the United States!!" It

*"A Pictorial Commentary Upon Gen. Lee's Proclamation to the People of Maryland."* As this political cartoon shows, Unionists in Frederick placed little faith in Confederate promises to treat the local populace as friends. COURTESY FRANK & MARIE-THERESE WOOD PRINT COLLECTIONS, ALEXANDRIA, VIRGINIA.

was a tense moment, but none of the Confederate soldiers present—including Jackson—responded. Jackson, who called Zacharias a "gifted" minister, wrote to his wife an explanation for his calm reaction: "I was not quite near enough to hear all the sermon, and I regret to say fell asleep." Henry Kyd Douglas, who referred to Dr. Zacharias as "my old friend," implied that this was a common occurrence: "As usual, the General went to sleep at the beginning of the sermon, and a very sound slumber it was. . . . The Doctor was afterwards credited with much loyalty and courage because he prayed for the President of the United States in the presence of Stonewall Jackson. Well the General didn't hear it; but if he had I've no doubt he would have joined in it heartily."[70]

After several days in Frederick, supplies for the Confederate army there were running low. Besides, Lee wanted to cross Catoctin Mountain and South Mountain, heading toward Hagerstown in Washington County—the mountain ridges would shield his movements, and the Hagerstown Road was a good path to Pennsylvania—and he hoped he could obtain more shoes in that city. Despite getting a thousand pairs in Frederick, many of his soldiers were still limping barefoot along the macadamized turnpike and

rocky side roads. Furthermore, Jeb Stuart—the army's "eyes"—reported the
Army of the Potomac was uncoiling from Washington toward Frederick,
with Major General George B. McClellan in command.

Lee also needed to take care of two Federal garrisons that had been isolated by the Confederate invasion, at Harpers Ferry and Martinsburg. The
Rebel general devised a plan calling for the split of his army. He and
Longstreet would begin the march to Pennsylvania with three divisions; the
remainder of the Southern army would attend to the Federal garrisons
before reuniting with Longstreet.

Although ready to move on, most of the soldiers were still in high spirits. "We were not afraid of [the Yankees]," wrote John S. Robson of Jackson's command, "but they might intimidate the Maryland folks, and prevent
them, from some extent, from joining us; and moreover . . . we wished to
enjoy ourselves a little while in this plentiful country, and get some fat on
our bones before breaking up another army for General McClellan."[71] The
men exchanged final souvenirs with pretty girls in paisley shawls and pert
straw bonnets, making blithe promises. "The fair ones, though coy, are very
agreeable," wrote William Owen, "and we each forthwith select one whose
colors we shall wear until we reach the next town."[72] Jackson's advance
force began moving out at 4:00 A.M. on Wednesday, September 10, heading southwest. Jacob Engelbrecht listened to the tramp and creak of an
army he estimated (rather generously) at seventy thousand men, on the
move for seventeen hours. Before leaving, Jackson confused the populace
by asking civilians misleading questions about roads and maps. Regimental
bands played "The Girl I Left Behind Me" while townspeople speculated
about Lee's ultimate goal: Pennsylvania? Washington?

>─┤─◆〉─○─〈◆─┤─�〈

The Confederate retreat sparked a hotly debated literary legend. In John
Greenleaf Whittier's stirring poem "Barbara Fritchie," the ninety-six-year-
old heroine waved a Union flag from a window as General Stonewall Jackson's troops were leaving Frederick on September 10. Seeing the flag,
Jackson halted his troops and barked an order: *"Fire!"* When the volley
severed the flagstaff, Barbara waved the flag herself with the immortal
words, "'Shoot, if you must, this old gray head / But spare your country's
flag,' she said." Her words supposedly shamed Jackson. "'Who touches a
hair on yon gray head / Dies like a dog! March on!' he said."[73]

Barbara Hauer Fritchie was real enough, an active and sharp-tongued widow, described by one contemporary as "a very ignorant German woman" and by another as "a small, withered old woman, with penetrating steel-blue eyes."[74] She was a fervent Unionist and not above caning loitering soldiers while shouting, "Off! You lousy Rebels!" Dr. Steiner wrote of "an aged crone com[ing] out of her house, as certain Rebels passed, trailing the American flag in the dust. She shook her long, skinny hands at the traitors and screamed, at the top of her voice, 'My curses be upon you and your officers for degrading your country's flag!'" Steiner later admitted that the "aged crone" was indeed Fritchie. But the incident involving Stonewall Jackson remains shrouded in contradictions.

By one account, a cry of, "The troops are coming!" sent Fritchie to her porch, flag in hand, in the mistaken belief that the Union army had arrived. When a Confederate threatened to shoot the flag from her hand, an officer rode forward and barked, "If you harm a hair on that old lady's head, I'll shoot you down like a dog." Later Fritchie exclaimed, "They tried to take my flag, but a man would not let them; and he was a gentleman."

The story spread so quickly, it was legend by the time the pursuing Federal army tramped through town. A member of the Third Wisconsin echoed, "The real heroine of the town was old Barbara Fritchie, who had kept a Union flag waving from her window during all the time of the Confederate occupation. . . . I heard the story told within twenty-four hours after the Confederate army had left Frederick, from persons who knew the circumstances."[76] When the 21st Massachusetts rested in the street, the story was quickly passed down the line. "Indeed, right opposite where Company K was resting," one soldier wrote, "was the house, the flag still flying."[77]

But the episode was also contested. Jacob Engelbrecht insisted, "The 'Barbara Fritchty [*sic*]' exploit . . . is *not true*. I do not believe one word of it. I live directly opposite and for three days I was nearly continually looking at the Rebel Army passing the door and nearly the whole army passed her door, and should anything like that have occurred I am certain some one in our family would have noticed it."[78] Stonewall Jackson's role in the poem angered and offended many Southerners—especially since Jackson was dead before the poem found published fame. His route through Frederick was dissected, with his champions maintaining that he was one of the few Confederate leaders who did *not* pass Fritchie's house. Henry Kyd Douglas sniffed, "As for Barbara Fritchie, we did not pass her house. . . . She never saw Stonewall Jackson and he never saw her."[79] The controversy

*Barbara Fritchie, a ninety-six-year-old widow and a slave owner, was a fervent
Unionist who became the catalyst for a legend still hotly debated.* AUTHOR'S
COLLECTION.

waged for years. In 1886 the beleaguered author published a letter: "The
poem 'Barbara Fritchie' was written in good faith. The story was no invention of mine. It came to me from sources which I regarded as entirely reliable. . . . I had no reason to doubt its accuracy then, and I am still
constrained to believe that it had foundation in fact. . . . I have no pride of
authorship to interfere with my allegiance to truth."[80]

Whatever Fritchie's experience, many similar incidents occurred during the 1862 occupation. Mary Quantrell, a widowed schoolteacher who
lived near Barbara Fritchie, waved a Union flag with some of her students
while the Confederate troops were leaving Frederick. An officer provided

protection for a time, but when he left, several Southern soldiers knocked the flag from Quantrell's hand and broke the staff in pieces.[81]

A Mrs. Nelson scolded several Confederate cavalrymen for treating Union flags with disrespect. "Young men, you are dishonoring the flag of the country under whose protection your fathers were born," she said. "Your forefathers fought for that flag—you should be ashamed." The soldiers listened in silence before bowing politely and trotting on, never realizing that Mrs. Nelson was a "lady of warm devotion to the Confederacy."[82] Anna Morris Ellis Holstein, a Pennsylvania woman who came to Maryland to nurse sick and wounded soldiers during the 1862 campaign, stayed with a Unionist family in Frederick who told of the scorn that Confederate soldiers had displayed for the national flag, at times trailing it in the dust as they rode through town. The Confederate retreat prompted "*their* hour of triumph; the flag which had been so cautiously concealed, and sacredly guarded, was brought from its hiding-place, and secured to a staff." When a line of Confederate prisoners was marched by the door, it was determined that "they *should* again pass under the flag they had dishonored. . . . The rebels could only threaten . . . that if again in possession of the city, they and their home were doomed."[83] But perhaps the best story comes from William Owen, a Louisiana artilleryman who passed a young woman with a small Union flag pinned to her dress as he entered Frederick. "Look h'yar, miss, better take that flag down," one of his fellow soldiers yelled. "We're awful fond of charging breastworks." She blushed and smiled, Owen said, "but stuck to her colors."[84]

>─◄►─◄─O─◄►─I─◄

As the Confederate army tramped west, their cavalry provided a rear guard and screen against the Federal army now pushing toward Frederick. Fitz Lee and Wade Hampton left Urbana midmorning on September 11. Von Borcke directed the retreat from Urbana in the name of Jeb Stuart, who, he wrote, "with the other members of the Staff, to my intense disgust, still lingered in the [Cockey] verandah with the ladies." As the Union troops pressed closer, the Cockey family began to worry about retribution for their kindness to the Confederates. Mr. Cockey decided to ride away with the Rebel column, "and so we galloped out of the village, in the direction of Frederick, amid the tears of women and children, who stood waving handkerchiefs to us as long as we were in sight." Ten minutes later the first Union troops reclaimed Urbana. The Confederate cavalry officers lodged that night at an Irish family's farmhouse east of Frederick, easing any regret that they felt about leaving the Cockey family by having a "lively little dance" with the daughters.[85]

Catherine Markell continued to feed Confederate soldiers as they slowly vacated, sometimes more than three hundred a day. On the twelfth her husband left home, presumably to avoid immediate recriminations and arrest. That afternoon Catherine entertained Stuart, Fitz Lee, Hampton, and their staffs. Stuart delighted the women by calling for his banjo player, signing autograph albums, and presenting pieces of his famous plume. The party continued until 4:00 P.M., when a courier reported that the advancing columns of McClellan's army were in sight. Markell described what happened next:

Hampton had left & Lee started, but the "Cavalier" Stuart waited until his hurried command was obeyed & then formed his men in line of battle immediately in front of our house. There a considerable skirmish occurred: The Confederates slowly retiring toward the mountain, up the Middletown pike. One of the Federal cannon burst at the end of Patrick St., killing several men. A piece of our railing was shot away. We all retired to the cellar.[86]

Though the initial skirmish took place east of town, the Confederates retired into the city. A lone Federal colonel, Augustus Moor, plunged after them with a cavalry troop and a single artillery piece. The two cavalry squads clashed in the street. Citizens peeking through shutters or watching with opera glasses saw the Confederate troopers retreat, then wheel magnificently, draw sabers, and countercharge. The clash was conducted, wrote Dr. Steiner, with "grand style. Saddles were emptied on both sides."[87] One Union supporter unfurled a flag as Jeb Stuart's men dashed by. Catherine Markell, who had climbed to the roof to see McClellan's army enter, wrote, "Someone hoisted a flag . . . which a Confederate officer spied & returning almost in the face of the enemy compelled them to take it down."[88] Heros von Borcke had earlier that day indignantly spotted "Mr. F." on his rooftop, "impudently" waving an American flag toward the approaching Federal column, and sent the Unionist word that he would be shot if he "continued his offensive course." Mr. F. retired but, von Borcke wrote, "as we were compelled to leave the city in some haste, he expressed his thanks to me in a charge of buckshot, which rattled from the front door of his house around my head."[89]

The fracas lasted only moments. While Union infantry poured into one end of town, the Confederate cavalry trotted briskly out the other. They left behind a few wounded soldiers and streets littered with ragged boots and uniforms discarded by the men lucky enough to buy replacements. They took with them a dozen prisoners (including Colonel Moor), a splendid plum cake tossed under fire at Captain Blackford by a "philanthropic young lady,"[90] and numerous tokens and mementos of a pleasant stay in Frederick.

# CHAPTER 3

# "What a Terrible Feeling This Is"

The stay in Frederick was the Confederate army's first experience north of the Potomac. Southern boys had enjoyed the sights and flirting with saucy Maryland girls. Many of the men had welcomed a taste of peach preserves or lemonade or biscuits and honey. Jeb Stuart's cavaliers had delighted in their ball. But on a grander scale, the Southern army's reception in Frederick was disappointing. Only about a thousand pairs of shoes had been found—hardly enough to refit the hobbling, barefoot army. And while Maryland was a land of plenty, most of the corn in the fields was not yet ripe, the wheat and barley not yet threshed. Nor did the adoration of Confederate ladies swell the army's depleted ranks or persuade stubborn Yankee merchants to open their shops. "This part of Maryland does not welcome us warmly," wrote a Virginian in a letter to his mother on September 6, while at Frederick. "I have long thought the State was a humbug."[1]

Throughout the countryside, many Unionists expressed their political sentiments with stony silence and locked doors. For the men with money to spend and empty bellies, the cold reception was galling. "I visited nearly a hundred farm houses during the day," one soldier wrote his father, "and did not succeed in buying a pound of meat or a bushel of corn. It is true that a considerable number of houses were deserted, but where I found the owners at home, they all told me they had nothing to sell. It is perfectly evident that the people of this section of the State are as hostile to us as if we were north of the Mason Dixon line."[2]

But even some of the secessionists didn't fulfill expectations. Some had little to give without risking starvation themselves. More than one hostess was horrified to discover that the soldier-guests gracing her parlor were crawling with the lice known as "gray-backs." But fear of retaliation certainly factored into the lukewarm reception. Secessionist citizens knew that, with all probability, the Southern army would quickly be replaced again by Federal troops. They had already seen too many friends and neighbors arrested and imprisoned because of their loyalties. It was a tense, dangerous time for secessionists. "They . . . seemed much constrained in manner," wrote one cavalryman, "as if feeling certain that Union men were in their midst quietly taking note of all actions or expressions, and ready to divulge names at fitting opportunities."[3] George Neese recalled a "bright-faced" woman waving a handkerchief at them from a window, "but she did it in a manner as not to be observed by her neighbors."[4]  Alexander Hunter observed, "There were many friendly people in the windows and doors, but they seemed afraid to make any manifestation of their feelings—only smiling covertly."[5] One Southern correspondent, traveling with the army, reported: "Only a few moments ago I met a lady who confessed that although she had Confederate flags ready to expose in her windows as we passed she was afraid to wave them, lest being discovered by her Union neighbors she should be reported to the Federals in case of our retreat, and be thereby subjected to insult if not imprisonment at their hands. . . . One of the Union men frankly confessed to me that he feared his own neighbors more than he did our troops, and he should regret to see us depart."[6] Few women had yet been arrested, however, and secessionist women were generally more ardent and vocal in their support than men. One cavalryman concluded, "While I cannot but despise the thousands [of men] standing with hands in pockets idly looking on . . . I must admire the beauty, kindness, and whole-souled fervor of Maryland women, who, in thousands of ways, evinced their loyalty and love for our cause."[7]

The Maryland men were a bitter disappointment to the Southern soldiers who had shared Lee's hopes for a strong rally, for hordes of new recruits. Marylanders in the ranks had done their best. Bradley Tyler Johnson issued a fiery call: "RISE AT ONCE. Remember the cells of Fort McHenry! . . . the insults to your wives and daughters, the arrests, the midnight searches of your houses!" Echoed Elijah White of Poolesville, "I am a Marylander! I have been in the service eighteen months opposing the tyranny which would have made of the South a subjugated and ruined country. I came to Maryland with the Southern Army to do what I can to carry her where she belongs—to the Southern Confederacy."[8] Some men did join the Southern ranks, including the former editor of *The Frederick Herald* (who issued his own proclamation calling for recruits on September 9) and a group of Poolesville men who had been waiting for an opportunity to enlist.

But while Southern correspondents blithely assured their readers that as many as seven hundred Maryland men had joined the ranks, the true number was closer to two hundred—perhaps less. A soldier from Virginia noted that "indications and . . . some expression of Southern sentiment" were not enough to satisfy the men that the Marylanders "were ready and willing to shed their blood for the Southern cause."[9] The First Maryland Regiment, CSA, had recently been disbanded, and some Marylanders were bitterly sure that the absence of a Maryland regimental flag—a rallying standard—was detrimental to the cause. Bradley Johnson was also disappointed that his dream of a Maryland Line had not materialized; he told Jackson and Lee that Maryland's "ardent sympathizers" had been "so crushed" by the long months of Union occupation that they could not expect much overt support unless the Confederate army could promise "an occupation [of] at least some permanence."[10] One soldier observed that Southern sentiments were found primarily among "the higher classes of society, who assign as a reason for not joining us that they fear we may not occupy this state permanently, and their property would be confiscated." He noted, perhaps wryly, that it was on their account that "our officers are particularly severe upon any of our men who depredate on the farmers or others, or take anything without compensation."[11]

Timing was off. If the invasion had come earlier in the war, when the Confederate army was fresh and the cause still imbued with a rosy patriotic glow, the results might have been different. Dr. Lewis Steiner speculated that even secession-minded youths would have thought twice about enlisting in the gaunt Rebel army. "If ever suicide were contemplated by anyone it must be by those civilians who propose to attach themselves to Jackson's cause," he wrote. Napier Bartlett agreed, concluding, "An advance after the First Manassas . . . would have carried Maryland to the cause of the Confederacy, but it was now too late. Her refined population could only see as the result of long soldiering, rags and filth, and barefooted soldiers . . . and so the sentiment of 'My Maryland' evaporated in poetry and paper."[12] John Stevens of the Fifth Texas put it more bluntly: "The romance had all vanished from their patriotic sentiments, war was now a reality; they had learned that war meant fight and fight meant kill and kill meant to be dead."[13]

"We had sung 'Maryland, My Maryland'. . . with a great deal of hope," wrote John Robson of the 52nd Virginia, "for this song asserted positively that 'She Breathes, She Burns, She'll Come, She'll Come,' but it didn't take 'us generals' of the ranks very long to see that . . . someone had blundered, for *she didn't 'come'* worth a cent."[14] A Georgian echoed years later, "Maryland remained a mute, inglorious Maryland. The state was sandwiched between the upper and lower millstone! The Eastern Shore . . . were Southern sympathizers. Western Maryland was for the Union."[15]

Most of the Yankee soldiers who would soon follow the Confederates into Frederick enjoyed a warmer reception. "There is no question of the loyalty of this part of Maryland," Brigadier General John Gibbon wrote enthusiastically in a letter after passing through Frederick, and many echoed the sentiments.[16] But ironically Maryland's political disunion was destined to cause disappointment in *both* armies. Because of Maryland's unique geographic and figurative role during the war, some Yankee soldiers also considered themselves to be on foreign soil during the Antietam campaign. Federal troops knew that only the unconstitutional arrest of pro-Southern legislators, before a secession vote could be taken, had kept Maryland in the Union. In addition, slavery was still legal in Maryland, which gave the state a troubling reputation throughout the North. Many Yankees viewed even sympathetic gestures with suspicion, fearful of being poisoned by every mug of water.

New Englanders in particular viewed Marylanders with distrust. "There was a lack of womanly delicacy in the feminine chivalry of Maryland," wrote Major Abner Small of the 16th Maine Volunteers, when his regiment was stationed near Washington before the Antietam campaign. "There was a coarseness, an absence of the nicety of manners that we had expected to find. . . . As for the young men, they looked and bore themselves like the greenest rustics, and exhibited a reckless indifference to dress and deportment, as well as to any opinion that we might form of Maryland youth."[17] A soldier from the First Minnesota stationed that autumn in Poolesville, while admiring the agricultural climate, observed coolly, "The people lacked that thrift and ambition that Northerners possess to make the most of their resources."[18] For some Union soldiers, the strong outpouring of support from pro-Union citizens in western Maryland was not enough to quell the unease prompted by the presence of divided loyalties and Confederate sympathizers. "This is a most miserable Secesh hole," one Yankee bitterly concluded that autumn, "and one is no safer here . . . than in Virginia."[19]

>─┤◆─O─◆├─<

By summer's end, Yankee soldiers in the eastern theater were reeling from the year's debacles. Early in the year George B. McClellan, once the overall commander of the Union armies, had been demoted to concentrate exclusively on the Army of the Potomac. McClellan excelled at training and he drilled a disorganized rabble into a well-trained army of a hundred and thirty thousand men. He made the men feel like soldiers, and they loved him for it. Abraham Lincoln was harder to please, however, and in February he had urged McClellan to leave the security of parade grounds. McClellan devised a plan that launched the Army of the Potomac for an assault on Richmond, the Confederate capital. By the end of March, 121,500 Union soldiers, 14,592 animals, 1,200 wagons, and 44 artillery batteries were poised just nine miles from Richmond. But McClellan didn't pounce. While he hesitated, Stonewall Jackson diverted Federal attention with his legendary Valley campaign, in which he successfully prevented Union reinforcements from reaching McClellan and maintained control of the fruitful and vital Shenandoah Valley. Ultimately the Army of the Potomac retreated toward Harrison's Landing, and when Union forces defending Washington started moving south under the command of General John Pope, Jackson's men contributed to another sound defeat of the Yankees on the old Bull Run battlefield. Dazed and embarrassed, the Union men on both campaigns retired in defeat.

Among them that August was the Third Wisconsin Infantry, camped at Tennalleytown near the city. "It was indeed humiliating," wrote Julian Hinkley, the regimental historian. "Here we were, after six months of campaigning, back again at the point where we had started. The Grand Army of the Potomac forced to seek the shelter of the fortifications of Washington!"[20]

In that atmosphere of confusion came word of the Southern invasion, delivered with flair by a Maryland farmer racing on horseback down Pennsylvania Avenue shouting, "The Confederates are coming!" Federal officials in Washington City were stunned at Lee's audacity. One member of the cabinet said, "The War Department is bewildered, knows but little, does nothing, proposes nothing."[21] The capital city was in an uproar. Telegraph operators delivered scores of messages from Philadelphia and New York and Boston, frantically petitioning the government for protection from the inevitable pillage and plunder. "The excitement in the north is tremendous," wrote Josiah Marshall Favill, an officer with the 57th New York Infantry. "That the rebel army should be advancing into the Northern states is something no one dreamed possible."[22] Hastily organized militias of clerks and storekeepers fumbled with muskets, ancestral swords, and any other weapon handy. Lincoln restored McClellan to command. "Again I have been called upon to save the country," the general wrote his wife. "The case is desperate, but with God's help I will try unselfishly to do my best."[23] The Army of the Potomac, again led by its beloved "Little Mac," scrambled to prepare for a march.

McClellan left a small force behind to defend Washington. The rest of the Union army began trudging west in pursuit while the Confederates were still enjoying themselves in Frederick. It was hot, the roads dusty. Still, those Yankees who had spent time in Virginia were happy just to be north of the Potomac. "It was a welcome change . . . to be greeted with smiles instead of frowns," wrote New Yorker Jacob Cole.[24] Along the march through the central Maryland countryside, civilians hurried to the roadside to cheer the boys on with refreshments and cries of, "God speed!" Farmers left their teams in the field to watch, black farmhands slipped to the roadside with baskets of peaches, children stood on porches waving tiny flags, pretty girls blew kisses. "The populace . . . made us feel proud to belong to the gallant army that was hurrying to place itself across the path of the invader . . .," Josiah Favill wrote. "Crowds of women and youngsters surrounded us, offering fruit, flowers and water, and gazed with admiration at our dress and accouterments. We took kindly to the glory of finding ourselves the heroes of the hour, and reciprocated the crowd's interest, parting with many of our buttons to the prettiest girls."[25] On September 11, the 56th Pennsylvania tramped through New Market and made camp on the outskirts of town. "The ladies carry water for the soldiers," Lieutenant Sam Healy wrote in his journal. "All want a drink whether thirsty or not."[26]

Most were thirsty, for the drought continued. Limping stragglers slumped against fences or dozed beneath trees. Lieutenant Colonel Rutherford B. Hayes of the 23rd Ohio summarized the march in his diary with three words: "Dust, heat, and thirst." He added, "Men were lost from their regiments; officers left their commands to rest in the shade, to feed on fruit; thousands were straggling; confusion and disorder everywhere."[27] Hayes missed his family desperately, and the excited little Maryland boys who marched with the troops now and then reminded him of his own sons.

McClellan moved slowly, cautiously, his army advancing only about six miles a day. He was hampered by fears that the Confederates were trying only to draw him from Washington, leaving the capital undefended. To counter those concerns McClellan spread his troops over a twenty-five-mile front to protect the approaches to Baltimore and Washington, with three main forces traveling toward Frederick on roughly parallel roads. Major

General Ambrose Burnside's men moved through Brooksville and New Market; Major General Edwin Sumner's troops headed through Rockville, Gaithersburg, Hyattstown, and Urbana; and Major General William Franklin's soldiers tramped southerly roads through Seneca, Poolesville, and Buckeystown. The reshuffling of troops into this widespread front further slowed McClellan's pace. In addition, he suffered from a lack of accurate intelligence about his enemy. Jeb Stuart's cavalry did such a good job of screening their army that McClellan wasn't even sure the Southerners were in Frederick until after Lee had left. Stories from civilians and prisoners (some evidently planted by Southerners) put Lee's force at a hundred and twenty thousand—more than twice the actual number. But despite McClellan's deliberate pace, the revitalized Union army was eager, and the Frederick Unionists, chafing under Confederate occupation, were just as eager. When swirling rumors began to promise their deliverance, "Old and young prayed with fervor that these rumors might be based on truth," Steiner wrote. "Bright eyes were growing dim and rosy cheeks pale from anxious watching, day and night, for the coming of our National army."[28]

Slowly, slowly, the Union army inched toward the spires of Frederick. The scenery was spectacular. Every pane of glass and the crosses on the church steeples shone like gold in the sun. Some men composed lyrical descriptions of the unrivaled landscape as they marched, to be recorded later in letters home. The less poetic ignored the view and fantasized about German bakeries and home-cooked meals. They'd been well treated along the route but were still eager to sample what Frederick City had to offer. One young man in the 118th Pennsylvania, spotting an elderly woman watching from her window on the outskirts of town, lifted his hat politely. "Madam," he asked anxiously, "what is there in the village?" "A college of some reputation sir," she replied. "Good heavens, madam, I can't eat a college!" he snapped testily and marched on.[29]

On September 12, after Jeb Stuart's cavalry clashed with the Union advance guard in the streets of Frederick, Confederate citizens sadly retreated indoors while the Unionist population exploded into a frenzy of welcome. "Such Huzzaing you never did hear," Jacob Engelbrecht rejoiced as General Ambrose Burnside, in the Federal vanguard, made his way through town.[30] American flags reappeared as Confederate banners were hastily whipped inside. "We thought you were never coming!" people yelled. "This is the happiest hour of our lives."[31] One of Burnside's Pennsylvanian soldiers described the scene:

Our reception by the people of Frederick City was an ovation. They illuminated their houses, the Stars and Stripes was thrown to the breeze, patriotic songs were sung, and refreshments were urged upon officers and men. General Burnside's passage through the streets was blocked up by citizens, eager to thank and bless him as their deliverer; ladies crowded about and insisted upon kissing his hands, and from the balconies of private residences bouquets rained upon him.[32]

After a hot, dusty march, the ovation stirred the men profoundly. Before entering Frederick, Hayes wrote that his Ohio men had "laid down in the road, saying they couldn't stir again. Some were pale, some red as if apoplectic. Half an hour after, they were marching erect and proud hurrahing the ladies!"[33] All the Federals, used to the taunts and jibes of the "vinegar visaged Virginians," gloried in the smiling faces and cheers.[34]

Beaming men and women stood on front steps with trays of fruit and tubs of lemonade; others zealously dragged passing soldiers inside for a proper meal. David Thompson, a New York infantryman, wrote to his family that by nightfall, "the place was alive with girls going around the streets in squads waving flags, singing songs and inviting the soldiers in for hot suppers." Thompson found that many establishments had been emptied by the Confederates, but eventually a Frederick woman provided a simple meal: "I gloat over the memory of that hot loaf & butter, for it was the most delicious meal to me—dusty & tired with a twelve miles' march—that I remember."[35] As evening descended, doors remained open wide and lamps burned extravagantly in every window of the Unionists' homes. "Women and children, as well as the men, vied with one another in extending a generous Southern hospitality," a Rhode Island soldier remembered fondly.[36]

The Union soldiers streamed through town and pitched their tents in the already-trampled fields ringing the city, prompting snide speculation regarding the results of breeding Northern and Southern gray-backs. But most men didn't take the time to bathe before hounding their officers for passes. The Third Wisconsin men, who had arrested the secession-minded Maryland legislators while on duty in Frederick the year before, were anxious to visit old friends. "We had been there so long during the past year," wrote one, "that it seemed to us almost like home."[37] The illumination, laughter, and hospitality lasted throughout the night.

*"The Daughters of Maryland Received the Sons of the North as They Marched Against the Rebel Invaders—Scene on the March." Along the lines of the Federal march west, civilians made sure that each soldier was fed and made welcome. "It was cheering to see their pleasant faces," wrote Maj. John M. Gould of the 10th Maine, comparing the ladies of Maryland with Virginia women, who had "ruined their faces by looking sour."* SKETCH BY F. H. SCHELL.

The tumult did not abate the following day as more dusty blue columns surged through town. The men marched crisply, with drums beating and bands playing and regimental colors unfurled. Men and women thronged the sidewalks and crowded into the streets, weeping, waving handkerchiefs. Young boys darted in and out of the ranks, delivering their mothers' pies and cookies. Young girls threw flowers. Officers on horseback labored to keep their animals from stepping on their admirers. "When [our] regiment reached the principal part of the town, it broke out into one of its sonorous and magnificent war songs, producing a wonderful effect," wrote one soldier. "This is our first real opportunity we have had of showing off to our grateful countrywomen, and we made the most of it, displaying our horsemanship to the best advantage."[38]

For the men used to taunts and cold silence from Southern ladies, the celebration was overwhelming. They were no longer invaders but defenders—a delivering army. Some enjoyed the fever pitch and fresh doughnuts and cold lemonade as a first-rate lark. But some, more thoughtful, were reminded of the patriotic urges, the deeply felt convictions, that had led them to the enlistment tent in the first place. For these, that first walk through Frederick's streets was an emotional experience. Every smiling face reminded them of loved ones waiting at home, every gesture of hospitality perceived as heartfelt thanks for what they were trying to do. "We could all see now something to fight for," Sam Healy wrote. "The Rebs were amongst us, our homes were in danger, for we felt as if we were at home by the greeting we got. We were soon leaving the town, but all with joyous faces and light hearts, every man anxious to meet the Rebs and felt capable of thrashing half a dozen."[39] The Union veterans had been thrashed themselves at Bull Run. Hopes had been dashed at Richmond. The first eighteen months of war had battered not only their army but their faith in their own ability to persevere. For many, being marched through loyal Frederick did more for morale than anything else George McClellan could have done.

The frenzy reached its zenith on September 13, when McClellan himself pranced into town on horseback. "I was nearly overwhelmed and pulled to pieces," McClellan wrote his wife. "I enclose with this a little flag that some enthusiastic lady thrust into or upon Dan's bridle. As to flowers!!—they came in crowds! In truth, I was seldom more affected by the scenes I saw yesterday & the reception I met with."[40]

For McClellan, it was the beginning of a wonderful day. Later that morning, members of the 27th Indiana, resting in a meadow on the outskirts of town, found a copy of Lee's latest orders to his chief subordinates wrapped around some cigars. Since leaving Washington, McClellan had been frustrated by the Confederate cavalry's effective screening maneuvers. This missive, known as Special Orders 191, detailed Lee's plans for the Confederate army—including his risky choice to divide his force, sending Jackson and twenty-five thousand men to capture Harpers Ferry while the remainder of the Southern army proceeded to Hagerstown. The find was a stroke of extraordinary luck for McClellan, and he wired an ebullient message to President Lincoln: "Frederick, September 13, 1862—I have all the plans of the rebels, and will catch them in their own trap if my men are equal to the emergency. . . . Received most enthusiastically by the ladies. Will send you trophies."[41]

*"General McClellan Entering the Town of Frederick, Maryland, the Popular Welcome." George McClellan received a hero's ovation when he arrived in Frederick. "I have never witnessed such a scene,"* one observer wrote. Harpers Weekly, *October 4, 1862.* COURTESY FRANK & MARIE-THERESE WOOD PRINT COLLECTIONS, ALEXANDRIA, VIRGINIA.

Blissfully ignorant for the time being of that unmitigated disaster, the Confederate troops shuffled west. Despite the disappointments, spirits were good. The farmboys among them marveled at the large prosperous farms they passed. "The barns . . . are truly an object of wonder," wrote one. "They are generally built of stone, often much larger, than our meeting houses, and several stories high. Such forage houses would be unnecessarily large in middle Georgia, but this is indeed a grain country."[42] The Maryland farmers were busy with fall harvest, and dusty Rebel stragglers, missing their own farms, hung over fence rails, chewing grass and critiquing the equipment and methods they saw.

Such convivial exchanges escaped the conjecture of many in the tiny mountain hamlets, where Unionist civilians waited for the Southern army's arrival with dread. A number of spectres loomed for the rural people. Unionists were afraid that spiteful Confederate neighbors would point them out, bringing the unimagined wrath of Southern soldiers upon their households. And many were convinced that all men, regardless of their politics, would be forced into service with the Southern army. "Impressment into the ranks as common soldiers, or immurement in a *Southern* prison—these were not attractive prospects for quiet, Union-loving citizens!" Dr. Lewis Steiner exclaimed.[43] A century after the war, the descendant of a newspaper publisher in Middletown wrote that his grandfather, a fervent Union sympathizer, suspended operations upon the approach of the Confederate army "to avoid being captured and pressed into service."[44] Men were occasionally impressed into temporary duty as guides, although there were usually sympathizers to provide that service, but Confederate soldiers were scornful of the Unionists' fears of actual draft. "Not a soldier wants Maryland, unless Maryland wants to go with us," a Georgian wrote. "We want no hand without the heart."[45] But with no reliable news from Frederick, the terrified citizens didn't know what rumor to believe.

Also dismal was the prospect of losing their horses. That fear was real, for transportation was becoming more of a problem for the military men. The cavalrymen needed fresh horses to replace mounts killed in battle, weakened by weeks of insufficient forage, or lamed by going shoeless. The honest among them offered cash; some tried to persuade secessionists to part with their mounts out of loyalty or by pointing out that the Federal army would likely impress their horses anyway. The wily citizens who did agree to sales insisted on bank notes or gold instead of Confederate money. Farmers who couldn't afford to lose their animals hid them in cellars or thickets far from the road. "Things look very serious," wrote John Koogle in his diary on September 7. "Some people are leaving for Pennsylvania and others look very grave." Koogle was trying to tend to his apple crop, but two days later, with news that the Rebels were very close, he abandoned his cider press and headed to Pennsylvania with his team of horses.[46]

Some prosperous farmers worried about another desperate loss, that their slaves or black hired hands would be abducted by one of the armies. It was not an idle fear. As early as January of that year, Washington County civilians had complained that Union soldiers were encouraging "insubordination and rebellion" among area blacks.[47] During the autumn campaign, when both armies moved through the area in quick progression, slave owners worried that if the Confederate men didn't abduct their workers for labor, the Union men would entice them to run away. George William Smith noted that a relative found his slaves "stolen" by the Union army. One Confederate private recalled, "A friend who had been wandering at his own sweet will, barefoot and without a shirt to his back, in the track of the army, hired and persuaded with his bayonet, an unwilling darky whom he met (driving a mule attached to a two-wheeled cart) to carry him a 'right smart distance'" to Sharpsburg.[48] Otho Nesbitt of Clear Spring noted, "The free Negroes nearly looked ashey, nothing like a laugh could be seen in any of their countenances. It was understood they were to be taken South and sold in place of the ones taken or run off by the Union army." Otho's brother Jonathan "watched his horses 2 or 3 nights for fear if the free Negroes started they might take the horses along."[49] Whether the blacks were taken or ran off, the result was the same.

The combination of fears instilled panic in otherwise sensible, stolid farmers when news of the Confederate crossing snaked through the mountain communities. Silver was buried in ash barrels and garden refuse heaps—and occasionally hidden in spots soon forgotten. One farmer put his coins under a setting hen for safekeeping—not an ideal cache when the impending foragers were more hungry than greedy. John and Mary Elizabeth Purdum buried their money in the firebox ashes of their kitchen cookstove, then built a fire on top of it.[50]

One of the towns in the Confederate path was Middletown, a pretty village six miles west of Frederick, nestled between the rolling ridges of Catoctin and South Mountains. Before the war, writers had described it in idyllic prose:

It is surrounded by a hundred oak groves, and there are hidden, romantic little valleys in all directions around the town where the farmers have their peaceful, comfortable and on the whole beautiful homes, among which are strewn orchards, farms and meadows. A little river winds crookedly by, and there is one mill after another, each swiftly and quietly swinging its ingenious wheelworks.[51]

War had brought inevitable changes to the valley. Some trouble had occurred in July, when the telegrapher employed by the U.S. Military Telegraph service was arrested for destroying an American flag.[52] But Middletown had its share of vocal Unionists, including Allen Sparrow, a merchant who frequently fumed in his diary that Rebels or secessionists "ought to be hung." When word came to Middletown that Southern troops were approaching, rumors flew that Unionist names had been supplied to the Confederate army in Frederick. Some people snatched what belongings they could carry and joined the exodus to Pennsylvania, further clogging the roads already jammed with military traffic. A group of thirty or forty farmers gathered at one home and decided to leave for Pennsylvania. Union men agonized whether to risk arrest, with its unknown consequences, or to take flight—leaving their families behind. Many believed their families would be safer without them. "Nearly all the men skedaddled, . . ." Allen Sparrow remembered, "very much scared, and making for some place where they thought that they would be out of the reach of the rebels." [53] One agitated man had to be reminded to put on trousers before heading for safety. The women stood in the road and watched their men disappear, clutching their children's hands, trying not to panic, trying not to cry. Sparrow joined the exodus, leaving his wife Eliza to cope with their eight children (the youngest only three) and the pending invasion.

But in 1862, along the lines of march as in Frederick, Robert E. Lee wanted to woo Marylanders, not frighten or infuriate them. Losing crops and food was not inconsequential, but farmers along the dusty lanes and turnpikes who watched helplessly while their sleek cattle were driven away were at least politely rewarded with a handful of bank notes—sometimes U.S. Treasury, more often Confederate scrip. Quartermasters bargained with farmers to purchase entire fields of corn or wheat. Just after crossing the Potomac a group of Confederates purchased a canalboat-load of melons, then marched along happily spitting seeds. Most storekeepers or farmers left clutching Confederate notes to show for their empty corncribs or storage rooms knew that the distinction between being paid and being robbed was more philosophical than practical. But to the Confederate commanders, it was an important distinction.

The policy was an unwelcome surprise to the troops, who chafed to root out better fare. "We had heard with delight of the 'plenty' to be had in Maryland; judge of our disappointment when . . . we were marched into a dank clover-field and the order came down the line, 'Men go into that corn-field and get your rations,'" wrote an officer in Stonewall Jackson's corps.[54] Edgar Warfield of Virginia remembered his dubious first allotment in Maryland: one skein of black thread and two smoked herrings. It was his first issue of rations in two weeks.[55]

Often the civilians took it upon themselves to improve the soldiers' lot. Throughout the Maryland campaign, civilians along the line of march were guided by personal mores of politics, economy, and compassion. One naive secessionist woman, hearing of the arrival of Confederate troops, vowed to give every one of Lee's soldiers something to eat; when she had stripped the smokehouse and used every ounce of cornmeal and was warned that only one division of the army had gone by, she gave up in despair.[56] Napier Bartlett of Louisiana remembered another good-hearted woman along the march through Maryland, who offered a tired soldier some fruit. "A mob of her own sex invaded her house and overwhelmed her with every reproach," he recalled. The grateful soldier pretended to have taken the fruit without asking, then skedaddled back to his unit.[57] Many Marylanders, regardless of politics, couldn't bear watching the skeletal boys pass without offering at least water. Some Unionists were still willing to sell food to the men, and those Southerners with money didn't hesitate to purchase anything in sight. William Thomas Poague, an artilleryman, got "first-rate meals" at a farmhouse where his unit was camped. "The inmates were not ardent Confederates," he recalled, "but all the same they took our Confederate money and gave us the best they had. I never enjoyed good things to eat, as much in my whole army experience."[58]

A hungry army of fifty thousand men could not pass and leave the land unmarred, and the temperaments of company officers, and individual soldiers themselves, made some violations inevitable. Several Texans came across three Georgians butchering a cow by the road, and the haggling that took place over the "rare and dainty gastronomic delicacies"—the sweetbread and marrowgut—was fondly remembered almost fifty years later.[59]

William Thomas Poague recalled the booty gained by "the most noted forager in the battery," which included a canteen of old applejack and a sack of food.[60] Another soldier recalled that a comrade had been "peppered with pigeon-shot whilst gathering our supper in a farmer's sweet-potato patch" soon after crossing into Maryland.[61] A Frederick woman told one of the Yankee soldiers who followed that "the Rebels had scared her by plundering her house for food & money, & not finding much of either, had rented their spite by tearing up her feather bed & pillows."[62] And when rations were not officially forthcoming, some officers gave latitude to their famished men. "We had nothing to eat yesterday, and, contrary to general orders, our lieutenant told us last night that if we could find corn or potatoes that we might take enough of them to satisfy the requirements of the inner man," George Neese wrote in his journal on September 12.[63]

High-ranking officers did what they could to protect the Maryland farm families they marched past. Guards were often posted at particularly tempting spots. Franklin Riley of the 16th Mississippi passed "numerous orchards along the way, but they were guarded so strictly that we had little opportunity to satisfy our appetites. Too bad. Fruit looked appealing."[64] The toll for disobedience could be high. Federal soldiers marching along a road that had recently been traveled by the Confederate army were horrified to find "two corpses in ragged gray uniforms" hanging on a tree. Shaken civilians reported that Jackson had ordered the men hanged for stealing. "Although the rebel army (ragged and half-fed) had just passed over the road . . .," one Yankee wrote later, "the ripe apples were left hanging untouched on the trees that lined the road."[65]

Many of the boldest Confederate scavengers found only field corn and apples, often not yet ripe. The men patiently punched holes in their cartridge-box tins with bayonets to make graters, boiled the coarse meal, then fried it on plates or baked it on flat stones among their campfire ashes. Unfortunately, whether the food was politely paid for or snatched from roadside fields, it was a poor diet for famished men. When several soldiers from South Carolina were taken prisoner, they assured their guards that they had been receiving "plenty of regular rations"; but when one of the Federals pawed through their haversacks, he found "their entire contents to consist of less than a dozen dirty little balls of corn meal, covered with the ashes in which they had been baked."[66] Another Confederate recalled, "Our menu consisted of apples and corn. We toasted, we burned, we stewed, we boiled, we roasted these two together, and singly, until there was not a man whose form had not caved in."[67] That soldier did find some more tempting fare while in Maryland. But twenty years after the war, another man described the invasion as the "green corn campaign."[68] The effects were made plain by epidemics of dysentery and diarrhea, a sanitation nightmare for landowners whose property bordered the lines of march. Terrified citizens fearing the wrath of invaders with each knock on the door instead found sick stragglers too weak to keep up with their regiments.

To a large extent, Lee's orders were followed during at least the first half of the Maryland campaign. Citizens experienced Southern occupation and Northern occupation in quick succession, and Unionist civilians were grudgingly forced to concede that the Confederate army was better disciplined than the Federal. "[The Confederates] behaved much better than we had any right to expect," Allen Sparrow admitted.[69] Echoed John Castle, also of Middletown, "It was not the army we looked for, for instead of an army of desperadoes, they were an army of gentlemen, the very pride of Virginia. Never was there an army under such discipline."[70] Some of the Rebels were surprised by the fear with which the civilians had anticipated their arrival. "People are kind enough generally, but they fear us with a mortal terror; many of them seem to think us Goths and Vandals and Huns, they tremble sometimes when spoken to, and are astonished to see us without torch and tomahawk," a Virginian wrote with some disgust in a letter to his sister.[71] "The people of Maryland were evidently disappointed to discover that the barbarians, of whom they had heard so much, could behave like gentlemen . . .," echoed a member of the 15th Georgia. "I am inclined to think the Yankee soldiers have been quite insolent to the people of Maryland." One old man told him, "I was really afraid of your army at first, but I am not now. . . . Our army took our horses and cattle and pressed them into service, but since I see so many of your guns, horses and wagons marked 'U.S.,' I am fully convinced that they only collected them and drove them down to be abandoned to your army."[72]

The Yankees had endured bitter times on the enemy soil of Virginia, and now they reveled in the abundance of friendly faces and fertile fields. They also had less to gain by polite behavior and in most cases were less disciplined. "Our boys are, like most privates in the army, disgustingly unprincipled and profane," wrote Edward Wightman, a New York recruit. "Hardly one of them hesitates at a theft."[73] Senior officers signed orders endeavoring them to "suppress pillage,"[74] but they were often ignored by both the officers and the men they commanded. Countless cows and hogs were shot "in self-defense." Cagey officers pointed at livestock and gave orders forbidding "taking one" pig or sheep—whereby cheerful volunteers quickly corralled two or more. Other Union officers, when asked for permission to use fence rails for campfires, replied, "Just take the top rail"—a juncture repeated until the fence was gone. Lieutenant Sam Healy of the 56th Pennsylvania noted that the Union soldiers did "not take anything out of their reach, but most of them have got a pretty long reach."[75]

And many felt it was their due. When the 23rd Ohio Volunteer Infantry bivouacked in an open field dotted with newly made stacks of grain waiting to be threshed, they helped themselves to the bedding. "The ground was a stubble-field in ridges of hard ground," Lieutenant Colonel Rutherford B. Hayes wrote later. "I saw it and made no objection." Major General Jesse L. Reno rounded on the foragers harshly: "You damned black sons of bitches!" Hayes assumed responsibility. "I . . . told him we had always taken rails, for example, if needed to cook with," Hayes wrote, "that if required we would pay for them. He denied the right and necessity; said we were in a loyal State, etc., etc." Colonel Eliakim Scammon of the same regiment recalled later, "General Reno, full of the idea of conciliating 'My Maryland,' was very indignant, and by no means sparing in rebuke to Colonel Hayes." Scammon and another officer appealed to Reno. "We told him something of the quality of the men whom he approached so roughly, and I added that it was certainly desirable that, on the eve of battle, no resentments should be engendered among us. . . . The General was . . . hardly ready to acknowledge that he had been too hasty. . . . At that moment, the idea of conciliating the Maryland farmers was uppermost." Hayes wrote later, "Men from Ohio [are] all in a talk about General Reno's abusive language. It is said that when talking with me he put his hand on his pistol; that many standing by began to handle their arms also! I am sorry the thing goes so far." Reno may have been venting frustration in an untenable situation: He was charged to protect the property of Maryland farmers on a campaign when even his subordinate officers—protecting *their* men's welfare—saw no harm in destroying a farmer's crop for the sake of a night's bedding.[76]

The issue produced unwanted results. A correspondent for the *New York Times* concluded that the indiscriminate pillaging by Union troops created local Confederate support among fence-sitters or mild Unionists.[77] Dr. Steiner, fervent supporter of the Union cause, admitted that compared with the Yankees, the Rebel army brought few stragglers or depredations on private property. Although he attributed their high state of obedience and discipline to fear of their officers (or in the case of Stonewall Jackson a "species of veneration" that prompted "a slavish obedience"), he felt compelled to add, "Some of our men have been less scrupulous."[78] David Strother, a Virginian on McClellan's staff, assessed the situation and reluctantly predicted that the Confederates had behaved "better than ours will do, I fear."[79] A member of the 21st Massachusetts agreed: "In sad contrast with rebel discipline, the straggling plunderers from our well-provided delivering army left few apples, chickens, or young pigs behind them on the march."[80] The Federals also brought unwanted baggage with them. Hundreds of prostitutes followed their bankroll out of Washington and pitched tents near the blue-clad troops. Unionists were shocked and embarrassed to discover that their own army was more of a trial than the dreaded Rebel horde. And secessionists buffered the dismal disappointments with their pride.

>-+-<>-+-O-<+-+-<

Leaving Frederick, the Confederate force split. James Longstreet and Major General Daniel Harvey Hill took their men along the National Road toward Hagerstown, passing through Middletown, over South Mountain, and through Boonsboro and Funkstown. Other Rebel columns under Major General Stonewall Jackson, Major General Lafayette McLaws, and Brigadier General John Walker headed toward Licksville and the Potomac or through Burkittsville and Brownsville to converge on Harpers Ferry. The columns inevitably moved accordion-style, with some sections bunching to a halt and others spread thin. Soldiers detailed to drive herds of cattle for the army hung their haversacks on the animals' horns and packed their knapsacks and muskets on the backs of the oxen and cows.[81] Their shuffling gait made a dull tramping sound, raising clouds of dust. They often accompanied themselves with favorite camp songs; "Gay and Happy" was a particular choice. Children at isolated farmhouses along the roads ran to their gates to watch the seemingly endless procession of shabby men, their bayonets glittering in the sun, flags bristling proudly from the column. Kind-hearted men and women dragged laundry tubs of water to the end of their lanes and stood ready with dippers. Their impression of the Rebel horde varied. "Many of them were from the far South and spoke a dialect I could scarcely understand," recalled one man. "They were profane beyond belief and talked incessantly."[82] But Angela Davis would later write, "As a general thing there was very little swearing among them."[83]

In one village, a group of Unionist women watched the column shuffle past from the porch of a tavern. One young lady had made an apron representing the national flag, which caused some Virginians to propose three cheers for the Stars and Stripes. The men answered willfully, and when the young lady finally retreated inside, they cheered her, too. "I did not hear a single ugly remark," wrote Edgar Warfield, "or see an act that would offend the most sensitive lady." Another young lady watched the whistling men pass from a fence post and called, "My Lord, you've got no music so you have to whistle to keep your courage up." The soldiers blithely cheered her, too, as they marched by.[84]

In Middletown, most Confederates quickly concluded that the town was predominantly loyal. The editor of the pro-Union newspaper had fled, but a few Rebels demanded the keys from his wife. When she refused, they threatened to burn down the building; General Hill arrived to order the men away and posted a guard around the home.[85] J. R. Boulware, a surgeon with the Sixth South Carolina, was glad to leave the town behind. "A *woman* . . . came out in her yard and bemeaned our soldiers at a terrible rate," he noted in his diary.[86] Another South Carolinian recalled, "Women, with Yankee effrontery from their windows, would make remarks of ridicule." Undaunted, still in good spirits, the Southerners parried every jibe. When asked why they were so dirty and ragged, a wag called, "Our mammas always taught us to put on our worst clothes when we go to kill hogs." Another bystander wanted to know why the men were barefoot. "We wore out our shoes running after the Yankees," came the reply. Few women won the verbal sparring matches.[87]

As General Jackson rode through the village, two young girls ran to the curbstone and waved tiny American flags defiantly. "We evidently have no friends in this town," Jackson said quietly to his staff, doffing his cap as he bowed to the young Unionists. A moment later their horrified mother hurried outside and shooed the girls back in the house.[88] Another flag caused more problems, when Stonewall Jackson wasn't close enough to maintain calm. A seventeen-year-old saddler's daughter named Nancy Crouse had a large national flag hanging from a second-story bedroom at her home on West Main Street. A dozen cavalrymen stopped to pull it down and were met by Nancy and a friend, Effie Titlow, who asked what they wanted. "That damned Yankee rag," said one, attempting to shove past the girls. But Nancy clattered up the stairs first and tried to protect the flag by draping it around her body. When the soldier threatened her with a gun, Nancy finally relinquished her flag. The trooper rode away with the flag tied around his horse's head. When the pursuing Yankee cavalry heard the story, they galloped indignantly after the Confederate squad, captured most of them, and gallantly returned the flag to Crouse.[89] Although never as famous as her Frederick counterpart, Nancy Crouse also inspired an enduring poem:

> Honor to the Maryland maid,
> Who the banner saved that day
> When thro' Autumn sun and shade
> Marched the legions of the Gray;
> Middletown remembers yet
> How the tide of war was stay'd
> And the years will not forget
> Nancy Crouse, the Valley Maid.[90]

Boonsboro was a little village at the western base of South Mountain, between Frederick and Hagerstown. It had once been a bustling stop on the main stage line, but since the railroad had bypassed the town, the arrival of an unreliable "coach and four" was usually the only excitement. Mail service had just recently started between Boonsboro and Sharpsburg, monitored by postmistress Eliza Beard. The whole district was home to only about 720 people in 1860. Most were laborers, although shinglemakers, welldiggers, confectioners, tinners, a liveryman, a glovemaker, a printer, a weaver, a gentleman, several hotelkeepers, and two hucksters were also duly noted by the 1860 census taker. Boys and girls attended different schools, and no fewer than five churches attracted parishioners.[91]

Boonsboro citizens had taken an active interest in politics as the secession crisis loomed. In September 1860, Bailiffs Davis and Gallaher finally arrested a number of hotheads who preferred fisticuffs to rhetoric, hauling them off to the Hagerstown jail. After the November election, local "boys and rowdies" made the night "hideous with noises and bonfires" for two weeks. Two American flags, including the one in front of O'Neal's saddlery shop, were torn down; the Confederate flag hoisted later on a hill outside of town met the same end. The Boonsboro Guards organized proudly in 1860 and went to some pains to recruit a good drummer boy, but Captain J. Brining resigned in July 1861; and when a company of Sharpsburg men marched through town a month later, en route to Frederick to join the U.S. Infantry, the Boonsboro Guards to a man refused to join. Perhaps fifty loyal Boonsboro boys ultimately enlisted on their own. Those of a different political persuasion slipped across the Potomac to find their band of brothers— or were arrested trying.[92]

When General Jackson and his staff arrived on September 10, 1862, they set up headquarters on the farm of Irish-born farmer John Murdock and his wife, Harriet, about a mile east of town. The Murdock children received Confederate buttons as souvenirs.[93] Some citizens enjoyed visits with old friends now in the Confederate army.

*John Murdock and his wife, Harriet, hosted Stonewall Jackson and his staff before the battle of South Mountain. After the battle, Murdock's farm near Boonsboro was used as one of the first field hospitals. Photo by Blessing & Company, Baltimore.* COURTESY DOUG BAST, BOONSBOROUGH MUSEUM OF HISTORY.

Colonel S. Bassett French and a friend also went to town and found a sizable number of townspeople and sightseers from the country milling in the plaza. The friend headed for Stonebraker's store while French decided to stop for refreshment at the United States Hotel, at the intersection of the National Road and the turnpike leading toward Sharpsburg. French was besieged by a crowd of the curious badgering him with questions, but the villagers' annoyance with his reticence didn't disturb his appetite. After a shot of whisky, he settled down to enjoy a hearty meal.

Henry Kyd Douglas went into Boonsboro against advice to visit a lady friend. Riding leisurely through town, Kyd Douglas and a courier were surprised to hear "the clatter of unseen cavalry coming up the other street, and in a moment a company of the enemy was facing us and proceeded to make war on us." French, hearing the commotion from the hotel, rushed to the window and was horrified to see a troop of Yankee cavalry pounding down the National Road, yelling like devils. While citizens peeped from their shutters or scurried for cover, Kyd Douglas and his companion made a hasty retreat with the Yankees in close pursuit.

Colonel French was cut off from his horse and companions, alone in a village where he had seen no signs of sympathy for his cause. While he tried to decide what to do, the terrified landlady rushed into the room and implored him to seek shelter in her chamber. "However inviting that might be under other auspices," French wrote later, "[I thought] better chances of escape might be found in some other . . . place of confinement." As Union soldiers began questioning civilians about Confederate stragglers, French's friend, in Stonebraker's store, quickly locked the door, put his pistol to the clerk's head, and whispered that he'd shoot the man if he made a sound. At the hotel, an elderly black man offered to conceal French, and the soldier reluctantly allowed himself to be locked in a coal cellar. Initially fretting about the apple pie he had left untouched on the table, his thoughts turned more ominous as a half-hour passed. Not knowing that the landlady had already told the Federal soldiers that he had run out the back door—"and feeling exceedingly uncomfortable . . . under the lock and key of a Maryland Negro"—French tried the windows and found them barred.

Meanwhile, retreating from town, Kyd Douglas had quickly come upon General Jackson leading his horse along the road. Kyd Douglas shouted a warning and, joined by several other cavalrymen, wheeled again. Excited Boonsboro citizens soon saw the pursuing Yankee horsemen driven back through town. French heard the commotion, and when the black man

opened the door, he joyfully bolted from the "dungeon." The tearful landlady thanked God for his escape, and entreated him to assure her protection
from the Confederate army, which he happily promised. "I could have put
my arms around her and heartily kissed this dear lady . . .," French wrote.
"I have a sneaking idea I did as I slipped my purse heavy with 'Confeds' to
the old darkey. . . . To be entirely honest . . . I ought to say that eye-wit-
nesses declared that I gave my purse to the lady and my embraces to the
Negro. N'importe! I would have hugged and kissed a dozen men or
women, white or black, in my grateful joy on escape from a twenty-mile
ride behind a Yankee trooper to a Yankee prison."[94] Kyd Douglas, in his
memoirs, delicately omitted mention of either embrace. He did say, however, that Colonel French emerged from the cellar irritated that the
"blamed Yankees" had interrupted his dinner.[95] To top it off, the pie he'd
left on the table had disappeared.

>-+-◇-○-◇-+-<

Funkstown was a milltown located on the National Road, two miles south
of Hagerstown, in a horseshoe bend of Antietam Creek. The stagecoach
driver who daily carried mail from Hagerstown to Frederick brought word
of Confederate invasion to the eight hundred or so people living in the
Funkstown district. The driver and his passengers had been surprised when
they stumbled into the Confederate picket lines ringing Frederick, and the
dutiful mail carrier tried to insist on passage. "[The pickets] threatened to
shoot him if he did not turn around," Angela Davis remembered, "and at
last he did, thus saving them as well as the U.S. mail from being captured."
Soon, northbound civilians from Frederick County, clutching passes that
allowed them to cross the lines "upon honor to give no intelligence to the
enemy," urged their friends in Washington County to take the same course.
Met with excited questions about the state of affairs across the mountains,
the refugees could only answer, "O, we are on parole and under oath not to
tell anything, or give the news."[96] With such honest friends, mail stopped,
and telegraph wires cut, the residents of the tiny communities in Washington County were left in agonizing suspense, fearing the worst.

Anxiety reached a fever pitch when a young man who had eluded the
Confederate picket line around Boonsboro rode furiously into town with
the news that the Confederate army was on its way. Mr. and Mrs. Davis
packed their goods and buried the store's account books, papers, and
money. A friend—described as "a very plain woman, but [with] one of the

best hearts, though she was a rebel"— took up her kitchen floorboards and buried a basket with the Davises' silver and china in it. Davis remembered, "Men were going in every direction, helter skelter, in the greatest confusion, hiding their horses, or taking them to Pennsylvania."[97] The "skedaddlers" packed saddlebags or piled wheelbarrows and carts with belongings and trundled north. Having heard that the Confederates had arrested many Unionist men in Frederick and shipped them off to a Richmond prison, Angela Davis convinced her husband to join the exodus.

The next morning the Confederates advanced. Henry Kyd Douglas returned to Boonsboro early to say good-bye to friends and wait for the army there. He breakfasted with Dr. O. J. Smith and again visited his lady friend, identified in his memoir only as Miss Rose. When the Confederate column passed through town, with Stonewall Jackson at the head, Rose "ran to the curbstone, drew one of [Douglas's] pistols from its holster, and presenting it in mimic salute, cried with her silvery voice, 'A Maryland girl's welcome to Stonewall Jackson.'" Jackson, showing a rare moment of sympathy for what he perceived as young romance, gave Kyd Douglas the opportunity to remain in Boonsboro while the column passed. But Kyd Douglas dutifully mounted and rode with the rest of Jackson's staff as they led the column toward Hagerstown.[98]

In Funkstown, a boy's cries of, "The Rebels are coming! The Rebels are coming!" summoned Angela Davis to her front door. She noticed how dashing Henry Kyd Douglas looked at the head of the riders leading the column.

*Confederate Henry Kyd Douglas visited family and friends during each Southern campaign into Maryland. After the war Douglas returned to Maryland and helped create a* cemetery for Confederate dead in Hagerstown. COURTESY DOUG BAST, BOONSBOROUGH MUSEUM OF HISTORY.

Several cavalrymen stopped at the house across the street from hers to visit a brother of one of the riders. Despite her political convictions, Davis's sympathy was aroused by the sorry state of the Confederate infantrymen:

> Poor forlorn looking set of men, who certainly had seen hard service, as they were tired, dirty and ragged; and had no uniforms whatever. Their coats were made of almost anything that you could imagine—butternut color predominating—their hats looked worse than those worn by the darkies; many were bare-footed, some with their toes sticking out of their shoes, and others in their stocking feet; their blankets were of every kind and description, consisting of drugget, rugs, bed clothes, in fact everything they could get, put up in a long roll and tied at the ends which with their cooking utensils, were slung over their shoulders. Poor, brave, uncomplaining men.

She so pitied their tattered state that she hauled buckets to the front door so that she could offer water. She tried to offer cheerful words to the infantrymen, "and when I felt quite courageous, would tell them that I was from New York, and was not in sympathy with their cause." Several of the Southerners worried that she had poisoned the water.[99] One of Davis's neighbors refused to accept any Confederate money for her produce because she was a staunch Unionist and instead gave it away. Another stood at her door with a bucket of water, offering it to the thirsty soldiers as they passed. *"Remember a Union lady* is giving you water," she told them. "Passed Funk's Town," a Confederate surgeon concluded, "a Union hole."[100] Young girls pinned ribbons on their bodices, arranged to declare whether they were for "the bars" or "the stripes." Some persisted in telling the Confederate boys they were for the Union. "I'm inclined to the same opinion," countered one Rebel, "provided the union consists of only two."[101]

It took several days for the Confederate army to pass—long, anxious days for the women alone. Angela Davis expressed their feelings:

> It seemed as if the men came out of the ground like locusts, and their terrible line of march would never cease. General Lee—who

was an elegant looking gentleman—passed through town in a very common ambulance, the Palmetto flag floating over it and guarded by six soldiers armed to the teeth. . . . Soldiers were encamped all around us, and we were completely hemmed in and cut off from the rest of the world. You can have no idea what a terrible feeling this is. It seemed as if there were a dark, thick, high, impenetrable wall between us and the rest of mankind.

Women like Davis, trying to guard their homes while their husbands were absent, suffered an agony of suspense. In addition to the occupation, they had no means of communicating with their loved ones. Conflicting rumors flew from village to village.

Lee's orders against pillaging still stood, and although hungry, most men were willing to pay what they could for whatever was offered. But as the divided Confederate columns moved through Washington County, more soldiers made their own rules. Several officers requested that Davis unlock her husband's store and allow the men to purchase (with Confederate money) any remaining food; if she refused, the officers could not, they said, take responsibility for the actions of their men, which would undoubtedly include breaking the door and ransacking the place. (She handed over the keys and "sold" the men several hundred dollars' worth of groceries, medicines, and dry goods.)[102] In the tiny crossroads of Keedysville, Confederates raided John Cost's store, "loading the store goods into the wagon, knocking the heads of the molasses and oil barrels in and running it over the floor."[103]

Illness still ravaged the Confederate army, and men dropped out to rest in cornfields or collapsed on porches, asking for assistance. "The situation, [from] a sanitary point of view, of our army was deplorable," recalled a Virginian. "The ambulances were filled with the sick. Not a man . . . had had a change of underclothing since . . . a month ago, and . . . they were dirty, tattered, and infested with vermin."[104] When Angela Davis made hot ginger tea for a man who had collapsed, it soon attracted such a crowd of sick men that she was forced to go inside and shut the door. "I never saw men endure so many hardships," she mused, "and yet complain so little."[105]

On September 11 the Confederate army marched "up the dusty, broad pike" and entered Hagerstown. The First Virginia Cavalry charged into the city and captured a small Federal force that had lingered too long. For the next five days, the streets of Hagerstown were thronged with columns of ragged soldiers. Many Confederates, who had named Frederick "the most loyal city in Maryland," found signs of support more in evidence. "The actions of the citizens of Hagerstown showed in vivid contrast to Frederick City," wrote Private Alexander Hunter, "for not only were the men and women outspoken in their sympathy for the Southern cause, but they threw wide open their hospitable doors and filled their houses with the soldiers, feeding the hungry and clothing the naked as well as their limited means allowed."[106] A man on the street, seeing a barefoot soldier limping by, took off his own shoes and handed them to the soldier. "There is secession here," wrote a Georgian. "I was not a little surprised at the enthusiasm shown by many of the citizens. . . . What a number of ladies plainly showed by smiles, the waving of flags, handkerchiefs, &c., one expressed in words, 'I am a rebel, every inch of me,' and I assure you she felt what she said." Well-coached children stood at the curbsides, cheering for Jeff Davis, Stonewall Jackson, and General Lee. Civilian men were cautiously reserved, but Southern-minded ladies flocked to see their arriving heroes. They complained of life under military rule, telling tales of spying neighbors and censorship. "These are dark days," one said, "and we are glad to see you come."[107] The vocal minority of Hagerstown civilians who were secessionists made the Southerners feel welcome.

Edgar Warfield, who had complained of the "scant welcome" his army received in Frederick, was more interested in necessities than politics. "The people [of Hagerstown] received the ragged 'Rebs' as if they were belted knights with victory on their plumes," he wrote, noting that every soldier was offered food.[108] The men seemed pleased enough to find anything, needed or not. More merchants in Hagerstown were willing to open their doors, and the Southern troops took full advantage. "Soldiers, on such occasions, are like children," Heros von Borcke observed. "They buy everything, and embarrass themselves with numberless articles which soon afterwards are thrown away as useless."[109] Soon residents of Hagerstown witnessed the bewildering spectacle of bedraggled men sporting beaverskin top hats, sucking lemons, puffing cigars, or tucking away ladies' dress patterns and packets of sugar. Men lucky enough to get new shirts or trousers often donned them in the streets, leaving their filthy rags in the gutters.

General Lee felt better about his army's reception in Hagerstown, as well. "The army has been received in this region with sympathy and kindness," he wrote to President Jefferson Davis. "We have found in this city about 500 barrels of flour, and I am led to hope that a supply can be gathered from the mills in the country."[110] He was disappointed, however, to collect only 400 more pairs of shoes. With the 1,000 gained in Frederick, and another 250 pairs from Williamsport, he still didn't have enough to provide for all of his soldiers.

The soldiers did what they could to improve their lot. Every evening, at campsites ringing the city, embarrassed civilian visitors found thousands of soldiers stripped and relentlessly pursuing the lice that made their lives miserable. "With trembling pen and an ashamed heart, I must confess that at that particular juncture in my career as a soldier I was, according to the polite but graphic language of our camp Chesterfields, quite insectuous,'" wrote a chagrined Texan in a letter. His camp near Hagerstown was on the banks of a beautiful stream, and he joyfully bathed. "The clear stream of water came in then most handily for the extensive and laborious ablutions rendered obligatory by my keen sense of the fitness of things."[111]

Once clean, the Rebels found other entertainments awaiting them. "During the short time that we were camped about the towns of Maryland," Napier Bartlett recalled, "the streets were full of soldiers, not to say the drinking saloons, which from time to time would mysteriously open and shut, though contrary to orders, and the jingling of spurs, sabres, and glasses, and the faint aroma of tempting drinks, would be born to the senses of the envious lookers on, compelled to remain upon the outside."[112] Despite lapses in discipline, the Confederate occupation of Hagerstown was generally orderly.

Most of the Southerners enjoyed their stay and were in high spirits. One orderly sergeant from South Carolina recalled "how one young lady, about sixteen years old, stood with a group of other girls and women in the doorway of Hager's store in Hagerstown and boldly waved a national flag at the Rebs as they passed. 'Why don't you fight under this flag?' she challenged them. One of the South Carolinians shouted back, 'Hagerstown, Hager's Store, Hager's daughter—hurrah for Hager.' At that the entire column gave the ladies a rousing Rebel Yell."[113]

>-+-+>-+-O-+<-+-+-<

Meanwhile, Frederick was adjusting to life with the Union army. Steiner noted that no arrests were made of secessionist citizens who had aided the Southern army, although prominent Confederate citizens' homes were searched for Rebel deserters. Squads of cavalry twice appeared at the Markell door, sent to search the house for concealed arms or soldiers. Each time they were talked out of such a search—evidently in part due to intervention from local Federal officers who knew the Markells—and left without further altercation.[114]

The streets were still thronged with troops, teamsters, and sightseers. Young girls' desire for romantic heroes was filled by "Rush's Lancers," the Sixth Pennsylvania Cavalry, who carried red pennants and long lances with medieval flair. At times the traffic was so congested that cavalry and artillery overflowed onto the sidewalks, scattering hapless passersby. It was noisy and cheerful, and the men were loath to leave. "I shall always remember with gratitude the good people of Frederick City," David Thompson wrote later. "They received us with open arms, took us into their houses, gave us to eat & to drink, & did everything in their power to make us feel at home."[115]

McClellan, however, had no reason to linger. On September 13 he set his first troops in motion, heading toward the beacon ridges of Catoctin Mountain and South Mountain beyond. Already trying to assess the damage done by the Confederates, the farmers who owned property along the route threw up their hands in despair as another army surged through. One soldier described the wake left by two armies:

> Most of the Confederate army and several corps of the Union had, the former preceding and the others closely following, gone over [the turnpike]. Each side of the road in the fields was well tramped out by the infantry, the main thoroughfare having been left for the trains. The fences were down entirely. Debris, broken wagons and abandoned property were strewn about everywhere. Telegraph poles and wires were cut and destroyed, and it was quite apparent the only purpose of the pursuers and pursued was to get along as rapidly as possible, regardless of what was lost, mutilated, or forgotten.[116]

Farm families could ill afford the destruction, but personal calamity was soon eclipsed by the first thunder of real war. In the western communities, nerves stretched thin were pulled tighter on Saturday when a fierce roar drifted north: Harpers Ferry was under siege from batteries mounted on the surrounding cliffs, including Maryland Heights, and Stonewall Jackson's men were beginning to pound the Federal garrison there into submission.

That night, Frederick Countians watched the flicker of a thousand Union campfires on the east side of the ridges, and Washington County residents watched the Rebel fires on the west—and everyone waited to see what happened next. Slaves considered casting their lot with the blue-coated redeemers. Children whimpered for their absent fathers. Farmers camped in damp mountain thickets with their horses, wondering if it was safe to go home. Adolescent boys eyed the soldiers' weapons with longing and dreamed of marching off to their own glory. Women at home alone in the midst of the armies prayed to see the soldiers leave, putting their children to bed that night and sitting through the long dark hours alone, afraid to sleep themselves, waiting.

The devout among them looked forward to Sunday services, hoping for consolation. That Sunday, September 14, in countless tiny churches in Funkstown and Boonsboro and Keedysville and Rohrersville, families tried to cast aside their worries as they knelt in prayer. But distant artillery clashed with their hymns, and their gazes drifted to a haze of smoke marking the line of battle unfolding among the rocky passes of South Mountain. The Federals had caught up with the Confederates.

CHAPTER 4

# "I'll Die First"

Robert E. Lee had left a division under the command of D. H. Hill at Boonsboro to guard the mountain pass at Turner's Gap, stall Federal scouts, and capture any Yankee troops eluding Stonewall Jackson's force circling Harpers Ferry. At the time, close pursuit by George McClellan's force seemed unlikely. Now, Hill's division stood in the Northern army's path. Hill's charge was critical. If the Army of the Potomac crossed South Mountain in force, the Army of Northern Virginia would be split, leaving Longstreet's command isolated well north of the Potomac River. The Confederates were in danger of being engulfed, one piece at a time.

Between the two armies were the rolling ridges of Catoctin Mountain, just west of Frederick, and South Mountain beyond. South Mountain, peaking at sixteen hundred feet, extends roughly fifty miles from the Potomac north into Pennsylvania. Several roads crossed South Mountain from the Middletown Valley to the east, and the Confederates grimly prepared to defend those mountain passes: Turner's Gap plus the National Road and Fox's Gap to the south, both near Middletown; and Crampton's Gap near Burkittsville. If Hill's Confederates could hold the Northern troops at bay long enough, Lee might have time to reassemble his army. Hill had fewer than five thousand men to dike the Yankee tide and protect the army's supply train at Boonsboro. To strengthen Hill's force, Lee recalled most of Longstreet's men from Hagerstown.

Meanwhile, McClellan was making his own plans at his Frederick headquarters. On Saturday Lee's Special Orders No. 191—the "Lost Orders" found by Union men in a field near Frederick—had trumpeted the astonishing news that Lee's army was divided, and signal stations west of Frederick reported sounds of cannonading from Harpers Ferry. The Confederate cavalry patrolling the ridges west of town made their presence

87

known to any Union soldier who ventured too far into the hills. Another general might have put his army in motion at once. McClellan ordered most of his Army of the Potomac to march west from Frederick and Middletown on Sunday morning, September 14, taking the National Road toward Turner's Gap. A smaller force was sent south toward Crampton's Gap with the ultimate goal of rescuing Harpers Ferry.

Sunday morning dawned hot, sunny, and dry. The Confederate rear guard and Federal vanguard bickered with artillery and musketry on Catoctin Mountain, and a civilian at the base of the mountain was struck by debris from a shell.[1] Troops were wheeling amidst the "rude and scattered" buildings of Hamburg on the crest of Catoctin Mountain, where "the manufacture of brandy seemed to be the chief employment of the villagers."[2] The Yankees slowly bullied the Rebel riders down the slope and across the valley toward Middletown.

Middletown Unionists were glad to see the end of the Confederate column, and not all retreated indoors when the fight moved through their streets. "I was one of the last horsemen that galloped through [Middletown] . . .," Heros von Borcke wrote. "The Yankee artillery threw a withering hail of shells along the main street of Middletown, from every by-street whistled the bullets of the sharpshooters, in our rear thundered the attack of the pursuing cavalry, while from the houses the Unionists fired at us with buck-shot and small-shot, and many fallen horses and riders impeded the road." The Koogle family lived near a bridge over Catoctin Creek a mile west of Middletown. Adam Koogle (known locally as A. C., to distinguish him from his father Adam) had enlisted in the First Maryland Artillery, USA, and was with his unit on the campaign. When the Confederate rear guard moved west from Middletown, they torched the bridge near his family's farm to slow the Federal pursuit. "The panic reached its height when we arrived at the bridge and found it blazing, through the premature execution of his orders by the officer in charge . . .," recalled von Borcke. "I forced my horse through fire and smoke across the burning bridge, which very soon after . . . fell with a loud crash into the water."[3] In the process the Koogles' barn, wagon shed, and blacksmith shop burned to the ground. Several shells struck the house, and only the arrival of Federal troops saved the farm from complete destruction. A seven-year-old slave girl "was found dead in her room, supposedly from fright," Adam Koogle Jr. wrote later. The family had also been caring for a Confederate boy severely wounded in an accidental explosion. "By great effort he was rolled up in a sheet and finally landed in the cellar," Koogle recalled. While the family huddled in the cellar, a shell landed in a bed just above their heads but did not explode.[4]

The Confederate riders galloped out of town. Though slowed by the burned bridge and artillery barrage, the Yankee vanguard pursued. While church bells in the valleys pealed, long columns of men in blue tramped toward the summit of South Mountain. From the ridge crest, D. H. Hill watched the Federals advance across the open Middletown valley. "The vast army of McClellan spread out before me," he wrote later. "The marching columns extended back as far as eye could see in the distance. It was a grand and glorious spectacle, and it was impossible to look at it without admiration." But he wished he had more comrades to share the view: Longstreet's men were miles away, and Stuart had taken most of his cavalry to Crampton's Gap, six miles south.[5]

That blue tide flowing from Frederick surged through Middletown's crowded streets. The men were stomping through ankle-deep dust, and dirty clouds announced their arrival. Residents braved the choking air and cheered the troops on. "Never was a more cordial welcome given to troops than was given to us," a Pennsylvanian remembered. "Bread, cakes, milk, water, fruit, and tobacco were freely given by the good people who crowded the doors and windows and lined the pavements, and flags and handkerchiefs were waved and flowers thrown as we passed. We felt then, for the first time during the war, we were fighting among friends."[6] All the Yankees received a warm welcome from the town Massachusetts troops fondly nicknamed "Little Boston." The 104th New York Volunteers passed through Middletown just as Sunday services should have been starting. "But the boys gathered on the front steps, with the girls and young ladies, did not go inside that church," one soldier recalled proudly, "and . . . even some of the older men and women lingered outside of the little church in Middletown that Sunday morning to watch and see Fighting Joe Hooker's corps march by on its way to the battlefield."[7]

At the base of the mountain, the Federal officers at the front of the column decided not to ascend the National Road and assault the Confederates at Turner's Gap directly, but instead flank them by turning onto the Old Sharpsburg Road and ascending to Fox's Gap, a mile south. They would crest the mountain and drive north toward Turner's Gap. The Union boys, so recently buoyed by the cheers, began a steep two-mile climb. By 9:00 A.M. the sound of the opening guns crashed through the valleys. In the

*"Middletown, MD., Near South Mountain."* The rousing welcome Yankee troops received in Middletown prompted Massachusetts men to dub the town "Little Boston." Sketch by A. R. Waud, Harpers Weekly. COURTESY FRANK & MARIE-THERESE WOOD PRINT COLLECTIONS, ALEXANDRIA, VIRGINIA.

little villages on either side of the ridge, timid residents scurried to their cellars while the bolder clustered on the street to watch.

Near the passes, a few hardscrabble farm families wrestled a living from hard-won fields among rocky ridges and dense stands of pine and cedar. Most of the stubborn mountain folks didn't leave until the shells began flying. Private Calvin Leach of the First North Carolina was among those trudging back up the western slope of the mountain that morning, when fierce fighting had already been under way for hours. "The citizens were leaving out," he wrote. "Those that lived on the top of the mountain came riding down in a carriage with tears in their eyes whose faces I recollected seeing as we passed before, who seemed gay and hapy surrounded by home and its comforts waving the southern flag at us as we passed before."[8] Soldiers were already pushing through the farmers' small orchards. Artillery fire plowed new furrows in their fields with a sound, one soldier recalled, "like the cutting of a melon rind."[9] Fences so laboriously constructed became sketchy shelter for those creeping forward—or obstacles for men crawling back to safety.

John Wise, twenty-four, and his sister Matilda, twenty-nine, who owned a rocky little farm near Fox's Gap, were evidently caring for a five-year-old niece named Cecilia in 1862. Their father, Daniel, also lived with them, supplementing family income by making pottery and practicing folk medicine for neighbors in need. After burying a trunk of belongings in the cellar, the Wise family prudently fled their home on the morning of the battle. Cecilia never forgot the sight of soldiers lining the old Sharpsburg Road as the family headed toward safety. Some of the soldiers urged them on by pointing their bayonets at the terrified girl. But the refugees evidently reminded one Rebel soldier of his own distant family, and he stopped Cecilia to give her a tiny ring that had belonged to his daughter. "I don't know if I'll ever get back or not," he said. "You keep it." He also gave her a precious jar of preserves.[10] She may also have been the child who caught General D. H. Hill's eye that morning: "Just then a shell came hurtling through the woods," he wrote later while describing a ride through the vicinity of the Wise cabin, "and a little girl began crying. Having a little one at home of about the same age, I could not forbear stopping a moment to say a few soothing words to the frightened child, before hurrying off to the work of death."[11]

On the ridge crest, some Alabama troops under the command of Colonel John B. Gordon formed a battle line in front of a tiny cabin. Recalled a member of the Sixth Alabama:

The hut was occupied by an old woman of ample proportions and her brood of white haired children. Standing in the doorway, she barred all entrance of soldiers or officers, seeking water. Glaring through her immense steel-bowed spectacles, she denounced all comers as "low-down thieving rebels." The soldiers cheer vociferously at each outburst of her wrath. Attracted by the uproar . . . Gordon rode up with his staff. Raising his hat in the most courtly manner, he said with the greatest politeness and deference, "My dear madam, fighting will begin in five minutes. Your life and that of your children are in imminent peril. You must leave here at once." The old woman, with arms akimbo, her eyes blazing with wrath replied, "I know what you want, you thieving rebels; you want to get me out of my house, and come and steal all I've got. I won't go, so there! I'll die fust!" The soldiers yelled, "Go it old lady! Hold the fort! Bully for you!" &c. . . . Gordon retreated amidst the ill-concealed laughter of his staff, for once speechless, utterly discomforted. I never knew the fate of this mountaineer Spartan mother, as at that moment my company was ordered to the foot of the mountain as skirmishers.[12]

An old stone inn and tavern called the Mountain House marked the summit of Turner's Gap on the National Road. The landlord, a staunch supporter, had probably skedaddled before the fighting began, but his inn became a landmark for the officers trying to coordinate battle plans among the tangled undergrowth and haphazard fields. When the battle neared Fox's Gap, three thousand Ohioans attacked one thousand North Carolinians commanded by young Brigadier General Samuel Garland. One of the Ohio artillery crews manhandled their gun close enough to spew canister at close range, taking a terrible toll on the Southerners. Rutherford B. Hayes's 23rd Ohio men fixed bayonets and charged, sending the demoralized Rebels down the mountain. Hayes fell with a shattered arm. Garland was among the men killed, and his body was temporarily laid out in one of the rooms where travelers had so often rested at the Mountain House.[13] Soon more wounded were finding shelter at the inn. The yard where coach drivers and freight haulers had tended their animals now teemed with Southern officers, couriers, aides, and dazed infantrymen looking for water.

Hill's position—and so the entire Confederate army—was in peril. In a desperate ploy he shoved the noncombatant rear echelon of cooks, drivers, aides, and messengers into line. "I do not remember ever to have experienced a feeling of greater *loneliness*," he remembered later.[14] The thin gray line held, keeping the Federal soldiers pushing from Fox's Gap from reaching the Mountain House.

>─┼─◇─○─◇─┼─<

For hours, while the soldiers in both armies struggled to force the opposing men down the mountain, Longstreet's Confederates hurried to help. It was a tramp of thirteen miles. Heat shimmered across the landscape. The men were soon caked with sweat and dust—and desperately thirsty. They heard the guns, saw the smoke, and pushed on with urgency. There was no time now to flirt with pretty girls, to barter for biscuits and apple butter, to relieve their homesickness by coaxing astonished women to let them hold their babies. Civilians in Boonsboro and Funkstown who had watched the Southern columns tramp west stared as the same men hurried back. At his headquarters near Boonsboro, General Lee sat astride Traveller, his familiar gray horse, beside the crammed road and tried to hearten his tired boys. It was a hard march, particularly for the men who had overindulged. "I was recovering from an attack of 'too much Maryland hospitality,'" admitted one man, whose stomach was "in a state of violent rebellion."[15] The soldiers sported whatever finery they had been able to acquire, but too rarely was it sturdy brogans. In the confusion, some of Longstreet's men went miles out of their way, and rural families peeping from shuttered windows were astonished to see columns of shabby men cutting through cornfields and farmyards. By the time the boys reached South Mountain, some were too exhausted to make the steep climb to the top. But most knew it was up to them to keep the Union army from swallowing the entire Confederate force.

Their comrades on the mountain were desperate for help. "The day was spent . . . marching and countermarching through deep ravines, dense thickets, and over abrupt hills and rocky precipices, in order that we might always have a force at any pass to oppose the advances of the Yankees," recalled one Confederate.[16] The Southerners were demoralized by the unending line of Yankee reinforcements marching steadily toward them on the eastern roads below. For too long the western roads remained empty. Then, finally, Longstreet's vanguard appeared on the turnpike. It was about 3:30 P.M. Some of the Confederates defending Turner's Gap had been fighting like demons for six hours.

As the reinforcements pushed toward the battle, the first ambulance wagons jolted toward Boonsboro. "Troops of demoralized stragglers are descending as we ascend," wrote John Dooley of the First Virginia, "and long lines of wounded limping down the road. The appearances of things are to say the least very discouraging."[17] The soldiers—those bloodied and those just joining the fray—jostled past each other uneasily.

Middletown residents had been in the middle of the armies for days. Many families were separated. Lonely wives, as well as their men waiting in Pennsylvania or hidden mountain hamlets, had no way of knowing if their loved ones were safe. The village had been under fire for much of the long Sunday, beginning when an artillery crew in McClellan's advance guard had unlimbered on the western edge of the village and lobbed some shots at the receding columns of Confederates. That gesture had drawn a resentful answering volley, and cannon shots crashed through the walls of several buildings.

No one knew what to do or where to go. "On Saturday when [the Rebels] were hiking through town . . . the people went in there cellers at first," Allen Sparrow remembered, "but soon got so reckless that they put themselves in danger. Some men nearly run their legs off to get out of the way and when they found themself was right in the midst of them."[18] Throughout that long Sunday the deafening, unending roar of artillery had been the worst. Women cringed with each shuddering boom, trying to calm screaming babies and howling dogs, aching with uncertainty.

General McClellan had expected to cross South Mountain before catching his prey, and he spent the morning at Frederick. When informed that a major battle was under way, he hurried to Middletown, galvanizing his proud troops as he cantered past the columns. In Middletown he climbed to the steeple of the Reformed Church and squinted through field glasses, trying to ascertain the Confederate position.[19] Some local civilians couldn't stand the suspense, either. They clambered to their barn roofs or trudged up nearby hills to squint toward the mountain as well. Isaac Hall of the 97th New York saw "spectators of both sexes . . . upon the hills witnessing the sublime but awful spectacle of contending armies."[20] In Sharpsburg, people listened to the distant crash of battle and stared at the ridge, wondering. "We could hear the guns," recalled Alexander Root, a young hired man working for Jacob Nicodemus, "but we couldn't figure out what was going on." Driven by curiosity, he rounded up several friends, and they walked across the fields to Keedysville, gathering more "recruits" as they went. In Boonsboro, the hotel keeper cautioned them against proceeding. "But we was nosey," Root admitted later, "and wanted to nose in." They continued toward the battle until they met their first wounded soldier. "He told us the troops was hot at it up there on the mountain. So we thought we'd let well enough alone, and we went back home."[21]

A young boy named C. C. Kaufman saw more of the battle than he wished to. The Kaufman family farmed near the eastern base of Catoctin Mountain, and the Confederate army had left a sick soldier from Florida in the Kaufmans' corncrib. Harboring a Confederate was cause for arrest, and Mr. Kaufman decided to haul the sick boy to his comrades in a farm wagon. He set out on Sunday morning with his son, C. C., and they caught up with the Confederate rear guard on top of Catoctin Mountain. C. C. stared, astonished, while his father and a Confederate commander haggled over the disposition of the hapless invalid. Mr. Kaufman agreed to loan the wagon to the Confederates and told C. C. to get out of the wagon. "I thought I was to be left with the soldiers," C. C. wrote, "so I asked him if I could stay in the wagon." Mr. Kaufman agreed and began walking home while a Confederate driver took the wagon, with the sick boy and C. C., on to South Mountain. The Kaufmans did not realize at the time that McClellan's force was also driving toward the mountain. "While Father was on his way home, the Blue Coats were coming up the pike, and the Rebel sharp-shooters on Jigger Hill were sending hot lead at them, bullets flying around my father like hail," C. C. wrote later. "A fine black horse was shot and killed from under an officer in front of our house." Most of the Kaufman family, frantic with worry about C. C., left home and trekked north through fields and woods to the home of friends, where they stayed until the following day.

Meanwhile, the Confederate driver delivered the sick soldier to a surgeon on South Mountain and headed back east with the wagon and C. C. They drove through Middletown and began climbing Catoctin Mountain. C. C. saw patches of smoking, burned grass left from exploding shells. As they reached the summit, a man on horseback rode toward them, yelling, "Take that horse and boy back, or they will get killed!" C. C. and the team were handily deposited at the Smeltzer house on the summit. The boy wandered miserably into the house, weeping, and found four women. "Hush!" one called Aunt Sally snapped, and C. C. tried to swallow his tears. A short while later a shell crashed through the house:

The four women came together in the middle of the room, crying, screaming and wringing their hands. I thought now was a chance for me to bawl, so I opened my mouth and let out a loud wail. Before I could let out another, Aunt Sally turned on me and said "hush" in such a fierce manner that I was afraid to bawl again, but I thought it was not fair for them to cry and not allow me the same privilege.

One of the younger women carried C. C. to a neighboring farm and left him. A twelve-year-old boy was assigned to watch him. At last "I could cry all I wanted to." C. C. tried to slip away repeatedly during the day but each time was hauled back by a vigilant black woman working at the farm. It was an interminable day for the youngster, finally relieved when his father found him in the late afternoon.[22]

>—·—‹›—·—O—·‹›—·—‹

On the east-slope roads, columns of Federal troops were still pressing toward the summit. "When we came nearer," wrote one, "we began to see something of battle. We passed the hospital on our way up—a little mud & log cabin hastily converted into one—& the ambulances were coming down with wounded. It . . . made my heart sick."[23] At 4:00 P.M. McClellan sent fresh troops north in a flanking maneuver and a single brigade in a new assault at Turner's Gap. The new troops shucked their knapsacks and scrabbled with burning lungs toward the combat. Some New Yorkers passed an elderly woman who had left her mountaintop cabin that morning. "Don't you go there!" she pleaded with the Union boys as they passed. "There are hundreds of 'em up there. Don't you go. *Some of you will get hurt.*"[24]

Dusk was descending when the Northern reinforcements arrived at Turner's Gap, and they met a barrage of gunfire blasted from Confederates waiting behind a stone fence. The Yankees sent north began hammering the Confederates there, who dodged from tree to tree bushwhacker-style to slow their enemies' advance. Smoke drifted through the trees. The air stank of powder. Sparks from rifles landed on the bone-dry tinder of fallen leaves and started small brushfires. Whimpering soldiers crouched in laurel thickets, trying to discern their own lines, unable to tell where their enemies were in the chaos. Amid the din of artillery and musketry, the feral yells and desperate pleas for help, the troops strained their ears to distinguish "whether the cheers [came] from friend or foe," as one Southern man wrote. "The Yankee cheer [was] 'Huzza! Huzza!' in deep, gruff tones, while ours [was] characterized by one continuous, unearthly yell, without pause or stop."[25] A colonel in the 20th North Carolina wrote later, "We were pushed on a level plateau about 100 yards wide in thick chestnut undergrowth, open fields in our front sloping down steep hills, the bottom of which we could not see; in our rear a precipitous rocky, wooded descent." When the 20th was flanked, they had nothing to do but give up. Some of the men were captured, although most tried to escape: "I was called upon frequently to halt . . . but instead of halting I made terrific leaps down that mountain."[26] In the howling confusion, officers lost their men; men, their pards.

As darkness descended the men at the summit kept at it, aiming at the enemy guns' firefly flashes. Fighting didn't die away until 9:00 P.M. Confederates were still on the mountain—and still held the National Road at Turner's Gap—but the Federals held the high ground.

>─┼─◆>─○─<◆>┼─<

Six miles south, another vicious fight had been unfolding at Crampton's Gap. Burkittsville, in the valley to the east, was a "pleasant village of neat brick houses, with one or two handsome churches."[27] It was also a bustling little agrarian service center for the farm families nearby. Oxcarts hauling charcoal to the Catoctin Iron Works often rumbled through its narrow main street, and burly market drivers heading from Virginia to Baltimore stopped for refreshment in the village. A tannery on West Main Street anchored a little cluster of industry, including stinking sheds and vats for processing hides, a pottery, a loom house, and a courtroom—handy, since the German saddler who had established the tannery also served as magistrate. During the Confederate occupation the tannery had been severely damaged.[28]

That morning Confederate gunner George Neese arrived in the gap at dawn, when the beautiful valley below was "reposing in the quiet calm of a peaceful Sabbath morning."[29] That peaceful calm was soon shattered. General Franklin's troops had been sent to relieve the beleaguered Federal force at Harpers Ferry and arrived about noon. Just as a few bold Unionists began cheering the arrival of the Federal vanguard, the Confederate artillery in Crampton's Gap and Brownsville Pass lobbed some shells at the village. Although some of the Rebel shells sailed over Burkittsville, others landed among summer kitchens, homes, and stables. Annoyed Union gunners established an artillery post east of town to throw shells back. A Yankee soldier heading through Burkittsville recalled that despite gunfire, the "women, young and old, with great coolness, waved their handkerchiefs and flags at us."[30]

While the Southern artillery held the ridge, a few Confederate infantry and dismounted cavalry waited along a country lane that ran along the base of the mountain, parallel to the crest. A low stone wall bordering Jacob Goodman's property provided cover for the waiting Rebels. Federal troops advanced toward the gap only after a lengthy delay. George Neese, watching the Federals approach, noted that the Yankees reminded him of "a lion, making exceedingly careful preparations to spring on a plucky little mouse."[31]

Residents along that road had also been waiting anxiously, and they watched in horror as Federal infantry troops advanced steadily through brushy meadows and cornfields toward the mountain. One person watching was Susan Tritt, a widow with two teenage daughters who had chosen to weather the storm in her own home—although a group of Georgians had turned her stone house into a fortress. A regiment of Schyulkill County coal miners, the 96th Pennsylvania, eyed the house warily as they advanced, noting the muskets bristling from every window and door. The Confederates opened a withering fire as the Pennsylvanians advanced. "When our men drew near . . .," one of the Northerners wrote later, "an ancient dame with nose all spectacle bestride showed herself at one of the windows waving her old calico sun-bonnet with both her hands, and with loud cries and frantic endeavors, strove to prevent our men from firing."[32] Despite Susan Tritt's pleas, the Pennsylvanians returned fire and, after a brief but vicious fight, captured her home.

The afternoon had slipped away before the Federal troops began to push the Confederate line up the steep mountain. Dozens of confused fights whirled among the trees and rocky ledges. A few local civilians living on the mountain had stubbornly refused to flee. Like the Confederates, they had watched the drama unfolding below with fascinated horror. Then the momentum surged toward their own homes.

Reverend Daniel Ridout, an African Methodist Episcopal minister living with his family on the east side of South Mountain, had been away when the troops arrived. He spent three frustrating days trying to cross the Rebel picket line from Washington County and had finally been permitted to travel on to his home. He arrived just before the battle began. His son later wrote of watching the battle unfold in the road below: "I seen them coming, bayonets glistening in the autumnal sun. They are nearing the rebel line . . . the command is given to the rebels to 'fire.' It seemed as if heaven and earth had collided." When a stray ball flew into the Ridouts' home and lodged in a wall, the family retreated to the cellar. But when the firing subsided, Daniel and one of his daughters ventured into the yard to "reconnoitre":

A rebel cavalier passing by sees them; maddened by the fact that the battle is almost lost to them, he aims a pistol at Father, pulls the trigger, but the weapon misses fire. Three times he aims and pulls the trigger, each time it only snaps, and refuses to kill "God's anointed." With an oath he rides on."[33]

Some Burkittsville civilians couldn't resist the show. Thomas Roger Johnson, who lived near Crampton's Gap, watched part of the battle from the roof of his barn "where I could see the discharges of the cannon and hear the whistling of the shells."[34] During three hours of hard fighting, the spectators stared at the mountain, trying to discern what was happening behind the veil of smoke, each hoping for the news that *their* army had won the day.

The Unionists were destined for good news, for the Yankees overpowered the outnumbered Confederates and seized the gap by 6:00 P.M. In the final confusion some Rebel soldiers fled south to Brownsville while a force of gray-clad cavalry pounded into Rohrersville. Frightened women cringed behind bolted doors as the Southern boys staggered onto their porches. The first to arrive begged for water. Then came the wounded.

The Union force scooped up almost four hundred prisoners near Crampton's Gap. They probably could have pushed on, smashed the flimsy Southern line thrown up in Pleasant Valley, and pressed through to Harpers Ferry just six miles away. Instead, General Franklin ordered his men to bed down for the night on the mountain.

The battle of South Mountain, destined to be forever overshadowed by the battle of Antietam Creek that quickly followed, was a bloody struggle that cost each army dearly: The Confederates lost 2,300 of the 18,000 men engaged and the Federals 1,800 of 28,000. Each army had lost a talented general, with Federal general Jesse Lee Reno falling near the spot where Confederate Sam Garland was killed. Although Lee still held Turner's Gap, he knew it could not be defended long after daybreak, and he ordered a retreat.

The Confederates had been bloodied, losing the opportunity to invade Pennsylvania and, ultimately, Washington City. But the Federals lost as well. The opportunity to save the Union garrison at Harpers Ferry slipped away, because while the Union army fussed and fretted, Stonewall Jackson calmly captured 73 artillery pieces, 13,000 small arms, and 12,500 men—the largest Federal capitulation of the war. And by lingering too long, McClellan lost the chance to gobble up Lee's army piece by piece. The desperate Confederates had stood game against overwhelming odds, tarnishing the

luster of the glorious triumph. McClellan counted the battle of South
Mountain a victory, but in the end he gave Lee a precious gift: time.

>–┼–◆>–O–<◆–┼–<

When night blurred the rugged contours of South Mountain, hundreds of
men were still on the ridge. Some had fought for hours without food or
water. A Massachusetts cavalryman recalled that a barrel of stolen rye meal,
mixed with water, spread on barrel heads, and cooked over a campfire "was
all that stood between the regiment and hunger."[35] Infantrymen dropped
where they had fought and slept, too exhausted even to forage. "Where we
lay wrapped up in our blankets we knew not who was our neighbor," Lieutenant Sam Healy wrote.[36] One man shared his blanket with what he
thought was a comrade, only to discover at dawn he'd been sleeping with a
corpse. After a day of searing heat, heavy dews cloaked the men in a damp
chill. Torch-bearing corpsmen stumbled through the undergrowth looking
for wounded—and quickly became lost themselves.

Campfires burned in the valleys throughout the night. On the west side
of the mountain, Confederate surgeons established a hospital at the Murdock farm on the Boonsboro Road. Straw from the barns was hauled outside and scattered over the yard to provide some meager comfort to the
wounded. Ambulances were quickly emptied so that the cursing drivers
could edge their team toward another load. By the flicker and flare of candle and lantern, hurting boys waited dully for attention.

Lee couldn't afford to take time with his casualties. The Federal army
held the ridge crest and had thousands of reinforcements waiting in the
Middletown Valley to the east. In the darkness, while thousands of
wounded soldiers still lay sprawled unseen among the craggy terrain, the
Confederates began their retreat from the slope. "We had been marching
and fighting all day and must now march and probably fight all night,"
wrote one Confederate later, remembering his exhausted reaction to the
withdrawal orders. "Captain Norton's company is reduced to *two members* . . .
that is, *himself* and *myself.*"[37] There was no moon, and understandably the
retreat was a bit jumbled. Survivors of the Fifth Alabama were sleeping so
close to their enemies that when their adjutant crept through his comrades,
shaking them awake with the muttered news that Federal troops were near,
he mistakenly roused several Yankee soldiers and was taken prisoner.[38]

The Confederates stole down the mountain, under orders to march to
Sharpsburg about six miles west. "It was impossible to prevent straggling

to a great extent," recalled one Rebel. "The men were exhausted, hungry and foot sore. . . . The greater portion of them managed to straggle through incredible hardships in getting back to Sharpsburg, and not a few continued the retreat on their own responsibility until they were safe across the Potomac and on Virginia soil."[39] The men hated leaving their wounded behind and plodded west in depressed silence.

Lee had not yet heard from Stonewall Jackson and did not know if his subordinate had captured the Federal force at Harpers Ferry. The Southern general may have learned that McClellan had found a copy of his Special Orders No. 191, which outlined his plan to divide his army. A delegation of Frederick citizens had witnessed McClellan's exultant reaction, and one of them, a Rebel sympathizer, managed to slip through the Federal lines with the news that some piece of intelligence had fallen into Yankee hands. After his outnumbered force had been pummeled in the passes of South Mountain, Lee planned to recross the Potomac and end his invasion into Maryland.

Once again Boonsboro residents heard the Confederates pass. Lamps still burned in most houses, where hundreds of wounded had already been taken. Soldiers banged on their doors, pleading for assistance, but many of the anxious citizens did not come to their doors. "Hundreds of our wounded are gathered in this little village, crowding the porches and steps of the houses and begging admittance; and we hear many voices from the various windows telling these poor victims of war to go away and not to get *them* in trouble," one Confederate related bitterly. "They are opposed to us all along this valley, and are or pretend to be fearful of punishment from the Yankees if they befriend us in any way."[40]

From Boonsboro the exhausted men shuffled through Keedysville. M. F. Rohrer, a boy of twelve at the time, never forgot the seemingly endless line of wagons rumbling by throughout the night. Before the column passed through, officers rode from house to house, advising women and children to leave.[41] They knew there was more fighting to come.

><>-O-<>-<

At dawn the Yankees still on South Mountain staggered to their feet and surveyed the carnage. Speechless, the men stared at the mangled bodies tangled in thickets, stacked like cordwood behind fences, sprawled among the rocks. "I have seen all of war I ever wish to," one boy wrote home. "The thing is indescribable. Oh, horrors!"[42] Farm cabins and outbuildings were riddled with bullets. Cornstalks dangled forlornly at breast height, nearly severed by shot. Shells had gouged ruts among the trees.

At the Mountain House, bleeding soldiers were packed into reeking farm wagons for the trip to Frederick hospitals. As the wagons jolted away, new drivers pushed toward the crest for more wounded. Federal officers also congregated at the old stone inn, to confer and advise and plan. McClellan paused from dictating heady telegraph messages to Washington and ordered the Federal cavalry to give immediate chase through the passes, with the infantry following. They knew that they were close on the heels of the Confederates. "The rebles run from the field & we have bin chaising them very cloce," Matthew Hurlenger of the 56th Pennsylvania wrote in his diary, "for I seen ware thay kild several oxen & leave the rest for thay had to run through the town of bonesborow & there fiers ware still burning so close we ware."[43]

Severely wounded Confederates were hauled away for care. But others were still on the mountain—men wounded slightly or lost. By dawn they were crawling after their army or toward the Potomac, trying to evade capture. Many of the desperate stragglers appealed to farm families for assistance, scrambling for cover when Federal regiments began scouring the field for prisoners. "Many soldiers . . . were found hiding in houses along the slope or in the valley," one Federal soldier recalled.[44] Others told civilians that they were ready to be captured. One civilian answered a pounding on his door and found a Confederate officer who had been cut off from his company. "We have been badly whipped," he said, "and I don't know where a single man can be found."[45]

The Old Sharpsburg Road bisecting the Wise family's property had been the scene of bitter fighting. The 12th Ohio had slept on the ground among the dead and wounded near the farm. In the morning they found Union and Confederate wounded in Wise's cellar, where they had crawled for safety the day before. "The little cabin and garden with its stone fences was the scene of the greatest and bloodiest conflict of the day," a lieutenant of Company A wrote.[46] According to Brigadier General Orlando Willcox, who had led his Yankee troops in battle at Fox's Gap, the Wise farm represented "such a picture of the killed and wounded as . . . was rarely seen during the war."[47]

On the fifteenth, Federal troops streamed over the ridge in pursuit of the Confederate army. The fresh reinforcements, breathless from their climb, stared in shock as they passed through the gap. The dead in the country road leading down the mountain had been run over by an artillery battery urgently careening toward the front. Captain Jackman, who passed through the gap with the Sixth New Hampshire, wrote, "It was a sickening sight after the last caisson had passed along."[48]

Surgeons were at work in the tiny Wise cabin, and additional amputation tables were set up in the front yard. Piles of limbs littered the lawn. A Pennsylvania soldier described what he saw: "[The dead Rebels] lay, actually two and three deep. . . . In a log house near by, [a dead soldier] sat with his eye to a chink between the logs with a bullet through his head."[49] In one of the Wises' outbuildings, a Massachusetts trooper found the bodies of a Union and Rebel soldier who seemed to have killed each other in a hand-to-hand fight.[50] A particularly macabre sight was noted in the diaries and letters of many of the Federals who passed over the Wise property on the fifteenth: The body of a Confederate soldier, killed just as he clambered over one of the farm's stone-and-rail fences, had been frozen by death mid-stride, still erect, one leg on each side of the fence. A Yankee had placed a biscuit in the man's open mouth.

The Wise family probably returned on that day from the church or school where they had sought temporary shelter. The only personal goods left in their cabin were those secreted in the buried trunk. In addition to the wounded "a hollerin' and a crying," young Cecilia Wise found a dead man sprawled across her bed.[51]

*This tiny cabin was home to Daniel Wise, two of his children, and granddaughter Cecilia, just five years old in 1862.* COURTESY MASSACHUSETTS COMMANDERY MILITARY ORDER OF THE LOYAL LEGION, THE U. S. ARMY MILITARY HISTORY INSTITUTE.

Other local residents were already milling about the gaps. "Citizens were coming from every direction to see the battlefield and saying the Rebs were getting out of the way as fast as possible," wrote Sam Healy, whose unit had stopped for breakfast near the Mountain House.[52] Another Federal recalled, "Some of the country people living thereabout, who had been scared away by the firing, ventured back, making big eyes at all they saw, and asking most ridiculous questions."[53] Otho Nesbitt noted in his diary on the sixteenth, "Many are going from the Clear Spring this morning to see the battlefield."[54]

Some of the locals returned to assess the damage, some to help with the wounded. And some braved the carnage to scavenge for souvenirs, ghoulishly robbing the dead and carrying away battle debris. John Long climbed up from Middletown for a look-see. "I picked up one gun to take home," he reported, "and they said I was not allowed to carry anything off of the battlefield and one man took it from me."[55] Most of the plunderers didn't meet such resistance: "[The farmers] collected as relics everything portable," recalled one New Yorker, "cartridge-boxes, bayonet scabbards, old muskets, and even cannon-balls were carried away by them."[56] One of the prizes found on South Mountain after the battle was an envelope decorated with verse:

May those Northern fanatics, who abuse their Southern neighbors
Approach near enough to feel the point of our sabres;
May they come near enough to hear the click of our trigger
And learn that a white man is better than a nigger.[57]

Jacob Hoke, a businessman from Chambersburg, also found a patriotic envelope bearing the inscription THE 51ST NEW YORK; ALWAYS READY WHEN WANTED and tucked it away for a friend. Hoke had ridden a special excursion train from Chambersburg to Hagerstown and managed to finagle a ride to Boonsboro before hiking to the battlefield. Soon after finding his souvenir, he got his first good look at a dead Confederate. "He had fallen with his head down hill," Hoke wrote later, "and pools of blood, which had run from his body, had collected in the hollow places, and were swarming with flies. His face was black, eyes open and glaring, tongue protruding, and his whole body swollen. . . . I ran from the place, but all around me were similar loathsome objects."[58]

The visitors who didn't run had steel resolve. Hogs were already rooting among the dead, adding to the "brutishness" of the stale carnage.[59] One group of civilians obtained a dainty souvenir when they found, a few days after the battle, a soldier's hastily made grave. The head was partially exposed, and they cut a lock of his hair.[60]

Burial details confronted the unsavory task of dealing with hundreds of dead in the vicinity. Disposal of the bodies on South Mountain was particularly troublesome. It was hot, and in addition to those dead in the fields and fencerows, men on the steep western slope had crawled under thickets and fallen into crevices between rocky crags. Accompanied by the groans of the wounded in the Wise cabin, burial parties faced the job of digging graves in the rocky soil and dragging bodies to them. By the sixteenth the heat had made the job so abhorrent that the soldiers, according to one observer, "could only endure it by being staggering drunk."[61] Some assigned to burial detail at Fox's Gap tried to make quick work of the job by dumping some of the bodies down a partially dug well on the Wise property. "The ground of the garden was literally covered with the dead and wounded," one man explained, "and the burial party which was left behind—by reason of the rapid decomposition of the bodies and of the stony character of the ground—were compelled to place about 60 of the bodies down the well at this cabin."[62] A Sanitary Commission officer a few weeks later came across the unsettling sight of a man's hand projecting through the earth shoveled on top of the well. Daniel Wise explained that he had caught some Ohio troopers in the act of ruining his well with the crude burial. Later exhumation proved that fifty-eight Confederates were jammed in before dirt was shoveled over the top.

In the tiny villages in the valleys, the dead waited for more respectable burial. Whimpering children stared at the forlorn rows of bodies lining the yards of the makeshift hospitals. The time it took to bury the dead men— and horses—took a sanitary toll on the local residents. The heat was unrelenting. Night breezes sweeping down to the valleys carried the odor of death. White-faced housewives stuffed rags beneath their doors, trying to keep the stench at bay.

>‑·◆·‑O‑·◆·‑<

Federal wounded had begun stumbling into Middletown by midafternoon on Sunday. They were haggard shells of men with powder-blackened faces and pleading, red-rimmed eyes. Civilians bedded dazed boys in their sitting rooms and barns, binding bloody wounds with heirloom tablecloths or cotton petticoats or whatever was handy. Recalled Isaac Hall, "The kind-hearted ladies, . . . like ministering angels anticipated every want, with that tender solicitude which woman only can feel."[63] Some of the wounded found shelter in the hard pews at the Reformed Church. In sanctuaries and stables, army doctors began their desperate work. Local physician Jacob Baer and his son Dr. James Baer rolled up their sleeves and pitched in. Jacob Baer was already serving as assistant surgeon in the First Regiment, Potomac Home Brigade; his other son, Caleb, was a surgeon in the Confederate army.[64]

As the sun set, an ambulance carrying Rutherford B. Hayes jolted slowly down the road. A surgeon—his brother-in-law—was trotting watchfully beside the wagon. As they reached Middletown, the officer stirred. "Joe!" he called to the surgeon. "Take me to the first respectable-looking private house we come to." The surgeon chose a tidy brick home on Main Street and knocked on the door. It was answered by Jacob Rudy.

That day had been especially difficult for Jacob and Eliza Rudy and their children, Daniel, Charlie, Kate, Laura, and Ella.[65] Eldest son Daniel and the two youngest girls, Laura and Ella, were in bed with scarlet fever. Kate, who had been taken into the country while the Confederate army passed through town, returned on Sunday "rather the worse for her journey." As the artillery's thunder rolled from the mountain throughout the day, Jacob and Eliza wondered if they should have tried to move their sick children out of harm's way after all. It was too late for second thoughts. Eliza already had three sick children to tend, but soon Rutherford Hayes was installed in a bedchamber next to Daniel.[66] The day after the battle, Hayes was hale enough to write a reassuring letter to his mother: "I am comfortably *at home* with a very kind and attentive family here named Rudy." And two days later he wrote, "It would make you happy about me if you could see how pleasantly and comfortably I am cared for." Young Charlie Rudy sat by the bedroom window and entertained Hayes by describing the traffic passing outside the window, and Eliza Rudy tempted the wounded man's appetite with her best currant jelly.[67]

On the morning of the battle, a Middletown woman named Mrs. Appleman was visited by her nephew, Lieutenant John D. Sadler of the First Pennsylvania Reserves. Sadler was filled with foreboding about the coming battle. "He declared it had been revealed to him in his sleep the night before that he would not survive the coming fight," his friend William Jobe recalled later. "I told him laughing that it was only a revelation of a streak of superstition in a highly educated gentleman."[68] Sadler was killed in the last moments of fighting on South Mountain. A wounded comrade, H. N. Minnigh, took the lieutenant's body back to his aunt.

Minnigh was determined to take Sadler's body home to Pennsylvania for burial. He changed into civilian clothes, managed to obtain a hearse, and started driving north. After passing through the picket lines near Emmitsburg, Minnigh changed back to his uniform and headed into town. When he stopped at a private well to bathe his wounded arm a woman rushed out of the house. "No Union soldier can have any water from that well!" she cried. Minnigh laughed lightly. "I think I know one who will," he answered. The woman grabbed the pump handle; he pushed her away. She called a dog to her assistance, and a large bloodhound rushed at Minnigh. "But I was ready," he recalled, "and a single shot laid him low. At this the woman commenced to cry bitterly, and said she would call the men; my reply was, that the men would be dealt with in the same way." No men appeared, and the determined soldier proceeded on his mission.[69]

>─┤◆>•O•<◆├─◄

By Sunday evening a long line of ambulances was slowly rumbling up and down the steep road from Crampton's Gap, hauling bleeding men to parlors and kitchens where their wounds were dressed. The first hospital was established at the home of Henry and Magdalena McDuell, Irish-born Southern sympathizers who lived on a farm outside of town. McDuell, who already was angry that his home had been taken over by the medical men, was enraged when in the ensuing chaos the home received an estimated three thousand dollars' damage. According to local lore, Henry's harangues were so annoying that a couple of orderlies eventually dangled him by the heels from a second-story window until he cooled down.[70]

Most residents handled the flood of wounded, and attendant medical personnel, with more grace. "The inhabitants of Burkittsville opened their houses with alacrity for the reception of the wounded," Dr. Thomas Ellis recalled, "and offered the kindest attentions to the sufferers."[71] The Christian Women's Association, a community organization, met at the redbrick tailor shop to organize medical supplies.[72] Lamps burned through the night, providing meager yellow light for the tired surgeons and the men and women providing aid. Children peeked into rooms suddenly barred to them, drawn by unimaginable sounds. The handsome churches were soon stripped of pews and overflowing with wounded, too, Northern and Southern boys lined on the floor in order of their arrival. "One or two of [the Rebels] positively refused to submit to the necessary operation," Ellis wrote later, "preferring death, the inevitable consequence of their obstinacy, to the supposed suffering of an amputation."[73]

A number of Confederate sympathizers in the area were concerned that the wounded Southern soldiers weren't receiving proper care in the Federal hospitals. Thomas Sim Lee (a distant relative of Robert E. Lee) found Sergeant Benjamin Mell of Georgia lying on the ground outside the German Reformed Church, where he had spent a cold, damp night; Lee took Mell home and nursed him until he died, five weeks later.[74] Several days after the battle, Thomas Roger Johnson, who lived near Crampton's Gap, traveled to Burkittsville and requested permission to take several of the Southern wounded into his home. Four Georgians were soon convalescing with Mr. Johnson. One of the men, named Cook, stayed for six months and helped Johnson smuggle Confederates across the Potomac. "I had so many applications for aid in crossing to Virginia it necessitated the forming of an underground railroad," Johnson wrote, "beginning with Mr. William R. Dorsey . . . then myself, thence to Mr. Oscar Crampton, near Burkittsville, Mr. Thomas Crampton at Crampton's Gap, and Mr. Grove at Sharpsburg, where they were crossed."[75]

The battle was over, but the Middletown Valley was in chaos. A member of the 16th Connecticut, which was hurrying from Frederick to catch up with the rest of the army, described the confusion:

The road was completely blocked up with army wagons and ambulances. The road was narrow over the mountain, and terribly dusty. The ambulances were filled with the wounded, and rebel prisoners under guard were trying to go to the rear. Infantry, baggage wagons, provision and ammunition trains, were eagerly pushing to the front. The result was a stand-still for over an hour. On both sides of the road, shot and shell had pierced the trees and houses. The fences were riddled with bullets, telegraph poles were down, and the earth was ploughed by solid shot. The dead lay by the road-side, and the ambulances were scouring the mountainsides with men detailed to pick up the wounded. The churches, houses, and barns were filled with the wounded. Parties were seen in every direction burying the dead.[76]

Some of the civilian men who had fled, or taken horses or other valuables to safety, headed for home when they heard the artillery. Allen Sparrow had trekked to Pennsylvania with some other men, a trip that included a few bad scares when they thought the Confederates had them. They were in Wolfesville on Sunday and could hear the guns. Their anxiety increased when someone assured them that Middletown had been burned to the ground, and they headed for home. "It was very hard to get any correct news," Sparrow wrote later. "We did not know how it was or wheather Middletown was burnt or not till we were coming down Harps Hill. Then we saw the church Stepels, then we were glad." The men stopped five miles from home, still not sure if the Confederates held the town or if it was safe to go home. Some were too anxious to delay and chanced the trip home. Sparrow hesitated, stopping to observe the unfolding battle, then retiring to the home of a friend where he thought he would be beyond the range of the guns. That evening some other men arrived with the news that Federals had driven out the Rebels and sent them scurrying down the mountain. Sparrow headed home the next day. "[I] found everything in excitement," he wrote. "Solders riding here and there. The wimmen baking pies and bread for the solders."[77] In the days to follow more men trudged home, hungry, travel-stained, thankful to find their homes and families intact. Children were scooped up by their fathers for hugs. Wives welcomed husbands home with dewy eyes.

Enduring the day of battle had been a horrible experience. Thousands of wounded men still jammed the makeshift hospitals and would for some time to come. Farmers had yet to tally their losses. Still, most civilians in Frederick County heaved a sigh of relief when the armies disappeared over the mountain. Their time of trial was over.

But across the brooding ridge of South Mountain more farm families, and country clerks and doctors and schoolteachers, waited. Their trial was just beginning.

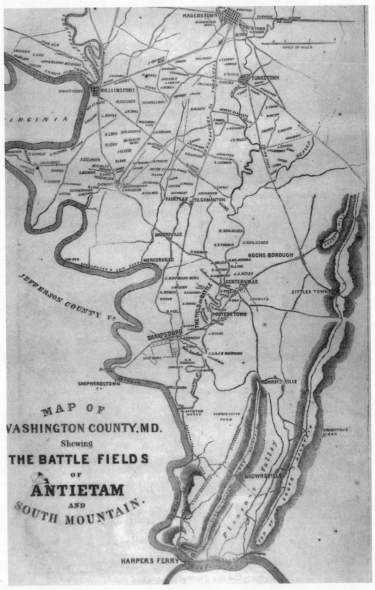

*"Map of Washington County, Md., Showing the Battle Fields of Antietam and South Mountain." Sharpsburg was not the only village engulfed by soldiers during the 1862 campaign. Zittlestown, Rohrersville, Centreville (Keedysville), and Tilghmanton were among the communities overwhelmed by the armies.* Harpers Weekly, *October 11, 1862.* COURTESY FRANK & MARIE-THERESE WOOD PRINT COLLECTIONS, ALEXANDRIA, VIRGINIA.

# CHAPTER 5

# "It Was an Awful Time"

The Confederate column trudging through Boonsboro was not the spirited band of brothers who had splashed playfully across the Potomac. "Our position was indeed a perilous one . . .," Heros von Borcke recalled of their retreat on September 15. "Every man felt this, and our lines . . . looked glum and desperately resolute. . . ." The tired soldiers had neither the mood nor energy for songs or banter. They plodded in a silence broken only by the "measured tramp of the column, the rumbling of the artillery wagons, and the booming of the heavy guns from Harpers Ferry." The siege guns' barrage reverberated through the mountains.[1]

Civilians in Boonsboro were still trying to cope with the wounded when they again heard the sound of skirmishing, and frayed nerves snapped. When the 17th Virginia halted on the outskirts for a short rest, Edgar Warfield knocked on the door of the closest residence and "asked the lady of the house as politely as I knew how if she would let me have some water so that I might make a little coffee" over the small cook fire that his very hungry comrades had started in the street. To his surprise she refused, using language "about as rough as could come from the mouth of anyone. She was simply vile." The Virginians were satisfied when, while she continued to scold, a Union shell sailed into her chimney, scattering bricks in every direction.[2]

Fitzhugh Lee had been set to the task of buying time for the Confederate army by slowing the Federal advance, which began at dawn. Lee set his artillery and the Ninth Virginia Cavalry at the east end of the village to harass the Federals with cannon and musketry. The eager Yankees were not long dissuaded, however, and Southern soldiers were quickly recalled to town. The cavalry tried to cover the withdrawal, but that proved tricky in Boonsboro's narrow streets. "In an incredibly short time the street became packed with a mass of horses and horsemen, so jammed together as to make motion impossible for most of them," wrote George Beale. "At the same time, the upper windows in some of the houses were hoisted and a volley of pistol shots poured down on our heads." The Federals mounted a charge. The retreat disintegrated into a wild stampede, while the impassioned citizens cheered from their windows and squeezed off a few last rounds. Fitzhugh Lee fell heavily to the turnpike when his horse was killed; bruised and dusty, he scrambled for concealment in a roadside field. One captain, also knocked from his horse, hid in a cornfield just out of town until darkness fell that night, when he appealed to a Boonsboro woman for assistance. Although she was a strong Unionist and had two sons in the Union army, she fed the famished trooper, giving him the sustenance needed to creep through the lines and catch up with his comrades.[3]

Soon the Union army poured through Boonsboro. It was, one soldier noted, a "quaint, old-fashioned village" that had been turned into a "charnel-house."[4] Most of the Yankee boys were in high spirits; some of the veteran campaigners had never before seen a Rebel's retreating backside, and despite the gore on South Mountain, they gloried in their victory. The army's reception among loyal citizens was even better than it had been east of the mountains; now they were an army triumphant, chasing the invaders back to the Potomac. "We have watched for you," a "respectable old gentleman" told Major Rufus Dawes of the Sixth Wisconsin, "and we have prayed for you and now thank God you have come!"[5]

But some of the Union troops were still unconvinced of the town's loyalty. A group of hot and thirsty Pennsylvanians was outraged to find every pump disabled, its handle removed. Assuming secessionist politics at work, they dumped stones, earth, and rubbish down every well they could find. Only later did they learn that "the inhabitants feared a permanent loss of their water supply. The demand from such a . . . sudden increase of population had taxed the wells beyond their capacity."[6] Unable to undo the damage, they shuffled sheepishly out of town.

The Boonsboro skirmish gave the footsore Confederate infantry the time needed to reach Sharpsburg. The columns had turned southwest and passed next through Keedysville. Oliver Reilly, then a boy of five, stood for hours by his Keedysville home watching the endless parade of shabby soldiers. According to local tradition, residents carefully hung Confederate flags while Lee's army trooped through, then later flew Union flags for the Yankees, avoiding trouble and striving for neutrality.[7]

In Tilghmanton, about five miles north of Sharpsburg, a group of Confederates broke down the door of the Moats home, where Sarah Ann Moats was alone with her infant son. While the soldiers ransacked the house, Sarah Ann ran to the home of her husband's sister, Lizzie Moats. Lizzie "marched back and told the Confederate soldiers they were taking food from the wife of a soldier who was away at war," Lizzie's youngest niece related later. Lizzie so shamed the men that they put the food back on the shelves, put the door back on its hinges, and disappeared.[8]

━━◆━◯━◆━━

In Sharpsburg people waited for news. That Sunday, worship services had been disrupted. First had come the ominous rumble of artillery, rolling down the mountain and across the valley and in open church windows. The reverberation reached the tiny German Baptist Brethren Church, where Elder David Long read from Psalms before preaching the sermon and leading a hymn. It followed the congregation as, eyeing the ridge uneasily, they walked to the nearby home of Elizabeth and Samuel Mumma for dinner. Some of the children hiked out for a look-see, edging as close as they dared to the smoke and roar, before running back to report.[9]

The war intruded again that afternoon when a squad of Rebel cavalry clattered through town while the Sharpsburg Lutherans were at Sunday school. "The whole assembly flocked out . . .," recalled Theresa Kretzer later. "The children ran home from church in terror. There was no dinner eaten that day. The people were too frightened."[10] Incredibly, the next horsemen they saw were Yankees. Although the Confederate force that encircled the Yankee garrison at Harpers Ferry was ultimately successful, a Southern-born Union officer named Benjamin Davis spent that night leading fourteen hundred cavalrymen on a daring escape across the Potomac. With a local civilian guide, the column threaded its way through Confederate lines in Washington County. John Shay, who lived at the edge of Sharpsburg on the Harpers Ferry road, was among the first to know of the Yankee cavalry escape. The horsemen had kept a killing pace, and Shay carried many buckets of water for the tired horses. So many came that he finally left the bucket, finding it the next morning at the public square, where it had been kicked. After capturing a Confederate ammunition train, the cavalry column ultimately made safe passage to Greencastle, Pennsylvania.

By the next day—Monday, September 15—thousands of Confederate soldiers began to descend on the little village. Robert E. Lee had chosen

Sharpsburg as the place for his scattered troops to converge before fording the Potomac back to Virginia in ignominious defeat.

Many of the Confederates limping toward Sharpsburg were roused by the sight of the beautiful valley sprawling before them. The farm fields presented a patchwork quilt of light-green nearly ripened corn, dark-green clover, and brown newly turned fields. "Numerous fine farm-houses dot the valley in every direction," wrote a surgeon, "some standing out plainly and boldly on the hill-tops, others half-hidden down the little slopes; and with the large comfortable barns about them, and their orchards of fruit-trees, these hitherto happy and quiet homes greatly enrich the view."[11]

The cornucopia was too much temptation for many of the men. "I could have eaten a plate of fried fish hooks," said one Sergeant Andrews from Georgia, who disobeyed orders and stole apples from a Sharpsburg orchard. General Lee happened by as the man was stuffing a haversack with the forbidden fruit. Andrews wrote later:

Right there I received the severest tongue lashing I ever had in my life. I did not know there were so many cutting words in the English language. . . . He had me so badly scared that I could only recollect three of them, a straggler, a thief, and a coward. A straggler I was, being out of rank; a thief, my haversack and pockets bulging with apples proved that; a coward, he had me scared to death, so he was correct on all three counts.

Lee ordered Andrews to be put under guard.[12] But General Lee couldn't personally oversee his entire army, and by the time the Rebel columns arrived on the hills around Sharpsburg, that army was using less constraint. Their grievances were mounting. Disappointment with Frederick's reception had been eclipsed by their bloody losses on South Mountain. In addition, the army was fragmenting, traveling on several narrow, rocky roads. Commissary wagons had not kept pace with the troops during the withdrawal toward the Potomac, and the men found it unbearable to pass the pretty farms. Orchards were full of green, yellow, red, speckled, and streaked apples. Cider mills powered by horse-pulled sweeps were visible in farmyards. The aroma of apple butter hung in the air. Porches were piled with pumpkins and squash, gardens neatly rowed with sweet potatoes and onions waiting to be dug, rows of tumblers gleaming with jewel-toned jellies lined cellar walls, peaches, cherries, pears, and plums were drying on scaffolding outside or hanging in neat muslin bags in attics. Even the pickle barrels were full. Some of the farmers had begun threshing their oats and rye and wheat; others had stacks of grain in the farmyard. Acres of corn still stood on the stalks on some farms or were laboriously tied into shocks on others. And the villagers kept chickens and cows, which were driven to a farmer's field each morning by boys paid a penny a day for the service.

It was a valley of plenty, about to be laid waste.

"Squads from different companies obtained permission to forage for themselves and comrades," remembered Virginian Alexander Hunter.[13] A canal boatman who had a home on the outskirts of Sharpsburg recalled, "The Southern troops . . . didn't pay any attention to the regular highways, but went across the fields the nearest way to where they wanted to go."[14] And a Rebel soldier even admitted later, "The fact is that we had no discipline, and at no time did we have a thoroughly-organized rear guard, the effect of which was that all those soldiers who desired to keep out of battles, or to drop out of the line, could do so without hindrance. It is a mortifying fact, yet true. "[15]

Citizens were besieged by the skeletal boys. "They nearly worried us to death asking for something to eat," a Sharpsburg woman said. "They were half famished and they looked like tramps." A slave who worked on the Otto farm remembered:

The hill at our place was covered with [the Rebels]. They'd walk right into the house and say, "Have you got anything to eat?" like they was half starved. We'd hardly fix up for a couple when a lot more would come in. The white people and my mother was in the kitchen givin' 'em bread and bacon. They was great fellers for milk, too. Some sat down at the table, and some would just take a chunk of food in their hands. They ate us out directly. The Union troops, who come onto our place few days later, wasn't so hongry. The Rebels was always hongry, and the men were miserable dirty.[16]

When the troops began foraging, they found some homes abandoned by panicked families. One soldier in Longstreet's corps wrote of finding such a deserted house: "Not an article had been carried off, the parlor door was open . . . there rested the cat on the windowsill, everything seemed so natural it was difficult to realize that the hostess would not enter and welcome us in a few moments." The men found milk and filled their canteens; found cider and poured out the milk; found apple brandy, poured the cider on the floor, and left happy. "I will . . . not mention how many lips were glued long and lovingly to the mouths of those canteens," the soldier continued. "The owner's health was honestly drank, however, none asking or caring whether he was Yankee or Reb."[17] One family left as soon as a company of the 27th Georgia made camp near their farmhouse. They prudently cleaned out their pantry before going, but the Georgians also found something just as appealing in the cellar: several barrels of prime hard cider. Soon the wooden barrelheads had been pried away, and the Georgia boys shoved forward with their tin cups. According to Captain Ben Milliken, they "drank until some of them was drunk or very near it. I know I was the drunkest I ever was. It was all I could do to get up the hill to camp."[18]

In Sharpsburg, tavernkeeper Delaney was finally forced to turn away a hungry Rebel, explaining, "You soldiers have e't us all out." The soldier silently left—and set the barn on fire. "The men jest had to get up on top of the house and spread wet blankets all over the roof to keep the tavern from burning," the slave cook recalled. "We couldn't save the barn. That burnt down to the ground, and the chickens and everything in it was burnt up. Oh! it was an awful time."[19]

>─┼─◆〉─O─〈◆─┼─�〈

The Southern army was as desperate for transportation as it was for food, and Sharpsburg was known for its horses. "All the people 'round had good ridin' horses then—lopers, rackers, and pacers," recalled one resident.[20] The Confederates weren't particular. But in a rural farm area, horses were among a family's most valued and needed property. They pulled the reaper and plow, and carried the family to church or town. During the 1862 invasion, most people were as determined to save their horses as the Confederates were to take them. Samuel Poffenberger hid his eight horses in a cellar, their feet muffled in feed sacks. Other cautious farmers did the same.[21] A young girl named Millie Landis hid her horse in the smokehouse on her family's farm near Beaver Creek, staying with him for the interminable hours that it took the troops to pass her farm.[22]

In Keedysville, Aaron Cost was forced to hand over his five horses at pistol point. Despite precautions, the Neikirk family had a more terrifying experience. Daughter Lizzie, seventeen, hid a purse containing several hundred dollars, and Henry Neikirk had prudently hidden his eleven horses behind some cliffs along Antietam Creek. A group of Confederates raided his home, possibly informed of his animals by Southern sympathizers. When they found the empty stable, and Henry refused to tell them where his horses were, they tried unsuccessfully to burn it down. Ransacking the house, they stole a small amount of silver, although Lizzie's hidden purse remained concealed. Finally the outraged soldiers dragged Henry outside and hung him up by a leather halter, trying to force his confession. The family story doesn't reveal whether Henry's wife, Mary Miller Neikirk (a niece of Jacob Miller's, who would give birth to a daughter two weeks later), was at home, but their fifteen-year-old son George cut Henry down just in time to save his life. Unfortunately, although Henry had managed to save his horses that day, they were taken later.[23]

Soldiers needed to replace dead cavalry mounts, and they also took horses and oxen to serve as draft for the countless supply wagons accompanying the infantry. Although the Confederate army moved through the area first, the Union army that came later was willing to scoop up animals that had escaped notice earlier. But in one instance, the owner triumphed. When storekeeper Jacob Cost's gray, Old Sam, was stolen and ridden to Frederick, Cost went to Union headquarters and tracked the thief down. They returned to Sharpsburg, and Cost instructed the soldier to remove the bridle in front of his store. If Old Sam didn't go to his stable, the soldier could take him again. "Old Sam ran direct to his stable," the story was related later, "kicking up his heels."[24]

While the privates scavenged, their officers went about the business of war. John Hebb, Joe Hoffmaster, and Moses Cox were impressed by several Union officers who needed help identifying local Potomac fords. William Logan might have joined them if he hadn't had the presence of mind to hide beneath his wife's voluminous skirts when the Confederates appeared, avoiding detection.[25]

Other civilians clashed with Confederates for political reasons. Theresa Kretzer's large American flag was still flying over East Main Street, suspended out of reach between the Kretzers' large stone house and the house opposite. Although the entire family was for the Union, Theresa, a diminutive young woman, was described by a contemporary as "more fiery and impulsive than the rest."[26] She recalled later, "In pleasant weather [the flag] was out all the time. But when we heard that Lee had crossed the Potomac, Pa began to be uneasy, and he says, 'Girls, what you goin' to do with that flag? If the Rebels come into town they'll take it sure as the world.'" Neighbors, fearful that the town would suffer from her gesture of defiance, also implored her to remove it. Theresa and a friend, one of the Rohrbach girls, finally folded the flag carefully into a strong wooden box and buried it in the ash pile behind their smokehouse. On Tuesday, September 16, she had a visit:

Early in the day two or three Rebels, who'd been informed by some one that a Union flag was concealed at my father's place, came right to the house, and I met 'em at the door. Their leader said: "We've come to demand that flag you've got here. Give it up at once or we'll search the house."

"I'll not give it up, and I guess you'll not come any further than you are, sir," I said.

They were impudent fellows, and he responded, "If you don't tell me where that flag is I'll draw my revolver on you."

"It's of no use for you to threaten," I said. "Rather than have you touch a fold of that starry flag I laid it in ashes."

Theresa's carefully worded explanation satisfied the soldiers, and they left without further confrontation.[27]

On the edge of town, the wife of a circuit-riding Methodist minister was alone with her children, although she expected her husband's return from his rounds at any time. The woman claimed distant kinship to Robert E. Lee and was shocked, therefore, when Confederate guards confined them to their house until her husband's return. "They had information that he had been carrying messages to the Northern forces," recalled a daughter years later. "Mother could scarcely believe this but knew he had mentioned an interest in the 'Underground Railroad.'" The guard remained through the long battle to come, penning the frightened woman and children inside their home. But a young son made friends with the sentries and somehow managed to escape their attention and run into the hills to alert the minister of his impending arrest. His father, though frantic about his family's welfare, turned back.[28]

By Monday afternoon, two days before the battle of Antietam exploded, General Lee had changed his mind about recrossing the Potomac. "We will make our stand on these hills," he told his staff, gesturing to a ridge just east of Sharpsburg.[29] News of the surrender of the Federal garrison at Harpers Ferry to Stonewall Jackson strengthened Lee's resolve, although until Jackson's column arrived the Confederates could muster only eighteen thousand men, less than a third of the force of the Federal army pursuing them. It was a bold, rather insulting, decision. When the news wigwagged east from Federal signal stations, George McClellan was astonished. Lee's army took up position in a line about four miles long and settled in.

Their line stretched across gardens and cornfields and pastures. The soldiers urged the farmers to leave the area for their own safety. It was a difficult decision for most to make: to stay in the line of battle or abandon their homes, their farms, their livelihoods. Some snatched a few valuables and fled, perhaps remembering other mementos too precious to leave before going far and turning back again. Others chose to take shelter at home—or even dismissed the idea of a battle commencing *right there*. The soldiers shook their heads at those who chose to stay. "[They believed] it impossible that the roar of battle should disturb their usual quiet," recalled one Confederate. "It was evident, though, to us who had been accustomed to seeing preparations made for a battle, that a storm was approaching."[30]

Samuel and Elizabeth Mumma lived with eight children just north of Sharpsburg, near the Dunker church; Mumma had in fact donated the land to the German Baptist Brethren.[31] One of the boys, Samuel Jr., already had a good—if perhaps apocryphal—war story: When he and a friend had ridden to visit the daughters of a man known locally as Isaac Smith on a fall evening in 1859, the girls had met them secretly by the road to warn them away. Their father, they whispered urgently, was about to make an armed raid on Harpers Ferry, seize the arsenal, and start a slave insurrection; and if the boys did not get quickly away, they would be impressed by Smith into bloody service that night. The boys retreated, learning soon after that Isaac Smith was none other than John Brown.[32]

Almost two years later, in 1862, the family was instructed to leave on Monday, September 15. Some clothes had been gathered, and the family silver was packed in a basket, but since some cannonading had begun, they took time only to snatch "a few small trinkets," leaving the rest behind. A granddaughter later wrote that as the family was hastily leaving, Mr. Mumma noticed a gold watch and "hung it around baby Cora's neck. That

*Samuel and Elizabeth Mumma and their eight children were given only moments to leave home as the Confederate line settled into place across their property.*
COURTESY WILMER MUMMA; ANTIETAM NATIONAL BATTLEFIELD.

watch was the only object saved except the clothes they were wearing." Daughters Lizzie and Allie (Barbara), angry about their eviction—and about leaving new silk dresses behind—refused a gallant offer of assistance by a Confederate soldier as they climbed over a fence. The Mumma family spent an uncomfortable night on a church floor. Samuel and Elizabeth decided to send their sons, Daniel and Samuel Jr., with a family friend back through the lines to get some necessities. After threading their way through thousands of soldiers on the four-mile trip, the boys found the house in shambles, ransacked. Samuel and the friend slipped away, but Daniel locked himself inside, hoping to discourage more looting. Sliding out a window, he crept into the loft above the springhouse and there, surrounded by the Southern army, he spent the night before the battle. Before daylight he crept outside and made his way back to his family.[33]

Joseph and Sarah Sherrick also decided to leave, but Joseph took the precaution of hiding his life savings of three thousand dollars in a stone wall in his yard. Jacob Grove also hid his money but, according to local historian O. T. Reilly, "forgot the hiding place and never did find it." Confederates advised William and Margaret Roulette to leave, as well. The couple had five children, ranging in age from two to thirteen, but they decided to risk the battle and stay rather than abandon their home to the foraging Confederates. Samuel Poffenberger took his wife, Catherine, to her father's house in Keedysville, then hurried back to his farm to hide his livestock.[34]

>–◄►–◦–◄►–◄

The Federals were still trotting toward Sharpsburg in pursuit, and the Union boys were pleased with the reception from loyalists as they hurried through the dusty villages like Keedysville along the route: "As in Frederick City, here too, we were received with tumultuous cheering," wrote one. "All the inhabitants apparently, being in the streets . . . showed their patriotism by serving out water, waving their handkerchiefs, etc."[35] John Cost, a "good Union citizen," earned the eternal gratitude of the 31st Pennsylvania by serving hotcakes and bread and a liquor ration.[36] While the sun-hammered soldiers gulped from dippers, the civilians related breathless tales of the Southern army's recent passage, of losing provisions and horses. The Rebels were only a short distance ahead, they said, urging the Yankees on.

Civilians living east of Sharpsburg saw the first two Federal divisions appear that Monday afternoon, September 15. Philip and Elizabeth Pry had a prosperous, 125-acre farm on a high bluff called Red Hill across Antietam Creek, east of town. After Philip and his brother Samuel had married sisters, Elizabeth and Mary Ann Cost, Philip remained on the family farm, and Samuel operated a mill within shouting distance of his brother's farm, at the junction of the Antietam Creek and a tributary, the Little Antietam.[37] That extended family's peace was broken when a Federal army officer pounded on Philip and Elizabeth's door. According to local history, the man identified himself as Captain George Armstrong Custer. General McClellan, he told the astonished Prys, had chosen their large, beautiful home for his headquarters. Soon couriers were racing furiously up and down the dusty farm lane. Aides hammered tent stakes into the lawn and mounted telescopes on them; the signal corps set up their flags; Philip's nearest fences were torn down, the rails being used to build a little redan around the command post. Even Elizabeth's best parlor chairs were hauled outside for the officers' use. Elizabeth was reportedly furious.

Like the Confederates before them, the Union soldiers needed food. One Yankee cavalryman noted that "rations for men and horses were issued only once from September 4th until September 19th. Both men and horses had to be fed from a country nominally loyal to the Union, but in reality to the Confederacy."[38] The men looked for cornstalks and leaves to feed their horses—and whatever they could find for themselves. The persistent belief harbored by some Yankees that they were in enemy territory took a toll on local residents of all sentiments. One resident recalled:

The locusts which settled down in clouds upon the land of Egypt could not have made things disappear before them as these soldiers did. Before the camp was organized the meat house was broken open and every mound of bacon was taken except a few hams, which had been concealed in the garret. Every ear of corn from the crib, and every pound of hay from the barn was taken by the soldiers. The horses had already been taken and now the hogs and poultry went. The fencing was swept from the farm as if by a conflagration.[39]

New Yorker Theodore Dimon, acting surgeon with the Second Maryland Infantry, USA, was hungry when he rode from South Mountain to Sharpsburg. "I sent off my black boy, Bob, to farm houses to get some food but, being black, he could get nothing." Dimon set out himself, and finally found a "good, honest-faced woman" baking bread in an outdoor brick bake oven, with a churn of fresh butter besides. Dimon paid the woman ten cents for a loaf of bread and a pound of butter, which he rolled up in a cabbage leaf for transport. Returning to his post, however, "such an eager crowd [gathered] around my saddle that I came near to losing my own share of the grub."[40] George and Margaret Jane Miller, who were also engulfed in the Yankee tide that day, had more serious problems. Their terrified children locked themselves in their bedrooms when Union soldiers, reputedly drunk, came to their house. The Millers ultimately lost most of the food carefully stored in their cellar and smokehouse.[41]

Another Federal surgeon, Abner Hard of the Eighth Illinois Cavalry, was told that a wounded Confederate was being hidden in a private home in the tiny crossroads of Mount Pleasant. Hard walked in and found the Rebel enjoying "a plate of cake and pie" and the adoring attention of three young ladies. When Hard produced a gun and demanded the Confederate's surrender, the boy came quietly. The young ladies were quite vocal, if unsuccessful, in their protests.[42]

The main body of the army didn't arrive until after dark. The next morning, people peeped from their windows nervously. The distant sounds of bugles echoed oddly with the roosters' calls, and the farm lanes were still busy with rumbling wagons and couriers pelting back and forth. A heavy mist hung in the valleys, obscuring at first the opposing lines. Many expected a battle to commence, but for most of that day the Yankees jostled into place on the hills east of the Antietam Creek.

The two armies stared uneasily at each other across the farmers' fields—"just a-feelin' for one another," a female slave later recalled.[43] The opposing artillery sporadically exchanged fire, tossing volley after volley toward the enemy and adding to the panic and chaos among the area residents. But if McClellan had hoped the sight of his blue line would send Lee scrambling across the Potomac, he—and the civilians—soon realized that the Rebels intended to stand and fight.

>─◆>─●─<●─<

For those civilians with loved ones in uniform, the armies' arrival was bittersweet. John Heck was a Boonsboro boy in the Union army; his brother, Jake, was in the Confederate army. As the Southern army retreated through Boonsboro after the battle of South Mountain, Jake stopped at his house on Potomac Street to visit his mother and sister, Sallie. He was enjoying his mother's cooking the next morning when John arrived. After that startling reunion, Jake finished his breakfast and slipped through the lines to rejoin his regiment.[44] Mrs. Heck and Sallie endured agonies of fear as the sullen rumble of battle shuddered two days later, knowing that the brothers were likely both engaged *and* facing each other.

Marylander Luke Tiernan Brien, on Jeb Stuart's staff, was reported to be "making exceeding merry" at his home near the Pennsylvania line, protected by five hundred cavalrymen.[45] In Sharpsburg, some families saw their

Confederate sons for the first time in two years. Joseph McGraw had crossed the river to join a Virginia artillery unit. When his battery arrived at Sharpsburg, he obtained permission to visit his brother and widowed mother, but the joy of reunion was tempered by his concerns for their safety.[46] General Stonewall Jackson sent his aide, Henry Kyd Douglas, home to report to his mother after he became ill. Kyd Douglas wrote later that he found Mrs. Douglas and her daughter Nannie providing first aid to Fitzhugh Lee, who had been injured from his fall during the retreat through Boonsboro, and several other disabled Confederate officers—"one of whom," he recalled later, "seeing me enter the parlor unhurt and with rather more freedom of manner than he thought becoming in a stranger, suggested to me pointedly I had better join my command; and immediately afterwards looked as if he would have a hemorrhage when my sister came in and I put my arm around her."[47]

Even for those Rebel residents without friends or family to greet, the presence of the Confederate army—after a year and a half of Union dominion—was thrilling. The officers, of course, garnered particular attention, and if Lee hadn't been busy at his headquarters—in a grove of trees just west of Sharpsburg on the Shepherdstown Road—he could have held court. Stonewall Jackson was invited to breakfast that morning at Dr. Jacob Grove's spacious brick home on West Main Street. Because Jackson was too busy to accept, daughter Julia Grove sent breakfast to him in camp. Jackson wanted to send a written note of thanks, but the bearer hadn't gotten her name, identifying her only as "the fair one." With a flash of rare whimsy, Jackson replied, "Well, as she has sent me my breakfast to the field, I will call her 'Miss Fairfield.'"[48]

Heros von Borcke and his staff spent the night of September 15 sleeping on the floor at the Grove home, von Borcke's saddle serving as his pillow. He recalled the family as "hospitable [people] who awaited with an indifference peculiarly American the momentous events that were so close upon them." The Groves were at home when the shelling began. Von Borcke ushered the ladies to the cellar for safety and settled down with his journal. "The ladies were running up-stairs every five minutes to witness the effect of the cannonade . . .," he recalled. "Accordingly, while the fire was every moment growing hotter, it was not long before the whole of Dr. G.'s family were again assembled in the room I occupied." The women watched the chaos of pounding couriers and jammed artillery wagons and ambulances and exploding shells until one of the missiles crashed into the house, and they took "precipitate flight" to the cellar once again. Von Borcke kept at his journal until a shell sent furniture flying and plaster and wood raining upon his head. One of the cavalry horses in the courtyard was killed. "Regarding further exposure of my own life and the lives of my couriers as now unnecessary," he wrote, "I gave orders for our immediate departure." Stumbling through blinding clouds of dust and smoke, the men managed to saddle their terrified horses and depart.[49]

Soon more shells fell among the rutted, narrow streets of Sharpsburg. Balls whizzed through the air, and bits of brick and timber spewed through the smoke. General Lee was eating breakfast at Delaney's tavern in Sharpsburg when a shell burst through the wall, which "busted and scattered brick and daubin' all over everything," recalled the cook, a slave. "There was so much dirt you couldn't tell what was on the table. I was bringin' in coffee from the kitchen and had a cup and saucer in my hand. I don't know where I put that coffee, but I throwed it away, and we all got out of there in a hurry." The slave woman was cleaning up her kitchen a short while later when soldiers advised her to take shelter, and everyone in the house retreated to the cellar. "We carried boards down there and spread carpets on 'em and took chairs down to set on," she recalled later. "There was seven or eight of us, white and black, and we was all so scared we didn't know what we was doin' half the time."[50]

The flying shells and debris weren't enough to keep troops from scouring the town for edibles—or

*"General Lee's Breakfast is Interrupted." An unnamed former slave, interviewed forty years later, told of trying to serve General Lee breakfast while shells were falling on Sharpsburg. Illustration from* Battleground Adventures, *by Clifton Johnson (Boston: Houghton Mifflin Company, 1915).*

something more gratifying. Louisianan Napier Bartlett pointed out that some troops were "ready to stand an unlimited quantity of shelling, provided they could thereby gratify what most soldiers acquire, a craving for liquor." But Bartlett and his comrades had trouble finding a storekeeper willing to conduct business under fire, and only threats of looting induced the tradesmen to open their doors and accept Confederate scrip for groceries. With precious coffee beans in hand, Bartlett went into a house next door to find a coffee grinder. The elderly woman residing there didn't seem perturbed by the intrusion. "She sat softly singing before the fire," Bartlett recalled, "rocking herself to and fro, and apparently heedless of the shells which were passing over her house." Her only relative was a son serving with Stonewall Jackson in the Rebel army, she confided to Bartlett; although certain he was going to be killed, she had no doubts of his bravery or duty as a soldier. When Bartlett ground his beans, he noticed that she was attracted by the smell, but "[no] entreaties could induce her to accept any . . . if she had possessed any [she] probably would have sent it off to her son."[51]

>━┤◆>━O━<◆┤━<

The true skedaddlers were already long gone by Tuesday, September 16, the day before the battle. They were safe across the Pennsylvania line, squeezed into hotels or in-laws' spare bedrooms or sleeping beside Northern roads with their valuables jammed into wheelbarrows and saddlebags. The Sharpsburg civilians advised to flee the day before the battle, when shells were already flying and the roads were hopelessly crowded, had to look closer to home for shelter. The Jacob Houser family was among the refugees on the road that day. As the Housers shepherded their children along, a few stray bullets whistled past, and a shell hit a nearby fence, making a lifelong impression on William Houser, then nine.[52] The Grice family lived near the Lutheran church. When they were advised to leave, Mrs. Grice packed some provisions for her brood, put them on Logan, their family horse, and set out, making their way to Killiansburg Cave, along the C&O Canal.[53]

Henry and Elizabeth Piper and their children lived on a prosperous farm north of Sharpsburg near the Hagerstown Turnpike, part of an old land grant known, ironically, as Mount Pleasant. Henry's fondness for fashionable headwear had earned him the local nickname Old Stovepipe. Although reputedly a Unionist, he also owned slaves who lived in a stone

*Elizabeth and Henry Piper. A descendant described Henry Piper as "an austere man of firm determination." He was no match for Confederate generals D. H. Hill and James Longstreet; Henry and Elizabeth Piper, and their family and slaves, left their farm near the Sunken Road when the officers commandeered their home.* COURTESY FLOYD W. PIPER, LOU AND REGINA CLARK.

building beside the farm's well. When the Confederate army appeared, most of Piper's fields were freshly plowed, ready for planting winter wheat, but a twenty-five-acre cornfield still awaited harvest. Piper also owned a fifteen-acre apple orchard.

The beautiful farm was in the center of Lee's battle line, and Generals James Longstreet and D. H. Hill commandeered the Piper home for their headquarters. Soon the yard was busy with couriers and staff, and maps and swords littered the tidy farmhouse. That evening the nervous Piper daughters served the generals dinner and, in an attempt to be courteous, offered the men wine. Longstreet initially refused, but when he saw General Hill drink some without ill effect, he said, "Ladies, I will thank you for some of that wine."[54]

After dinner the generals urged the family to leave. The Pipers quickly packed what they could carry into a wagon, and Elizabeth buried her dishes in the ash pile. As the family set out, one of the female slaves cried, "Oh, my God, take me along!" She made the trek walking beside the wagon, carrying Henry and Elizabeth's six-month-old grandson, Elmer, in her apron. "We left everything as it was on the farm," Mary Ellen recalled later, "taking only the horses with us and one carriage."[55] After leaving their home to the dubious protection of James Longstreet and D. H. Hill, the family headed toward Killiansburg Cave, but they ultimately decided to seek shelter at Henry's brother Samuel's farm near the Potomac.[56]

A group of Keedysville women and children, including little Oliver Reilly, left their homes and made their way to Samuel Pry's mill. The Pry home proved to be nebulous haven; while there, seven Confederates asked Mrs. Pry for supper. She set their table on the porch and as they were eating (all but one, who was sick and lying in the corncrib), a group of Union cavalry clattered down the road and ordered their surrender. When one refused, a Yankee pointed his revolver and called, "Come out or I will shoot you down." Remembered Oliver Reilly, "Mrs. Pry threw up her hands and cried, 'For God's sake, don't kill him on the porch!'" The Rebel reluctantly conceded defeat, and the lot of them trudged away under guard.[57]

At McClellan's headquarters, the Phillip and Elizabeth Pry family—including Samuel (fourteen), Alfred (twelve), Ellen (nine), Jacob (five), Charles (three), and a year-old daughter—was still in residence. Elizabeth Pry was cooking breakfast for General McClellan and General Hooker when an ambulance arrived, intended as transport for Hooker. Instead, McClellan ordered Elizabeth to take her children away to safety, and with the ambulance at their disposal, they trundled away to a friend's farm in Keedysville.[58]

After capturing Harpers Ferry, most of Jackson's men hustled back across the Potomac to provide critical support to the outnumbered Rebels already poised on the hills. A Georgia regiment arriving the morning of September 16 halted in a peaceful grove outside of town near a small, plain sanctuary: the Dunker church. Captain James Nisbet asked, "Who are the Dunkards?" A civilian explained, "They are German Baptists. This is a German settlement."[59] Any "Germans" lingering near the lines that day were treated to a strange performance. As Harpers Ferry veterans greeted South Mountain veterans, regimental bands struck up their beloved anthem, "Dixie," and the rough, reverent chorus swelled. It was, William Poague recalled, "inspiring, soul-stirring music."[60]

That afternoon, Federal commanders were still jockeying their divisions into place. Several crossed the Antietam near Samuel Pry's gristmill. Most of the I Corps bivouacked on the Poffenberger farm near the Hagerstown Turnpike. General McClellan ordered Jeptha Taylor of Keedysville to provide supper for himself and his staff officers, paying Taylor two and a half dollars in gold for his trouble.[61] Around dusk, a fierce artillery barrage erupted, and civilians crouched in cellars trembled with each deafening roar. About nine o'clock it began to rain, and Albert Richardson, correspondent for *The Tribune,* wandered into a farmhouse, occupied now only by some pickets. Using his saddle as a pillow, he lay down on some farm wife's scoured parlor floor to get some sleep. Richardson was fortunate. The XII Corps didn't bed down in the tidy cornfield of Martin Line's farm until midnight. Surgeons had already established a field hospital in the house itself.

McClellan had ordered no fires and complete silence among the troops, and no one in any of the homes near the lines dared light candles or lanterns for fear of drawing fire. The dark blanket that settled over the tense valley was punctuated sporadically by bursts of gunfire as jumpy pickets fired at each other and threatening shadows. A big battle was coming, and no one got very much sleep.

CHAPTER 6

# "Too Afraid to Cry"

Most mornings, farm people near Sharpsburg were milking cows and frying eggs by 5:30 A.M. That Wednesday, September 17, those who hadn't fled looked out nervously from behind shutters, sniffing the damp air. It was 65 degrees—cool after the hot spell the valley had been enduring. The rain had stopped, but mist hung foglike in the hollows.

Dawn came at 5:43. It spread over the Confederate army, which was occupying a line east of Sharpsburg between the town and Antietam Creek. Stonewall Jackson's troops, fresh from their victory at Harpers Ferry, held the left flank. General James Longstreet, Lee's warhorse, known by his troops as "Old Pete," held the center. Lee left his right flank—the area between Sharpsburg and the creek's lower bridge—only lightly defended; he was expecting the arrival of Major General A. P. Hill's Light Division, which had handled the final details at Harpers Ferry and was still somewhere south of the field. Lee's headquarters remained in the grove west of town.

The new sun also found the Federal army—most lined on the east side of Antietam Creek, some across and north of town—facing the Confederates' bow of defense. McClellan planned to make his main attack on the enemy's left; a diversionary attack against the right was to follow. If either assault succeeded, McClellan would send any available resources to strike the Confederate center.

Major General Joseph Hooker was selected to launch the Federal attack. He had spent the night in Joseph Poffenberger's musty barn and rose before dawn. Riding out to survey the line that morning, he looked over the terrain and picked out a landmark to guide his advance: the Dunker Church, the small one-story whitewashed building where the German Baptist Brethren gathered for worship.

The Union assault was launched at first light. Confederate gunners met the barrage with a blast of cannons from the Jacob Nicodemus farm. Federal artillery, four batteries of 20-pounder Parrot rifles, roared back. A reporter calculated that the Yankees were firing sixty rounds a minute—a shot every second. A group of women and children had sought shelter in the Nicodemuses' sturdy stone house, and the earth-shaking, deafening bombardment was unendurable. In the midst of the barrage the door burst open, and the terrified women flew outside "like a flock of birds . . .," Southern cavalryman William Blackford wrote later, "hair streaming in the wind and children of all ages stretched out behind." Snatching skirts high, clutching little ones, the women stumbled across the rough earth of a freshly plowed field. "Every time one would fall," Blackford recalled, "the rest thought it was the result of cannon shot and ran the faster." The cavalryman galloped into the field, brought several of the children up behind him, and escorted the women to safety behind the Southern lines. He noted with approval that gunners on both sides held their fire during the rescue.[1]

The first tide of battle ebbed and flowed through cornfields and barnyards. Stacks of grain waiting to be threshed were hit by shells and set ablaze. Fences were dismantled. Livestock not already driven away was stolen or hit by stray bullets. One soldier recalled seeing a mare and a colt, several cattle, and some sheep in a pasture that became the deadly fire zone between lines. All but the colt fell during the first barrage of fire; fifteen minutes later the colt ran from the smoke, apparently unhurt. The next day the soldiers found "the little thing" half a mile away, riddled with bullets.[2]

The Mumma family's beautiful home was so potentially enticing to Yankee sharpshooters that a Confederate general ordered it to be destroyed. Several men from the Third North Carolina volunteered, and Sergeant Major James F. Clark led the detail. One of the men picked up a chunk of burning wood from a cook fire, carried it to an open bedroom window, and dropped it on the painstaking piecework of a quilt covering the bed.[3] Soon a column of black smoke rose into the morning sky as the house burned. The fire added to the chaos for the men fighting in the Mumma yard, fields, and family cemetery. One New Yorker described the scene for his family: "Just in front of us a house was burning, and the fire and smoke, flashing of muskets and whizzing of bullets, yells of men, etc., were perfectly horrible."[4]

Several woodlots provided some cover for the scrambling troops that morning. The Dunker church stood on high ground adjacent to what became known as the West Woods. Hooker led his first assault from the North Woods near the Poffenberger farm. Major General Joseph Mansfield was mortally wounded leading a second Federal charge from the East Woods. And in the middle of that triangle was the prosperous farm occupied by David R. Miller, known as D. R. The farm, mostly open pasture, straddled the Hagerstown Road. On the west side a number of haystacks stood near the large barn and stable, and there may have been an old tenant house south of the barn. On the east side was the farmhouse, a springhouse, an orchard, and a garden sprawling with pumpkins and potatoes and beans. Miller's livestock had been driven north to safety before the armies arrived— all except one angry bull that refused to be herded. Mid-September was a bad time to interrupt a farmer's labors, and Miller had a twenty-acre cornfield ready to harvest, the dry stalks higher than a man's head.[5]

That cornfield stood between Hooker and the Dunker church. In the battle's opening hours, screaming Confederate and Union troops pushed each other back and forth through Miller's corn, charging and countercharging. Bullets rattled like hail through the stalks. Artillery raked the field. Ranks of privates dropped as they had marched: together. The barrage was so savage that, General Hooker reported later, "every stalk of corn in the northern and greater part of the field was cut as closely as could have been done with a knife."[6] Soon a dirty haze of smoke hung over the corn. Men stumbled over cobs and bodies as they advanced. More than once the enemies exchanged savage fire at forty, even thirty, yards. Musket barrels got so fouled from the fierce fire that some boys needed rocks to pound their ramrods home. Desperate soldiers scrabbled among the wounded and dead for extra cartridges. Mobile wounded tried to drag themselves to cover; those who couldn't walk cringed helplessly as the fighting swept back and forth over them. A Wisconsin soldier later wrote home that the fighting was "a great tumbling together of all heaven and earth—the slaughter on both sides was enormous."[7] The 12th Massachusetts claimed a grim honor by losing 224 of 334 men engaged, the highest proportion of casualties of any Union regiment that day. The Louisiana Tigers lost 323 of 500 men in fifteen minutes of fighting. Men in both armies dropped their rifles and were killed trying to protect their sacred flags among the bloody cornstalks. On the deadliest day in American history, D. R. Miller's cornfield was the scene of more vicious fighting than anywhere else on the field. Miller would survey his field after the battle and find not a single stalk left standing. The tillage

*"The Battle of Antietam—Burning of Mr. Mumma's House and Barns." The Mumma family home was deliberately burned so Yankee sharpshooters couldn't take refuge there. The Mummas left home with little more than the clothes they were wearing, and lost everything. Sketch by A. R. Waud.*

where he had picked rocks and cultivated corn and built shocks would be forever known as *The* Cornfield.

More than eight thousand men were killed or wounded in the first surge of battle in the East Woods and on the Mumma and Miller farms. Hooker, who had started the morning's drive, was shot in the foot just as the Dunker church seemed within his grasp and had to be carried from the field. It was 9:00 A.M.

In huge thatch-roofed grain barns, surgeons eyed their supplies with concern. Stretcher bearers managed to bring a few men off the field, but many of the wounded were still under fire, calling piteously for help. Soldiers panting behind limestone rills and woodpiles stared at the writhing wounded in The Cornfield, choking with helplessness.

One of the wounded was Sergeant Major James Clarke of the Third North Carolina, who had led the men detailed to burn the Mumma farm. He managed to reach a field hospital at the rear, where he lay for some time unattended. Finally, dazed, he opened his eyes and found a beautiful black-

*D. R. Miller and his wife. Little is known about D. R. Miller, the Sharpsburg farmer whose twenty-acre cornfield was the scene of such carnage that it became known forever as* The Cornfield. COURTESY WILMER MUMMA.

haired woman bending over him. As the woman bandaged his arm, he wondered if she had lived in the home he had destroyed.[8]

Adam Koogle of Battery A, First Maryland Artillery, whose family's farm in Middletown had been so damaged during the Confederate withdrawal, was also wounded in the morning's fight. He was carried to a field hospital, but after hearing that the surgeons intended to amputate his left arm, he crawled away and hid behind one of Mr. Mumma's strawstacks throughout the long afternoon and night to follow. At first light he stumbled three miles to the home of an aunt, where he waited until his father was able to fetch him home.[9]

During the morning artillery barrage, Sharpsburg came under heavy fire. The first balls came before dawn. "It made such a racket you'd think the earth was opening up," wrote Jacob McGraw. He had been feeding his horse when a Federal shell burst directly overhead, sending debris crashing through the barn roof onto him. It "came mighty near gettin' me," he said. "It . . . stunned me right smart." Jacob retreated to the Kretzers' strong cellar.[10]

Remaining civilians were urged to leave by concerned Confederates, including one Rebel who had observed a number of residents "chatting about the causeless alarm" the evening before. The morning's barrage prompted a panicked stampede:

> It was sad to see so many people deserting their homes . . . but in all the uproar and confusion I could not restrain a hearty laugh at the many ludicrous sights presented. Narrow souled men were seen nailing up their cellars and smoke house door to prevent starved soldiers from taking advantage of their absence and helping themselves to something to eat. . . . I saw middle aged women running through the streets literally dragging their children after them; the little fellows had to take such tremendous strides that it seemed to me they hit the ground but seldom. Then came a dozen young ladies, each with a stuffed sack under each arm, some of which in their haste they had forgotten to tie, and as they ran the unmentionables were scattered behind them.

With "cannon shot from the enemy literally rak[ing] the streets and batter[ing] . . . houses," and women and children "running, crying, and screaming so loud that their combined voices could be heard above the roaring battle," the ever-resourceful soldier stopped to examine the ladies' undergarments. "I was in need," he concluded, "but could get none that would fit."[11]

One family had barely left their house when a shell ripped into the building and exploded, "tearing things to pieces."[12] A few other late skedaddlers tried to scramble from town; one old black man made his way through the streets with a kettle on his head. But the earth-shaking, ear-splitting roar of artillery drove most to their cellars. "Such thunderen and roaring you never heard since you been born," a Sharpsburg man wrote after the battle in a letter to his brother. "You would have thought the day of Judgement had fully come if you would have been here."[13] In addition, a signal station that Rebels had established in the Sharpsburg Lutheran Church's belfry on East Main Street was drawing heavy Union artillery fire to the already beleaguered village.

The Kretzer family had chosen not to flee, and their large house on East Main Street became a community gathering place. When the shelling started, they retreated to their spacious cellar, which had four rooms, a dirt floor, thick stone walls, and was fed by a spring. Some neighbors had arrived the afternoon before to take shelter there, including women and children of varying ages and elderly men. The Kretzers and their five children did what they could to make everyone comfortable. "We carried down some seats," daughter Theresa remembered, "and we made board benches around, and quite a number of us got up on the potato bunks and the apple scaffolds. We were as comfortable as we could possibly be in a cellar, but it's a wonder we didn't all take our deaths of colds in that damp place."[14] The damp was particularly hard on Mrs. Henry Ward, who had delivered a baby girl on September 10. Her neighbors fretted about her delicate health, so she and her newborn were carried up into the kitchen. She had been there only a short time when a shell crashed into the house, sending debris flying and setting up a choking cloud of dust and smoke. The terrified mother begged to be returned to the cellar. Bundled into an armchair, she was carried back downstairs. "I'd rather take my chances on taking cold and dying," she said, "than to be killed with a shell or cannon ball."[15]

Shells splintered trees, shattered windows, crashed into chimneys and walls, and sent bricks raining to the streets and yards below. One shell came through Aaron Fry's house on Antietam Street and passed through a chest of bedclothes, leaving a neat hole in every layer of the folded sheets. Henry Hebb wanted to watch from his doorway on the public square but had a scare when a 12-pound solid shot crashed through that spot only seconds after he moved away. Another family seeking refuge in a cellar had a shell land in a featherbed, setting it afire. Two civilian men quickly extinguished the blaze.[16]

*"Women and children of Sharpsburg, MD., taking refuge in the cellar of the Kretzer Mansion, during the Battle. Bursting of a shell in the window of the cellar." A number of Sharpsburg civilians sought shelter in the Kretzer family's large cellar, which had the advantage of a natural spring flowing through one room. Several Confederate soldiers, unable to endure the fighting, also found safety in the cellar. Sketch by F. H. Schell.* COURTESY FRANK & MARIE-THERESE WOOD PRINT COLLECTIONS, ALEXANDRIA, VIRGINIA.

The wife of Davis Smith was cowering in her cellar with her three daughters and son when a shell exploded in the front of their home; a chunk of shrapnel passed "through the front door, hit the floor, on through the back door, into a closet, broke a jar of honey, struck the side of the closet, and lay on the shelf." Her son saved it as a souvenir. His sister Sue ventured into their yard to retrieve a 20-pound Parrot shell for the same reason and carried it down to the cellar. After a Confederate soldier who sought refuge with them told them it might explode and kill them all, the children carried it outside and poured water on it.[17] Dr. Augustin Biggs, the community physician, lived with his family on West Main Street. A shell went into the front window and burst in the dining room, nearly destroying everything in the room. Another shell hit the gable end of the house, which Dr. Biggs used for his office. A sick Confederate soldier sitting in the doorway was hit by a stray bullet and killed.[18]

During a late-morning lull, word again passed that the women and children should try to leave town. The slave cook at Delaney's tavern was one of those who emerged, ready to make an escape. The first thing she saw was a dead horse lying in the street. Ambulances were lurching through town, blood dripping from the floorboards. She could hear the wounded men whimpering inside; one cried, "O Lord! O Lord! O Lord!" as the vehicle passed. Her party hadn't gone far when a shell exploded above their heads, and they scurried back to their cellar. "The way they was shootin' and goin' on," she remembered, "we might have been killed before we was out of town."[19]

Jacob Miller, the ardent secessionist, refused to take flight during the battle. One of his daughters had also "determined to remain at home and go in the Seller [sic]," but two doctors boarding with her family prevailed upon her to leave the house to them. She wrote later:

I was standing at the window when a shell exploded in [the] Russel's house between the roof and ceiling; [it] sent the shingles flying every direction, cut several rafters in two pieces, went in the floor driving the end of a feather bolster in so tight they could scarcely get it out. It was that, that unnerved me at the moment. I gave way and we left, going out the back way to Gerry Groves Town woods, with the shells flying over our heads and around us, we were in more danger than if we had staid at home.[20]

Savilla Miller, Jacob's youngest child, spent at least part of the day at their village home on Main Street. When a shell burst near the Miller family's house, a piece of shrapnel severed the strap holding up a parrot cage on the back porch; the bird reputedly cried, "O Poor Polly" as it went down. Henry Kyd Douglas rode through Sharpsburg during the heavy barrage, and in the middle of the destruction and desolation he was surprised to see Savilla standing on the porch. "It gave one an odd sensation to witness it," he wrote. Concerned, he urged her to seek shelter. "I will remain here as long as our army is between me and the Yankees," she replied in a calm voice, although there was excitement in her face. "Won't you have a glass of water?" She took a pitcher to the well and in a moment was handing the astounded Kyd Douglas a glass of water. "As she approached me," he wrote, "a shell with a shriek in its flight came over the hill . . . [but] over the face of the heroic girl only a faint shadow passed." Kyd Douglas got his refreshment, repeated his warning, and trotted away, leaving Savilla "at her post." She was still there at noon, when three Confederates walked unhurriedly up Main Street. As they passed the Miller house a shell exploded in front of them, "horribly mangling and killing the one in the center and stunning the other two. . . . Miss Savilla was standing in the door at the time and escaped unhurt." The soldiers dragged their dead comrade into the Millers' orchard and buried him there.[21]

Several other young women in Sharpsburg that day were not easily cowed. About noon, when an exploding shell set Aaron Good's house on East Antietam Street on fire, four young women staying at the Miller house on Main Street, Jeanette Blackford, Maggie Hart, Jennie Mumma, and Clara Brining, of Boonsboro, "rushed to the scene and amidst flying shot and shell and whistling bullets, and armed with basins and buckets, carried water from the little spring in the lot adjoining the house and put out the fire. In a short time it caught again. These young ladies again repaired to the scene and this time [were] successful in thoroughly extinguishing it."[22] Their heroics inspired a local bard:

> If deeds of daring should win renown
> Let us honor these ladies of Sharpsburg town;
> Who, while the battle was raging hot
> 'Midst whistling bullets, and flying shot
> They braved the danger, then let their names,
> Be inscribed in gold on the scroll of fame.

During the shelling several Confederates passed through Sharpsburg, "on a tour of sight-seeing and touring generally," apparently at ease with the accompaniment of "war music" echoing from the surrounding hills. They found the place "forsaken, not so much as a stray dog being seen upon the streets," but when the barrage reached its peak, "a young girl of apparently sixteen years appeared on the street bareheaded, her long hair streaming wildly. The Sharpsburg maiden was mad, it seemed, not from love but with terror, and tore frantically along, screaming piercingly as a shell exploded over her head." In odd contrast, the Rebels also found on a back porch "an old couple, as calm and composed as if the war and carnage had been a thousand miles away." When warned for their safety, "the old man replied that they had no place to go, that this had been their home all their lives . . . and they would rather die here than leave it; he had not done the Rebels any harm . . . that they should not come and drive him out of his house; no *they would not go;* they intended to stay. 'Do we not?' he added, appealing to his aged spouse, who only answered by an emphatic nod."[23]

Many civilians had sought protection in Killiansburg Cave, along the C&O Canal and the Potomac about two miles west of town.[24] Killiansburg was a shallow cave beneath some cliffs, about twenty feet high, thirty feet across, and thirty-five feet deep, reached by a steep climb from the towpath. During the battle it "was crowded with a variety of people of all classes," reported a family who had sought haven there.[25] The shelter faced away from the battle, so shells passed safely overhead without doing more than terrifying the refugees huddled below.

Bud Shackleford, eighteen in 1862, was among a group of some two hundred women and children sheltering in a farmhouse at Snyder's landing about a mile upstream of the cave. Conditions were so crowded that he slept on a piece of bark the night before the fight. The children had had nothing to eat until someone thought of getting flour out of a warehouse nearby, and the women made shortcakes.[26] Several families took shelter in the Canal Company's boardinghouse near the Potomac. Little William Moore and his friends were entranced with a fine brass-mounted revolver that a Confederate had left hanging on a fence, and they took it. Soon, however, the soldier returned. After accusing the boys of taking the revolver, he told them he "would cut their damned heads off" if they didn't tell where it was. The terrified boys returned it.[27]

The artillery thunder reverberated for miles. Civilians listened and wondered, praying that *their* army was carrying the day. "A tremendous battle has been going on today from daylight till dark near Sharpsburg, Keedysville, and Bakersville," Otho Nesbitt wrote in his diary that night. "The cannons and musketry have been roaring all day."[28] Angela Davis of Funkstown recalled, "We heard the cannonading distinctly. . . . When it was very loud . . . we would know that McClellan's army was being driven in toward us, and when faint like distant thunder then General Lee's army was retreating. Thus the day was spent in an agony of suspense."[29]

In Keedysville, a "poor widow" and her daughters, who had given supper and lodging to a Union colonel and two other officers the night before,

*"Killing's Cave, on the Banks of the Potomac, Near Sharpsburg, MD, Used as a Place of Safety During the Battle of Antietam."* With local roads clogged, dozens of civilians sought shelter in a shallow cave near the Potomac. Protected by the rocky overhang, the hungry refugees waited out the battle. Sketch by F. H. Schell.
COURTESY FRANK & MARIE-THERESE WOOD PRINT COLLECTIONS, ALEXANDRIA, VIRGINIA.

had breakfast on the table for their boarders when the opening artillery salvo shook the ground. "The women looked flurried," the colonel wrote later, "and as the sounds continued several neighbors came running in exhibiting great alarm. Being for some time past accustomed to eating and sleeping to the sound of cannon, I continued my meal indefinitely, quite amused at the fidgety struggle between politeness and terror manifested in my entertainers." After his meal, the colonel packed a lunch, harnessed his mare, and paid his bill. "By this time the guns were pounding away rapidly, and the women, who had broken down entirely, were wringing their hands and weeping aloud." Before trotting to the front himself, the colonel, not completely heartless, tried to bolster their courage by telling them that the Rebels would soon be driven back across the Potomac.[30]

Those who couldn't bear the suspense were inevitably drawn to the field of battle. One reporter estimated about five thousand spectators massed

on the hills behind Antietam Creek that day.[31] Jacob Hoke, the Pennsylvanian who had traveled south to tour the South Mountain battlefield, had
made his way from Boonsboro and sat on a rise two miles away from the
field. "The whole valley below us was like a seething caldron of fire," he
wrote, "and smoke rose up and hung like a dark pall, as if heaven were
shutting out the terrible scene." When he asked the Reverend W. R.
Coursey of Boonsboro to predict the outcome, the reverend didn't hesitate.
"I have no fear of the result," Coursey said with a smile. "I saw both armies
as they marched through here on Sunday and Monday, and the Boys in
Blue are able to pick the rebels up one by one and smack them."[32]

Oliver Reilly was among the crowd near the Union Signal Station near
the Pry farm on Red Hill to the east; that vantage provided a good view of
the battlefield, but Reilly saw little besides clouds of smoke and dust.[33] The
gregarious visited McClellan's headquarters at the house, although one officer noted with amusement that these citizens were as eager to see the general's famous horse, Dan Webster, as the Union leader himself.[34] For his
part, McClellan was busy with his aides and with George Rohrer, who had
been summoned from his Keedysville home by an aide who appeared with
a saddled horse. George spent the day locating the visible puffs of smoke on
McClellan's map.

>─I─◆>─0─◆<─I─<

The Southern line was spread desperately thin. The Confederates had been
able to meet each Union charge only by quickly pulling troops from other
places on the field. Every man was engaged. By midmorning General Lee
was already watching the southern road, longing for a glimpse of A. P. Hill's
troops. He knew that a single, concerted attack from the Union force could
destroy his army and perhaps end the war. Hill's men were still pushing
grimly toward the battlefield from Harpers Ferry. Usually, ten minutes of
each hour were given to rest on the march. That day there was no rest.
Officers coaxed, cajoled, threatened. Under the broiling sun the men
tramped on and on, choking on dust, falling out only when their legs
would simply no longer move beneath them.

Meanwhile, thousands of Union men were held in reserve all day, doz-
ing, writing letters, brewing coffee, playing chuck-a-luck, waiting for orders
to fall in that never came. On that blood-drenched day, a third of the Federal army never fired a shot. The only man who didn't seem to know how
close he was to complete victory was George McClellan. He committed his

forces "in driblets," as one disgusted officer put it, instead of striking the scraggly Southern line in a concerted attack.[35]

One of the driblets was a division of Federal troops led by Brigadier General William French, which splashed across the waist-deep Antietam near Pry's Mill and marched onto the field shortly after 9:00 A.M. Some confusion on his part helped him escape a bloody scrap in the West Woods. French veered south instead, headed toward the Roulette farm and the center of the Confederate line.

Surgeons had already taken charge in the barn, scattering straw for the wounded and fashioning operating tables from planks. The Roulette family—William, Margaret, and their six children ranging from twenty months to thirteen years—had found dubious shelter among pickle barrels and potato bins in the cellar, already enduring several hours of ferocious battle. Suddenly the cellar door banged opened and a group of Confederate skirmishers plunged inside, chased by men of the 14th Connecticut, who gleefully barricaded the door behind them.[36]

An aide found French and panted out new orders to continue on toward the Confederate center. Most of French's troops were green, their banners clean and whole, and their advance was glorious. They marched in parade formation through the apple orchard and across the farmyard, although the 132nd Pennsylvania was distracted when a shell landed in the Roulette apiary. Yelping Pennsylvanians scattered as thousands of angry honeybees swarmed over them.

The Roulette property was separated from the Piper farm by a narrow, rutted farm lane known locally as Hog Trough Road, or the Sunken Road. Years of travel by heavily laden farm wagons and washout from hard rains had worn the lane into a natural trench. Confederates held the Sunken Road, piling fence rails on the embankment to enhance their defensive position. They watched the Yankees advance across the open ground toward them with awe, waiting until they could see their cartridge boxes before firing. Their first volley "brought down the enemy as grain falls before a reaper," a colonel of the 30th North Carolina wrote later.[37] It was the beginning of three and a half hours of new slaughter. French got reinforcments, and the Federals launched assault after assault against the Sunken Road. In the midst of the deadly storm William Roulette came out of the cellar to see what was happening, and he cheered the men in blue on: "Give it to 'em! Drive 'em! Take anything on my place, only drive 'em!"[38]

*William Roulette. The Roulette family weathered the battle in their cellar, although William did emerge at least once to cheer the Yankees on. "Drive 'em!" he shouted, before retreating back to safety.* COURTESY EARL ROULETTE.

The Confederates brought reinforcements through Piper's cornfield and orchard and pastures. Roulette's pasture was littered with Union corpses and wounded; when Confederates died, the entrenched Rebels used the bodies as breastworks. Finally a group of New Yorkers managed to reach a rise over a bend in the road, which in the confusion had mistakenly been left poorly defended, and rained fire down on the Southerners. "We were shooting them like sheep in a pen," wrote Charles Fuller of the 61st New York.[39] The lane that had provided such good cover now became the scene of horrible carnage. The Confederates broke ranks, clambering out and racing back through Piper's corn. Federals tumbled into the Sunken Road and, kneeling on the grisly carpet of Southern bodies, poured fire into the routed Rebels. The battle might have ended there if General Longstreet, still headquartered at the Piper house, hadn't patched together an artillery barrage to slow the Federal plunge. Desperately short of men, he ordered his staff officers to handle the guns, and he directed the defense while holding their horses. The Federal rush faltered, then stopped.

The fighting at the Sunken Road had claimed almost fifty-six hundred casualties. The Southern line was holding, Longstreet said later, "only by sheer force of desperation." McClellan made his sole visit of the day to the battlefield, issuing orders to his generals at the center and Federal right to "hold their positions." He also sent a telegram to his wife: "We are in the midst of the most terrible battle of the age."[40] It was not yet 1:00 P.M..

Thousands were dead, thousands more torn and bleeding, crawling painfully toward whatever shelter they could find. The surgeons were already tired; their makeshift hospitals in barns and country kitchens already full. At the farm at Snyder's landing, the warehouse that had furnished barrels of flour to the hungry refugees became a hospital as well. The doors were torn off their hinges and mounted on the empty flour barrels to make operating tables.[41]

The Reel farm was directly north of Sharpsburg. David Reel's wife, Ann, had died in 1859, leaving half a dozen children behind. David and his family had probably fled before the battle, but local lore suggests that a young woman—possibly a stepdaughter or a relative of Ann's—remained at home to care for wounded soldiers. If so, she witnessed a particular horror when David's barn, which was serving as a Confederate field hospital, suffered a direct hit. Sparks flew among the hay and straw, and the structure immediately went up in flames. The wounded men who had been carried inside died in the fire; days later, some boys poking around the ashes found their bones.[42]

Henry Piper's son Samuel heard that the Piper barn had also been torched, and he decided to investigate. Making his way back toward the family farm, he saw the smoke coming from the Mumma house instead. A sharpshooter in a nearby tree was surprised to see a civilian about when bullets were still flying. "Get out of here!" he yelled, and Samuel retreated.[43]

Years after the battle, Martin L. Moats of Tilghmanton told his daughter that he had "waded through blood up to his shoetops" to bring water and food to the wounded.[44] Martin Eakle, a forty-seven-year-old miller from Keedysville, also ventured onto the battlefield that day. Captain William Graham's Federal battery, the First U.S. Artillery, took some heavy losses near the Sunken Road. Ordered to pull back but still under enemy fire, the grimy, bloodied, exhausted men were astonished to see a civilian driving a buggy and two-horse team approach their guns. Eakle, a renowned Southern sympathizer, emerged from the buggy with a hamper of biscuits and ham, which he calmly passed around; the flask of whiskey that appeared next was probably even more appreciated. Graham wrote in his official report, "This gentleman drove his carriage to my battery while under a severe artillery fire, and carried off my wounded, who were suffering very much for want of proper surgical attendance." Graham wrote that Eakle made a second trip to his battery; and—according to a civilian watching from Red Hill—he made several more trips of mercy to the field that day. Eakle escaped injury, although one of his horses was wounded.[45]

Hearing the artillery, a number of Hagerstown civilians also set out with provisions. Matthew Barber and J. Dixon Roman found a number of "faint and broken down" Confederates at Lappans Cross Roads north of Sharps-burg and gave what aid they could. But the battle's roar became so ominous, they changed course, veering east on the Boonsboro Road. A Federal picket stopped them outside of Boonsboro but was "induced by the gift of a bottle of wine to let them pass," and the men proceeded on into the village, where they distributed their supplies to the wounded already there.[46]

*This postwar photo shows Eakles Mills. Martin Eakle, a Confederate sympathizer, was commended for driving onto the field repeatedly to deliver water and food to exhausted soldiers.* AUTHOR'S COLLECTION.

It was a long day for the hundreds of civilians trapped in their cellars—the third day of shelling for many of them. A few of the mothers had thought to carry enough food for their children, but most of them went hungry as the hours passed. "We had to live on fear," Theresa Kretzer remembered. Many of the women and children cowering in the dark cellars were further terrified that day when six Southern soldiers, deciding they'd seen enough of the battle, crept down the damp stairs and pushed their unwanted company on the group in the Kretzer cellar. One was wounded, his ear "nearly off." When Theresa and her mother slipped to their stable at noon to milk their cows, they found several more hiding in the haymow: "We're tired of fightin'," one explained.[47] Other civilians found deserters under sacks of wheat, in outhouses, in grain bins. Jacob Houser spent the day hiding in his cellar with eight Confederates. A shell came through the wall and burst, killing four of the soldiers and wounding the others.[48]

Confederate troops who weren't seeking shelter were seeking water and food. The "intolerable dust" intensified thirst, and water supplies were "inconvenient."[49] Hunger still plagued the Rebels as well, and as the brutal hours inched by, some took what steps they could to alleviate that particular discomfort. The Confederates driven from Bloody Lane, fleeing for their lives, snatched apples from Piper's trees as they raced through the orchard. A man in the Second North Carolina was helping the regimental surgeon on the Piper farm but managed to get a kettle of stewed chicken going, too:

> There wasn't a surgeon on the battle field from Our Brigade but Gus Stith. He stayed there to the last. He, his two assistants, and myself dressed wounds until the Yankees got in 30 yards of the house. . . . The house in which we were was the hottest part of the battle field; we were exposed to a cross fire of two Yankee Batteries, and from the front by musket balls. The house, kitchen, trees, and everything else was torn and shot all to pieces. We had a large pot full of chicken on the stove, cooking for dinner, when a bomb took off one-half of the kitchen and turned the stove bottom upwards. That stopped the splendid dinner we had in preparation.[50]

A. H. Osborne of the First South Carolina Sharpshooters ventured into a deserted house with a comrade during a lull in the fighting and found it on fire from a bursting shell. "It's not the General's rules to try to save burning property," Osborne observed. But as they were very hungry, the men doused the fire before ransacking the house.[51]

At dawn that morning, George M. Beale's company was moved from their bivouac and passed an orchard, beyond which stood a large brick house. "Through this orchard were fleeing in consternation and most piti-fully, the female part of the family, without their breakfast, with most hastily arranged attire, and bearing nothing in their hands that I noticed, of the cherished contents of their home." That pitiful exodus didn't keep Beale's comrades from trooping inside. They emerged again with "their hands filled with meat, cans of fruit, honey, jars of pickle—whatever was eatable found in the building." The house, Beale was sure, was left "as bare as Mother Hubbard's fabled cupboard."[52] A Georgia soldier confiscated a crock of apple butter and went into battle with it rolled into his blanket, slung over one shoulder. When his company regrouped, "the famished soldier scooped the contents out by the handful and shoveled them into his grimy mouth. When the line bolted forward, the Georgian shoved the rest of the apple butter into his mouth and raced in to the fray with dirty face."[53]

General Lee's nerves were raw, and he had no patience for soldiers dis-obeying his orders against foraging. When he saw a soldier dragging a stuck pig toward the rear during the fight, the usually soft-tempered Virginian ordered the man taken to Stonewall Jackson with orders that he be shot immediately. Jackson, generally known as a much harder man, ordered the thief to the front instead.[54] The forager survived, known ever after as the man who lost his pig but saved his bacon.

>–·◄►·–O–·◄►··◄

Antietam Creek was fringed with sycamores and waterwillows, its sloping banks in many places covered with tangles of blackberries and wild roses, pawpaws, and hazel and elder thickets. Fish in the muddy waters were so prized by locals that a bill had once been introduced in the Maryland leg-islature to prohibit fishing there with nets, baskets, and gigs. The creek was spanned by three graceful stone bridges near Sharpsburg.

Waltons Grove Farm was located near the lower bridge, known locally as Rohrback's Bridge. In 1862 it was home to Henry Rohrback, his wife, and their daughter Jane Rohrback Mumma's family. That family included young Ada Mumma, whose paternal grandparents, Samuel and Elizabeth Mumma, lived on the farm near Hog Trough Lane and the Dunker Church. Ada's day began by helping haul mattresses to the cellar, where she was ordered to stay. "It seemed great fun to me to have the beds in the cel-lar," she recalled years later, "but soon General Burnside and his staff rode up to the front porch and dismounted." The officers' horses, and coats bedecked with braid and brass buttons, were too enticing for the child, and she crept to the porch. The Yankee general was astonished to see her. "Your family is not in the house . . .?" he asked her grandfather. "Send them away at once!" All of the family's horses had been stolen except one too lame for army use, but Burnside insisted the risk of leaving was less than the risk of remaining. Henry was adamant about staying, but Ada's father decided to take Ada, her slave nurse, Mary, and Ada's mother and grandmother away in their lightest carriage, a rockaway. Ada wrote:

> We were soon on our way. Grandfather, his brother, and the col-
> ored people stayed at the house. We had the orchard to cross first.
> The bullets were whistling all around us. One went through my
> father's hat and several went through the curtains on the carriage
> but passed us by. Then I heard a terrible whistling and an explosion
> which sent the earth and stones in every direction, which I was
> told was a shell exploding. It was not very far from us and we were
> all terrified but the old lame horse carried us safely to the home of
> a good neighbor at the foot of the mountain, where we were out
> of the line of battle.[55]

It was a frightening experience, but Burnside's warning had been prophetic. McClellan ordered Burnside's corps of eleven thousand infantrymen and fifty cannons to hold the ridge overlooking Rohrback's Bridge, "in readiness to assault the bridge in his front."[56] Local farmers told Union officers about a good crossing spot less than a mile downstream, Snavely's Ford, but no one gave it much attention. Burnside's men spent the earliest morning hours nervously eyeing the narrow bridge that would take them across Antietam Creek. After Lee had pulled most of the Southern troops in the area north to help in the morning's bitter fighting, only some 520 Rebels stared back across the creek at the Federal guns.

The Confederates minimized the imbalance by making the most of the high, rock- and tree-studded bluff on the west side of the creek. Well-protected Georgia sharpshooters poured a hail of lead down on any Yankees who dared venture out in the open. By noon, several attempts by Federal troops to cross Rohrback's Bridge had failed. McClellan sent repeated couriers with withering orders to cross the creek at all costs.

The Snavely family lived along the creek south of Rohrback's Bridge. During that difficult day a wounded soldier was taken into the house, where he soon died, and when troops from the opposing army approached, the frantic family—fearing arrest or retaliation—dumped the body in the creek. When the current of war shifted, the body was retrieved and brought back into the house—a sequence repeated two more times as soldiers clawed over the land.[57] One of those watery burials may have been precipitated by the Federal troops who finally found Snavely's Ford. At the same time, another group found a second passable ford just upstream of Rohrback's Bridge. At about 1:00 P.M., the 51st New York and 51st Pennsylvania crested the ridge and marched staunchly down the slope to the bridge. But before plunging across the span they were driven to seek shelter behind a stone wall and a rail fence. "We were then ordered to halt and commence fireing," one of the soldiers remembered, "and the way we showered the lead across the creek was noboddys business."[58] Supported by artillery, they finally managed to punch across the bridge.

The Confederate soldiers on the ridge beyond were almost out of cartridges. Breathless aides reported more Federals wading the creek downstream, poised to outflank the thin Southern line above Rohrback's Bridge. The Georgians retreated after stubbornly stalling the Federal attack on the Southern line for three hours. Rohrback's Bridge would soon be called Burnside's Bridge in dubious honor of the general who lost five hundred men trying to get across.

McClellan had by this time abandoned his idea of breaking the Rebels' northern flank, and the fighting in the center near Hog Trough Lane was foundering. He shifted his attention to the bridge. Inexplicably, the fords were again ignored, and it took two critical hours to get Burnside's troops across the dearly captured bridge and begin a concerted march toward Sharpsburg. Still, almost in spite of himself, George McClellan was poised to destroy the Southern army and end the war. At that decisive moment A. P. Hill galloped up to Lee's headquarters and reported that his troops were close behind. Lee was so relieved that he embraced Hill, praying that his poor boys defending Sharpsburg could hang on.

Yankees and Rebels skirmished on the undulating farmland around the village. A group of New Yorkers encountered strong fire from Confederate soldiers sheltered behind stone walls on the Sherrick farm—the same stone walls where Joseph Sherrick had hidden his life savings, three thousand dollars in gold. Jacob McGraw had at some point left the refuge of the

Kretzers' cellar and taken shelter in his brother's old brick hotel at the northwest corner of Antietam and Mechanic Streets. As the skirmishing line hit the outskirts of town, he peered around a corner of the hotel, hoping for a glimpse of the action; just then a shell hit the wall above him, showering him with mortar and broken bricks. He said later that he was "admonished to beat a hasty retreat."[59] Some of those still huddled in the Kretzer cellar were on the edge of hysteria. "A number of babies were there," Theresa Kretzer remembered, "and several dogs, and every time the firing began extra hard the babies would cry and the dogs would bark. Often the reports were so loud, they shook the walls. Occasionally a woman was quite unnerved and hysterical, and some of those old aged men would break out in prayer."[60]

Finally, painfully, the Federals pushed the line back to the outskirts of Sharpsburg. Scores of Confederates turned and ran through town. Caissons careened through the narrow debris-choked streets, the exhausted drivers on a desperate mission to replenish ammunition. Ambulances continued to jolt mercilessly toward makeshift hospitals. Wounded men staggered along clutching fenceposts for support. Edward A. Moore, a Confederate cannoneer, described the view from a ridge overlooking the village: "[Sharpsburg was] almost enveloped in the flames of burning buildings, while flocks of terrified pigeons, driven hither and thither by the screaming and bursting of shells, flew round and round in the clouds of smoke."[61] Jacob Miller's oldest daughter, Elizabeth, who had reluctantly retreated to safer ground, watched with dread: "That night I thought the whole town was on fire. You may imagine my feelings, thinking of dear papa and all I left. I did not expect to see anything but embers when I returned the next day."[62]

Theresa Kretzer, trapped under fire and behind Confederate lines for days, was experiencing different emotions. When the cellar became too stifling, she and a friend climbed to the attic. Although bullets were "raining on the roof," they opened the shutters and looked east. "On all the distant hills around were the blue uniforms and shining bayonets of our men," she said, "and I thought it was the prettiest sight I ever saw in my life. Yes, there were our men, advancing cautiously, driven back again and again, but persistently returning and pushing nearer. My! it was lovely, and I felt so glad to think that we were going to get them into town shortly." The girls stayed at their post until a neighbor scolded them back to safety.[63]

Union skirmishers crept through alleys on the outskirts of Sharpsburg. Several Federal divisions were within half a mile of the village—and of cutting off the Confederate army's escape route, the road to the Potomac. There were no more Rebel boys to throw in line. But just then A. P. Hill's exhausted men arrived. They had crossed the Potomac at Boteler's Ford and pushed cross-country toward Sharpsburg. The Confederates struck at the Federals crossing John Otto's cornfield at about 3:40 P.M. Brigadier General Maxcy Gregg so understood the urgent need that he didn't pause even to reform his column. "Commence firing, men," he bellowed, "and form the line as you fight."[64] Another fight ripped among the rustling of cornstalks. It was hard to see, and the confusion was intensified because some of the Confederates had traded their lice-infested rags for fresh Union sack coats at Harpers Ferry. One by one the vanguard Union regiments fell back, stunned by the fresh onslaught from Hill's force of almost three thousand.

Formal orders to withdraw reached the Union flank about 5:00 P.M. They included the Ninth New York, a gaudy Zouave regiment still bedecked in baggy red trousers and short blue jackets and tasseled fezzes. That afternoon they had advanced under a brutal rain of artillery, withstood a face-to-face shoot-out with a Confederate line fifty yards away, pushed into a swarming maelstrom of hand-to-hand combat with bayonets and musket butts wielded like clubs, and yipped in triumph when the Southern boys broke and ran. In their climb to high ground, the Ninth New York Zouaves had lost sixty-three percent of their force. They were also dangerously low on cartridges, but Lieutenant Colonel Edgar A. Kimball knew how close they were to victory. The regiment had to be ordered again, personally, to march to the rear. "Look at my regiment!" Kimball fumed. "They go off this field under orders. They are not driven off."[65] Kimball was among the frustrated Union officers fighting two forces: aggressive Confederate gambles and overcautious Union leadership. Burnside still had more than twice the number of Confederates on the field, but he withdrew his men all the way to Antietam Creek.

Sharpsburg Unionists were dismayed to realize that the Confederates still held their village. The group in the cellar at Delaney's Tavern crept upstairs when the shooting subsided. The slave cook stepped outside when she heard the Confederates passing and asked, "Did you have a hard fight today?" One answered, "Yes, Aunty, the Yankees give us the devil, and they'll give us hell next." The woman went back inside and tried to rest, "but I couldn't sleep none because I didn't know when they'd break in on me."[66]

The fighting didn't completely fade away until after dark, but a few brave souls ventured out as the sun was setting. They found a smoldering

*The Lutheran church on Main Street was used as a Federal signal station and subsequently was shelled heavily during the battle. By the time this photo was taken several days after the battle, it was being used as a hospital. Photo by Alexander Gardner, 1862.* LIBRARY OF CONGRESS.

landscape. Smoke stained the sunset eerie shades of red, and flames from burning buildings still writhed against the sky. George Neese, the Confederate gunner, bivouacked on the battlefield that night. "Some of the enemy's shells set some buildings on fire in Sharpsburg," he wrote in his diary, "and the flames threw a red glare on the sky that reflected a pale ghostly light over the battle plain strewn with the upturned faces of the dead."[67]

Several civilians hitched their horses to old farm wagons and began assisting the grim task of transporting the thousands of wounded men into the homes, barns, schools, and churches being used by the surgeons. One pregnant woman who lived on the edge of town, alone with her young children during the interminable battle, had spent much of the day tearing their clothes and bedding into strips and packing lard and goose grease into every shard of crockery they could find, while jugs and gourds were filled with water. When the fighting subsided, the little group ventured onto the battlefield, lugging baskets and quilts. One of her daughters later recalled:

> There was a red haze from the sunset . . . the brick of the church was red, and as far as I could see were suffering, crying, or dead men . . . red, red, red. It was a red stew. I can remember my mother laboring with three big baskets and I holding her pettiskirts . . . pulling a large bundle along the ground . . . and all of us, my brothers and sisters, too afraid to cry.[68]

Theresa Kretzer and her mother slipped out to the stable that evening to milk their cows, but occasional firing didn't completely fade away until 10:00 P.M. They dared another trip above ground to fetch some bread and butter, then quickly returned to the damp cellar. Their neighbors didn't go home, either. The elderly were tucked in makeshift beds; a few others lay on the floor. "But the best part of the people sat up all night and watched," Theresa explained, "for we didn't know what was going to come on us."[69]

That evening General Lee and his lieutenants assembled at the Jacob Grove House on West Main. Lee's first worry was the absence of General James Longstreet. Longstreet finally arrived, explaining that he had stopped to help a family whose house had been set on fire from a shell. "How bad is it?" Lee asked each commander in turn. "As bad as it can be," General D. H. Hill answered.[70]

Despite the reports, Lee decided not to retreat. Soldiers and civilians alike held their ground, wondering if dawn would bring renewed fighting.

# CHAPTER 7

# "A Smell of Death in the Air"

As the hour of midnight passed, the bloodiest day in American history went with it. But the horrors were far from over. In farm kitchens and barns and churches and schools, bleary-eyed surgeons manned their saws. Torches and lanterns bobbed through the night on both sides of the field where thousands of men lay dead or in mutilated agony. Moans, cries for help, pleas to God or mother or sweethearts mingled through the darkness. Lost, dazed soldiers searched for their regiments, men groped for missing friends, medical corpsmen hauled away the wounded, and the inevitable scavengers robbed living and dead of anything worth stealing. Officers and correspondents huddled in little farmhouse kitchens, writing hasty reports by the flickering light of candle stubs, surrounded by the injured and dying. More than *twenty-three thousand* men had become casualties that day—twenty-three thousand men needing medical assistance or burial in the once-pastoral Sharpsburg Valley. Men still on the field wondered if dawn would ever come. "I never want to spend another night on a battlefield," Theodore Vanneman of the First Maryland Light Artillery, USA, wrote his wife. "The cries of the wounded and dying cannot help but melt the hardest heart."[1]

The next morning, local residents cautiously crept from the cellars. "It . . . was unearthly quiet after all the uproar of the battle," Theresa Kretzer recalled.[2] The silence was broken only by occasional gunfire as a few Confederates used their remaining ammunition to shoot pigs, chickens, and other livestock wandering the streets. "Poor little things," they murmured, "they have nowhere to go, and we ought to take care of them." Heros von Borcke watched a Texan shoot a pig galloping down the street sixty yards away. Although admiring the "capital shot," the officer felt compelled to rebuke the man for his "wanton disregard of the rights of property." Flabbergasted, the private stared at von Borcke. "Major, did you have anything to eat yesterday? . . . I haven't tasted a morsel for several days." Von Borcke didn't have the heart to object further and left the man to his breakfast.[3]

Most soldiers and civilians alike expected a renewed contest. If George McClellan acted decisively, he might crush the Army of Northern Virginia and end the war along the meandering banks of Antietam Creek. McClellan had more than eighty-six thousand troops at hand, many of them fresh. Lee could muster fewer than forty thousand spent men, although he arrayed his line to make optimal defensive use of the rolling terrain. At 8:00 A.M. on September 18 General McClellan sent a portentous telegram to his wife: "The spectacle yesterday was the grandest I could conceive of—nothing could be more sublime. . . . I am well nigh tired out by anxiety & want of sleep."[4]

Few understood McClellan's hesitation except, perhaps, General Lee, who knew his enemy intuitively. Lee had practical reasons for being on the field that day: It took time to arrange for the care of his wounded, to begin moving his battle-weary soldiers back across the Potomac, to arrange for transport of the vital supplies captured at Harpers Ferry. Throughout the long day of September 18 the two armies stared uneasily at each other across the battlefield. Some struck informal truces in order to search for comrades, aid the wounded, or retrieve bodies for burial.

As the morning hours lengthened without the dreaded rumble of artillery, the civilian refugees began to emerge. Stumbling from whatever shelter they had found, they scarcely recognized their homes. Chaos reigned in every direction. Smashed caissons, overturned wagons, muskets, cards, Bibles, and haversacks littered the ground, left by what one soldier called "the awful tornado of battle."[5] Dead men were in neat rows or hidden under thickets, turning black, bloating, awaiting burial. Dead horses dotted the landscape. Amputated limbs piled up outside the makeshift hospitals. Incessant buzzing flies tormented the living by tormenting the dead.

Most of the hungry, tired civilians who had sought temporary refuge were anxious to return home, though fearful of what they would find. Many had to first find the appropriate officer and get a pass: "There was pickets all along the road who would stop you," one man explained.[6] Some of the apprehensive refugees were turned away without the vital pass, a maddening experience for people desperate to return to their own homes—or what was left of them. Anyone who had made the mistake of seeking refuge across the Potomac faced even greater difficulties. John

Hoffman, a Sharpsburg clerk, had sent his wife to Shepherdstown during the battle; when she tried to return, she was arrested as a spy and held for questioning before being permitted to leave.[7]

The refugees at Killiansburg Cave picked their way back through a gruesome landscape. One young girl later told her grandchildren of having to step over corpses as they walked.[8] The Grice family started for home that morning with their children and Logan, their old pony. One of their daughters was carried by Robert Lakins, a black barber who had also taken refuge at the cave. The daughter recalled that "the dead lay so thick that old Logan would be very careful not to step on any of the dead." That grim debris was too much for Mr. Grice, who was riding Logan. "But [my] mother, a thoroughbred Irish woman of pluck, would shake [my] father and cause him to recover, and make fun of him and tell him to get back on the horse and continue the trip."[9]

On Friday Henry Piper shepherded his family home from his brother's mill along the Potomac. "On our return the Union forces were encamped upon the farm and in the vicinity, and the Union cavalry were moving along the Hagerstown pike in great numbers towards Sharpsburg," recalled daughter Mary Ellen. "We had some difficulty in passing across the pike to get to our house."[10] When the family reached the hill where the sharp-shooter had warned son Samuel to safety the day before, they saw the soldier hanging in the same tree, dead. Their barn had been shelled, and only the fact that the hay stored inside was too green to burn had saved it from destruction. Union soldiers were camped on the farm, busily butchering the Pipers' remaining cattle as the family arrived. Wounded soldiers were lying on the floor of every room. One had the family Bible propped up in front of him, tearing out each page as he finished reading.[11] The Pipers brought several horses that they had concealed during the battle with them. "The horses had not been in the stable long, probably not two hours," a farmhand testified later, "before a squad of Union cavalry came to the stable and took the roan mare."[12]

The group of Keedysville women and children who had sheltered at the Pry Mill decided to walk home in the evening. Little Oliver Reilly was among them, and he remembered meeting Union soldiers at the Sharpsburg Pike. "General McClellan and his staff were just passing," he wrote later. "[I remember] well the little brown horse of General McClellan's, Dan. . . . The women and children had to make way for the horsemen, and the road was completely blocked with soldiers, some lying down, some sitting down, others resting on their guns, cheering little Mack, as he was called."[13] When the Reilly family got home, they found two dead soldiers in their yard and three more in the house. Mrs. Reilly checked the barn and found another body under some hay. "There's a dead man in the hay-mow," she called. She was astonished when the man sat up and cried, "For God's sake don't make this known as I have a wife and eight children which I surely want to see!" Their cupboards stripped bare by the passing soldiers, the Reillys had nothing to eat but bread spread with beef tallow until neighbor Levin Benton stopped by later with a basket of provisions.[14]

Sharpsburg residents returned to find their tidy village horribly scarred by the shelling, skirmishing, and looting. Bricks and stones littered the ground. Liberty poles were shattered. Windows were smashed, larders ran-sacked. "I verily believe every door in town was broken open, and every-thing that could be eaten . . . consumed," observed one Southern soldier.[15] Confederates had used the Lutheran church's belfry as an observation sta-tion, and as a result it had been a steady target for Yankee artillerists. One soldier counted and found only five dwellings, in the town of thirteen hun-dred people, that had escaped damage.[16] A Yankee noted that "the small wooden hotel and tavern . . . was perforated like a honeycomb."[17]

When describing structural damage, most observers singled out the Mumma house. The blackened ruin of the formerly lovely and prosperous farm was horribly compelling. "I saw Samuel Mumma's fine brick house and barn that was burnt . . .," Otho Nesbitt noted in his diary after visiting the field, adding, "Another barn was burnt close by, 4 or 5 small houses, and stables in Sharpsburg."[18] But an early historian noted that in Sharpsburg the homes of "Widow Holmes and the Widow Shackleford" had burned to the ground, as had a large barn in the middle of town; Surgeon Ellis also confirmed that two village homes had been burned.[19] Elizabeth Miller mentioned that "a few" houses had burned.[20] The Mumma house was the only home *deliberately* destroyed during the battle. Sketch artists, diarists, correspondents, and the claims records left from the family's attempt to receive compensation documented well the Mumma family's dear losses. But there is no way of knowing how many poor families also lost every-thing. Tenants, illiterate people who scratched their living in rude cabins, who didn't attract the particular attention of sightseers and didn't make damage claims, left no documentary evidence of their misery.

>·+◈·◦·◈·+·<

*"Union Cavalry Ferreting Out the Rebel Stragglers and Fugitives After the Battle of Antietam." After both battles of the 1862 Maryland campaign, Confederates who had been wounded or separated from their commands sought shelter from local residents. Sympathizers formed an "underground railroad" to help spirit a few of these men across the Potomac to safety.* COURTESY FRANK & MARIE-THERESE WOOD PRINT COLLECTIONS, ALEXANDRIA, VIRGINIA.

Among the debris the returning citizens found men: sick or wounded soldiers huddled inside; dead men lying where they had fallen. Some of the Confederate snipers, unwilling to believe that either army had won a decisive victory, stayed in the trees around Sharpsburg, with corn-husk mattresses pulled among the limbs for protection. One young Sharpsburg girl soon got them down: "To lure them from their perches we left water, home-bread, and new peach jam beneath the trees," she recalled, "and with the smell of it they came down and gobbled like animals."[21]

Emory Smith, who lived on Main Street, came home to a grisly tableau: two Confederate soldiers had been in his family's kitchen and a third drawing water from their well when a shell had come through the building and exploded. The man at the well had been killed by the impact; the men inside had been "literally torn to pieces" by the explosion, one still holding a bunch of onions.[22]

Sixteen-year-old James Snyder and his mother had carefully hidden their American flag, locked all the drawers, and bolted every door before taking refuge with friends during the battle. The next day James, "against his mother's protest but impelled by a boy's courage and curiosity, insisted on going up to town to see what conditions were at the house." James made his way to Sharpsburg and was dismayed to find his home looted, like every other house left vacant by its owners. Inside he found "little heaps of dusty rags"—the discarded, filthy Confederate uniforms shucked by the soldiers who had exchanged them for the Snyder boys' clothes. James was astonished to find one of the offenders lying in bed, stark naked. Irate, James demanded, "What are you in bed in that condition for?" The soldier looked up at him almost pleadingly. "Young man," he replied, "I am here because I'm sick, and I didn't want to spoil the clean bed with my dirty clothes, so I took them off." James evidently let that pass, but he remarked indignantly to another Confederate outside, "Well, you fellows used this house pretty rough!" "Rough!" replied the soldier. "We ought to have burned the damned thing down. We found a Yankee flag in there as big as a barn door."

Amid the devastation was ample evidence of mindless looting. James's father had taken refuge at Killiansburg Cave. He was making his way home when one private said, "Here, old man, you can have this," and tossed him a daguerreotype. Mr. Snyder was astonished to find himself holding an image of his own wife.[23] Civilians trudging home passed some soldiers still hauling not only food but women's bonnets, silver spoons, and other knick-knacks plundered from vacant houses.

In the outlying farms, it was much the same. The farmers who had presided over tidy, fruitful tracts found complete desolation. Fences had been torn down, fields of ripe grain and corn trampled, livestock driven off or butchered, prim orchards stripped bare, beehives destroyed, and root cellars emptied. And everywhere, in all directions, was a sea of broken men. "The house was full of wounded Northern soldiers, and the hogpen loft was full, and the barn floor," recalled Alexander Root, who worked for the Jacob Nicodemus family. "The wounded was crowded into all our buildings. I looked around to find something to eat, but there wasn't enough food in the house to feed a pair of quail."[24]

Gussie Rohrback and her family returned to their stone house near the Dunker church to find a dead Confederate lying in their doorway and others nearby in the street. The Dunker church, the eye of such a fearful storm the day before, was now overflowing with wounded—and dead. Martin Snavely, who helped there, recalled a pile of limbs several feet high outside the church window nearest the amputating table. Some of the men who did not survive were embalmed there as well; Mr. Snavely needed a six-horse hitch to haul the loads of coffins from the Dunker church to the railroad station at Hagerstown, where they would be shipped home.[25]

Those residents whose homes had been commandeered by the surgeons faced the appalling sight of bloodied men on parlor carpets, on kitchen tables, on porches and lawns. There weren't enough bandages; the men used cornstalk leaves to bind their wounds while waiting for better care. Overwhelmed surgeons worked frantically, fighting fatigue. "On the porch where the amputating tables were," recalled one man who had been a young boy in 1862, "the blood was thick against the walls for weeks after."[26] A Southern journalist visiting a hospital was sickened by what he saw. "There is a smell of death in the air," he wrote, "and the laboring surgeons are literally covered from head to foot with blood of the sufferers."[27]

The exhausted surgeons tried to fight off the horror that touched them to their core and keep working. Dr. William Child, serving with the Fifth Regiment of New Hampshire Volunteers, poured out his feelings in letters to his wife. "The days after the battle are a thousand times worse than the day of battle," he scribbled. "And the physical pain is not the greatest pain suffered. . . . I pray God may stop such infurnal work."[28]

Young Ada Mumma, who returned to her home near Burnside's Bridge, found her grandparents helping the surgeons with dozens of wounded. "I could not sleep," she recalled. "I could hear those poor men calling for 'water . . . for God's sake, give me a drop of water.'"[29] Her grandmother had returned a day earlier and found the farmhouse so jammed with wounded that she had to climb in a window. Federal brigadier general Isaac Rodman was cared for in the Rohrback's farmhouse until he died in early November. Jacob McGraw, who helped the family clean up the debris, recalled that Rodman's wounds "became so offensive . . . [we] were obliged to set the dining table on the porch, as it was impossible to partake of food in the house." McGraw also believed the surgeon attending the general was incompetent.[30]

Stewards were attempting to determine which of the wounded should be lined up for the surgeons, which should be left alone, which to assign to the dismal parades of ambulance wagons already making their way to better facilities at Hagerstown and Frederick. Two Sisters of Charity who had traveled from Emmitsburg to help found themselves "in constant danger from bomb shells which had not exploded and which only required a slight jar to burst. The ground was covered with these and it was hard to distinguish them when the carriage wheels were rolling over straw and dry leaves."[31]

Many civilians pushed aside their own shock and willingly helped the overwhelming needs of the wounded who, at any of the field hospitals, were already waiting in rows in the yards, packed so closely together that there was scarcely room to pass between them. By morning on September 18 women were already binding wounds, holding hands, making tea, distributing whatever provisions they could scare up. Dying men, terrified of being lost among the unknown dead, begged the women to write down their names.

In Funkstown, Angela Davis and her husband quickly packed some provisions and journeyed to the battlefield. "As we stepped out of our carriage, a ghastly, gruesome sight met our gaze," she wrote later. The Davises made their way to one of the hospitals:

[Mr. Line's house] was used by the surgeons for amputating purposes, and dressing wounds, and there were one or two tables in the yard being used for the same purpose, and a pile of severed hands, arms and legs lying on the ground. . . . A horrible and sickening scene to behold such as I never wish to see again. I staggered from the carriage, but exercising all of my will power, kept from fainting.

One [of the wounded men] who seemed to be dying, looked up at me and exclaimed—"Oh; Thirza, is that you?" The surgeon near, nodded to me to say "Yes." As I knelt down by his side and took his cold, clammy hand in mine, he again said excitedly "Oh; Thirza, is it you? I am so glad you have come. I knew you would. I—knew—you—would—come," and in a few moments his spirit quietly and sweetly passed away. . . . I have often wished I could meet *this Thirza* and tell her that her husband supposed she was with him in his dying hour.

Soon after, a mortally wounded man was carried in on a stretcher, "lying in a pool of blood, dripping from every side." The scene was too much for Angela, and as she fainted, there was a scurry at the pump, which had been locked to prevent precious water from being wasted. Revived, she moved on to comfort another wounded soldier.[32]

As civilians appeared on the field to help, local legend tells of a little old lady who stopped by the sunken Hog Trough Road, now piled deep with bodies, the living entwined with the dead. Overwhelmed, she descended from her carriage, knelt in prayer, and asked God's blessing on the men who had fallen in that "bloody lane."[33] Her benediction gave the local byway its enduring name: Bloody Lane.

Many of the men in Bloody Lane were beyond the help of surgeons, for hundreds of men had died in that rutted trench. With several thousand men already lying dead in the cornfields and country lanes and more dying in the hospitals, the need for burial details was enormous. While many civilians labored to help the living, others took on the odious task of burying the dead. Although some may have volunteered, the army was grateful enough of help to hire local men to assist.

Because of the number of bodies, only shallow trenches were dug, and the corpses, most already stripped of shoes or other valuables, laid to rest. Sometimes local people stopped to say a prayer over the bodies; one veteran recuperating at one of the hospitals hobbled outside as soon as he was able and daily sang over the graves.[34] But most of the fallen men received a rough burial at best. A local man wrote that the surrounding property was "as common for graves as the cornstalks are on a forty acre field."[35] Seven hundred men killed in or near Bloody Lane were buried on William and Margaret Roulette's farm.

The job had to be hurried, for the hot weather continued. "The stench was terrible—terrible!" remembered one man who was hired to help the soldiers assigned to burial detail.[36] With kerchiefs tied over their noses and mouths, the men worked as quickly as they could, digging long trenches about six feet wide and eighteen inches deep. Corpses were placed on blankets and dragged; if the job was too repugnant, the retching men on grave detail heated and curled bayonets into hooks to help with the hauling. "The trenches was so shallow," Alexander Root recalled, "that after the loose dirt which was thrown back had settled down, heads and toes sometimes stuck out."[37] Oliver Reilly and his father visited the field days after the battle and saw "the dead soldiers that had crawled into the bushes and died there and

*This Union burial detail was at work on the D. R. Miller farm. Many civilians come home and found dead men in their kitchens, fields, and outbuildings. Because the volume of dead necessitated that only shallow graves be dug, residents lived with ghastly reminders of the battle for years. Photo by Alexander Gardner, 1862.*
LIBRARY OF CONGRESS.

had not been buried yet. Some of those that were buried had their feet out, some their hands, and some were buried so shallow that their heads could be seen."[38] The inevitable tourists stared with horrified fascination. "The country people flocked to the battlefield like vultures," wrote one soldier detailed to a burial party, "their curiosity and inquisitiveness most astonishing; while my men were all at work, many of them stood around, dazed, awe-stricken by the terrible evidence of the great fight."[39] One of the gravediggers was stopped by an officer, who asked if by chance he had found the body of one Jimmie Hays, 19th Massachusetts. "I told him I thought I had it in a blanket at that very moment," the man replied, who had looked to letters in the dead boy's pocket for identification. "I uncovered the face and he examined it carefully, then wept a little, and finally said, 'That boy is my brother.'"[40]

Men on the fields were buried first; those who had crawled under thickets or behind haystacks weren't found for days. Soldiers left the burial of men who had died near dwellings up to the property owners, who did the best they could scratching makeshift graves in gardens and country lanes. Children were set to the task of finding flat stones to lay over the shallow graves, to keep the chickens away. In the press, a few bodies were left in gutters, covered with brush and leaves.

The Federal army held the field, so Yankee dead were attended to first. Confederate dead were piled in mass graves. When Angela Davis and her husband visited the field, they saw "any number of new made graves, the Union Soldiers . . . having little pieces of board with their names written with a pencil, put at the head. In one of the fields, there were a great many rebel soldiers buried, but their graves could not be marked, as their names were not known."[41] Civilians who buried men on their property usually left no record, so many of the fallen were never identified.

Adding to the grim task of human burial was the need to dispose of hundreds of dead horses also decomposing under the September sun. Samuel Fiske of the 14th Connecticut observed, "There are hundreds of horses . . . all mangled and putrefying, scattered everywhere!"[42] Here, too, civilians were needed to help. "We'd hitch a log-chain around a dead horse's neck, and it was all that the four horses could do to drag the carcass [away]," remembered one of the men who helped.[43] Mr. Mumma, whose property had seen such bitter fighting during the battle's morning hours, dragged fifty-five dead horses from his farm to the East Woods and burned them.[44] Most of the animals were disposed of in this manner, which only intensified the smell. "The stench was sickening," Alexander Root recalled. "We couldn't eat a good meal, and we had to shut the house up just as tight as we could of a night to keep out that odor. We couldn't stand it, and the first thing in the morning when I rolled out of bed I'd have to take a drink of whiskey. If I didn't I'd throw up before I got my clothes all on."[45]

&gt;━◆&gt;━○━◆━&lt;

During the evening of September 18 civilians living west of Sharpsburg heard the shuffling tramp, the creaking and jingling and rumbling, of an army on the move: Lee's Army of Northern Virginia, leaving the field. It continued through the night as the column pushed down to the Potomac ford on the narrow country lanes. People living on the bluffs above Boteler's Ford could see the flicker of torches held by cavalrymen posted midstream.

Spirits were low as the men forded the Potomac "in the pitchy darkness . . . floundering among sharp and dangerous rocks."[46] Confederate captain Greenlee Davidson wasn't sorry to leave. "The people [of Maryland] almost without exception are soul and body Union shriekers. . . . I doubt whether there was a man in the army that did not rejoice that he was out of Maryland. For my part, I have had enough of Maryland. I don't want to hear anything more of 'Maryland, My Maryland.'"[47] At dawn the next morning, when the regimental band of the 18th Mississippi tried to cheer the departing troops with its rendition of that song, it was shouted down.

Unionists were overjoyed. Theresa Kretzer, who had buried her American flag in the ash pile, quickly retrieved it so that the Yankee troops could see it aloft as they entered town. "I hurried to get it swung across the street," she said later, "and after that, as the officers and men passed under it they all took off their hats. Their reverence for the flag was beautiful, and so was the flag." Theresa stood watching and waving as the men passed, and she was there when a group of Confederate prisoners was herded by:

Bless your soul! Among them I saw the very men who had demanded the big flag that was now suspended across the street. They looked at the flag and looked at me and shouted, "You said it was burned!" and they cursed me till some of our men drew their swords and quieted 'em down.

"No," [I] shouted back. "I told you the exact truth. When you tried to get that flag the other day, it was in ashes."[48]

The Yankees were gratified by their reception in Sharpsburg. "The people were beginning to return as we were coming through the town and they treated us very kindly; the ladies gave us fruit and coffee and such refreshments as the rebels did not find or could not carry away," wrote one.[49] One New Yorker advanced through Sharpsburg on the nineteenth, while artillery and cavalry were already flying toward the ford in hot pursuit of the Confederate rear guard. He recalled seeing civilians emerge as soon as the Yankee men took possession of Sharpsburg, "the ladies displaying the Stars and Stripes, which they had secreted about their persons. . . . Old gray-headed men would shout, 'Three cheers for the Union!' and the Yankee volunteers responded with a will."[50] Another New Englander serving in the Federal army recalled his reception after the Confederate evacuation of Sharpsburg: "The people welcomed the arrival of the Union army with every evidence of gladness, and hailed them as their deliverers. 'Bless God!' said one old lady, 'you've driven them away. I've been down in my cellar three whole days!'"[51] An old man seized the hand of another New Yorker as he passed, saying simply, "I am so glad you have come."[52]

Only one army remained in Maryland. Whether for secession or union, the Marylanders prayed the tides of battle would not again wash their way.

>⋅⋄⋅○⋅⋄⋅<

In the days after the battle, more civilians proceeded to the valley. Scores of sightseers pushed their way past the endless parades of ambulances. "Was to the Battle Field of Antietam to-day," wrote John Koogle in his diary. "The road was so full of men and wagons that we could hardly travel. We saw plenty of wounded and dead, a most lamentable sight, the worst I ever beheld."[53] One incredulous officer wrote, "Hundreds [of tourists] were scattered over the field, eagerly searching for souvenirs in the shape of cannon balls, guns, bayonets, swords, canteens, etc."[54] Another Union soldier was on the field on September 19, when the Confederate army was across the Potomac and a few shells were still flying as Southern rear guard and Northern vanguard quarreled. One shell that fell near the Roulette's orchard, he noted, was dug up later that day by a civilian relic hunter.[55]

Otho Nesbitt of Clear Spring was among a group who toured the battlefield on the eighteenth, before the Confederate army had even retreated. After watching the burial details at work, Nesbitt left the others and rode toward Hagerstown, stopping once to dissuade "a young trooper who had a notion to [im]press my horse." Unable to find lodging in a tavern, he bunked with a group of other tourists at a farmhouse. The next day he returned to the battlefield and was allowed to go where he pleased. He wandered to the Confederate lines, where the dead had not yet been buried, and coolly surveyed the carnage, which he recorded in some detail later in his diary. "I left about 12 o'clock for home," he concluded, "having satisfied myself in regard to falling humanity." After passing a friend walking along the road—who explained that his horse had been impressed and waved a certificate intended to eventually provide recompense—Nesbitt and a traveling companion rode out as fast as they could in fear of losing their mounts as well. After dodging among the troops of both armies, they retired to another farmhouse, where they obtained permission to spend the night. The next day Nesbitt and his companions had further adventures evading soldiers intent on impressing horses, including one wild scramble when several troopers arrived in a yard where the men were watering their

*"Maryland and Pennsylvania Farmers Visiting the Battle-field while the National Troops were Burying the Dead and Carrying off the Wounded." The Federal soldiers tending the wounded and burying the dead were astonished by how quickly visitors arrived on the field for sight-seeing and relic-hunting. Sketch by F. H. Schell.* COURTESY FRANK & MARIE-THERESE WOOD PRINT COLLECTIONS, ALEXANDRIA, VIRGINIA.

mounts at a trough. The men eventually "got home safe without losing mare, horse, or gelding, life, leg, or limb, and notwithstanding the difficulties didn't begrudge the trip."[56]

But many of the newcomers were volunteers, wanting to provide aid. In Hagerstown, members of the Ladies' Union Relief Association collected supplies, ripped heirloom linen tablecloths into bandages, and sent well-laden nurses to Sharpsburg. Miss Mollie Magill, daughter of a Hagerstown physician, provided such tender care in Sharpsburg hospitals that the men called her "the Angel of the Confederacy."[57] In Funkstown, the Davises organized a bipartisan relief effort, letting neighbors know that they would transport to the field anything brought to their home by 9:00 A.M. "So we sat up most of the night, killing and cooking chickens, &c.," Angela wrote, "and the next morning our dining room, kitchen, and wash house were all filled with jars or crocks of mashed potatoes, fried ham, chicken and beef sandwiches, and in fact everything that was available in a small country town."[58]

The men were immensely grateful for the women who persevered through their shock and horror, remembering them for the rest of their lives. Jacob Lair of the 20th New York had lost an arm during the battle and was taken to the Hoffman farm. For the next several weeks he lay among the wounded and dying in their barn, his days brightened only by "the good ladies of the Hoffman family, bringing fruits, cake, pies, etc. to the wounded."[59] Another wounded soldier wrote home gratefully, "A lady, Mrs. Lee, a resident here, is around amongst the men, with chocolate and other luxuries, writing letters for some, taking mail matter to the Post in the next village, and in other ways kindly ministering to the wants of the soldiers."[60] And later:

> In addition to ordinary nurses, there are at Smoketown three ladies, whose self-sacrificing benevolence deserves honorable notice. Mrs. Husbands, Mrs. Lee, and Miss Hall, are rendering gratuitous service to the soldiers, receiving and distributing supplies from Home Aid Societies. To their labors much is due in promoting the comfort and recovery of the sick. The gratitude of the soldiers for their attentions is expressed in the warmest terms. The place of women at the bedside of suffering, can never be supplied by more professional attendance of the other sex.[61]

Among the women stanching wounds was Clara Barton, who had traveled from Washington. One of the patients she tended was a young Frederick woman named Mary Galloway. When the Third Wisconsin had been stationed in Frederick in 1861, a lieutenant named Harry Barnard had been quartered at Mary's house, and the two had fallen in love. The 1862 campaign had briefly brought the regiment back to Frederick, and Mary and Harry had enjoyed a fleeting, bittersweet reunion. Unable to bear her anxiety when the Wisconsin men marched on to South Mountain and Sharpsburg, Mary found a Yankee uniform and set out to join them. She caught up with the army, but she was still frantically searching for the regiment on September 17 when a bullet struck her in the neck. Clara nursed Mary until she was well enough to make the journey home to Frederick but was unable to learn if Harry Barnard had survived the battle.[62] Clara Barton went on to well-deserved fame as an army nurse. Unsung were the hundreds of Maryland farm women who didn't have to follow the army to the field, but performed with equal valor.

*"The Ladies of Hagerstown, MD, Ministering to our Wounded." In Hagerstown and other communities, ladies began preparing baskets of food and medical supplies even before the battle ended. The relief efforts were monumental. Sketch by Theodore R. Davis.*

More than seventeen thousand wounded soldiers were in need of medical attention, and the valley was overwhelmed. Most suitable buildings east of Sharpsburg were still inundated with the soldiers wounded at South Mountain. Hagerstown was already flooded as well. One Sanitary Commission officer arrived there on the twenty-fourth and wrote in his diary, "Rooms at the hotels not to be thought of; it was not easy to get inside their doors. Soldiers and officers were bivouacking in the streets."[63] A physician from the Sanitary Commission reported, "Indeed there is not a barn, or farmhouse, or store or church, or schoolhouse, between Boonesville, and Sharpsburg, . . . and Smoketown, that is not gorged with wounded—Rebel and Union. Even the corn-cribs, and in many instances the cow stables, and in one place the mangers were filled. Several thousands lie in open air upon straw, and all are receiving the kind services of the farmers' families and the surgeons."[64] Another volunteer wrote, "Those were fortunate who were in barns, where they were sure of a little hay or straw upon which to rest their shattered limbs."[65]

The magnitude of suffering was hard to grasp. For example, 1,396 wounded men from both sides passed through a hospital established on a farm near Keedysville owned by Southern sympathizer Otho J. Smith, a physician practicing in Boonsboro. Oliver Reilly, who lived in Keedysville, carried meals to some of the wounded men in the schoolhouse and German Reformed Church, and evenings, when things were still, he could hear the moans of the wounded echoing from those buildings to his home "some distance away."[66] Captain William H. Harries of the Third Wisconsin was taken to a large barn in Keedysville after being wounded. "Until the Sanitary Commission came along we were in horrible condition," he wrote. "I do not care to describe my own; suffice it to say I felt like a new creature when I got on a clean shirt."[67]

The largest field hospital was at Smoketown, a tiny settlement consisting of "three small houses and a pig pen" north of Sharpsburg, where more than six hundred men were simultaneously cared for in tents. A surgeon had selected the ground, attracted by a gentle elevation (allowing drainage), a sparse grove of oaks (which supplied some shade), and room for one hundred tents, arranged neatly in wards, with additional room for kitchens, store tents, a camp post office and dispensary, a chapel, and ambulances. Mrs. Kennedy of Hagerstown was among the women who organized relief efforts for the Smoketown hospital. She once took a visitor from New York with her, who later described the experience:

We went to the ladies' tent, while the attendants unloaded the ambulance, and I wish you could have heard the exclamations as the various articles appeared. "Oh, Mrs. K. there is some of your good bread—they get so tired of the hard bread and what the baker brings is so often sour and heavy!" "Onions; we have needed them so much!" "Oh; there are lemons, now we can do so and so," and so on, and I am sure it would have moved you to have seen the eyes of ladies and attendants glisten over the flannel garments, few as they were, and heard their remarks as they took up for instance the grey flannel drawers, (there were only two pairs of them) "won't these be grand for some of those poor fellows who are lying in bed for want of clothes to get up in?"[68]

*Dr. Anson Hurd, regimental surgeon for the 14th Indiana Volunteers, stands among makeshift shebangs providing feeble protection for the wounded at the field hospital on the Otho Smith farm near Keedysville. Photo by Alexander Gardner, 1862.* LIBRARY OF CONGRESS.

Surgeons tried to keep the evacuation moving, and officers of the Sanitary Commission, including Dr. Lewis Steiner, were on the field within hours of the battle. Ambulances journeyed endlessly over the rough mountain roads, carrying wounded men to Frederick and returning with loads of medical supplies. Dr. Jonathan Letterman, who had recently been assigned as medical director of the Army of the Potomac, faced the overwhelming challenge of coordinating the movement of soldiers and supplies. The removal of so many wounded from the field to general hospitals was, he wrote, an "arduous undertaking." Railroad service from Greencastle, Pennsylvania, and Harpers Ferry was unreliable, so he determined that all of the wounded should be sent in ambulances to Frederick, then on to Baltimore, Washington, or elsewhere. It was a mammoth endeavor:

> It was imperative that the trains should leave at the proper hours, no one interfering with another; that they should halt at Middletown, where food and rest, with such surgical aid as might be required, could be given to the wounded; that food should always be prepared at this village at the proper time, for the proper number; that the hospitals in Frederick should not be overcrowded, and the ambulances should arrive at the railroad depot in Frederick at the required time to meet the Baltimore trains. With rare exceptions this was accomplished and all the wounded, whose lives would not be jeopardized, were sent carefully away.[69]

Letterman put in motion innovative systems of triage and helped implement other changes designed to maximize efficiency while improving care. The two-wheeled "gut-buster" ambulances had been replaced with four-wheeled vehicles designed to carry up to a dozen men. When fully loaded, the heavy vehicles needed four-horse hitches to haul them over the winding mountain roads. Although the Federal army had been wrestling with the dilemma of removing wounded men from the field since the war began, the design improvements made so far provided a passage still painful at best; some of the wounded had to hang on with both hands to keep from being dumped on the floor. Volunteered or commandeered farm wagons, smelling of sweet clover or manure, provided transport for many other wounded men. The trip was agonizing for the men inside, hard on the farmer-drivers who could do little but listen to the groans. Several civilians witnessed a more horrifying sight: An ambulance whose draft animals could not make a steep hill had tumbled down the embankment.

But no matter how quickly the vehicles bore the wounded away, more were carried in to take their place. Dr. William Child, noting the jubilance that swept through the North with news of victory, wrote, "The masses rejoice, but if all could see the thousands of poor, suffering, dieing [sic] men their rejoicing would turn to weeping." While Child labored at Smoketown the local family that was providing his lodging came to visit the hospital. "As we were going through the wards a man with an amputated leg called the little boy to him and took him by the hand. A flood of tears rolled down his sunburnt face. . . . I was then vividly impressed with the fact that every soldier in this vast army however humble has an invisible but strong cord reaching away back to his loved ones at home."[70]

>—+—◆>—•—O—<◆—+—<

Many of the men suffered from hunger and exposure as well as their wounds. And the shortages were soon intensified, for telegrams and news reports of the battle brought even more people—frantic fathers and wives and friends, desperately searching for wounded or missing soldiers. Their carriages were shoved off the road by passing ambulance trains; wheels broke, horses were impressed. The desperately anxious travelers were often stranded and forced to leave their luggage beside the road amid the other rubble of war, trudging on to the nearest wayside with whatever they could carry. There was no place to house them and little to feed them. Still, they came. "We had a good many to stop with us," Allen Sparrow remembered. "They were always willing to pay well for what they got. . . . We had nine men for supper, lodging, and breakfast, they said they were willing to put up with any thing so they could get some place to stay for every place was full." The visitors were from Massachusetts, and despite being terrified of being poisoned (since they were, after all, in the South), they paid Sparrow ten dollars a day to take them over the battlefields while they searched for their loved ones. One man found his son in a field grave at Sharpsburg, "partly buried, one foot sticking out," Sparrow said. "I do not want to witness such a seen again."[71]

Captain Oliver Wendell Holmes Jr. of the 20th Massachusetts had been shot in the neck and left for dead among the corpses in the West Woods. A friend found him, bandaged the wound, and sent a telegram to Holmes's father in Boston. Holmes was tended in a little white-washed log cabin in Keedysville by Margaret Kitzmiller and her daughters before being sent on to Hagerstown. Anna Kennedy saw him stumbling toward the train station, sent one of her sons to bring the captain inside, and nursed him there for several weeks. Holmes Sr., meanwhile, arrived in Maryland and began a desperate search for his son. Beginning in Frederick, he made his way from ward to ward, from field hospital to field hospital. "Many times . . . I started as some faint resemblance—the shade of a young man's hair, the outline of his half-turned face—recalled the presence I was in search of," he wrote later. Hearing that his son had gone to Hagerstown, he assumed they would meet at a friend's home in Philadelphia. Arriving there and learning that there had been no sign or word of his son, he went to Harrisburg. After more waiting and dozens of anxious telegrams, the father and son were finally reunited.[72]

Telegrams had clattered to all corners of the Union, and from Maine and Ohio to Connecticut and Michigan, mothers and brothers and wives came to take personal charge of a wounded man's care. "In the crowd of ambulances, army wagons, beef-cattle, staff officers, recruits, kicking mules, and so on," wrote George Templeton Strong in his diary, "who should suddenly turn up but Mrs. Arabella Barlow . . . unattended, but serene and self-possessed as if walking down Broadway. She is nursing the colonel, her husband. . . ."[73] In Middletown, Rutherford B. Hayes was impatiently awaiting the arrival of his wife, Lucy. "Had hoped to see her today," he admitted to his diary on September 20, "probably shan't. This hurts me worse than the bullet did." He fretted for days, watching and waiting. Finally, on September 26, he was able to write, "Lucy is here and we are pretty jolly. She visits the wounded and comes back in tears."[74] Lucy Hayes divided her time in Middletown between tending her husband and visiting the wards.

All of the relatives who made their way to the Antietam valley were well-intended, lugging parcels of chocolates and tumblers of marmalade. Many insisted on arranging transport for their loved ones, sure they would mend best at home. Those who found their men in cattle barns or granaries were especially insistent, and timid Victorian women who had never before left their own village found themselves far from home, arguing with short-tempered blood-stained surgeons. "It was impossible to make them understand that [the wounded men] were better where they were," Dr. Letterman wrote, "and that a removal would probably involve the sacrifice of life. Their minds seemed bent on having their friends in houses. All would, in their opinion, be well if that could be accomplished."[75] Determined to get their men home, the visitors haggled with farmers for wagon rental, bullied their way onto train cars in Frederick and Chambersburg, and were on their way.

If the relatives agreed to let the men recuperate at the hospitals, diet often prompted additional arguments. The civilians found it hard not to treat their long-suffering men with whatever rich dainties could be obtained. For men weakened by wounds and illness, gaunt from hard campaigning, the sudden change in diet could be disastrous. In Frederick, Assistant Surgeon Keen kept a journal that included entries about Private

Richard Brown of the Second South Carolina, who was wounded in the skirmish on September 12. "Patient got diarrhea from fruit smuggled in by a Confederate friend," Keen noted on October 30; and on November 7, "Pvt Brown died."[76] Major General Israel Richardson had been mortally wounded by a minié ball at Antietam and taken to the Pry house, where he lingered in an upstairs bedroom until November 3. His wife and sister soon arrived to tend him, and Elizabeth Pry watched them hover helplessly during those agonizing weeks. She believed the overeager women contributed to Richardson's death by providing the general with more delicacies than the doctor thought wise.[77]

Too many of the civilian arrivals were too late to even tend their boys' last hours. Too many mothers and wives spent days or weeks searching hospital wards, arriving in Sharpsburg only after their loved ones had died. One man recalled a widow who "threw herself prostrate upon [her husband's grave] and wept in bitter agony." A woman related another sobering tale:

Among the many who came to visit the Battlefield was a young wife whose frantic grief I can never forget. She came hurriedly as soon as she knew her husband was in the battle only to find him dead and buried two days before her arrival. Unwilling to believe the facts that strangers told her—how in the early morning they had laid him beside his comrades in the orchard—she still insisted upon seeing him. Accompanying some friends to the spot she could not wait the slow process of removing the body but in her agonizing grief, clutched the earth by handfuls where it lay upon the quiet sleeper's form. And when at length the slight covering was removed and the blanket thrown from off the face, she needed but one glance to assure her it was all too true. Then passive and quiet beneath the stern reality of this crushing sorrow she came back to the room in our house.[78]

One New York woman who had lost her brother wrote a letter of thanks to those who had cared for him and buried him; several months later those caretakers received another letter, begging them to "once more look upon the body we had placed [in the grave], and know that it was *indeed* her brother. Painful as it was, her request was complied with to the letter."[79]

Countless Sharpsburg women opened their homes to the desperate people searching for their loved ones—feeding them, taking them to hospitals, comforting them in their grief, making arrangements for coffins and transport. Their own losses—of crops and horses and clothes and potatoes—sometimes dulled in comparison.

Over the mountains in Frederick, civilians were stunned by the mounting horrors. "I can recall standing on Market Street, which was a dirt road then," wrote Lavinia Hooper, who was nine in 1862, "and how we used to watch the wagons bringing the wounded into Frederick for us to look after. There was so much blood dripping out of the back of the wagons and falling on the dirt road, that eventually the mud became red as the wagon wheels ploughed through the streets."[80] Surgeons and nurses who had felt overwhelmed with casualties after the battle at South Mountain were dazed by the new influx of broken men. Hundreds of barns and farmhouses in

*Charles F. Johnson, a Zouave from New York, made this sketch of the Presbyterian Church hospital in Frederick while he convalesced there. "I am still in Frederick City, experiencing kind attention from its people," he wrote, noting that he expected to be sent on any day, "but I don't think I care very much about going." Johnson spent some of his time composing verses, "Lines to a Lady in Frederick," to a local woman named Hattie Wilson, who reminded him of a former sweetheart. Sketch by Charles F. Johnson.* COURTESY CARABELLE BOOKS.

Frederick County were carpeted with wounded. In the city, the huge army hospital quickly overflowed. Schools, hotels, seminaries, even the almshouse were pressed into service. Members of altar guilds doggedly packed away hymnal books so that their husbands could install planks and cots over church pews. (Only St. John's Catholic Church, with its deep walls and high windows, wasn't impressed for hospital duty. It became a prison, instead.)

Many townspeople opened their homes, as well. Women bathed blood-soaked boys, boiled mountains of laundry, and prepared meals for some four thousand sick and wounded men being fed and cared for in town. "You must speak well of old Frederick hereafter," Rutherford B. Hayes wrote his uncle on September 22. "These people are nursing some thousands of our men as if they were their own brothers."[81] A New York Zouave named Charles Johnson wrote in his diary of the "kind attention" he received from civilians, adding, "I am well contented to stay in this city, and I don't think we could be better off anywhere else." When he was well enough to move back to his regiment he noted sadly, "My nice time in that darling little city of Frederick is over."[82]

After a bout of typhoid fever, Clara Barton arrived in Frederick to help with the nursing there. While visiting one of the hospitals she came across an extremely agitated soldier with a gangrenous arm wound. "I want Mary!" he cried deliriously, and when Clara read the card attached to the bed she was stunned: H.B., 3d WIS. The suffering man was Harry Barnard, beau of the young wounded woman Clara had tended at Sharpsburg. Clara quickly fetched Mary Galloway, who was able to comfort her beloved before the surgeons amputated the arm. When Clara left the hospital, Harry was recuperating quietly, with Mary by his side.[83]

The happy reunion was an amazing coincidence of war, for men were moved on as soon as they were medically able to withstand the trip. Each day seven hundred or so men were carried to the depot, loaded into railroad cars, and sent rattling away. But the incessant wagons inevitably brought more men to take their place in the hospitals. "Town in Commotion," Engelbrecht observed. "Our little City is all day long & part of the night one Continued bustle of moving Wagons, Ambulances bringing Wounded Medical & Hospital Stores. . . . Some days about from 500 to 1,000 wagons pass our Street." Just as busy as the hospitals were the morgues. Many of the dead were tended in the Whitehall and Company building on East Patrick.[84] The new process of embalming, the invention of sealed metallic coffins, and Frederick's access to quick rail service made it possible for relatives to send remains home for burial. Elsewhere in the city carpenters worked feverishly, though some of the bereaved were thankful to find even rough-hewn caskets. Pastors spent hours conducting one funeral after another. Gravediggers expedited the process by digging trenches for multiple burials.

Like Sharpsburg—and every other village in western Maryland—Frederick was jammed. A "floating population" of desperate wives and mothers, mourners, teamsters, officers, and sightseers more than doubled the population. The streets were filled with refugees and visitors and soldiers hobbling about with canes. Some of the Federal soldiers captured at Harpers Ferry by Stonewall Jackson's force and now paroled stumbled bitterly into the city. Hundreds of Confederate prisoners of war were marched east through the streets. Thousands of lowing beef cattle were herded west, destined for McClellan's army.

Some Frederick citizens found time to wander curiously through the abandoned campsites ringing the city, now putrid with buzzing piles of offal and bones left from butchered cows and pigs and sheep. They were also among those tourists who flocked to the battlefields—some to help, some to stare, gazing with lurid fascination at the Rebel dead, still unburied in South Mountain's gaps five days after the battle. They brought home haversacks and broken swords and shells—some of which were set too close to cookstoves and inconveniently exploded.

The Sanitary Commission set up shop in Tyson's warehouse to store and package food and supplies. Donations were "too numerous to describe," noted *The Examiner,* and by October 1 the organizers had enough assembled to send forty wagonloads of goods on to Middletown, Boonsboro, Keedysville, and Sharpsburg.[85] Steiner was pleased to report the prompt arrival of "28,763 pieces of dry goods . . . 30 barrels of old linen bandages and lint; 3,188 pounds farina; 2,620 pounds of condensed milk; 5,000 pounds beef stock and canned meats; 3,000 bottles wine and cordials, and several tons of lemons and other fruit, crackers, tea, sugar, rubber cloth, tin cups, and hospital conveniences."[86] The Sanitary Commission shipments alleviated untold suffering and helped speed ill and wounded men toward recovery. "You need not send fruit and things," Rutherford B. Hayes wrote his mother. "I get all I need without trouble."[87]

In Sharpsburg, civilians were glad enough to receive the additional supplies—and to send the wounded on to Frederick as soon as they could. The hospitals slowly emptied as the weeks passed following the battle of Antietam. The ambulances creaked over the winding mountain roads with less frequency. But Jeremiah Kuhn, who kept the post office, and James Snyder, who hauled the mail to and from Sharpsburg by stage, were kept busy handling the convalescent soldiers' letters. Packages of books, pickles, religious tracts, and cordials arrived from all over the country. Gravediggers were still in demand. New cemeteries blossomed and grew near the hospitals. Aaron Fry, a carpenter who helped with many of the burials, developed a grisly sideline: digging up bodies when grieving relatives came to find their loved ones. Hundreds of the dead were retrieved and sent home for burial, although it was not always possible. One father, a member of the 21st Connecticut, got leave from his unit in order to search for the grave of his eighteen-year-old son, who had been killed at Burnside's Bridge. It could not be found. "Oh how dreadful was that place to me," he wrote, "where my dear boy had been buried like a beast of the field!"[88]

In field hospitals, churches, and schoolgirls' bedrooms, seriously wounded men lingered for weeks. Local people did what they could. Some

*Like most churches in Frederick, the Evangelical Lutheran Church was hastily converted into a hospital after the battle of Antietam. This rare photo shows how planks were placed over the pews, then cots put on the planks.* COURTESY THE EVANGELICAL CHURCH, FREDERICK.

mothers took their children to help cheer the lonely men, far from their own families. "Though being but a little tot I was a daily visitor in the Lutheran church," wrote a Middletown woman in 1899, "and it was my delight to take something to the wounded soldiers." Wounded fathers who were well enough told stories to the children, gave them gifts of testaments or carvings, and wondered if their own children had grown so tall.

Otis Smith of the Sixth Alabama remembered with gratitude an "old German farm couple" who came to the schoolhouse near South Mountain where he was being tended with wagonloads of food for the Southern soldiers. The farm wife cooked nourishing meals for the emaciated boys, serving them up on Delft china. Once they brought a niece with them, "so pretty, modest, gentle, sunny and helpful," wrote Smith, "that in less than half an hour every mother's son of us had broken the first commandment." Smith's clothes had been so saturated with blood when he was carried from the field that they had been removed, and he sweated through the hot days clad only in a wool blanket. Smith and the young lady both suffered an embarrassing moment when she unknowingly tried to remove the blanket, but she later sent her sweetheart, a young schoolteacher, back with spare clothes.[89]

The women visiting the hospitals each day ached for the suffering men. They sang hymns for the wounded, wrote letters for them, let the home-sick boys talk of mothers and sweethearts. They cut locks of hair from dying men to send home and carefully placed the frail comfort of blurry tintypes of wives and children in the men's hands as they passed away. One Massachusetts boy asked a woman to help him learn the Lord's Prayer before he died.[90] Mrs. Thomas Maught helped Benjamin Prather, a seriously wounded Georgian, write a letter to his wife:

The women and men are so good to me. They bring us hot bread, soup and meat for all meals. They cook in three big butchering pots in the carriage yard. The boys bring us ice from the ice house up the street. . . . The Dunkard preacher Pastor Emmanuel Silfer sees us every day. He loaned me his pen and ink. Mrs. Amanda Silfer, the pastor's wife, brings me her bible every morning. The women and girls sing for us every evening and Pastor Moses A. Stewart of this church prays.[91]

For the enlisted men, without refined quarters and care, the lengthening autumn created new hardships. "The nights grew bitterly cold," remembered one New Englander camped near Sharpsburg until the end of October. "The sick grew numerous. Many were sick with typhoid fever, and our condition at all times in this camp was mentally, morally, and physically bad."92 Disease swept mercilessly through the field hospitals, swelling the number of patients needing care. "In a miserable little log-house near the Potomac," one volunteer wrote, "thirty men lay upon the floor, ill with fever; some had a little straw, but no pillows were to be found; at that time it was unavoidable, but their food was hardly fit for well men; medicines very scarce;—this house the counterpart of many others, both as to occupants, food, etc."93 Isabella Morrison Fogg, a Maine volunteer who arrived in early November to inspect the hospitals, described Smoketown Hospital "in the midst of [a] driving snowstorm . . . the poor fellows huddled together, with their pallets of straw on the ground, their tents connected by flyes . . . many without walls and no stoves. Those who were able to creep out of their tents were crouched over fires, built in the woods, their heads covered with snow. And *all* I may say, almost without exception with thin muslin shirts on." Of another stop she wrote simply, "The misery and suffering beggars all description, the heart sickens at the sight."94

Taking care of soldiers in such conditions was not an easy task. At one farm north of Sharpsburg, sixty sick and wounded soldiers shivered in the barn. When the farm wife became ill, it fell to her young daughter to feed the surgeons staying there and tend to other domestic needs, as well. The girl's father, who had some medical training, administered quinine and whiskey to the patients. When he got sick, too, the daughter also took up that duty. "[Father] showed me a chart of the barn [that] showed the position of each patient on the floor and he indicated in that way which medicine I was to administer to each," she explained later. "I successfully performed this duty but it was not an agreeable one for after each visit I would be covered with vermin. . . . The hospital made it sickly at our home. Although the greatest care was taken and disinfectants were used liberally all about the house, my little sister was taken with typhoid fever and was very ill."95

The shock of those September days took a toll on anyone of fragile health. On October 26 the Roulettes, who had huddled in their cellar while the armies literally fought over their heads, lost daughter Carrie May—"a charming little girl twenty months old . . . just beginning to talk," William Roulette wrote.96 Ada Mumma's mother, Jane Rohrback Mumma,

The tents pitched in a grove of trees about two miles north-northeast of the Dunker Church became known as Smoketown Hospital, the largest field hospital in the area. The woman walking beside the stretcher bearers has been identified as "Miss Hall." A reporter who observed Miss Hall and two other ladies dispense supplies and tend the wounded wrote, "The place of women at the bedside of suffering, can never be supplied by more professional attendance of the other sex." Photo possibly by A. H. Messinger. COURTESY EDWARD G. MINER LIBRARY, UNIVERSITY OF ROCHESTER MEDICAL CENTER, NEW YORK.

was pregnant when she was forced to flee her home with her family. On October 10 Jane delivered a baby girl, Mary Jane, who was either stillborn or lived less than a day. Jane herself died on November 10, her fifth wedding anniversary. Ada explained later, "My mother, due to the great amount of excitement, was taken ill and died." Ada was raised by her grandparents.[97]

The army doctors' authority to take charge of many houses in Sharpsburg and the surrounding area brought additional layers of misery to families already in shock. It was bad enough to come home and find surgeons at work on their kitchen tables, severed limbs piling beneath windows; it was even worse to learn that their homes might be unavailable to them for days or weeks. "The doctors would huddle the family all into one little room or turn 'em out," Jacob McGraw said. "The house across the way from mine was a hospital, and the family there got what the doctors called camp fever, and some of 'em died."[98] Wagonmaker Adam Michael's family was hit hard. During the battle Adam and Nancy Michael and five of their six children— Samuel, Elizabeth, Ann, Catherine, and Caleb—lived on the corner of East Main and North Church Streets. Another son, David, had moved to Indiana. The Michaels were staunch Confederates and resisted the Federal surgeon's plan to turn their home into a hospital. Samuel, a farmhand, told David in a letter how it happened: "Elizabeth took sick and died from the tyfoid fever. She had been sick . . . I was certain that she was going to recover. . . . They forced a Hospital in our house. Kate and Mother fought them hard. And she heard it upstairs and it frightened her and she just gave way and . . . died."[99] Elizabeth died of fever on October 24, 1862. Her mother, Nancy, died a month later, on November 25. Caleb Michael was also afflicted with typhoid fever, and although he survived, he "never fully recovered."[100] The Michaels lived across the street from Jacob Miller. The provost guard detail had been billeted in Jacob's cellar and inexplicably added to the Michaels' grief by not immediately allowing them to remove Elizabeth's body for burial.

Jacob had weathered tremendous losses on his agricultural properties, but he and daughter Savilla managed to stay well. Still, they had their own loss to mourn: Jacob's brother Daniel. "He departed from us on Sunday 16th day of November . . .," Jacob wrote his daughter. "He was not well when he left home, the day before the big battle. . . . After he got back he was taken with a diarear [sic] which was a very comon complaint with the troops and Citizens. Both armies were afflicted with the disease. . . . He appeared anxious this warfare should be settled but now it is nothing to him whether it is settled or not." Jacob noted the Michaels' losses before continuing the litany of illness:

> Hellen and Janet have had a severe attack of tayfoy fevour. . . . Jacob and Annmary's children nearly all or perhaps all had Scarlet fevour . . . Henry Mummas wife is no more, she departed this life about two weeks since, she had the same fevour. Nearly all or quite all of John Smith family wore down but are getting better. Many other citizens and hundreds of soldiers have been taken with the same, and many died. It is an army disease thus adds an addition to the Horrors of war.[101]

Epidemics ravaged the county for months. "The small pox is in town . . . ," Otho Nesbitt noted four months after the battle. "'Tis said there is one or 200 hundred cases in Hagerstown, Persons are getting vaccinated everywhere."[102] A young woman at the Hagerstown Seminary, which was used as a hospital until January 1863, wrote, "The small pox that terrible disease is fearfully on the increase in town and even those that have been vaccinated have taken it. I dread it very much."[103]

It was hard for civilians to piece their lives back together when the devastation and horror seemed to linger. The shallow graves weren't sufficient, and residents frequently came across gruesome reminders of September 17. "It was a common thing to see human bones lying loose in gutters and fence corners for several years," Mr. C. M. Keedy recalled, "and frequently hogs would be seen with limbs in their mouths."[104] Blood needed to be scrubbed from walls, from floors, from doorsteps, from kitchen tables. The mess of ransacked homes—broken crockery, torn clothing, splintered furniture—had to be dealt with. Shattered trees had to be hauled away and scattered bricks gathered. One man came home to discover that the soldiers who had butchered the family's sixty chickens had done so in their kitchen. "They were dirty butchers," he wrote, "and the floor was ankle deep easy with heads and feet, entrails and feathers."[105]

The litter of battle also had to be removed. Once the dead humans and horses had been disposed of mountains of equipment remained: broken caissons, discarded haversacks, overturned supply wagons, all needing to be carted off or burned. Alex Davis remembered hauling wagonloads of broken guns, swords, cartridge boxes, shells, old canteens, and other debris to the Nicodemus farm and pitching them down an abandoned well.[106] More were burned, thrown in refuse heaps, or carted off as relics. "I never remember seeing a stove poker in my grandmother's home," wrote Virginia Mumma Hildebrand in 1958. "She used bayonets instead."[107] For years Sharpsburg children played with the debris of war as other children played with dolls or jacks.

The debris also included an abundance of weapons and other deadly souvenirs of war that the local children found irresistible. In Middletown, little boys found a wealth of guns theirs for the taking after the battle at South Mountain. "Frequently the cartridge and cap boxes of the soldiers at the Hospitals here have been rifled by some of them for ammunition," reported the *Valley Register*. When little Melvin Corrick was shot by another boy, the town commissioners passed an ordinance prohibiting all boys under the age of sixteen from carrying or discharging any firearm.[108]

Shells were another potentially lethal find. After the battle of Antietam, hundreds of shells were carted from farm fields and dumped in Antietam Creek. Still, farmers kept turning them over with their plowshares and picking them out of wheat stacks when threshing. The shells sometimes broke the machinery, but the farmers considered themselves lucky if they didn't explode. In addition to the exhausting and numbing work with soldiers in the hospitals, local physician Augustin Biggs was too often called to attend civilians who had become latent shell victims. And again, children were irresistibly attracted to these deadly souvenirs. Young William McDermot of Porterstown found a shell and placed it in the kitchen cookstove; the resulting explosion blew the stove to bits, blinded him, and tore off his arm. George Reilly carried a shell down to the stream near Keedysville before setting fire to it, but the explosion sent shrapnel flying within a few inches of several civilians some distance away. Reverend Shuford and his wife, who lost three children to diphtheria sometime between 1857 and 1864, lost their oldest son, Alvah, when a shell he was playing with exploded. Mr. John Keplinger, who lived near Bloody Lane, reputedly gathered and destroyed ninety-nine shells before the hundreth one exploded. He "was terribly torn," recalled the Newcomer daughter who helped Dr. Biggs attend him, and he died from his wounds.[109] Ada Mumma Thomas said later that numerous people were killed handling shells after the battle.

Some confusion exists about whether any civilians were killed outright during the battle of Antietam. Virginia Mumma Hildebrand, who collected civilian accounts in the twentieth century, wrote confidently, "Strange as it may seem, not a single citizen of Sharpsburg was killed during the entire bloody battle."[110] But by several accounts, a young Sharpsburg girl was killed on September 17.[111] And Adam Koogle wrote of the young black girl who died during the fighting in Middletown. A number of civilians died of disease in the days and weeks following the battle, and trauma was believed to have contributed to several other civilian deaths, such as Ada Mumma's mother and newborn sister. Compounded by the dormant devastation of exploding shells, the civilian death toll was high enough.

*A woman, possibly "Miss Hall," can be seen tending patients in one of the tents at Smoketown Hospital. Dr. William Child, assistant surgeon of the Fifth New Hampshire Infantry, was one of the surgeons who labored at Smoketown. "To the feeling man this war is truly a tragedy," he wrote, "but to the thinking man it must appear a madness." Photo possibly by A. H. Messinger.* COURTESY EDWARD G. MINER LIBRARY, UNIVERSITY OF ROCHESTER MEDICAL CENTER, NEW YORK.

# CHAPTER 8

# "Broken Hearts Can't Be Photographed"

President Abraham Lincoln arrived at Sharpsburg on October 1, where he spent four days viewing the field and prodding General George McClellan. While visiting several hospitals, he shook hands with Union and Confederate men alike. One of his stops was Stephen P. and Maria Grove's beautiful farm, Mount Airy. The Grove children had been sent to Shepherdstown during the battle, but Stephen and Maria had stayed to protect their property, despite repeated requests to leave by the Union soldiers establishing a signal station on their roof. According to family lore, when a well-intentioned officer told Maria that a lady couldn't stay at the house, she responded, "Sir, if a lady can't, a woman can!" Confined to a single room, Stephen and Maria weathered the battle safely. They later saw wagonloads of wounded men brought to their house and barns. Within a week of the battle, four hundred soldiers were recuperating or dying there. Federal major general Fitz John Porter had also located his headquarters at Mount Airy during the Confederate retreat.

During his visit, Lincoln reviewed a detachment of Michigan cavalry camped in the Groves' orchard, then met the family. With his hand resting on the head of seven-year-old Louisa, Lincoln expressed regrets to the Groves. The wounded Confederates lying on piles of straw in Maria's parlor also had the opportunity to shake Lincoln's hand, and most were deeply moved by the president's expression of goodwill.[1] Lincoln then visited McClellan in the commander's tent on the Groves' lawn. Photographer Alexander Gardner captured that awkward meeting on one of his glass plates, with the farmhouse just visible in the background. Those photographs are the enduring record of Lincoln's visit. Evidently none were made of the president visiting the wounded. But as the *New York Times* reviewer wrote when Mathew Brady exhibited Gardner's work later that month, "Broken hearts cannot be photographed."[2]

President Abraham Lincoln hoped to wring some greater good out of Sharpsburg's devastation. Emancipation of the slaves had long been on the country's mind, and Lincoln—who held preservation of the Union above any other cause—had written a draft of the Emancipation Proclamation two months before the battle of Antietam. At that time, however, the Union army was retreating, and government officials feared the proclamation would appear to the world as a desperate last bid for victory. Lincoln agreed to wait.

Tactically, the issue of who had won or lost at Antietam was debatable. In the campaign as a whole, the Confederate army lost roughly fourteen thousand men; the Union army, almost twenty-seven thousand. The South considered the battle a draw. But strategically, many Federals interpreted the retreat of Lee's army back to Virginia as a Union victory.

That "victory" at Sharpsburg, nebulous as it had been, also provided the momentum Lincoln needed to emancipate the slaves. He hoped the proclamation would prohibit European powers from aiding the Confederacy and unite the politically divided North. The preliminary proclamation was made public a week after the battle. The great proclamation, however, freed only the slaves in those states presently in rebellion against the government. Slaves in loyal border states—including Maryland—remained slaves.

>─┤◆├─○─┤◆├─<

In addition to the hundreds of patients lingering in makeshift hospitals, the Yankee army remained on the field for weeks. The Union presence, at first so reassuring, became a source of tension even for the loyal families. Men got drunk, got loud, got boisterous. Provost guards raided saloons that served soldiers, dumping barrels of whiskey in the streets. "Some of the boys . . . dipped it out of the gutter with tin cups," wrote Daniel Mowen of the Seventh Maryland with some disgust, after a raid in Williamsport.[3] Boys visiting the camps stared with fascinated horror at soldiers bucked and gagged for unruly conduct.

Continued thievery was another cause of strain. "An old woman came up this morning examining all our tents for a tin bucket she had lost," wrote David Strother in his diary on September 20. "She says a soldier borrowed it for General McClellan. Some waggish thief has doubtless visited her."[4] It was a time when the loss of a tin bucket could be catastrophic.

And families trying to tend business, help haul wounded, clean up, or find relatives still had to guard their horses carefully. The cavalry of both armies grew more desperate for horses as the campaign wore on. In addition to battle casualties and horses crippled by being ridden shoeless on the limestone-rich soil and rough roads, an equine epidemic swept through the camps. "The result was disastrous," recalled a member of the First Massachusetts Cavalry. "Nearly half of the horses of the Army of the Potomac were rendered unserviceable, and vast numbers died. The same disease raged in the horses of the Confederate army. . . . The regiment within two weeks from the battle of Antietam was practically unhorsed."[5]

Above all else, troops and their horses needed food. The same cavalryman noted that between September 4 and September 19, rations were received only once. Unfortunately, the families near Sharpsburg had little to spare, but officers continued to order the seizure of some livestock. Union men bivouacked on the Piper farm for several weeks after the battle. "During this time," Mary Ellen Piper said later, "all cattle and sheep on the farm were taken and used by U.S. military forces. The sheep were all taken the day after we returned home. The hogs and cattle were slaughtered at different times. I remember four of the calves were slaughtered in the orchard back of the blacksmith shop."[6]

Even men who received rations looked for better fare. Civilian entrepreneurs quickly tried to fill the gap between soldiers' appetites and army food. Some farmers removed from the armies' path but close enough to haul produce made tremendous profits. John Koogle lugged apples, potatoes, and a barrel of cider to Sharpsburg on October 17; he got seven dollars for the cider.[7] Some of the local women also charged the men for plates of stew or loaves of bread, much to the professional sutlers' dismay. Austin Stearns of the 13th Massachusetts was willing to pay cash, but the going price was around fifty cents for supper, twenty-five cents for a loaf of bread, and some civilians were reluctant to accept the new "greenbacks" he had to offer. "I remember waiting 2 or 3 hours for my turn to get a corn-cake baked," he wrote, "and then after I received it could not make change. I took the cake and gave my promise to pay the next time I came around, but thus far have not been around since."[8]

The soldiers resented wartime inflation. One Yankee camped on Stephen Grove's farm complained that the sutlers and traders "asked exorbitant prices for everything. One dollar a pound for butter, six small cakes for fifty cents, etc. was a fair sample of the outrageous advantage and monopoly which these non-combatant sharks seized upon."[9] Some of the soldiers vented their ire on the peddlers themselves, stealing when they could or looking for other means of mischief. Allen Sparrow (who made a quick fourteen dollars hauling knapsacks from Middletown to Clear Spring for some soldiers) noted that some of his neighbors, who made "considrabal money" baking pies for the troops, were taken to task when the customers felt the price rose too high:

> The soldiers served some that they thought wanted to take advantage of them . . . they would give them what they cald a winding. . . . They would take a blanket and lay the one on it and then one at each corner, they would toss him up in the air till the breath was nearly out of him. Sometimes one would let his corner go and let [the] victim fall. The one that got treated to a winding hardly ever went to trade with that regement again but would look out for a new place to sell his pies.[10]

But the final burden of inflation fell not on the sutlers or soldiers but on local farm families, for high prices simply compelled most soldiers to look elsewhere. "Foraging was resorted to," admitted Austin Stearns, who objected to the farm wives' prices. "To a considerable extent Turkeys, Geese, and Chickens were taken whenever found, corn-cakes, bread, ham, and smoked sides with butter, apple butter, and in fact every thing that was eatable was procured."[11]

Six-year-old Hanna Marion Johnson long remembered the day soldiers came to his family's home along the C&O Canal and began tearing down the hog pen:

> Mother told one of the boys to run up over the hill and get an officer. She grabbed an axe and ran out after the men. She bluffed them away from the hogs until the officer came. He sent the men back to the camp and told her if any more came to molest her, she would be within her rights to kill them because they had orders not to destroy or steal.[12]

Hogs were prized bounty, and not all owners were as bold—or fortunate—as Mrs. Johnson. Henry B. James of the 32nd Massachusetts Volunteers stood patiently with his comrades while an officer read general orders forbidding all foraging in Maryland. But while on the march, they couldn't resist temptation when they passed a pigsty. Waiting until he thought a passing general was out of earshot, James shot one of the pigs—and was promptly arrested. The dead hog was not given to the family, however. The vigilant officer ordered the culprits to carry the hog on their long march and, much to their dismay, it became supper for the general and his staff that night.[13] Some civilians appealed to military authorities to help protect livestock and late crops, although if guards were furnished, the family was expected to feed those men as well. But few residents were even given that choice. "Perhaps we were better enabled to obtain the services of guards," recalled one woman, "from the fact that generally there were officers occupying the house who were anxious upon their own account to keep something in the larder."[14]

Warren Goss, a New Englander who published his recollections in 1890, had harsh words for the Southern soldiers who had preceded his unit in occupying Sharpsburg. "The people had had a hard time, and the contrast between our treatment of them, and that of the Confederate army (who had made levies of food upon them, and their marauders who had plundered them unmercifully) was so great that I think it must have cured them forever of any desire to make common cause with those in rebellion." And yet, he went on to add, "The corn which we gathered in the fields (oft-times without permission) gave us hasty-pudding and johnny-cake."[15]

The countryside was full of stragglers, men too sick or disheartened to remain with their regiments, and they were a particular source of concern to the rural residents. Three men deserted from the 13th Pennsylvania Cavalry and embarked on a thieving spree in Boonsboro, for example, and two local men had to chase them to Waynesboro, Pennsylvania, before they were apprehended.[16] As the number of depredations increased, armed patrols were established and directed to arrest any soldier found absent from his unit without a written pass. When that proved ineffective, General McClellan reminded his subordinate officers that the Union army was occupying a "loyal state" and announced that he was holding them responsible for any violations of his orders against foraging. A correspondent for *The New York Times* had perhaps the most unbiased observation. "The indiscriminate plundering by soldiers," he wrote, "has resulted in creating and increasing local support for the Confederates, even among many of the area's lukewarm Unionists."[17] McClellan did not move his army until October 26, almost six weeks after the battle. Although a few Federal troops remained in the area to guard the vulnerable fords, most civilians were relieved to see the bulk of the army cross the Potomac.[18]

And when the cursing teamsters and tramping infantry and jingling cavalry finally departed, the valley was silent. One man recalled:

> You couldn't hear a dog bark nowhere, you couldn't hear no birds whistle or no crows caw. There wasn't no birds around till the next spring. We didn't even see a buzzard with all the stench. . . . The farmers didn't have no chickens to crow. . . . When night come I was so lonesome that I see I didn't know what lonesome was before. It was a curious silent world.[19]

Like those in flesh and bone, the wounds lingering in the Antietam valley's landscape would take time to heal. Those left behind were left to confront, as one observer put it, "the whole country forlorn and desolate."[20] A twelve-mile stretch of the C&O Canal had been severely damaged with floodgates destroyed, and an attempt had been made to blow up the Monocacy aqueduct. In addition to the Middletown bridge, which had been burned by the retreating Confederates, the B&O Railroad bridge over the Monocacy had also been destroyed. Miles of railroad tracks had been rendered useless, telegraph lines cut.

Familiar landmarks were gone. Residents out after dark often got lost in the torn landscape. Farmers born and raised near Sharpsburg and who had seldom been farther from home than Hagerstown could scarcely recognize their own land. With fences demolished, it was hard to tell where one man's land ended and another's began, and supply trains and artillery caissons had made new roads across fields in every direction.

Indeed, the very earth—the soil so revered by true farmers—was despoiled. Years after the battle two sisters recalled how, when walking in the Sunken Road near the Roulette farm, they had slipped in pools of blood that still remained. "This story is vouched for by many other residents and soldiers," wrote Oliver Reilly, "for at the time of the battle there was blood that pushed its way through the dust for some distance."[21] According to local tradition, for months after the battle when it rained, "the water was red running down Bloody Lane"—an ever-present reminder of the physical and emotional stains of the battle.[22]

Winter came early in 1862, with an October snowstorm that surprised everyone. It was a grim warning of the hard months ahead for families who had lost everything. The Federal government was willing to take responsibility for damage caused by Federal troops, but those families whose homes had by chance been damaged or destroyed by the Confederate army were unable to make claims.

On October 6 Brigadier General John F. Reynolds appointed three soldiers to survey the farms of Samuel Mumma, William Roulette, and Henry Piper to assess the damage. They determined that foodstuffs and personal goods had been destroyed by the Confederates, but Union troops were responsible for most of the loss of or damage to fences, grain, and hay. Samuel Mumma was still petitioning the government for payment in 1867. The Union officer who had confiscated supplies had assured him that no receipt for his goods was needed—a point hard to prove five years later. A letter explained that Mumma hadn't pressed the officer for receipts because of "his feebleness in body and inexperience in such matters . . . as well as the great distress and trouble which . . . [he] would necessarily have on account of the great destruction of his property, the fruit of a long life of labor, toil, and trouble."[23]

Most claims required years of litigation before the supplicant received even part of what had been lost. Henry Piper finally sued the Federal government for damages in 1886. Piper had submitted an initial war claim itemizing just twenty-five dollars for his house and barn but requested over four thousand dollars for the destruction of his household furnishings, clothing, supplies, crops, livestock, and fencing. The detailed inventory reveals vandalism and theft, for listed among the hay and bacon and chickens are goblets and decanters, daguerreotypes, two fine shawls, and sixty dollars worth of "ladies' wear." In 1863 most of the Piper clan moved into Sharpsburg, leaving son Samuel to tend the farm. Samuel purchased the property from his father in 1892.[24]

The Jacob Houser family wasn't able to move back into their home until extensive work had been done, and they had lost all of the food stored up for the coming winter as well as eight hundred bushels of threshed wheat. Soldiers had turned a drove of cattle loose in the Houser cornfield, and their hay had been lost, as well. "The only thing my wife and I had left," Mr. Houser said, "was five hungry children." Jacob totaled his losses and submitted a bill for nearly three thousand dollars. After years of fighting with the government, he received a little over eight hundred dollars.[25]

The Sherrick house had been occupied by Rebel sharpshooters on September 18 and was subsequently attacked by a cavalry squadron, which quickly drove the "Johnnies" out of the house like *"rats."* The next morning, one of the Yankee soldiers visited the house: "It had been hastily evacuated, as it was between the lines. The foragers ahead of us had pulled out what edibles it contained, and among them a splendid assortment of jellies, preserves, etc. the pride of every Maryland woman's heart." The soldiers seized the sticky crocks, shoveling whatever was left into their mouths with happy abandon. "No crowd of schoolboys . . . ever acted so absurdly as did these rough, bronzed soldiers and recruit allies, on that death-strewn ground about Sherrick's yard and orchard."[26] Joseph Sherrick and his wife, Sarah, returned to a shambles, but at least they had a home—plus three thousand dollars that Joseph had hidden in the stone wall. A house was more than their neighbors the Mummas could claim, so the Sherricks generously moved to Boonsboro, allowing the devastated Mumma family to stay in their rural home until the following spring. The Mummas' home and barn had been burned, destroying all of the family's personal belongings, crops, and livestock. Samuel Mumma's damage estimate exceeded ten thousand dollars, but since the house had been torched by Confederates, the Federal government simply absolved itself of any responsibility. The following spring Samuel managed to begin construction of a new dwelling and barn.[27]

The Pry family, who had left their home in the hands of George McClellan and his staff during the battle, returned to find relatively few battle scars. But the Union occupation of the Pry land was another matter: All crops were destroyed, all fields trampled, all edibles consumed. Pry estimated the loss at $2,459. He did not receive his first payment until 1865.[28]

Jacob McGraw, whose brother was in the Southern army, lost almost everything to the Confederates. "Stragglers were running around robbing the houses of people who'd gone away, and they got in my house and just took everything," he said. "Besides, they took five mules of mine out of a field where I kept 'em. Them were mules that did my towing on the canal."[29] That loss destroyed McGraw's livelihood as a boatman on the C&O Canal.

The battle had many lingering effects on the local economy. Some people started carrying two purses—one filled with U.S. greenbacks and the other filled with Confederate scrip, never sure who would demand what type of currency. The agricultural and mercantile losses plus the influx of currency while the Federal troops were in the valley combined to bring sharp inflation to the local economy; staples such as salt, sugar, and coffee were unavailable at any price. To survive their losses, many men mortgaged their land, bearing interest charges of 8 to 10 percent. Others borrowed money at a rate of fifty to seventy-five cents on the dollar, which had to be repaid at one hundred cents on the dollar. Speculators descended quickly, buying Confederate notes at a fraction of their worth before crossing the Potomac and spending the money on supplies.[30] Many farmers and merchants were left with fistfuls of Confederate money, and local currency fluctuated wildly. In Frederick, Dr. Lewis Steiner fumed about merchants who took advantage of others. "The wealthiest grocer in town raised the price of coffee to 75c., and brown sugar to 40c/lb., to be paid in gold or our own currency," he scribbled in his diary. "This outrageous attempt to take advantage of the troublous condition of the community has excited considerable indignation."[31] Desperate women watched prices rise, felt the cold weather descending, and wondered how they were going to feed their families.

The 1862 Maryland military campaign was as politically complex as the state itself—and educational for many of the men who marched there. George Templeton Strong, for example, received lodging in Hagerstown with a family who offered "a frank cordiality and kindness beyond all my experience. They only knew we were Union men and engaged in some kind of work for the army. . . . They have a son in the rebel army! But one must go into the Debatable Land to see full-blooded, genuine Union feeling."[32]

On the other hand, in the numbing hours after the battle, a Southern surgeon and a Northern medical steward became involved in a dispute that led to challenges of an immediate duel, and only intervention by a Sister of Charity—who took their pistols—put an end to it.[33] Fortunately the surgeons working at the Stephen Grove farm after the battle experienced a different cultural meeting. "A large tent was erected in [Mr. Grove's] yard for the wounded and the medical officers of both armies ate together, drank together, and slept together, and had a high old time," wrote one North Carolina surgeon wistfully in 1901. "Several of us slept in the garret of Mr.

Grove's house." Surely that camaraderie was as unexpected and pleasurable for the Northern surgeons as well.[34]

The campaign had produced some memorable reunions. Southern soldiers came home to visit friends and family, some for the first time since the war's beginning. Young women saw their sweethearts, mothers their sons. After Harpers Ferry fell to the Confederate army, Joseph McGraw, the Sharpsburg soldier serving with a Southern artillery unit, visited the camp to call on old friends and schoolmates who had been captured.[35]

But not all the meetings between Northern and Southern sympathizers were pleasant ones. The military occupation heightened fears and suspicions. Many of the Rebel soldiers' depredations took place, the victims believed, at the urging of sympathetic civilians. Aaron Cost was ordered "at the point of a pistol" to hand his five horses over to soldiers or sympathizers.[36] Mr. Neikirk's ordeal, with Confederate soldiers attempting to hang him for hiding his horses, was believed to have been prompted by sympathizers, as well. The Grice's pony Logan was one of reportedly only three horses left in Sharpsburg after the battle, and he was stolen five times— several times by neighbors, who ransomed him back to the family.[37]

The animosity went both ways. Although Jacob Houser was described as being pro-Union, neighbors told the Federal soldiers camped on the Houser farm that he was a Confederate. The troops destroyed much of the Housers' personal property, "and what was left was hauled away by their neighbors and kept. Mrs. Houser was so terrified by that turn of events that she became ill, and kept to her bed for weeks."[38] Several neighbors visited Mayberry Beeler one night after the battle, threatening to burn his barn because he was "a Rebel sympathizer." By fortunate chance a Union officer who had been wounded and helped by Beeler intervened. "A man that does for the Union soldier as Mr. Beeler has done for me is no Rebel," he said—and the barn was saved.[39]

In Frederick, four young secessionist ladies made secret plans to take clothing and delicacies to Confederate friends being held prisoner in Hagerstown. Enroute they were surrounded by a squad of Union riders, who promptly escorted them to the Hagerstown provost marshal. "After much questioning, we were taken into another room and a strict search was made of our persons by a hard-eyed woman . . . ," wrote one of the girls. "Every article of clothing we wore was subjected to the strictest scrutiny, and we were even compelled to remove our shoes and stockings and take down our hair, before she was satisfied that we had no contraband articles on us." The gifts were confiscated and the women were detained overnight before being sent home. "We returned to Frederick burning with indignation, and a high resolve to discover who had informed on us, but we were never any the wiser."[40]

Numerous arrests had taken place before the Antietam campaign; numerous men had been hauled before the provost guard to answer questions or sent rattling off to the dank cells of Fort McHenry in the cars. But having the Confederates on Maryland soil, with all the incumbent opportunities to visit or assist, provided new names for informers. People accused of aiding the Confederates during the campaign were arrested. Union guards arrested civilians for offering food or unauthorized medical aid to Rebels. Known Confederate sympathizers like Fred Markell made themselves scarce. In October the editor of *The Examiner*—back from his skedaddle—published the names of fifteen Frederick men who, he claimed, had promised General Lee that Maryland would rise in support of the Confederate army, then faded from sight, prompting feelings of betrayal among the Rebels. Among the names was Frederick Markell: "Fred Markell marched away with the rebel horde, and appears to be the only man among them with a grain of spirit." The other men were painted as cowards, some greedy or drunken, as well.

Fred hadn't joined the army, but his absence was an agony of suspense for his wife, Catherine. "The anniversary of our wedding day," she wrote in her diary on November 27. "I cannot join in the general thanksgiving, my heart is too sad—I'd rather fast and pray—my beloved husband is absent and I know not where he is." Her anxiety continued for several more weeks. Then, on December 19 he came home: "About ten o'clock PM whilst gazing at my dear husband's picture I heard footsteps. . . . I went to the back hall door and there he stood, my beloved one—Thank Heaven he has returned safe and sound." The next day she visited the provost marshal to ascertain if Fred could safely remain at home. Fred evidently escaped arrest, but on February 4, 1863, *The Examiner* printed a telling notice: "Mr. A. B. McCaffrey purchased stock, etc of Frederick Markell's Dry goods establishment."[41]

Fred Markell was a prominent businessman and Confederate sympathizer, likely to attract attention. But in the after-battle excitement, fingers were pointed in many directions. In October a Frederick coal dealer named Benjamin Brown was arrested, taken to Washington, and charged with "aiding and assisting the Rebels"—or, as Jacob Engelbrecht noted, "for Some offence against the 'Peace, Government & dignity of the United States.'"[42] In 1861 Brown had received permission from local authorities to make a trip to Lynchburg, Virginia, to pursue an insurance claim, and the family had been asked to care for some Confederate wounded during the 1862 campaign. Upon his arrest, his wife, Dorcas, found herself abruptly alone, left to tend to the children—Florence, Fannie, and Willie—and to manage business affairs until her husband's return. Dorcas went to Washington and tried without success to obtain a pass to see Benjamin. "The Sec. War refused me a pass," she wrote to him on November 6. "I really thought my heart would break. . . . I felt as though I was coming from your grave." Three days later she sent another letter. "We all miss you badly. Home is not home without you. I hope you will soon have a hearing, and be permitted to come home to your distressed family. Bennie I am sad and lonely, the world looks dark and gloomy, if it were not for our dear little children who occupy my attention, I should lose my senses." Dorcas and the children sent packages and mail, and were further upset with the news that Benjamin hadn't received any of them.

The letters jump from 1862 to 1864. It isn't clear whether Brown was incarcerated for that entire time or arrested twice, but in May 1864 he wrote to Dorcas that the charges had been explained to him. "I had an interview with my counsel Mr. Wills yesterday," he wrote. "He informed me I am charged with having gone to Lynchburg. Also with having Rebel sick in my house &c." He asked Dorcas to look for letters of passage he had been given by the proper authorities regarding the trip to Lynchburg, and to ask the medical director to provide a certificate affirming that the Browns had been asked to care for the Confederates by military authorities. The Browns were able to provide the needed certification, including a list of prominent citizens willing to testify that Benjamin was a "loyal citizen of the United States," and on June 17 the attorney wrote Dorcas the news she had been aching to hear: Her husband had been acquitted. "Allow me to congratulate you all and especially Mrs. Brown," he wrote, "for the glorious privilege of her husband being again restored to her companionship and to the bosom of his family—God bless her! and may she never be called upon to undergo such trials again."[43]

The Browns' ordeal was painful but not uncommon. After the Confederate retreat, the Federal army quickly occupied Henry Kyd Douglas's beautiful home, Ferry Hill, high on the prominence above the Potomac, ripping down fences, running artillery through the wheat field, seizing hay and corn and fodder. He wrote:

My father, mother, and sister were prisoners in their own house, without the freedom from danger which prisoners usually enjoy. Unfortunately, there were two sons in the Confederacy and the sufferings of those at home must be vicarious; there are harder things to endure than battles and wounds. To invade his house at pleasure and search it as a whim, to enter the chambers of his wife and daughter, looking through the contents of bureaus and wardrobes and pitching beds upon the floor with bayonets, using brutal language to all the inmates—this was scarcely the way to improve the loyalty of the man of the house.

One evening in October, when the wind blew open a shutter, Mrs. Douglas passed in front of it with a candle while on her way to a sickroom. A sentinel spotted the brief flicker, and Mr. Douglas was arrested for "giving signals to the enemy." His frantic family was not told where he was being taken; the elderly minister was held for six weeks at Fort McHenry in Baltimore without being formally charged, an ordeal that Kyd Douglas believed robbed him of health and led to his death shortly after the war.[44]

A lockkeeper named Johnson was accused of sending messages to Rebels "when all he was doing," his son explained, "was checking the water level in the canal with a lantern." Mr. Johnson was held for several weeks.[45] Solomon Lumm, who operated a small mill near Sharpsburg, was arrested by members of the 45th Pennsylvania and accused of assisting Confederate sharpshooters who had occupied his mill. "They were going to use rough means with him," Oliver Reilly wrote, "but several of the citizens of this town interceded in his behalf and he was let go free again."[46]

Samuel Michael itemized his losses at "Yankey" hands as "upwards of 2 thousand dollars" and provided a sense of the times in a letter:

They have refused to pay us anything yet I have been arrested frequent[ly] by them. They held me once in Williamsport a while and in Martinsburg nine days. I was marched in the rain one whole day in water four feet deep and had to sleep in my wet clothes until they dried on me, and had to sleep on the floor in mud two or three inches deep. I was arrested by such men as Eli H—[illeg.] and Ed Saylor. These men you know have good caracters as well as I do. The charges was for helping the Rebels to capture a cannon. All of them was false and forged against me.[47]


Through bitter experience, men and women had lost faith in people who for years had been trusted neighbors and friends. "It realey does look as though some people are possessed with the devel or they have lost there cences," Allen Sparrow concluded in his diary in December 1862.[48] But in the tension of occupation and battle, emotions ran high and political differences exploded. Though financial losses were bad enough, those that couldn't be tallied in a ledger were perhaps even worse.

# CHAPTER 9

# "Deliver Us From This Terrible War"

The winter of 1862-1863 was a harsh string of snow, hail, mud, and more snow. By spring, people were yearning for warm weather. They were also yearning for peace. Men lingered over their newspapers. Women wrote letters to husbands who were becoming strangers. Children looked for distant places like Vicksburg, Mississippi, in their atlases. "This wicked & Sinful Rebellion must be Crushed-out, whether it takes ten years or twenty years, and no matter at what Price of money or lives," Jacob Engelbrecht wrote in his diary; but many of his neighbors felt the toll had already been high enough.[1]

In March 1863 the U.S. government, desperate for fighting men, instituted conscription. Five months earlier a local draft in Frederick—called since that county had not provided its portion of Maryland's quota—came to an ignominious conclusion when Dr. J. Moran, examining physician, was arrested for selling certificates of exemption.[2] The 1863 conscription met with little more success. Having gotten a good taste of war on their own doorsteps, many western Maryland men resisted the idea. Samuel D. Piper, Jacob Snyder, and Jacob Myers of Sharpsburg precipitated the idea of a possible draft by riding on horseback to Canada. They nearly drowned in a river crossing but ultimately succeeded in hiring Canadian men as substitutes, paying five hundred dollars for each.[3] Martin Line, who had lost one thousand dollars worth of horses to Confederate soldiers, paid eight hundred dollars for a substitute for his eldest son, Daniel.[4] A number of men found the necessary cash to hire substitutes; three brothers in the Kefauver family were drafted and purchased the services of other men to fill their places.[5]

Some Hagerstown businessmen made money from army contracts, and farmers removed from the battlefield watched with satisfaction as prices for their wheat and wool climbed. But those Sharpsburg farmers who hadn't already given up labored that spring to coax new life into fields "beaten down as hard as a turnpike road" by the army traffic the preceding fall. Men struggling to guide their plows found that the land broke only into "great clods and lumps."[6] They proved too much for the harrow, and farmers attacked them with axes and mallets as if mining for good soil. William Roulette, who had already provided the land needed to bury seven hundred soldiers, amended his damage claim to include nine acres of ground that could not be seeded "in consequence of the army."[7]

Many western Maryland civilians were still struggling to recover when they heard with dread the unwanted cries: "The Rebels have crossed the Potomac!" Once again the Confederate army plunged north, with the Federals panting in pursuit. Rumors raced through the valleys and hamlets. Herds of cattle and horses were driven north by dour farmers; in Clear Spring, thirty head of cattle stolen by Rebels were jubilantly retaken by Unionists and driven to safe haven in the mountains. "The Rebels have gutted all the towns around about except Clear Spring," Otho Nesbitt noted on June 25. "Everybody is buying all the groceries and everything they want for the next 6 months to come."[8]

The Federal troops guarding Frederick retreated only reluctantly. "We in our good City of Frederick are of Course all agog," Jacob Engelbrecht wrote in his diary.[9] On June 20 a squad of Confederate cavalry galloped into town. Some of the Confederate girls on West Patrick Street had been "sitting on the front stoop, looking down [their] noses at the Yankee Cavalrymen," eagerly awaiting their heroes. One described the sudden adventure in a letter:

> We were expecting [the Yankees] at any moment to get news of the approaching Confederate Army, and turn tail and run for the east bank of the Monocacy. . . . We heard the sound of musket fire coming from Bentztown, and soon here came the Yankee Cavalry galloping towards us with our boys in close pursuit. Both sides were firing as they galloped, and we girls were so excited we failed to realize the danger we were in. Fortunately, we became aware of people shouting at us from behind shuttered windows, and we ducked into the doorway.

The girl's sister and cousins sought shelter in the hall, and tugged at her skirts to follow them, but she was so thrilled she kept her head poked outside—until a minié ball hit a rainspout, inches from her head. "I didn't need any more tugging on my dress," she wrote. "I jumped in the hall and slammed the door."[10] Jacob Engelbrecht also happened to be on the street that morning as the cavalrymen "came by in full speed firing as fast as they Could."[11] Ultimately the Confederates retreated west of town. People held their breaths, wondering if the unthinkable could happen twice.

For a brief time it looked like the confrontation might come at Emmitsburg, a pretty Maryland community near the Pennsylvania line. The soldiers who passed through took note of the large convent there. Most of the students had long since been sent home, and most of the Sisters of Charity residing there had left for nursing service in army hospitals. William Ballentine of the 82nd Ohio referred to the town as "one of the worst secesh holes in Maryland," but he was impressed with the convent grounds and fascinated by the sisters. Despite their attire of hoopless black dresses and scoop-shovel-shaped bonnets ("the ugliest piece of furniture I ever saw"), he noticed how pretty some of the young nuns were. "And it seemed to me to be a shame to keep them immured in a gloomy building like that," he wrote, "with no appropriate society."[12]

The arrival of the Federal troops brought a flurry of activity to the quiet grounds. Soon the residents eyed the strange sight "of guns in battery, of stacked muskets, of sentinels walking back and forth with their guns in hand, of soldiers making coffee in the gardens, of horses ready saddled eating their oats under the apple trees." Colonel Phillipe de Trobriand settled his brigade on the grounds of the convent, then ascended up to the belfry to survey the terrain—startling a group of nuns who had already climbed there to view the spectacle. "We had cut off their retreat," he wrote with some amusement, "and they were crowded against the windows like frightened birds, asking Heaven to send them wings with which to fly away. 'Ah! Sister,' I said to them, 'I catch you in the very act of curiosity. After all, it is a very venial sin.'" After teasing the embarrassed women, the officer had one request: "Ask St. Joseph to keep the rebels away from here; for, if they come before I get away, I do not know what will become of your beautiful convent."[13]

De Trobriand credited the prayers of the "pious damsels" for Maryland's deliverance when Lee this time led his men through the western Maryland panhandle and into Pennsylvania. The two armies clashed at a little town called Gettysburg, ten miles north of Emmitsburg, where the fighting lasted for three days. People in Emmitsburg and Hagerstown lingered on street corners or climbed to their roofs, watching a cloud of smoke grow in the northeastern sky and wondering. Lutie Kealhofer's future husband and many friends were in the Confederate army. "What an anxious time for those who have friends engaged," the young Hagerstown woman wrote in her diary on July 4. "I scarcely allow myself to think of it and yet thoughts will arise unbidden. God have mercy on them and spare them." The next day she learned that her Willie was safe, but news of the fighting (including an erroneous account that her friend Henry Kyd Douglas had received a mortal wound) did little to calm her fears. "Maryland has suffered deeply—dreadfully," she wrote. "Last night I felt as if my brain was on fire—the constant anxiety is fearful to one deeply interested."[14]

The battered Confederate army trudged back through Maryland. The destruction of the Harpers Ferry bridge, plus a Federal force stationed at Frederick, funneled the escaping army back through Washington County. When the first Rebels arrived back at Williamsport after the battle at Gettysburg with a vulnerable wagon train of several thousand wounded soldiers, two thousand men, ten thousand draft animals, and almost no provisions, they found the Potomac River ten feet above fording level. "The highest water ever known," Otho Nesbitt reported from Clear Spring, where local creeks were angrily overflowing their banks and women had been carried clear of the floodwaters in wagons and on horseback. The grim Confederate force bottled in the area was an unwelcome burden. "A few minutes ago the ladies were all dressed up and the Union flags flying from nearly every house," Nesbitt added. "Now they were pulled in, and the ladies' faces are a different hue."[15]

Inevitably, Williamsport's muddy banks became an impromptu hospital camp. Officers watched the floodwaters, tensely waiting for the pursuing Yankee army to descend. All the women in the area were ordered to cook for the wounded, some of whom had not eaten in thirty-six hours.[16] While the Rebels were trapped on the Potomac River's north bank, the few remaining residents of Williamsport wondered if their town would become "another Sharpsburg." The frequent skirmishing had been deadly enough. "The houses are all riddled and almost all deserted," observed one Virginian on the 1863 campaign, "and the country for a mile about is fetid with beef offal and dead horses."[17]

Jeb Stuart's cavalry shielded the ambulance wagons, sutlers, and battered army on the rocky roads that they had learned the year before. Soldiers and civilians alike lived through each day burdened with anxiety, watching the northern roads, waiting for the Yankees to pounce. The Confederate army was close to annihilation.

The Federal army did not allow the Confederates to pass completely unmolested. A dozen minor battles were fought in western Maryland between July 5 and 14 as the Confederate rear guard fended off pursuit and as Lee tried to get his army across the Potomac. On July 6, Hagerstown residents found the war erupting in their own city streets. "At this moment fighting is going on in our very town & balls are whizzing through the streets . . .," Lutie Kealhofer wrote in her diary. "Oh God, of Heaven have mercy upon us and deliver us from this terrible war."[18]

The tumult began when some Union cavalry clashed with the Rebel picket line. The infantry's stubborn defense gave the Southerners time to deploy a regiment of their own across the city's main street. While some civilians huddled in cellars and others peered from behind their shutters, the cavalry charge was mounted. "The cutting and slashing was beyond description," wrote W. W. Jacobs, who watched from the roof of a hotel. Jacobs helped carry a mortally wounded trooper from the 18th Pennsylvania Cavalry into a private home for care. Before he died, the cavalryman managed to say that he had been shot by a young woman standing on her porch.

Amid the close-pitched melee an artillery duel "shook the city to its very foundation and terrified its inhabitants," recalled Jacobs. The battle slowly shifted through the streets of Hagerstown, the Federal troops led by Brigadier General George Armstrong Custer. The flamboyant general "rode by us . . .," Jacobs recalled, "his long yellow curls flowing over his shoulders, his hat in his left hand, waving it and bowing to the ladies in the windows, who were waving handkerchiefs, while bullets were sweeping his ranks."[19] Romantic Union ladies were thrilled by Custer; and when sixteen members of the First Vermont were cut off from their troops, civilians concealed them for six days while waiting for the return of the Union army.[20] Fierce Confederate ladies, meanwhile, such as the one firing from her porch, enjoyed their own taste of the drama. But several Hagerstown civilians were killed that day, including John Stemple, a local artist who had climbed to a roof to sketch the fight.[21]

The Confederates held Hagerstown until July 12. Their cavalry formed an arc protecting Boonsboro, Sharpsburg, Williamsport, and Clear Spring.

Funkstown was the scene of several bloody engagements between July 7 and July 12. On the tenth Union cavalry tried to dislodge Jeb Stuart's cavalry, with some infantry and artillery, who held the town. Nearly five hundred men were killed, missing, or wounded before dusk brought an end to the fighting. Many residents opened their homes to the wounded. At the Chaney houses, slaves sang spirituals for the dying.

The Gettysburg campaign brought the same odd juxtaposition of joy and sorrow to the politically diverse communities. On the way north, the courageous and optimistic Confederate army was plunging deep into enemy territory. On the trip back south they were bloodied and close to obliteration. The civilians they encountered cheered and mourned, or mourned and cheered, as the tides of war quickly shifted.

As he had done the year before, General Lee issued strict orders forbidding foraging, and some of the exchanges between resident and soldier were downright convivial. George William Smith, a Confederate sympathizer and farmer who lived on Jefferson Road near Frederick, was cutting wheat with a McCormick reaper. "It was one of the first used in the county, and a curiosity for the troops," he wrote. Soon soldiers were following him around the field, trying to get a closer look at such new-fangled technology, evidently more interested in acquiring agricultural knowledge than looting.[22] Added one Mississippian in his journal, "We are to make war on soldiers but leave private citizens alone. So far—except for some rails, a few overly friendly chickens, and some hats which we have long-armed from citizens in the towns—we have obeyed General Lee's order to the letter."[23]

Nonetheless, when the Confederate army moved through Sharpsburg while advancing to and retreating from Gettysburg, many civilians experienced additional losses of crops, livestock, and food. Henry Piper amended his initial claim to include 7 1/2 cords of wood, 10 acres of hay, 15 shocks of wheat, and 10 dollars' worth of "pasturage of cattle and sheep."[24] Martin Eakle received an order from Major General Edward Johnson: "Mr. Eakle will at once proceed to grind flour for the Confederate States or his mill will be impressed for that purpose." Eakle was the Confederate sympathizer who had hauled refreshments to the field, including to some Union men, during the battle of Antietam.[25] The farmers who had lost their apples the previous autumn now found their cherry crops in jeopardy, and dusty harvest crews watched helplessly while entire fields of grain were commandeered.

*In this wartime photograph of the Sharpsburg Square, the Grove house can be seen at left and the Biggs house second from the right. Some veterans of the 1862 campaign passed through Sharpsburg in 1863 with a sense of superstitious awe; others didn't hesitate to scavenge again.* COURTESY MARIAN AND SID GALE.

Many of the troops who passed through Sharpsburg in 1863 had done so the previous September. They eyed the valley with reverence and curiosity, remembering fallen comrades, noting the still-visible signs of damage. When some Yankee prowlers visited the area where they had fought, they found the corn growing much taller than in other parts of the field; "Our regiment had furnished an inexpensive fertilizer for the thrifty Maryland farmers," a comrade noted. The same soldier's friends returned from a late-night scavenging foray with less plunder than expected. "They had been almost to Sharpsburg and told with superstitious horror of a luminous haze which they said overhung the field of Antietam. All concurred in saying but for the terror which this strange misty light had caused them they would have brought back more that was good to eat and drink."[26]

An aggressive Union general might have forced another great battle in Washington County, perhaps ending the war for good, but the Union commander at that time, Major General George Meade, was exhausted. So after more than a week of waiting for the floodwaters to subside and fending off

Yankee harassment, the tattered Rebel troops managed to slip back to Virginia. Once again the Confederate army had survived.

For some farm families trying to hang on, the 1863 campaign was too much. "Washington County is trampled down, run over, and eaten up," Otho Nesbitt recorded gloomily that summer.[27] More than one woman looked at once-again empty shelves and knew with certainty that this time the catastrophe could not be met. More than one man threw up his hands, sold his land for whatever he could get, and moved his family on.

The campaign was over, but civilians living near the Potomac seldom felt safe. The Confederate cavalry, including rough-riding bands of partisans, often splashed across pebbly fords by moonlight to snatch horses or meet an informant. Jesse Dixon credited neighbors who were rabid Southern sympathizers with keeping damage done in his community to a minimum.[28] But although violence was rare it did happen; and most rural people lived with a constant cloak of fear as the war dragged on. Major campaigns were heralded by rumors and warnings; partisans struck with lightning swiftness and could not be predicted.

In Sharpsburg, grief-stricken Henry and Martha Rohrback, whose daughter Jane Rohrback Mumma and youngest granddaughter had died shortly after the battle at Antietam, sold their farm near Burnside's Bridge and moved to town with Henry's twin brother, Jacob, and Jane's husband and surviving children. The family was asleep one night when several of Mosby's Rangers, a Confederate partisan band, banged on the door and demanded the keys to the stable. While they were being fetched, one raider shot Jacob Rohrback in his bed, killing him instantly, and the family had yet another death to mourn. There weren't enough horses in town to pull the hearse to the cemetery, and the pallbearers were obliged to take on that job as well.[29] Mosby's band made more than one visit to Washington and Frederick Counties, usually moving independently of the armies. "Mosby's men . . . represented a species of ignoble warfare," said a Frederick woman. "In reality they did not benefit the cause which they professed to serve, but merely molested inoffensive farmers by carrying off their stock and thus depriving them of their means of livelihood."[30]

The tangle of politics and loyalties deepened as the months passed. During the 1863 Gettysburg campaign a spy was captured and hung from a tree outside Frederick. "[He had been] frequently seen in our camp selling maps, books, etc.," wrote Daniel Mowen in his diary on July 6, 1863. "The evidence against him was found in his boots."[31] The body dangled for almost a week, drawing a stream of tourists from the city. "Hundreds of people went to See him," Engelbrecht noted, "& every body (nearly) wanted Some memento, in consequence of which all his Clothes, were Cut up by piece meals & when they were exausted, they commenced at the Rope which hung him which caused him to be Cut down then they commenced at barking the tree which was Completely barked as far as they Could reach up."[32]

Among the morbidly curious must have been some civilians also engaged in clandestine work—if not outright spying, then passing contraband mail or otherwise aiding the Confederate cause—and perhaps the forlorn end of "Spy Richardson" gave them pause. Still, the work went on. Many Frederick men were arrested several times; some were carted off to prison, some hauled before the proper authorities, where they politely provided an oath of loyalty. A lively smuggling operation was carried out throughout the war from Frederick and other points. Some merchants, such as Hugh McAleer, were arrested when contraband goods were traced to their store shelves.[33]

And the ladies continued to do their part. By April 1863, "because of the obnoxious demeanor of the Tory females," the provost guard was not giving passes to anyone not known to be loyal.[34] Teresa Jamison of Frederick was arrested when she obtained permission to care for two Confederate prisoners in her boardinghouse, then later could not furnish either the prisoners or a plausible reason for their disappearance.[35] In September of that year Mrs. Pettit's three daughters were arrested for singing secessionist songs. When Unionist neighbors entertained "a very pompous group of Yankee officers," the Yankee songs drifting through the open windows became annoying. "We stood it as long as we could," one young woman wrote, "and then one of our visitors exclaimed with a grin, 'Let's set up some opposition music to that Yankee concert. It would . . . make the evening complete, don't you think?'" Everyone agreed, and one of the girls settled at the piano. A new batch of music drifted out over Second Street, including "Bonnie Blue Flag," "Dixie," and "Maryland, My Maryland." Soon, "in strode a Yankee Officer in high dudgeon. He demanded the names of all present, and told us we were all under arrest for insulting our loyal neighbors by singing secession songs." The girls were ordered to appear at the provost marshal's office the following day, where some Unionist relatives intervened on the girls' behalf, and they were released on parole with a stern warning not to repeat their offense. "Served them right," sniffed the editor of *The Examiner,* "Maryland is a loyal State."[36]

>—<♦>—○—<♦>—<

The winter of 1863–1864 was harsher than the previous one. Pumpkins and potatoes and apples froze solid in unusually frigid cellars. Water froze in bedside basins and pitchers. Women who had emptied their linen chests to warm sick soldiers in the hospitals now huddled their children around cookstoves with whatever quilts or covering they could find. Federal cavalrymen passing through the area camped on D. R. Miller's farm and burned three thousand hard-split fence rails.[37]

A Federal major general named David Hunter, who had been assigned to Virginia's Shenandoah Valley that spring, instituted a policy of total war, burning the territory as he moved up the valley. Confederate officer Henry Kyd Douglas, whose own family near Sharpsburg had felt the oppression of Union anger, was in the vanguard of the force chasing Hunter. "It was a scene of desolation," he recalled of his painful ride in the Northern force's wake. Those houses not burned had been ransacked. The Southern cavalry passed women weeping in the road, their clothes and belongings carried off or destroyed. "I had never seen anything like this before," Douglas added, "and for the first time in the war I felt that vengeance ought not be left entirely to the Lord."[38] Hunter was despised by the South—and soon would be despised by many north of the Potomac as well.

Robert E. Lee planned another offensive in 1864. This time plans were made to invade Maryland and strike east, threatening Washington City and relieving the pressure Union forces were putting on Petersburg. The Southern force was led by Major General Jubal A. Early, "the meanest of all rebels."[39]

The Confederate force began crossing the Potomac near Sharpsburg on July 6, and within two days it was occupying that village plus Williamsport, Boonsboro, Hagerstown, Jefferson, and Middletown. Once again, some families rejoiced as Confederate soldiers took advantage of the opportunity to slip home. Boys who had aged beyond their years were petted and pampered—and sometimes hidden behind closed shutters from neighbors' prying eyes. While on this campaign Henry Kyd Douglas stopped by Sharpsburg to briefly visit family and friends. He took General Lee and an entourage of officers and staff with him, delighting in introducing them to Savilla Miller, "the only person who in the battle of Sharpsburg was never driven back a foot."[40]

But most people cringed, bracing for further disaster, for by now war-weary rural residents knew exactly what any campaign might bring. Farmers and merchants headed to secret camps in the mountains to wait out the invasion with their horses and goods. Free blacks, fearing that Confederates would ship them south, fled as well. Heirloom china and silver spoons were buried, unburied, and buried again. The Piper girls, who had lost new silk dresses to the troops in 1862, were determined not to let that happen again. "Henry Piper's girls had packed up their clothes two or three times," Jacob Miller reported, "to be ready at a moments warning."[41]

Upper-class women who lost their kitchen help with each such exodus fed their families stale bread and awaited their servants' return. Capable women with supplies to spare—and an eye toward profit—locked their chicken coops and fired their bake ovens. One soldier recalled:

[The boys] kept the farmers' wives busy through this whole neighborhood baking the much coveted soft bread, which they buy at fabulous prices (75 cents or $1.00 a loaf). You wouldn't think soldiers' wages would hardly hold out at such rates. They, however, don't mind prices if they can only get the articles. Soldiers are utterly regardless of expense when they see anything they want, especially after they have been campaigning a while.[42]

Horses, as always, were in high demand. In Sharpsburg, Rebels raided the secessionist Miller clan's farm, snatching every horse but one. (A month later, Yankee soldiers trotted into the field and, while the helpless harvest crew watched, unhitched the lone survivor from the threshing machine and led him away.)[43] "The Rebels are making their appearance, 2 being here this evening for horses," John Koogle wrote in his diary on July 6; the next day he added, "The county is running full of rebels, not much work done, horses all gone." Confederates stole a horse worth $125 from Koogle and another from his mother worth $150. "Hard times," Koogle concluded gloomily on July 9, "looks like worse coming."[44] Koogle was right. Angered by the wanton Union destruction of civilian property in Virginia, the Southern men trudged onto Maryland soil with retaliation in mind. On prior campaigns, the Confederates had been given orders to damage only what commanders deemed necessary to slow the pursuing Yankees. The 1864 campaign was pointedly destructive.

Rebels dug out portions of the C&O Canal walls, releasing the waters to the Potomac and bringing traffic along the canal to a halt. Locks were destroyed, canalboats burned, mules stolen—livelihoods ruined. Many of the boatmen were so terrified that they refused to venture out on the canal, further interrupting the flow of coal from western Maryland to the capital city, where it was sorely needed. They were perhaps shamed by one Mrs. Neill, who cooked for a canal company repair gang on a houseboat. When a group of Confederate raiders boarded her boat in July 1864, she refused to leave and instead, in a "resolute and determined manner," dared the Southern men to burn the boat with her on it. Ultimately cowed, the troopers sheepishly left. Mrs. Neill's boat was the only one on that section of the canal left untouched during that destructive raid.[45]

The destruction was not limited to the canal. Hagerstown citizens, especially those who had risked retaliation themselves to welcome the Confederate soldiers in 1862, were stunned when Brigadier General John McCausland of the Confederate army presented a written demand for twenty thousand dollars in United States currency and an additional list of supplies—and two hours to furnish them, or else the city would be burned. Despite a flurry of effort, town officials were still short when the appointed hour came. McCausland prepared to carry out his threat, ordering the evacuation of women and children. Frenzied civilians besieged his staff with pleas for clemency, and several officers persuaded McCausland to accept what had been raised and move on. Although he relented, when the main body of Confederates marched toward Frederick, a marauding rear unit ransacked the city anyway. Men of all political persuasions found themselves collared and set to work burning Federal government stores. Women hugged their children tight as soldiers slammed through their homes, stealing what they could carry and damaging what they could not.[46]

Middletown was also ransomed. General Jubal Early demanded five thousand dollars to keep from burning the village—a sum beyond the ability of the local people to pay. After frantic negotiation, the village portion was lowered to fifteen hundred dollars, with the balance to come from the surrounding countryside. In the confusion the rural citizens' allotment was never formally collected. "But [the Confederate soldiers] would go into the people's houses in the country," Allen Sparrow related, "and if they did not give them what they wanted they would threaten to set fire to the house, and in some places they carried coles on a shovel in the rooms before the people would give up their money." The Confederates also raided stores, emptying shelves and filling their pockets with booty. Molasses barrels were particularly prized bounty, and once the heads were knocked in, delighted infantrymen shoved to get in line. "[They] would take it in any thing that they could get hold of," Sparrow noted, "old pots and pans, some said they saw one fellow with a shoe full. I saw one with a plug hat full and it was runing over and he was licking it off the out side."[47]

Other Rebels ranged through the countryside, kicking in doors, threatening bloodshed, driving off sheep and cows, stealing silver spoons and parasols, and generally terrifying the farm folks. Most watched mutely but one, seventy-year-old George Blessing, had had enough. Blessing lived on a farm called Highlands on Catoctin Mountain; when five Rebels arrived, he was ready. "As they rode up, I gave my son two guns and I took six and went in the name of the Lord God of Hosts to meet them," he wrote, "and as they rode up in haste, we fired upon them in quick time." Two of the Confederates were wounded, one mortally, and a third was killed as the survivors retreated. When they returned with reinforcements Blessing settled in a grove of cherry trees and exchanged wild fire with the enraged soldiers. The Confederates were threatening to shell his farm when a detachment of the Potomac Home Brigade's Coles Cavalry arrived, bringing the affair to a close. Blessing was known for years after as "the Hero of the Highlands."[48]

Often during those hot, difficult days skirmishing erupted along county turnpikes and rutted lanes, sending farm families to their cellars as Confederate cavalrymen pushed east and a few Union men tried to delay their progress. The Yankees ultimately fell back to Frederick, adding to the chaos that had erupted with news of the Confederate crossing. Eight hundred sick and wounded Federal soldiers rattled into the city on the cars from Harpers Ferry. A number of Union men skedaddled, packing saddlebags and kissing wives and trotting away in a routine that was becoming all too familiar. In Frederick, the editor of *The Examiner* prudently left town: "Skedaddlers," he wrote upon his return. "Not relishing the idea of falling victims to the tender mercies of the Southern Chivalry, we skedaddled to Baltimore on their approach to this city, hence no issue of *The Examiner* last week."[49] Jacob Engelbrecht noted with some disgust in his diary that "Union stock is down with me about 5 percent," since the "soft shell Union men" lacked the carapace needed to stand to their convictions when Confederate occupation was imminent. "Rebel Stock," he added, "is up 50 or 60 percent to

Judge from their Countinances."[50] Hard-shell secessionists held their breath, waiting for their friends and praying that this time—*this time*—the Southern thrust would succeed.

They thought it had on July 6, when two Union riders wearing gray doublets trotted blithely down Patrick Street. Someone took up the cry: "Rebels are in town!" Country people in town whipped their horses east. Women snatched their children's wrists and jerked them toward home. Anyone still owning a horse ran to padlock the stable or pounded out of town altogether. Union cavalrymen dashed for their horses, Unionist civilians loaded their guns—and Southern women pinched their cheeks and ran outside. Once the cause of excitement was ascertained, things settled down. The secessionists went back inside, went back to waiting for their men.

Former resident Brigadier General Bradley T. Johnson was trying to oblige them. A key participant in the 1864 campaign, he arrived on the hills west of his old city leading fifteen hundred cavalry and dreaming of a quick thrust east to liberate the fifteen thousand or more Confederate prisoners held at Point Lookout, on Maryland's Eastern Shore. For a brief time he camped on the Gouveneur family farm near Frederick, where the family had hidden their horses in the cellar. "I called [the children] to me," wrote Marian Gouveneur later, "and in my sternest tones . . . gave them to understand that if they said 'horse' or rebel 'devil' in [the soldiers'] presence I should punish them severely." The children held their tongues.[51]

Johnson didn't find the horses or make it to Point Lookout—although he did lead his column of horsemen close enough to Baltimore and Washington to induce a general panic. But before commencing his ride east, Johnson assumed the honor of opening the fight for Frederick. "Battle in progress at west end of town," Catherine Markell wrote in her diary on July 7. "Cannonading from 4 A.M. to 8 P.M. All stores closed, shells thrown by Brad Johnson's men into the town."[52] Some excited citizens clambered to rooftops to watch the puffs of smoke from batteries on the hill west of town and the meager Frederick defense line trying to organize on the outskirts. A group climbed to the courthouse cupola to watch the Confederates approach, and one of the eyewitnesses later described the experience for his grandson:

> We stood on the cupola fascinated, as the guns and caissons reached the hilltop and wheeled into position . . . and even though we

were aware that the cupola was their target, we were still too fascinated by the spectacle, to take in its significance for us. In a moment however we saw three large puffs of smoke with centers of flame . . . and almost instantly the air around us was full of the shrieking of shells.

The young men beat a hasty and undignified retreat down the ladder.[53] Shells damaged a number of buildings in town, including the Presbyterian church and, Unionists smugly noted, the former home of Bradley T. Johnson. Since the house had been confiscated and sold at a sheriff's sale in February 1863, he probably didn't care.[54]

Warned that Frederick was about to fall, Union major general Lew Wallace hurried west from his Baltimore headquarters bringing twenty-five hundred men with him, and he soon mounted a thin line of defense south and west of the city. Some civilian men resisted the dangerous lure of spectating and helped the city's commissary troops cram every train car available with supplies to be sent on to Baltimore and Washington. The barracks hospital buildings were emptied of all except those convalescents too ill to move, and the parade of sick and wounded soldiers continued north and east.

On July 8, sightseers ventured out to the farms west of town to ghoulishly gawk at dead horses and cows and barns riddled "in Style" with shells and balls.[55] More skirmishing took place near the city that day, providing an additional show for the battle-hardened citizens still in the area. General Wallace stared with disbelief when someone called his attention to a group of men, women, and children perched on a fence behind the line. "Good Heavens!" he cried. "Those people are in the range of bullets. Ride, some of you, and order them away!" One of his men explained that the civilians had already been warned to leave: "They were here all day yesterday. We tried driving them off, but they would not go." Wallace sent several men to urge the civilians to withdraw. They rode back and forth, waving their arms, exhorting the onlookers to seek safety, but although the crowd watched with interest, it did not disperse. "I could think of but one explanation of the very remarkable indifference to danger thus displayed," Wallace mused later. "Frederick City and the region around it had been a playground for the game of war from its first year and the people had grown so used to it in all its forms that even battle had ceased to have terrors for them."[56]

At midnight on the eighth, with word that a Confederate force was threatening to cut off the road to Washington, the Yankees evacuated Frederick. Civilians listening from behind their shutters heard the last cavalrymen retreat around 2:00 A.M. Soon after dawn, the Confederates marched eagerly into Frederick.

The Federal force retired to the Monocacy River, protecting the roads leading to the eastern cities. The Unionists remaining watched stony-faced as the Confederates seized Frederick. Making matters worse, Jubal Early, having heard tales of the aid provided the Union troops by loyal citizens, demanded a ransom of two hundred thousand dollars. While waiting for a response, the Southern troops emptied store shelves, stole horses and livestock, and generally took what they wanted. Bankers met and grimly made arrangements for the ransom to be paid. "These are awful times," lamented Jacob Engelbrecht. "One day we are as usual & the next in the hands of the enemy."[57]

Meanwhile, nervous farmers were trying to gather their wheat crop during those hot July days. To the accompaniment of artillery, the reapers cut, bundlers made shocks, and drivers edged the wagons through the fields and carried loads of grain to the barns or to the men deftly building roof-high stacks. Boys carrying jugs of vinegar water to the dusty workers dawdled, turning their heads toward the sounds of skirmish. One of those boys was Glenn Worthington, who lived with his parents, John and Mary Ruth, near the Monocacy River southeast of Frederick. He wrote later of a harvest abruptly halted: "Boys, fill up the middle of the stack high so as to turn the rain that may fall," one man told his field hands. "Then unhitch your horses from the wagon, unharness them, and take them all, including those in the stable, to the Sugar Loaf Mountain, and tie them by their halters in the darkest and loneliest place you can find."[58] With half of the crop still waiting desolate in the fields, the Worthington family nailed boards over their windows and carried tubs of water to the cellar. By the time they were finished, blue-clad squads of cavalry could be seen taking position on the adjoining farm.

On July 9 Confederate soldiers skirmished with the Yankees southeast of Frederick near the Monocacy River. The fracas escalated into the battle of Monocacy, fought in part among the stubble grain and waist-high cornfields of the Worthingtons and their neighbors. "In comparison with other battles, this was but a drop in the bucket,'" acknowledged Jesse Dixon, whose family weathered the battle on their farm four miles away; still, "we were frightened almost to death."[59]

Wallace was so desperate for soldiers that a chance comment about local men sitting out the war led to the impressment of several startled young men from Araby, a large farm owned by the Thomas family, neighbors of the Worthingtons. Two were fiancés of Alice Thomas and a friend, Mamie Tyler; the third was Mamie's brother. In the middle of the chaos the two young women marched into headquarters, looking for Wallace. "Two extremely attractive young women are very much in evidence as they flit from place to place," a soldier wrote, "obviously in deep distress over something." The women may not have caught up with General Wallace, but in time they were happily reunited with their fiancés and brother.[60] Ultimately Wallace scrounged up about seven thousand men to meet a Confederate force almost twice that size. He knew he could not defeat the Southerners in battle, but the unspeakable spectre of capture was looming over Washington, and Wallace hoped to delay the Rebels long enough to allow Union reinforcements to arrive in the capital city.

By the time the fighting commenced, most of the civilians near the Monocacy had fled or taken refuge. John and Margaret Best, first-year farmers who tended leased land, lost much of their year's labor when their barn burned during the battle; Union artillery positioned on the east bank of Monocacy Creek aimed their guns to scatter the Confederate sharpshooters crouching by windows in the house. The C. Keefer and Evelyn Virginia Thomas family, and Antoinette Gambrill and her children, huddled in the Thomas cellar while Confederate artillery showered that house, trying to dislodge Union sharpshooters. Antoinette's husband, James Gambrill, who owned a flour mill nearby, sheltered there during the battle. Like C. Keefer Thomas and John Worthington, James Gambrill was a Confederate sympathizer—despite the fact that his brother George was serving in the Union army.

John Worthington watched the battle from a second-story window in his home. The rest of the family and their slaves peered through cracks in the boards nailed over cellar windows, listening to shouted orders, the tramp of feet, explosions of artillery, the moans of the hurt and dying. When the sounds of fighting died away, they crept out to survey the scorched landscape. Although their house had received little damage, dead and wounded men were lying in the fields, in the garden. Some of the stubble fields had caught fire, and blankets were brought to help smother the flames before they engulfed more whimpering, blood-stained men. Glenn and his brother were sent to the harvest field, where armfuls of the

*Frederick women such as Sarah Adams and Soffia Reich, who hoped they had seen the last of war in 1862, found themselves with more wounded to tend after the battle of Monocacy. Photographs by Marken's Gallery, Frederick, Maryland.*
AUTHOR'S COLLECTION.

carefully bundled sheaves were grabbed and brought to the yard to make improvised pallets and sun shields for the wounded.[61]

Yipping and howling, the jubilant Rebels pushed the outnumbered Union soldiers east in a confused retreat. A thousand Yankee boys were captured and marched toward prison camp. Wounded soldiers stumbled into Baltimore, sending the panic there to a fever pitch. The Union army suffered sixteen hundred casualties; the Confederate force, seven hundred. The battle of Monocacy was a Confederate victory. Jubal Early herded his army through the dust and heat toward Washington, and by July 11 the Confederates were poised to attack the capital. But Wallace's stand delayed the Confederate army just long enough. Even as the Rebels moved into line, Federal reinforcements could be seen pouring into the vast but weakly manned network of forts defending the city. Early held his position for a day, waiting for Johnson's cavalry expedition to withdraw from its push into southern Maryland, letting his army feed on Maryland produce instead of Virginia's, and maximizing the psychological harm he was inflicting by lingering so close to the capital. Then Early ordered a withdrawal back to Virginia. "Major, we haven't taken Washington," he told Henry Kyd Douglas, then serving on his staff, "but we've scared Abe Lincoln like hell!"[62]

>—+◆>•O—<•+—<

Skirmishing took place frequently that summer along the Potomac River and county turnpikes. General Early, not satisfied with his Maryland campaign, sent two cavalry brigades across the Potomac on July 29. After a few raids into western Maryland, the Southern men rode on to Chambersburg, Pennsylvania, and demanded a ransom of one hundred thousand dollars in gold or five hundred thousand dollars in Union currency. City officials refused to pay, and the pretty town was burned. Maryland civilians who had argued against raising the ransom money in Hagerstown and Frederick quieted down in shocked disbelief. Frederick City would spend the next century trying to recover its financial loss. But at least its civic buildings and records, its high-spired churches and shady residential streets, were still intact. Residents shuddered, realizing how close they had come to total devastation.

Their losses had been dear enough. Four years of war—and the wanton destruction of the final campaign—had exacted a heavy toll on the once-prosperous communities. Hired hands were scarce, harvest wages high. "Many are talking about stopping farming or farming less," Otho Nesbitt wrote.[63] The price of coffee had climbed to sixty cents per pound; brown sugar twenty-five cents per pound.[64] More and more widows crept through the streets in black crepe.

James Montgomery, a member of the Union army's signal corps, was briefly stationed in western Maryland that year, and he kept a diary. He found his first camp near Hagerstown "an awful place. . . . Everything in confusion, nobody in charge. Horses scattered over three square miles. . . . No rations for the men or feed for the horses." During that summer's campaign he was stationed at Fort Duncan, a Union stronghold near Maryland Heights, the mountain overlooking Harpers Ferry across the Potomac and the tiny village of Sandy Hook below, which he described as "one of the most forlorn looking places I have ever seen." In July Montgomery wrote, "Nothing to be seen but marred and blackened ruins. Here the ground is plowed by the enemy's bursting shell, before us a house in ruins, its blackened walls as if it were laughing at its former occupants who have been turned into the wide world homeless." A few days later, he noted tersely, "A little girl shot by a drunken soldier at Sandy Hook."[65]

The political toll of frequent occupation was high. Almost everyone suffered during the 1864 Confederate occupation, and many who had always strived for tolerance, for neutrality, found their resources stretched thin. The brutality of total warfare scattered bitter seed on Maryland soil. More fingers were pointed, more old friendships severed, more arrests made.

In Sharpsburg Jacob Miller, his daughter Savilla, and sons Morgan, Samuel, and Andrew Rench were arrested and taken to Harpers Ferry. "Savilla and I were conducted to a boarding house Some distance up town where there ware two ladys kept the house," Jacob wrote in a letter. "We had excellent quarters, but the boys were Sent up the Shanandoer to a guard house however they did not complain much of their boarding and treatment and I had to pay our boarding Six dollars per weak we were there two & a half weaks which cost $30." An officer on General Hunter's staff "examined into the matter and found that there was no charge against either of us, then the provost Marshal discharged us without asking a word." The Millers had more trials waiting. The day after their return home, "some fiendish rascal Set fire to our barn, and burned it to the ground, with all its contents, wheat, rye, oats, timethy & clover Seede, three Sleighs one wheat drill and many other things of value." A Confederate column arrived in Sharpsburg while the Millers were incarcerated, sending a wave of panic through Unionist civilians who feared retribution for the Millers' arrests. There were some frightening moments, but no real harm was done. "Perhaps in the whole our arrest has done Some good," Jacob concluded, "as the disunion party (as I call them) have been mute as a fish ever since."[66]

The Millers' experience was, as Jacob calmly described it, mild compared to some. General Hunter was commanding the district. His policies had already created grief in Virginia, and his net was now cast over western Maryland as well. A new policy called for anyone who had given aid to the Confederates or openly expressed Southern sympathies to be imprisoned. Their homes were to be confiscated, their belongings sold at public auction to benefit Unionist civilians who had suffered during the invasion. The families of such miscreants were to be escorted to the Potomac and left on the south shore. Many Unionists were stunned by the policy's severity.

In the confusion a number of families whose ties to the Confederacy were dubious at best were singled out for punishment. As always, some of the military leaders viewed all Maryland residents with suspicion, creating further resentment. "Although Northern in our sentiments," Marian Gouveneur wrote, "we sometimes preferred the visits of the Confederate to those of their adversaries, owing to the greater consideration which we received from them." Union soldiers frequently descended upon the Gouveneurs to search their house for "Concealed rebels . . .," she added. "The Union soldiers took it for granted that, owing to the locality of our home, we were Southern sympathizers, and accordingly at times seemed to do everything in their power to make us uncomfortable."[67] An early Maryland historian noted that the provost marshals directing this policy went about their business with zeal. "Under their rule spies and informers swarmed like vermin in Egypt. . . . Private letters were broken open, dwellings ransacked, women treated with the grossest personal indignities, and men of unimpeachable characters subjected to arrest by ruffians and protracted imprisonment without trial."[68]

In part due to protests by loyal citizens, some leniency was shown. On August 1, for example, a number of people were arrested and given notice that their families would be evicted. One on the list was errant grocer Hugh McAleer. When the provost marshal arrived at the McAleer residence, he seized a pair of velvet slippers, with a "Rebel flag . . . handsomely and conspicuously worked . . . [displaying] a remarkable degree of skill and taste on the part of the fair sympathizer," McAleer's daughter Clara. Although the slippers were confiscated, and Hugh was charged, Clara evidently escaped harsh punishment.[69]

But some women were among those rowed across the Potomac, including Ellen Swann and Alice Magill of Hagerstown, who were relocated south after being charged with "harboring Rebels and giving information" to the Confederates. It was better than prison but no light punishment, for by 1864 conditions in Virginia were deplorable. Richmond was crammed with refugees, and thousands more wandered homeless past barren fields and burned-out barns.[70]

Some of the women arrested had openly defied Federal authorities by flaunting their Confederate sympathies and perhaps done more than just sympathize. But the policy also affected women who had done no more than love a son who had chosen to fight for the South—or even less. "General David Hunter . . . was regarded with terror by those in sympathy with the Southern cause . . .," wrote Marian Gouveneur. "Many of his victims were elderly people and it is difficult for me . . . to describe the amount of distress these orders occasioned." The August 1 list included Dr. Thomas

McGill, whose wife was in "delicàte health." Unionist leaders appealed for clemency for the McGills, which was ultimately granted, but "the fright caused by such summary proceedings . . . resulted in [her] death."[71]

The winter of 1864–65 crept by. Impoverished young widows wrote letters to a bewildering array of military officials, trying to procure their husbands' pensions. Men of "copperish" sentiments, opposing the war, dared derision to voice their sentiments.[72] Despairing housewives found old, tough chickens selling for fifty to sixty cents; cabbage, Jacob Engelbrecht noted, was "too dear to eat."[73] Homeowners sprinkled ashes on their sidewalks so that growing numbers of veterans hobbling through town on crutches wouldn't slip on the ice. Families of soldiers haunted the post office, aching for mail. Children stared at blurry daguerreotypes of strange men named Father whom they could not remember. Lamp oil was dear, and families crowded together in the kitchen at night, listening to the latest war news read from the newspaper. And in the faint light women knitted socks and mittens for the hospital, wondering when it would all end.

CHAPTER 10

# "When That Time Comes, All Hearts and Hands Will Unite"

While the war was grinding painfully through its second half, western Maryland—like the rest of the state—was still wrestling with the question of slavery. Although Abraham Lincoln's Emancipation Proclamation exempted Maryland, some owners evidently tried to honor its spirit—perhaps by conscience, perhaps seeing the inevitable, perhaps because financial losses from the 1862 campaign made welcome the excuse to absolve responsibility for a few extra mouths to feed. In Sharpsburg, John Otto's slave recalled, "After emancipation his son said to me, 'Now, Hilary, you're your own man. Pap wants to hire you, but you can go and work wherever you please. If you decide to go away, and it happens that by and by you have nothing to do, come back and make your home with us.'" This evidently happened in early 1863, because Hilary stayed and was subsequently drafted; Otto took him to Frederick and paid three hundred dollars for an exemption.[1] Other owners took a more prosaic view to the notion of blacks serving in the army, such as Josiah Smith of the Middletown area, who paid his black field hand six hundred dollars to serve in his place.[2]

Farmers who owned slaves or employed black field hands, or townspeople with house slaves, had struggled to hang on to their workforce as the armies moved back and forth through western Maryland. In 1861 a slave belonging to Samuel Horine of Boonsboro had found shelter in the Fourth Connecticut's camp, although on appeal the slave was returned; and in 1862 a Hancock slave marched away with the 19th New York.[3] Two of the Kealhofers' slaves ran away from Hagerstown during the tumultuous summer of 1863. "I've learned something new today—for the first time in my life I've had to work & got along very well," a somewhat dumbfounded Lutie Kealhofer wrote in her diary on August 25. "Nancy & Harriet left Sunday night for parts unknown & we've not yet been able to get anyone in their place."[4]

In 1862 Otho Nesbitt had recorded, "Free Negroes taken by the army." During the frequent alarms in 1863, he often sent his horses to safety, in care of his slaves; and on July 1 he noted, "The Rebels about 75 or 100 strong went past . . . this evening with about 500 cattle and about two dozen Negroes and some horses." During the final invasion in 1864, when his male slaves were once again safely away, he wrote, "Rebels took Mary Jane and her mother." And six weeks later: "Rebels . . . found my horses in the mountains but the negroes escaped."[5]

Although Nesbitt blamed the trouble on the Confederate army, many feared the Union army as well. Jerry Summers, who worked for Henry Piper, was reportedly "carried off" by the Yankees. Henry tracked him down to Frederick, where he somehow negotiated successfully for his release.[6] Some evidence indicates that men in the Confederate army occasionally used force with the blacks they encountered. A Wisconsin soldier who arrived in Williamsport just after the Confederate army had slipped back across the Potomac in July 1863 noted in his diary, "In a barn we found a Negro branded with hot irons because he refused to flee with the retreating rebels."[7]

A few slaves continued to be bought and sold in Washington and Frederick Counties during the war's final years.[8] But for the first time the

*The diary kept by Otho Nesbitt, the staunch Unionist and slave owner from Clear Spring, reveals how often daily life was interrupted by the almost constant passing of troops. In addition to the major campaigns and minor skirmishes, frequent rumors of trouble prompted Otho to send his slaves and livestock to hidden mountain hollows for safety. Despite these precautions, Nesbitt's farm economy was hit so severely by the war that he never recovered. When the slaves he inherited were freed by Maryland law, they stayed on for a time, working for room and board.* COURTESY CLEAR SPRING DISTRICT HISTORICAL ASSOCIATION.

issue was involving the community at large. Voices calling for emancipation had grown to a chorus, and that chorus was finding popular support. The Unconditional Union Men of Frederick County recognized the higher cause fueling the war and sponsored emancipation meetings. Other men were driven into the debate by sheer economic necessity. Marylanders had already suffered enormous pecuniary losses. Unwilling to confront further financial blows, many slave owners demanded recompense for the looming loss of their labor force. An editorial published in *The Examiner* on October 1, 1862, summarized both that argument and the need for advanced planning:

The value and utility of slavery in Maryland have already been destroyed by the war. . . . Emancipation would afford relief to thousands of slave holders and if accompanied with Federal compensation for the public and private inconvenience attendant upon a change of system . . . would promote the welfare and prosperity of the State. The time has past when we could delude ourselves with the hope that slavery would survive the ordeal of rebellion and come out of the fire unscathed. Every reflecting man now sees that its doom is written, let us, therefore, devise and pursue such prudent counsels as may prepare us for the impending social revolution and avert its calamities.[9]

Maryland was entitled to financial compensation for emancipated slaves because of the "conspicuous and steadfast loyalty of the people of Maryland," argued proponents of the plan—a dubious argument at best. Still, some slave owners *had* remained loyal to the Union; that was certainly the case in western Maryland. The Federal government had supported their right to own slaves during the war's early years by returning runaways, and it still couldn't afford to jeopardize its precarious support in Maryland by antagonizing even a small percentage of Unionists.

At the same time, the Union army's desperate need for fighting men was hammering at the chains of Maryland's slaves. Conscription among whites had not gone well, and by 1863 abolitionists and black leaders were agitating for authority to enlist willing black fighters. The first Maryland recruitment efforts were focused in Baltimore, although a group of black musicians from Hagerstown enlisted as a regimental band. Soon, the enlistment appeals spread to western Maryland—with mixed results. When one Colonel Creager enlisted black recruits at a black church in Frederick he got twenty-five to thirty volunteers. Evidently a few were slaves, however, eliciting such an angered response from their owners that Creager was arrested and jailed for three months.[10] Slave owners, believing the recruitment officers were careless about differentiating free blacks from slaves, were outraged.

In October 1863, President Lincoln succumbed to both arguments by agreeing to provide three hundred dollars to owners for slaves who enlisted in the army; the same order declared that "all persons enlisted into the military service shall forever thereafter be free."[11] Most slave owners greeted the law with tired tolerance, pleased at least to receive compensation, and began filling out the new deeds of manumission. Blacks from western Maryland ultimately served in a number of regiments.

But the state of Maryland had yet to act. The Unconditional Union Men continued to agitate for abolition, sponsoring speakers at its public meetings. Jacob Engelbrecht applauded their efforts. "Hardly any Speaker would have attempted to Speak on that Subject 4 or 5 years ago," he noted in his diary on April 5, 1864, "—what wonderful Changes have taken place in Maryland . . . since the Rebellion."[12] Six months later a new constitution was adopted, and on November 1, 1864, slavery ceased to exist in Maryland. "The foul blot of Slavery will be stricken from the Constitution of Maryland," Engelbrecht rejoiced the day before the law went into effect. "Huzza for Liberty."[13]

Those owners still clinging to their slaves greeted the day with less enthusiasm. Jacob McKinney's owner made him strip, giving him the choice of leaving the farm naked or staying until he worked off the price of the clothes. McKinney was still working there when the owner realized the law specified that freed slaves be provided a set of clothes.[14]

Most owners weren't quite so cruel. Some offered their freed slaves wages; in some cases, particularly on small farms where owner and slave had worked together in the fields, relations were cordial and the blacks readily agreed. In Sharpsburg, Jerry Summers had chosen to stay with the Piper family after he was legally freed; years later he testified in Piper's behalf when Henry Piper sued the government for war damages. When Henry died, Summers and his wife, Susan, were rewarded for their loyalty with a cabin and garden plot near Bloody Lane. Emory Summers and his family were also given lodgings, and Emory continued to work for the family, as

*Jeremiah Summers was born a slave but was freed prior to the Civil War. He worked as a farm laborer for the Piper family for many years, and after the war made his home with his wife in a cabin near Bloody Lane.* COURTESY DOUG BAST, BOONSBOROUGH MUSEUM OF HISTORY.

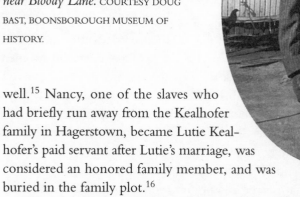

well.[15] Nancy, one of the slaves who had briefly run away from the Kealhofer family in Hagerstown, became Lutie Kealhofer's paid servant after Lutie's marriage, was considered an honored family member, and was buried in the family plot.[16]

Owners who couldn't afford to offer wages gave their freed slaves the option of staying on in exchange for food and housing. Otho Nesbitt's opinions and actions exemplify the complexity of owner–slave relationships in western Maryland. Nesbitt, the Unionist who had bitterly opposed emancipation, revealed his situation in his diary: "The negroes all set free in Maryland without compensation to their owners . . . the work of Abolitionism," he wrote on November 1; he valued his seven slaves at two thousand dollars. The next day he presented his situation to the newly freed blacks:

Told the negroes that I had nothing more to do with them. It was now near winter and they had no house, no home and probably could get no work this time of year and if they cared to work on as they had been doing till spring they might do so, that I couldn't pay a whole family of negroes to cook a little victuals for me after all that I had lost to both Armies. They said it was so and they would work on until spring as they had been.

Although records indicate that a woman named Hannah Temperance Robison gave birth to his first child in 1865, Nesbitt was evidently living a bachelor existence in 1864. Nesbitt, who had provided some schooling for his slaves, fed and housed the family until members began to leave in search of employment in 1865; they all stayed in touch, and sometimes worked for him, for years to come.[17]

In 1864 "freedom" had a hollow ring for many Maryland blacks. Like Nesbitt's slaves, most were destitute, freed with winter imminent in a local economy with little latitude for a suddenly available workforce. Scant documentation illuminates the painful choices confronting the black families or the trials endured as they struggled to create their own identity and home. Certainly some succeeded, creating small colonies of freedmen and -women in rural hollows and village outskirts. Others did not succeed, perhaps watching their children starve when food was scarce or fading away from fevers when there was no money for medicine. And some swallowed their pride and asked for help, like George and Hannah, who had been owned by an Urbana family. "They slipped away for a month or two," Jesse Dixon remembered. "At the end of that time they were both back, wanting to be hired. They showed hard usage and poorer food than formerly, and their late owners gladly put them on wages." Years would pass before George and Hannah were able to save enough money to leave the farm where they had been enslaved and make their own way in the world.[18]

With these social upheavals happening amidst the carnage, political stress, economic devastation, and emotional trauma of civil war, race relations in the Antietam Valley remained complex. For every affable relationship, another was tainted with intolerance. And for that minority angered by Lincoln's Emancipation Proclamation raising the war to a more noble plane, the blacks became the target of all frustration, loss, and anger. At war's end Samuel Michael, the Sharpsburg secessionist who had lost his mother and sister during the 1862 campaign, wrote a letter to his brother:

I suppose you are satisfied with the Nigger war. I suppose you are satisfied that you helped to whip Jeff Davis and company out. The South lost no honor, only property. They fought all the combined powers of Europe and the damned Abolitionists of the North and the Nigger to boot and came very near whipping out after all. . . . The Yankee Abolitionists have destroyed the property of the people better than they dare[?] be for the purpose of freeing the negroe and establishing Negro equality, a race that never ought to be free, but to be held as servants from generation to generation. . . . You cannot pick a meaner set in hell to compete with the Yankee Abolitionist, that as many as Old Abe has already sent in yonder who are now quarreling with Old Abe there about Negroes equality.

The family had, Samuel also reported, "the same colored woman yet keeping house for us."[19]

>––>–•–O–•–<––<

While slave owners and abolitionists wrestled with those issues, the bulk of the populace was trying to survive each day and yearning for the war to end. On February 1, 1865, *The Examiner* printed a notice of PEACE RUMOURS AGAIN—THE NATION'S HEART BEATS ANEW WITH NERVOUS ANXIETY AT WHAT SEEMS TO BE A GLEAM OF HOPE LOOMING UP FROM BEHIND THE DARK HORIZON OF WAR. The Confederate army was sinking to its knees, battered, starving, exhausted. The Civil War finally ground to a painful halt in April 1865. Frederick politicians celebrated by staging a grand illumination. Flags hung from homes and shops; bunting draped shops and office buildings. As dusk fell thousands of candles and lamps and gaslights glowed. Some civilians rejoiced; others wept. Most were only too thankful simply to see peace come at last. They dug up their silver, built new fences, visited cemeteries, and took stock. The war had dragged on far longer than anyone had anticipated, and the cost had been dear.

Most western Maryland residents were still trying to heal from four years of bitter fighting. They had endured three campaigns, including the two horrendous battles of 1862. "We are getting along in the house on the rough and tumble," wrote Samuel Michael. "Things are very gloomy here [compared] to what they once were."[20] The joy of peace was tempered with devastating losses—emotional and financial. Men spent decades petitioning the government for compensation from war damage, searching for witnesses who could testify on their behalf, trying to regroup. Marylanders were still viewed with suspicion by Federal authorities, and some legitimate claims were contested, postponed, denied.[21] After hanging on through the war years, some people were eventually forced to admit that they couldn't keep going. In Sharpsburg the Prys never recovered from the 1862 campaign's blows, and in 1874 they sold their farm and moved to Tennessee.[22] The Reel family, whose barn had burned while in use as a hospital, also sold their farm after the war and moved west.[23] "For ten years after the close of the war the work of liquidation went on . . .," noted a local historian. "Many farmers sold their property and emigrated to the West. For years each spring two or more special trains left Hagerstown each Tuesday carrying emigrants away from their old homes. In this way Washington County lost several thousand of valuable and industrious citizens."[24]

But for every person who left, others wanted to come back. For those who had been waiting at home, the best news of all was that the beloved brothers and sons and husbands who had marched away to war had survived and were coming home. Union boys returned to public welcomes and joyous receptions; they were feted and pampered and proclaimed heroes. Mothers and wives were horrified by the physical changes in their men. "[I was] not the hale, hearty young man of three years previous, knowing nothing of pains and aches," wrote Daniel Mowen of the Seventh Maryland, "but [I came home] with hollow cheeks, sunken eyes, a weak, gaunt creature, like the flickering of a candle, ready to go out."[25] Their women looked in their eyes and saw other changes, the changes wrought in men who had endured and suffered and seen too much—but unlike most of the North, the men saw these things mirrored in their women's eyes, as well.

There were other Maryland veterans, too. Among the dazed, beaten Confederate troops were hundreds of Marylanders, dreaming of home. By May 1865 these weary boys were trudging north. They crossed the Potomac to a place that no longer felt like home, unsure of their reception—unsure of many things. Their first stop was the provost marshal's office, where they raised their hands and woodenly recited the oath of allegiance, just wanting to begin putting their lives back together.

It wasn't that simple, of course. Officers faced particular challenges. Dr. John Forney Zacharias, son of beloved Frederick pastor Daniel Zacharias, returned in May but was not permitted to practice medicine, and he spent the next five years in Virginia.[26] Although Jane Claudia Johnson, who had spent the war years in the South with her husband, General Bradley T. Johnson, came home to Frederick with her young son in July 1865, the Johnsons spent the next thirteen years in Richmond.[27]

But most anonymous privates were permitted to return to their families. Among them were men who had found romance during the desperate days of war. Lucky girls like Lutie Kealhofer, who had sent their sweethearts to war and watched them come and go during the Maryland campaigns, wept with joy when they marched home for good, and married them. Other Maryland women had met their future spouses during the campaigns. Dr. John Mutius Gaines, a Confederate surgeon, had remained in Boonsboro with his wounded men after the armies moved on in 1862 and was subsequently captured; in October 1865, he returned and married Helen Jeanette Smith of Boonsboro.[28] Daniel Mowen of the Seventh Maryland had suffered a broken heart when he heard that his girl had married another man while he was in the service, but during the 1862 campaign he met a Frederick girl whom he later married.[29] Frederick County native Luke Tiernan Brien, who had been Jeb Stuart's chief of staff during the 1862 campaign, purchased the Urbana property where the glorious Sabres and Roses Ball had been held.[30] Captain Chauncey Harris of the 14th New Jersey married Clementine Baker, who had nursed him to health after the battle of Monocacy. A Frederick widow later married the father of a mortally wounded Pennsylvania boy she had tended in her home.[31]

The men carefully folded away their tattered, cherished uniforms and began learning how to be civilians again. Soon Union and Confederate veterans were passing on the streets, meeting in shops, sitting in adjoining pews at church. It was awkward at best, painful for many—and painful, too, for the civilians who in their own ways had fought and suffered for the cause that they believed in. It took time for the tensions to ease, even a little. Citizens relived each battle, each snub, each affront in tales often told. They knew that some things would *never* be the same.

But time did eventually soften even the harshest memories. "The time of bitterness will soon pass away," Bradley T. Johnson told his former comrades in 1874, and he went on to summarize his vision:

This generation will see the day when the soldiers, and the widows and the orphans, of both sides, will stand as equals . . . equally honored, equally respected, and equally cared for. It will then be understood, that the vast mass of the men and women, North and South, who supported the war by their blood, by their prayers, their works and their substance, were alike impelled by the same high considerations of patriotism and love of liberty. When that time comes, all hearts and hands will unite. . . . Here in Maryland, we can do so now.[32]

Veterans began swapping stories with the men who had opposed them. Altar guilds and charity work brought together women who had worked for opposing causes. Farmers once again headed to their nearest neighbor to borrow a needed tool, without considering politics first. "I remember how the passing years tempered even the more unpleasant memories of my grandparents," wrote one Frederick man, "and that their eyes had a half-amused look when they were telling of occurrences which had once aroused their angriest emotions, years before."[33]

As they tried to rebuild their lives, the particular horror of September 1862 remained with them. The young children who had lived through that time were particularly scarred, haunted forever by the scenes and experiences that had shattered their world.[34] But adults were haunted, too, and those who didn't move on could not escape the residue of war. In Sharpsburg, members of the Lutheran church, which had been so badly damaged in 1862, laid the cornerstone for a new church in 1866.[35] And in nearby Keedysville, the German Reformed church had been only ten years old in 1862, but the piles of amputated limbs buried directly outside the building—and the endless buckets of waste and dirty water poured out windows—eventually weakened the foundation, and walls began to crack. By 1892, seven thousand dollars had been collected to rebuild that church, as well.[36] These building projects were not insignificant for the tiny communities, and the struggle to raise funds was a constant reminder of what had happened.

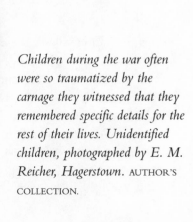

*Children during the war often were so traumatized by the carnage they witnessed that they remembered specific details for the rest of their lives. Unidentified children, photographed by E. M. Reicher, Hagerstown.* AUTHOR'S COLLECTION.

And there were other lingering reminders of those September days. In 1934 a historian named Fred Cross visited the Stephen and Louisa Grove farm, then home to a family named Poffenberger. "The lady . . . took me into the parlor," he wrote, "raised the curtains, and turning up the corner of the large rug which covered the floor, showed me a big blood stain which told the story of some poor sufferer who lay there after the battle. 'I have washed and scrubbed that spot again and again until I have thought I had got it all out,' she said, 'but as soon as the floor dried the spot would reappear as plain as ever.'"[37]

The bloodstains and bones confronted many residents for years. In the years after the battle it was not uncommon for Sharpsburg or South Mountain residents to unearth human remains while plowing or pulling stones or after a hard rain. In 1865 the state of Maryland established an eleven-acre cemetery for the men who had fallen at South Mountain and Antietam. Augustin Biggs, the Sharpsburg physician who had tended so many of the dying, was made superintendent of the cemetery, and he carefully supervised each burial. Two years later, on the fifth anniversary of the battle, President Andrew Johnson dedicated the ground as a national cemetery. All known Union dead—who numbered 4,776, including 1,836 unknown soldiers—had been reinterred there. For years the caskets of Union soldiers being buried there were draped with the flag Theresa Kretzer had kept hanging over Main Street during the war and hidden from the Confederates—until, she said later, "it was completely worn to shreds."[38]

Some Confederate soldiers remained buried in shallow battlefield graves until the early 1880s. Most Confederate remains were interred in a portion of Rose Hill Cemetery along South Potomac Street in Hagerstown (where Henry Kyd Douglas arranged the official Confederate Cemetery Dedication in 1877) and in Shepherdstown, West Virginia. All identification of Southern skeletons—the bones of twenty-five hundred men—was lost.

>+⟨⟩+O+⟨⟩+⟨

Like the bones and blood, the endless rows of quiet graves were merely tangible reminders of the emotional stains that would never fade. Over the years the veterans of Antietam were drawn back to the field again and again, to weep for fallen comrades or to remember old glories. They did not forget what had been won and lost on the field. And they didn't forget the people. They wanted to meet the preacher who had given them a Bible, the woman who had nursed them through typhoid, the man who had sung hymns in the barn where they had lain among the wounded, the child who had read to them. They came to inquire about unnamed women who had tended their wounds—or to apologize for damages done. They presented civilians with certificates bearing formal resolutions of thanks tendered by veterans' societies: "Resolved that the names of these Good Samaritans be honorably enrolled among our archives and the memory of their Christian Actions be sacredly cherished in our hearts," said one.[39] Survivors of the 16th Connecticut contributed a stained-glass memorial window, featuring the dove of peace, to the Sharpsburg German Reformed Church when it was remodeled in 1890; the blood of fallen members of that unit still stained the floorboards of that little church.[40] Years after the battle, veterans of the 107th New York Regiment returned to the Dunker Church the pulpit Bible, which had been carried off by a member during the campaign.[41]

One war widow, whose husband had died in Samuel and Catherine Poffenberger's bedroom, came to visit the couple after the war, painting pictures of the house where her captain had lived his last hours.[42] Mr. Roulette and one Captain Wright of Boston made frequent visits to each other's homes.[43] John Van Horn of the 130th Pennsylvania Volunteers returned twice to express his gratitude to the woman who had provided special care for him in one of the hospitals when he had been wounded.[44] Middletown civilians also kept in touch with some of the soldiers who had marched through their little community. Effie Titlow Heron, who had nursed a Pennsylvanian thought to be mortally wounded at South Mountain, was invited to a regimental reunion by the man whose life had been saved.[45] Kate Rudy, who had helped care for Rutherford B. Hayes after he was wounded, was later invited to visit the Hayes family.[46] These bonds were precious to civilian and veteran alike.

Hundreds of veterans returned over the years, some many times. Oliver Reilly, who had been a boy of five in 1862, moved to Sharpsburg in 1877, married Annie Katherine Spong, and became a shopkeeper and tour guide. A straight-spoken Irishman, he wore a white shirt and bow tie even when plowing his garden and never started morning chores before raising the flag. From his store on the Sharpsburg square he advertised his relic collection and guide services with a hand-lettered sign. Lucky customers got to hear him play his Civil War drum, kept on top of a Coca-Cola case in the shop basement. Through the years he escorted hundreds of veterans over the battlefield. Their memories ranged from inspirational to mundane. One soldier brought a comrade to the field in 1895 and suddenly "spied the old rough casted

*Oliver T. Reilly, a five-year-old in 1862, later became a battlefield guide, collected relics, and wrote a battlefield guide for tourists. "He always had an answer when asked a question," remembered his granddaughter.* COURTESY MISSY KRETZER, ANTIETAM NATIONAL BATTLEFIELD.

house that belonged to Mr. Moses Poffenberger. . . . 'Look, Brown,'" he said to his friend, "'there is the house where we got the white bread and apple butter.'"[47]

Railroad service arrived in Sharpsburg in 1880, which increased the stream of veterans making the pilgrimage. From the station it was a sun-baked two-mile walk through town to the cemetery. Within a decade two graceful rows of Norway maples were planted along the route to provide shade, and walkways were added beside the dusty highway. The soldiers came alone with their own thoughts or in groups for reunions and memorial services. When the hotels overflowed, civilians boarded the veterans. The children who had been terrified by the soldiers in 1862 now opened their own homes, and *their* children listened for hours to the stories. They helped the veterans sort out their memories, knowing they had experienced something enormous, something important, and the stories were passed along. Many wrote them down. "Now I am writing this for the young people and if the older ones don't want to read it they need not," Allen Sparrow noted when he added a postwar reminiscence to his diary. "There is no person living that did not live here during the war that could form an idea of the times."[48]

Hard as they may have tried, the local civilians knew they would never, *should* never, forget what had happened in 1862. As time passed they realized that something more important than the finger-pointing and tale telling among one-time friends eclipsed personal trials and petty injustices. Survivors of the 1862 campaign, both military and civilian, understood that more than a battle had been decided on Sharpsburg's bloody fields. They knew that the war might have been ended on that September day. "If a Grant, a Sherman, or [a] Sheridan had been in command," wrote Jacob Hoke, who had surveyed the carnage soon after the battle, "the after bloody battles with the army of Northern Virginia would have never occurred. The Potomac would have been its grave and winding sheet."[49] A bold leader had *not* been on the field in 1862, so the war ploughed on. But the Northern states' impression of the war would never be the same after Antietam—in part because of the sheer magnitude of the losses, in part because of Alexander Gardner's photographs, in part because anyone believing the Confederate army would never cross the Potomac had been forced to acknowledge their error.

The troops trudging through western Maryland recognized that the civilians they encountered lived in neither the true North nor the true South; and because of the ambivalence, they viewed the Marylanders with both admiration and suspicion. During the campaign some perceptive Yankees had realized that these folks were experiencing war as their own families in Maine and Vermont and Indiana did not. "Patriotism in this border State was not confined to sentiment, it was a living principle—intensified by what it cost," wrote Isaac Hall of the 97th New York. "It is an easy matter to be a patriot where all are patriots, but not so easy nor safe when surrounded by traitorous neighbors."[50] Echoed a female relief worker who arrived from Pennsylvania, "They *felt,* what we at the North knew nothing of, that loyalty meant life was at stake, homes deserted, property destroyed, and the friends of early, happier years, *all* given up,—for what? Devotion to the country, and the flag!"[51] Still, many of their comrades were never able to set aside their suspicion, their fear, of even vocal Unionists. Northern soldiers marching through Maryland experienced for the first time the confusing and painful experience of true civil war, forever blurring the distinction between friend and enemy.

But the South was disillusioned, too. The 1862 campaign was the first of three that ventured north of the Potomac—and the last truly embodied with the idealistic chivalry so romanticized in popular culture. The Southern soldiers who splashed onto the Maryland shores were an eager, liberating army, waiting for the chance to free Maryland, waiting for the promised hordes of new recruits. It was a fleeting, glorious time. "A rosy light hovers around it still," wrote William Blackford wistfully in his memoirs, "illuminating the vista of dark and lowering clouds of war overhanging the past."[52] They reforded the Potomac two weeks later, disillusioned, jaded, battered. For Maryland boys in the ranks, the retreat was a particularly "severe trial . . . to leave their native state," wrote one, "maybe never to return as was the case of many of them."[53] The Confederates lost more than battles on that campaign. They lost some of their faith.

And the civilians lost their innocence. The 1862 campaign provided Maryland civilians their first opportunity to test their political convictions against not just the noble ring of rhetoric but the fire and brimstone of battle. Those of opposing sentiments had initially taken divergent paths with "sadness, rather than hatred; [with] regret and sympathy, rather than wrath and vengeance," noted an early historian.[54] As tensions rose during the campaign, that good faith was eroded. When the Confederate armies arrived, Unionists feared that their neighbors would point fingers and bring the army's wrath upon them; secessionists feared the same fate as the tides turned. "This was one of the vilest evils produced and encouraged by our Civil War," wrote a Confederate veteran about the first Maryland campaign, "that it often made the oldest and nearest neighbors the bitterest enemies and mutual spies."[55] Still, when the armies marched on and the hospitals slowly emptied, most of the raw ugliness subsided. Relations were often painfully strained—and Major General David Hunter's late-war policies prompted a spate of harsh reactionism—but western Maryland did not descend into the violent mob rule that terrorized citizens in other border areas, such as Missouri and east Tennessee.

Those September weeks, when the distinction between civilian and soldier faded, taught many civilians that self-preservation was the wisest course. Allen Sparrow of Middletown noted that some of his neighbors "were on either side acording to circumstances," cheering for whatever army seemed dominant.[56] A Hagerstown girl complained bitterly about a teacher who was "one of the blackest secessionists" when no Union troops were in town, but "tried to pass for a pure Unionist when they were here."[57] General Ulysses Grant, asking a young Urbana girl about her parents' sympathies during the 1864 campaign, was amused by the frank, if revealing, answer: "Mama, she's a Rebel, but Papa, he is a Rebel when the Rebels are here and a Yankee when the Yankees are here."[58] The Marylanders had learned that decent men and rogues could be found in each army. They had seen for themselves the result of fratricide, and the memory of the soldiers—those who had marched on and those whom they had buried—was haunting.

The soldiers lying in the western Maryland cemeteries fell during what remains the single bloodiest day in American history. They had fought, in the words of noted Antietam scholar Stephen W. Sears, "to the limits of human endurance and beyond."[59] Two great armies—two *American* armies—had collided on the peaceful rolling fields around Sharpsburg. Then the dead were buried, and the troops moved on. But the civilians remained. Their rutted streets and cornfields had provided a crucible for the great American tragedy and watershed that was civil war. They provided a metaphor for not only border states but for the nation in those bitterly divided years of fratricide. Politics were not simple for Martin Eakle, the slave-owning Confederate sympathizer who carried food to Union troops under heavy fire and later had his mill impressed by the Southern army. Or Mr. Delaney, who invited Robert E. Lee to breakfast and had his barn burned by an irate Confederate soldier. Or the minister, a cousin by marriage to Robert Lee, who was reported to Southern troops for carrying information to the Union army. They were not simple for Stephen Grove, who owned five slaves and shook hands with the man about to issue an Emancipation Proclamation. They were not simple for the families divided, the brothers and cousins who had somehow become enemies, the people reported to one army or the other by once-trusted neighbors.

The civilians had been tested as surely as any grizzled veteran, and most had not been found wanting. They had lived through more than battle, as horrendous as that had been. Women whose war work in 1861 had been stitching flags and baking cakes were by the end of 1862 competently managing monumental relief efforts. Farmers who had worried over drought and insects confronted complete devastation. Women left alone while their husbands skedaddled, children witnessing carnage beyond comprehension, and parents huddling by candlelight in the late autumn to total financial losses and wondering how they would survive the coming winter—all dredged up a rare courage to confront what they must. They were not sol-

*This postwar postcard shows the Unionist Kretzer family's large stone house on the right and the stone side of the secessionist Miller family's home three doors away.*
AUTHOR'S COLLECTION.

diers trained to face battle; they were ordinary people facing extraordinary challenges. And most survived, symbolizing a million Americans, engulfed in an unendurable war, somehow finding the courage to face each new day.

"I favored the South early in the war," Jacob McGraw once said, "but later I didn't care which side won if only they put a stop to the fighting."[60] His wish for peace was fervently echoed by men and women throughout western Maryland, and this was their greatest triumph. Some fought political battles, angrily opposing their neighbors' loyalties with any means at their disposal. Some were so bitter by war's end that they never recovered. But many struggled to keep some shred of humanity alive in a hellish time. When they provided water to enemy soldiers, when they helped wounded boys say their prayers, and when they opened their homes to devastated mothers and widows, they managed to wring some goodness from overwhelming tragedy.

# NOTES

## CHAPTER 1: "This Conflict of Opinions and Sympathies"

1. John N. Ware, "Sharpsburg," *Confederate Veteran* (April 1921), 133.
2. *New York Times*, 20 October 1862, quoted in William A. Frassanito, *Antietam: The Photographic Legacy of America's Bloodiest Day* (New York: Charles Scribner's Sons, 1978), 14–16.
3. Angela Kirkham Davis, "War Reminiscences: Letter," Western Maryland Room, Washington County Free Library.
4. Thomas J. C. Williams, *History and Biographical Record of Washington County, Maryland* (John M. Runk and L. R. Titsworth, 1906), 173.
5. Joseph R. Stonebraker, *A Rebel of '61* (New York: Wynkoop Hallenbeck Crawford Company, 1899), 32.
6. J. Thomas Scharf, *History of Western Maryland* (Philadelphia: L. H. Evarts, 1882), 194. Scharf served in the First Maryland Artillery, CSA, before being appointed to the Confederate States Navy.
7. Some discrepancy exists regarding the Miller children. Jacob's biographical sketch (Williams, 911–913) provides the names and birthdates for ten children. Savilla is not listed among them, but elsewhere in the same material an anecdote refers to "[Jacob's] daughter, Miss Savilla." Jacob's letters clearly reveal Savilla as his youngest child, as do other period accounts, and a gravestone for Savilla Susan Miller (1839–1917) is listed in the records for the Mountain View Cemetery in Sharpsburg. The Eighth Federal Population Census, 1860, lists Jacob, seventy-seven; Helen, twenty; Thomas, thirty-five; Samuel, twenty-four; and Cicilia (Civilla), twenty-one. Helen was not one of Jacob Miller's children but may have been the daughter of his oldest child, Elizabeth. The names of two of Elizabeth's daughters, Helen and Jeanette, appear as residents of the Jacob Miller household at various times during this period.
8. Jacob Miller letter, 1 July 1859, Miller Family Letter Collection, Antietam National Battlefield Archives, courtesy of Harold R. Decker. The letters written during the 1850s and 1860s were written to Jacob's daughter Catherine Amelia and her husband, Christian Houser, who lived near Muscatine, Iowa. Some punctuation and spelling have been edited for clarity.
9. Williams, *History and Biographical Record*, 912.
10. Main Street was known as Front Street by contemporary residents. The Miller home was located where the gas station now stands, two lots removed from the Kretzer home, which is still standing.
11. Kretzer family genealogical information courtesy Linda Irvin-Craig, of Hagerstown; from Eighth Federal Population Census, 1860; and from Williams, *History and Biographical Record*. Leonard Kretzer, who died in 1821, may have had more than one wife,

242

for his children were born over a twenty-five-year span. The death record of John Kretzer (b. 1812; d. 1901) lists his children as Anna Mary, Maria Theresa, Margaret Civilla, Malinda Elizabeth, and Stephen Philip. Aaron was evidently not listed due to his premature death in 1867. For the purposes of this book, I am using the common names listed in the 1860 census, which in several cases are the person's legal middle name. Savilla/Civilla was not an uncommon name in Sharpsburg.

12. Fred Cross, "Story of Flag Woman Saved at Antietam" (1929), Antietam National Battlefield Archives.

13. Angela Davis, *War Reminiscences*, 10–13.

14. Stonebraker, *Rebel of '61*, 41.

15. James B. and Dorothy S. Ranck, Margaret R. Motter, and Katharine E. Dutrow, *Unto Us: A History of the Evangelical Reformed Church* (Frederick: 1964), 101. Florence Trail wrote about her mother, Ariana McElfresh; the other two known abolitionists were "Dr. Jencks and Mr. Henry Schley."

16. Williams, *History and Biographical Record*, 250.

17. Dennis Frye and John W. Schildt, *Antietam Remembered: A Guide to Selected Historic Sites in the Antietam Valley* (Hagerstown: Tri-State Printing, 1987), 33; and Marguerite Doleman, *We the Blacks of Washington County* (Hagerstown(?): Washington County Bicentennial Committee, 1976). A large stone can still be seen on the corner of Church Street and East Main in Sharpsburg on which, according to local tradition, slaves stood while being auctioned; some historians consider that legend to be apocryphal, suggesting that the stone served instead as a mounting block.

18. Michael L. Spaur, "What's in a Name?" *The (Frederick) News*, 2 May 1979.

19. J(esse) W. Dixon, "Slave Days on the Farm," *The (Frederick) News*, a collection of undated clippings from an ongoing column, Historical Society Frederick County.

20. Doug Bast Collection, Boonsborough Museum of History.

21. Williams, *History and Biographical Record*, 457; and Eighth Federal Population Census, 1860. The census schedules noted the race of each individual as w(white), b(black), and m(mulatto or mixed), and recorded blacks and mulattos as "colored."

22. Dixon, "Slave Days on the Farm."

23. Otho Nesbitt diary, 25 April 1861, Clear Spring District Historical Association.

24. Williams, *History and Biographical Record*, 838; and Eighth Federal Population Census, 1860.

25. Carl F. Bowman, *Brethren Society: The Cultural Transformation of a "Peculiar People"* (Baltimore: Johns Hopkins University Press, 1995), 86.

26. J. Maurice Henry, *History of the Brethren in Maryland* (Elgin, Ill.: Brethren Publishing House, 1936), 364–367.

27. E. Russell Hicks and Reverend Freeman Ankrum, "The Church on the Battlefield: Part 1: The Brethren Congregation," *Morning Herald*, 21 April 1959.

28. Samuel Mumma had two slaves in 1850 and one in 1860; John Otto owned one twenty-seven-year-old male mulatto and one forty-four-year-old black female in 1860.

29. (Doyle Moore), *Odds and Ends by Gum*, typed compilation/summary of *The (Boonsboro) Odd Fellow*, 5 April 1860–25 September 1862, Western Maryland Room, Washington County Free Library. Moore's summary cites a notice of 22 November 1860: "A Mrs. Feltz of Mt. Pleasant ran away with a negro slave belonging to a Mr. Witmer. They got as far as Harrisburg before capture."

30. Allen Sparrow diary, copy in George Brigham Jr. Library. The diary also contains an informal reminiscence, written late in life, about Sparrow's war experiences. Some punctuation and spelling have been edited for clarity.

31. Ora Ernst, "Slaves Passed through Here on Way to Freedom," (Hagerstown) *Daily Mail*, 18 December 1978.

32. Williams, *History and Biographical Record*, 251.

33. James A. Helman, *History of Emmitsburg, Maryland* (Frederick: Citizen Press, 1906), 90–91. A large group of slaves fleeing to Pennsylvania in 1861 raised such a cloud of dust that local residents thought Confederate troops were on their way. W. P. Conrad and Ted Alexander, *When War Passed This Way* (Greencastle, Pa.: A Greencastle Bicentennial Publication, 1982), 41.

34. Dixon, "Slave Days on the Farm."

35. Williams, *History and Biographical Record*, 794–795.

36. John W. Blassingame, ed., *Slave Testimony: Two Centuries of Letters, Speeches, Interviews, and Autobiographies* (Baton Rouge: Louisiana State University Press, 1977), 405.

37. Blassingame, *Slave Testimony*, 108–109. James and Stephen were the second and third of Bazil and Nelly Pembroke's thirteen childen. The source information does not reveal why James had a different surname.

38. Williams, *History and Biographical Record*, 249–250.

39. Jacob Miller letter, 10 August 1859. According to census records, Jacob Miller owned an eighty-year-old black male and a seventy-five-year-old mulatto female in 1860. Local legend also names the Miller house as a stop on the Underground Railroad. A cellar crawl space is believed by a former resident to have once sheltered runaways.

40. (Moore), *Odds and Ends.* The 26 December 1861 issue contained notice that Margaret Simms was sentenced "by the Court of Hagerstown to be sold outside of the State" for burning a white man's barn.

41. Blassingame, *Slave Testimony*, 167. Fourteen slaves owned by the Claggetts were sold south in 1860 and observed being driven through Boonsboro in an omnibus. (Moore, *Odds and Ends*).

42. Clifton Johnson, *Battlefield Adventures: The Stories of Dwellers on the Scenes of Conflict in Some of the Most Notable Battles of the Civil War* (Boston: Houghton Mifflin, 1915), 104–105.

43. Eighth Federal Population Census, 1860; untitled manuscript, Antietam National Battlefield Archives; Virginia Mumma Hildebrand Collection, "Antietam Remembered" (typed manuscript, 1958), Western Maryland Room, Washington County Free Library; Francis F. Wilshin, *Report on the Piper Farm "Slave Quarters"* (28 September 1969), Antietam National Battlefield Archives. According to the 1860 census, Henry Piper owned a female, fifteen; a male, thirteen; a male, seven; and a female, four. Also living in the household was a sixteen-year-old free black listed as "John." The free black was in fact Jeremiah Cornelius Summers, born in 1846, a former slave. It is not clear whether the other slaves were related to Jeremiah Summers.

44. Robert J. Brugger, *Maryland: A Middle Temperament* (Baltimore: Johns Hopkins University Press in association with the Maryland Historical Society, 1988), 244.

45. Nesbitt diary, 1851–1856. Slaves had been passed along in Otho's grandfather's will, executed in 1807; and in 1855, Nesbitt's father gave one family of slaves to Otho and another family to Otho's brother Jonathan, who lived on a neighboring farm. The 1860 census shows Otho Nesbitt as owner to six slaves: a man and woman, each forty; two boys, twenty and seven; and two girls, seventeen and six.

46. Angela Davis, *War Reminiscences*, 25.

47. Scharf, *History of Western Maryland*, 214.

48. John Koogle, Diaries for the Years 1861–1868, with notes by Fred S. Palmer, Western Maryland Room, Washington County Free Library. Koogle lived between present-day Route 40 and Route 70 near the junction of the Appalachian Trail. John's brother Jacob served in the Seventh Maryland during the war, and in his absence John tended his widowed mother's farm on Canada Hill Road.

49. Jacob Miller letter, 20 August 1861.

50. Daniel D. Hartzler, *Marylanders in the Confederacy* (Westminster: Family Line Publications, 1986), 43–44; Williams, *History and Biographical Record*, 318.

51. Stonebraker, *Rebel of '61*, 39.

52. Stonebraker, *Rebel of '61*, 40.

53. Scharf, *History of Western Maryland*, 213–214.
54. Jacob Miller letter, 20 August 1861. DeWitt Clinton Rench was the son of Jacob's first wife's brother. Williams's *History and Biographical Record* includes a slightly different account, in which Rentch [*sic*—spelling varies] had already conducted business in a Williamsport store and engaged in some socializing before a mob demanded that he leave town; when he mounted his horse to comply, hot words were exchanged, and shots were fired. "The reason for this was Rentch's well known sympathy for the South of which he never hesitated to give very free expression. It was also believed that it was his intention to join the Southern army." Williams also referred to Rench's father, Andrew Rench, as "the wealthiest farmer of the County" (Williams, *History and Biographical Record*, 309).
55. Henry Kyd Douglas, *I Rode With Stonewall*, ed. Fletcher M. Green (Chapel Hill: University of North Carolina Press, 1940), 7.
56. "Tragedy and Death," *Williamsport Ledger*, 1861; clipping in Jacob Miller Letter Collection.
57. Miller letter, no date. This letter is very difficult to read.
58. Williams, *History and Biographical Record*, 300.
59. Stonebraker, *Rebel of '61*, 40; Conrad and Alexander, *When War Passed This Way*, 60.
60. Keith O. Gary, *Answering the Call: The Organization and Recruiting of the Potomac Home Brigade Maryland Volunteers* (Bowie, Md.: Heritage Books, 1996), 78–92.
61. Angela Davis, *War Reminiscences*, 14.
62. Jacob Miller letter, 17 February 1862.
63. Nesbitt diary, December 1861–January 1862.
64. Scharf, *History of Western Maryland*, 225.
65. Scharf, *History of Western Maryland*, 225.
66. Quoted in Ronald H. Bailey and the Editors of Time-Life Books, *The Bloodiest Day: The Battle of Antietam* (Alexandria: Time-Life Books, 1984), 8.

## CHAPTER 2: "In a Small Commotion"

1. Quoted in William C. Davis and the Editors of Time-Life Books, *Brother Against Brother: The War Begins* (Alexandria: Time-Life Books, 1983), 89.
2. *(Frederick) Examiner*, 17 April 1861; 17 July 1861. Several other flag-related stories made the news in the first months of war. See also the Reverend Freeman Ankrum, *Maryland and Pennsylvania Historical Sketches* (Masontown, Pa.: The Times-Sun, 1947), 9–10.
3. Julian Wisner Hinkley, *Service with the Third Wisconsin Infantry* (Madison(?): Wisconsin History Commission, Original Papers #7, 1912), 11.
4. T. J. C. Williams and Folger McKinsey, *History of Frederick County, Maryland* (Frederick: L.R. Titsworth, 1910), 369–370.
5. Stonebraker, *Rebel of '61*, 42–47. He was later moved to Fort McHenry in Baltimore, where he stayed for several miserable months before he and a friend decided to "swallow the pill" and take the oath. After informing the Federal commander that taking the oath did not change their sentiments, they recited the words and were released. Stonebraker later joined the Confederate army.
6. *The Examiner*, 11 December 1861.
7. Jacob Engelbrecht, *The Diary of Jacob Engelbrecht*, ed. William R. Quynn, (Frederick: The Historical Society of Frederick County, 1976), 4 July 1861.
8. Charles Camper and J. W. Kirkley, comp., *Historical Record of the First Maryland Infantry* (Washington: Gibson Brothers, Printers, 1871), 19.
9. *The Examiner*, 16 October 1861.
10. George William Brown, *Baltimore and the Nineteenth of April, 1861* (Baltimore: Johns Hopkins University, 1887), 70.

11. Johnson's troops, however, were orphans in a war where each Confederate unit was armed and equipped by its state government. His wife, Jane Claudia, a native of North Carolina, saved his fledgling regiment from an ignominious end by successfully appealing to the North Carolina legislature to provision her husband's troops. Throughout the war, Jane Claudia was a supportive wife and compatriot. She was, Johnson wrote, a "splendidly handsome, brilliant, and intellectual woman. . . ." ("Memoir of Jane Claudia Johnson," *Southern Historical Society Papers*, Vol. XXIX [Richmond, Va.: 1901], 32–47). Johnson ultimately served as major, lieutenant colonel, and colonel before the unit was disbanded in August 1862—a tremendous disappointment to him.

12. Catherine Thomas Markell diary, 29 May 1861, microfilm, C. Burr Artz Public Library, Frederick, Maryland.

13. Engelbrecht diary, 17 November 1861.

14. "Life in Frederick During the Civil War," typed manuscript, Historical Society of Frederick County Archives.

15. Paul and Rita Gordon, *Frederick County, Maryland: A Playground of the Civil War* (Frederick: M&B Printing, 1994), 206.

16. Sparrow diary.

17. Ernest Helfenstein, *A History of the All Saints' Parish in Frederick County, Maryland* (1932), 99; Engelbrecht diary, 5 November 1862. The Reverend Dr. Ross, minister of the Presbyterian Church, did not resign until 1862. One of the main arguments against Stonewall Jackson interacting with Barbara Fritchie (see pp. 50–52) was his detour to visit his friend, the Reverend Dr. Ross. Jackson's early-morning visit on his way out of town—although he could do no more than leave a note for Dr. Ross—may have exacerbated tensions in the Presbyterian congregation.

18. Jeremiah C. Cramer letter to Colonel Dennis, 24 November 1861, Historical Society of Frederick County Archives.

19. Engelbrecht diary, 2 August 1861.

20. *The Examiner*, 16 April and 27 May 1862.

21. *The Examiner*, 14 May 1862.

22. *The Examiner*, 3 September 1862.

23. Quoted in James V. Murfin, *The Gleam of Bayonets: The Battle of Antietam and the Maryland Campaign of 1862* (New York: Yoseloff, 1965), 65.

24. J. B. Polley, *A Soldier's Letters to Charming Nelli* (New York and Washington: Neale Publishing, 1908), 80.

25. John W. Stevens, *Reminiscences of the Civil War* (Hillsboro, Tex.: Hillsboro Mirror Printing, 1902), 66.

26. Heros von Borcke, *Memoirs of the Confederate War for Independence*, Vol. I (1867; reprint ed., New York: Peter Smith, 1938), 185.

27. Randolph McKim, *A Soldier's Recollections: Leaves from the Diary of a Young Confederate* (New York: Longmans, Green, 1910), 157–158. McKim was not part of the 1862 Maryland campaign. Many Confederate Maryland soldiers were completely cut off from news of families and loved ones for the duration of the war. John Goldsborough White of the Second Maryland Infantry, CSA (reorganized from the First Maryland CSA), did not receive any news of his family in Talbot County, on Maryland's Eastern Shore, from the time he enlisted in 1862 until his internment in Point Lookout in 1865. (John Goldsborough White, "A Rebel's Memoirs of the Civil War," *The Baltimore Sun*, 19 May 1929.)

28. Jonathan Thomas Scharf, *The Personal Memoirs of Jonathan Thomas Scharf of the First Maryland Artillery*, ed. Tom Kelley (Baltimore: Butternut and Blue, 1992), 48.

29. Douglas, *I Rode with Stonewall*, 147. Evidently White's wife, Elizabeth, spent much of the war years at her parents' home in northern Montgomery County; the couple's children divided their time between their mother's and their father's parents, who were also

local. (Roger Brook Farquhar, *Historic Montgomery County, Maryland: Old Homes and History,* Silver Spring, 1952, 226–227.)

30. Polley, *A Soldier's Letters,* 80.
31. Quoted in John M. Priest, *Antietam: The Soldier's Battle* (Shippensburg, Pa.: White Mane Publishing Company, 1988), 103.
32. Franklin Lafayette Riley, *Grandfather's Journal,* ed. Austin C. Dobbins (Morningside Press, 1988), 103.
33. Edgar Warfield, *A Confederate Soldier's Memoirs* (Richmond: Masonic Home Press, 1936), 128.
34. Quoted in Murfin, *Gleam of Bayonets,* 93.
35. Greenlee Davidson, *Diary and Letters, 1851–1865* (Verona, Va.: Virginia McClure Press, 1975, c. Charles W. Turner), 48.
36. Mollie Hays Jones, "Reminiscences of the Civil War, *The Montgomery County Story,* Vol. IV, No. 2, February 1961, 1–3. Fitzhugh Lee, Robert E. Lee's oldest son, was promoted to brigadier general on 15 September.
37. Engelbrecht diary, 5 September 1862.
38. *The Examiner,* 24 September 1862.
39. Nesbitt diary, 9, 10 September 1862.
40. Williams and McKinsey, *History of Frederick County,* 376.
41. Lewis H. Steiner, M.D., *Report of Lewis H. Steiner, M.D.* (New York: Anson D. F. Randolph, 1862), 6.
42. Markell diary, 5 September 1862.
43. Steiner, *Report,* 8.
44. Alexander Hunter, "A High Private's Account of the Battle of Sharpsburg," *Southern Historical Society Papers,* Vol. X, 508.
45. J. J. McDaniel, *Diary of Battles, Marches and Incidents of the Seventh South Carolina Regiment* (186?), 10–11.
46. William Ellis Jones diary, n.d., copy in George Brigham Jr. Library.
47. Steiner, *Report,* 8.
48. Quoted in Hunter, *A High Private's Account,* Vol. X, 508–509.
49. *The Land We Love,* September 1867, 432, copy in George Brigham Jr. Library.
50. Hunter, *A High Private's Account,* Vol. X, 508.
51. George Barton, *Angels of the Battlefield: A History of the Catholic Sisterhoods in the Late Civil War* (Philadelphia: Catholic Art Publishing Company, 1879), 60–61.
52. Engelbrecht diary, 6 September 1862.
53. Davidson, *Diary and Letters,* 47.
54. Steiner, *Report,* 9.
55. A Confederate, *The Grayjackets: and How They Lived, Fought and Died, for Dixie* (Richmond: Jones Brothers & Company, 1867), 273.
56. Engelbrecht diary, 9 September 1862.
57. Markell diary, 8 September 1862.
58. Quoted in Murfin, *Gleam of Bayonets,* 101.
59. Markell diary, 9 September 1862.
60. Douglas, *I Rode with Stonewall,* 149.
61. Markell diary, 9 September 1862.
62. Von Borcke, *Memoirs,* 193.
63. W(illiam)W. Blackford, *War Years with Jeb Stuart,* (New York: Charles Scribners' Sons, 1945), 141.
64. Von Borcke, *Memoir* 196–197.
65. Blackford, *War Years,* 142.
66. Quoted in Bailey, *Bloodiest Day,* 18.
67. Steiner, *Report,* 11.

68. *Grayjackets,* 275; *The Examiner,* 24 September 1862. The editor was most concerned about the destruction of a "fine full length picture of the Immortal Washington, in their attack upon *The Examiner* office. . . . We did not think they would mutilate that picture. But they did; they kicked it about in the street, and tore it into tatters.—Further comment is unnecessary!"

69. Hartzler, *Marylanders in the Confederacy,* 38, 315. The Maryland Guerrilla Zouaves were organized in Richmond and assigned to Louisiana troops by the Secretary of War.

70. Markell diary, 7 September 1862; Mrs. Mary Anna Jackson, *Memoirs of Stonewall Jackson* (Louisville, 1895), 332; Douglas, *I Rode with Stonewall,* 150. Zacharias also requested a hymn called "The Stoutest Rebel Must Resign."

71. John S. Robson, *How a One-Legged Rebel Lives: Reminiscences of the Civil War. . . ."* (1898), 119.

72. Quoted in Murfin, *Gleam of Bayonets,* 101.

73. John Greenleaf Whittier, "Barbara Frietchie," *Atlantic Monthly,* October 1863.

74. Dorothy McKay Quynn and William Rogers Quynn, "Barbara Frietschie," *Maryland Historical Magazine,* September 1942, 231; C. Sue Markell, *Short Stories of Life in Frederick in 1830* (Attic Treasures, 1948), 44.

75. Caroline H. Dall, *Barbara Fritchie* (Boston: Roberts Brothers, 1892), 27–36.

76. Hinkley, *Third Wisconsin Infantry,* 48–49.

77. James Madison Stone, *Personal Recollections of the Civil War* (Boston, 1918), 84.

78. Engelbrecht diary, 6 April 1868.

79. Douglas, *I Rode with Stonewall,* 151–152.

80. John Greenleaf Whittier, *Century,* (10 June 1886); quoted in "General Jesse Lee Reno at Frederick: Barbara Fritchie and her Flag," Civil War Papers Read before the Commandery of the State of Massachusetts, Military Order of the Loyal Legion of the U.S., Vol. II (Boston: Printed for the Commandery, 1900), 554.

81. "General Jesse Lee Reno at Frederick," 562; Quynn and Quynn, "Barbara Fritchie," 251–252. Some Quantrell descendants believed Quantrell's episode was actually the basis for the Whittier poem.

82. "Life in Frederick During the Civil War."

83. Mrs. [Anna] H[olstein], *Three Years in Field Hospitals of the Army of the Potomac* (Philadelphia: J. B. Lippincott Company, 1867), 24–25. *The Examiner* related several similar incidents.

84. William Miller Owen, *In Camp Life and Battle with the Washington Artillery of New Orleans* (Boston: Ticknor and Co., 1885), 133.

85. Von Borcke, *Memoirs,* 201–202.

86. Markell diary, 12 September 1862.

87. Steiner, *Report,* 23.

88. Markell diary, 12 September 1862.

89. Von Borcke, *Memoirs,* 202–203.

90. Von Borcke, *Memoirs,* 205. Blackford was visiting the Ross family home (where his father had lived while studying law in Frederick) when the cavalry became engaged, and one of the young ladies there ran outside "under a skirmish fire" to present the cake she had made for him. "There was nothing to do with it but strap it to my saddle," he wrote later, "to be enjoyed around our campfire that night." (Blackford, 142–143.)

## CHAPTER 3: "What a Terrible Feeling This Is"

1. Ham Chamberlayne, *Ham Chamberlayne—A Virginian: Letters and Papers of an Artillery Officer in the War for Southern Independence, 1861–1865* (Richmond: Dietz Printing Company, 1932), 105.
2. Davidson, *Diary and Letters,* 48.
3. An English Combatant, *Battle-fields of the South, From Bull Run to Fredericksburgh* (New York: John Bradburn, 1864; reprint ed., Time-Life Books, 1984), 467.
4. George M. Neese, *Three Years in the Confederate Horse Artillery* (New York and Washington: Neale Publishing Company, 1911), 117–118.
5. Hunter, *A High Private's Account,* Vol. X, 508.
6. A Confederate, *The Grayjackets,* 274.
7. An English Combatant, *Battle-fields of the South,* 467.
8. Proclamations quoted in Steiner, *Report,* 15–16.
9. David E. Johnston, *The Story of a Confederate Boy in the Civil War* (Portland, Or.: Prudhomme Company, 1914), 138. Johnston made this observation in Hagerstown.
10. Bradley Tyler Johnson, "Address on the First Maryland Campaign," *Southern Historical Society Papers,* Vol. XII, 504. A Southern correspondent agreed, observing the Maryland men to be "between two fires" and choosing to "sacrifice principal" to "secure [their] homes." (Quoted in Fletcher M. Green, "A People at War: Hagerstown, Maryland, June 15–August 31, 1863," *Maryland Historical Magazine,* December 1945, 253.) The First Maryland Regiment, CSA, was disbanded in August 1862 when its numbers were whittled to about two hundred fifty men. Johnson had always hoped to have a strong Maryland contingent in the Confederate army, but many Maryland men had enlisted with friends or kin in the regiments of other states.
11. Quoted in Hildebrand Collection. This unfinished, bloodstained letter was found on the field at Antietam.
12. (Napier Bartlett), *A Soldier's Story of the War, Including the Marches and Battles of the Washington Artillery and of Other Louisiana Troops* (New Orleans: Clark and Hafeline, 1874), 130.
13. Stevens, *Reminiscences,* 68.
14. Robson, *How a One-Legged Rebel Lives,* 118.
15. James Cooper Nisbet, *Four Years on the Firing Line,* ed. Bell Irvin Wiley (Jackson, Tenn.: McCowat-Mercer Press, 1963), 101.
16. John Gibbon, *Personal Recollections of the Civil War* (New York: G. P. Putnam's Sons, 1928), 74.
17. Abner Small, *Road to Richmond: The Civil War Memoirs of Major Abner Small of the 16th Maine Volunteers,* ed. Harold Adamson Small (Berkeley: University of California Press, 1939), 46.
18. Quoted in "The Civil War in the Poolesville Area," typed manuscript, November 1961, Frederick County Historical Society Archives.
19. William Watson, *Letters of a Civil War Surgeon,* ed. Paul Fatout (West Lafayette, Ind.: Purdue Research Foundation, 1961), 25. Dr. Watson, a Pennsylvanian, added, "There are plenty of scamps here willing and ready to put a bullet through a 'Yankee soldier' any time, could they do it in safety. . . ."
20. Hinkley, *Third Wisconsin Infantry,* 46.
21. Quoted in Bailey, *Bloodiest Day,* 13.
22. Josiah Marshall Favill, *Diary of a Young Officer Serving with the Armies of the United States During the War of the Rebellion* (Chicago: R. R. Donnelly and Sons, 1909), 181.
23. George McClellan, *The Civil War Papers of George B. McClellan: Selected Correspondence, 1860–1865,* ed. Stephen Sears (New York: Ticknor and Fields, 1989), 435.
24. Jacob H. Cole, *Under Five Commanders, or A Boy's Experience with the Army of the Potomac* (Paterson, N. J.: News Printing Company, 1906), 77.
25. Favill, *Diary of a Young Officer,* 182.

26. Sam Healy journal, Gettysburg National Military Park, copy in George Brigham Jr. Library.

27. Rutherford B. Hayes, *Diary and Letters of Rutherford Birchard Hayes, Nineteenth President of the United States*, Vol. II: 1861–1865, ed. Charles Richard Williams (The Ohio State Archaeological and Historical Society, 1922), 346.

28. Steiner, *Report*, 22.

29. The Survivors' Association, *History of the Corn Exchange Regiment, 118th Pennsylvania Volunteers, from the First Engagement at Antietam to Appomattox* (Philadelphia: J. L. Smith, 1892), 35.

30. Engelbrecht diary, 13 September 1862.

31. Hayes, *Diary and Letters*, 352.

32. Joseph Gould, *The Story of the Forty-Eighth* (Philadelphia: Printed by A. M. Slocum Company, 1908), 77.

33. Hayes, *Diary and Letters*, 352.

34. Thomas Francis Galwey, *The Valiant Hours*, ed. W. S. Nye (Harrisburg: Stackpole Company, 1961), 35.

35. David L. Thompson letter, Western Maryland Room Archives, Washington County Free Library. Thompson was a private of Company G, 19th New York Volunteers.

36. Henry J. Spooner, *The Maryland Campaign with the 4th Rhode Island* (Providence: Snow and Farnham, 1903), 14.

37. Hinkley, *Third Wisconsin Infantry*, 48.

38. Favill, *Diary of a Young Officer*, 183.

39. Healy journal. This unit passed through on 14 September.

40. McClellan, *Civil War Papers*, 458.

41. McClellan, *Civil War Papers*, 453.

42. Ivy W. Dugan, 15th Georgia, letter, 1 October 1862, copy in George Brigham Jr. Library.

43. Steiner, *Report*, 6.

44. George C. Rhoderick Jr., *The Early History of Middletown, Maryland* (Middletown: Middletown Valley Historical Society, 1989), 13.

45. Dugan letter.

46. Koogle diary, 7–9 September 1862.

47. Charles Branch Clark, *Politics in Maryland During the Civil War* (Chestertown, Md.: n.p., 1952), 160.

48. Warren Lee Goss, *Recollections of a Private: A Story of the Army of the Potomac* (New York: Thomas Y. Crowell & Company 1890), 103.

49. Nesbitt diary, 9 September 1862. He noted on 12 September that one of his slaves "came down out of the mountain and went to work."

50. A. Thomas Fleming account, April 1996, Frederick County Historical Society Archives.

51. Johann Jakob Rutlinger, quoted in Rhoderick, *Early History of Middletown*, 32–33.

52. Telegram, 5 July 1862: "Mr. Burns has been arrested for tearing down a Union flag last night and there is no one to relieve me. Shall I close the office tonight?" Frederick County Historical Society Archives.

53. Sparrow diary. The Eighth Federal Population Census, 1860, lists "Trade" as Sparrow's occupation.

54. Murfin, *Gleam of Bayonets*, 93.

55. Warfield, *A Confederate Soldier's Memoirs*, 109.

56. Francis W. Dawson, *Reminiscences of Confederate Service, 1861–1865*, ed. Bell I. Wiley (Baton Rouge: Louisiana State University Press, 1980), 140–141.

57. Bartlett, *A Soldier's Story*, 130.

58. William Thomas Poague, *Gunner with Stonewall: Reminiscences of William Thomas Poague*, ed. Monroe F. Cockrell (Jackson, Tenn.: McCowat-Mercer Press, 1957), 41–42.

59. Polley, *A Soldier's Letters,* 81.
60. Poague, *Gunner with Stonewall,* 42.
61. Goss, *Recollections of a Private,* 103.
62. Thompson letter.
63. Neese, *Three Years in the Confederate Horse Artillery,* 117.
64. Franklin Lafayette Riley, *Grandfather's Journal,* 104.
65. Charles F. Walcott, *History of the Twenty-First Regiment Massachusetts Volunteers in the War for the Preservation of the Union, 1861–1865* (Boston: Houghton Mifflin, 1882), 188.
66. Walcott, *History of the Twenty-First Regiment,* 193.
67. Quoted in Murfin, *Gleam of Bayonets,* 94.
68. Quoted in Murfin, *Gleam of Bayonets,* 93.
69. Sparrow diary, September 1862.
70. "Reminiscences of the Civil War," *The Valley Register,* n.d., clipping in George Brigham Jr. Library.
71. Chamberlayne, *Ham Chamberlayne,* 105.
72. Dugan letter.
73. Edward King Wightman, *From Antietam to Fort Fisher: The Civil War Letters of Edward King Wightman, 1862–1865,* ed. Edward G. Longacre (Cranbury, N. J.: Associated University Presses, 1985), 34.
74. David Hunter Strother, *A Virginia Yankee in the Civil War: The Diaries of David Hunter Strother,* ed. Cecil D. Eby Jr. (Chapel Hill: University of North Carolina Press, 1961), 102.
75. Healy journal.
76. Hayes, *Diary and Letters,* 346–347; E. P. Scammon, "The General Reno Story," Address delivered at the 23rd Regiment OHVI Annual Reunion, 22 August 1888, reprinted in *Fremont Journal,* 29 March 1889.
77. Richard Ray Duncan, *The Social and Economic Impact of the Civil War in Maryland* (Ph.D. dissertation, Ohio State University, 1963), 244.
78. Steiner, *Report,* 26.
79. Strother, *Virginia Yankee,* 106.
80. Walcott, *History of the Twenty-First Regiment,* 188.
81. Goss, *Recollections of a Private,* 103.
82. Quoted in Murfin, *Gleam of Bayonets,* 93, written by a man who had witnessed the river crossing.
83. Angela Davis, *War Reminiscences,* 35.
84. Warfield, *Confederate Soldier's Memoirs,* 110.
85. A. C. Koogle, "Fiftieth Anniversary of South Mountain Battle," *The (Middletown) Valley Register,* 13 September 1912.
86. J. R. Boulware diary, Virginia State Museum (Richmond), copy in George Brigham Jr. Library.
87. McDaniel, *Diary of Battles,* 11.
88. Douglas, *I Rode with Stonewall,* 152; "Jesse Lee Reno at Frederick," 561.
89. Rhoderick, *Early History of Middletown,* 15; Eighth Federal Population Census. According to the 1860 census, Nancy was one of six children in the household of George W. and Catherine Crouse. There are no records of other family members during the incident.
90. T. C. Harbaugh, "The Ballad of Nancy Crouse," *Middletown Valley in Song and Story* (1910), 24. This is one stanza of the poem.
91. John H. Bast Sr., *The History of Boonsboro,* Western Maryland Room, Washington County Free Library; Eighth Federal Population Census, 1860; (Moore), *Odds and Ends.*
92. (Moore), *Odds and Ends.* The 4 September 1862 issue noted that of 508 men enrolled in the Boonsboro militia, "about fifty" enlisted. John Christian Brining, first captain of the Boonsboro Guards, was father of Clara Brining, who stayed in secessionist Jacob

Miller's Sharpsburg home during the battle of Antietam (see p.139–140). Although Boonsboro gained a reputation among Union soldiers as a stoutly loyal town, the news items gleaned from this manuscript indicate that Boonsboro had its share of Southern sympathizers. In September 1861, Franklin McAuly of Boonsboro made news for being arrested while trying to "escape to Virginia with wagons and horses," and Reverend William H. Wilson was arrested for smuggling medicine to Confederates. On 10 April 1862, the editor summarized his perspective on divided loyalties in Boonsboro by noting that "the confederates and southern sympathizers have tried to put us out of business. Lots of our patrons have deserted us on our union sympathies, but we have joined two-fold in subscriptions."

93. Doug Bast, 7 January 1994.
94. S. Bassett French, *Centennial Tales: Memoirs of Colonel "Chester" S. Bassett French, Extra Aide-de-Camp to Generals Lee and Jackson, The Army of Northern Virginia, 1861–1865,* comp. Glen Oldaker (New York: A Reflection Book, 1962), 62–66.
95. Douglas, *I Rode with Stonewall,* 153.
96. Angela Davis, *War Reminiscences,* 22–23.
97. Angela Davis, *War Reminiscences,* 29–30.
98. Douglas, *I Rode with Stonewall,* 154.
99. Angela Davis, *War Reminiscences,* 31–32.
100. Boulware diary.
101. Dugan letter.
102. Angela Davis, *War Reminiscences,* 32–33.
103. Oliver T. Reilly, *The Battlefield of Antietam* (Hagerstown, 1906), 20.
104. Hunter, *A High Private's Account,* Vol. X, 509.
105. Angela Davis, *War Reminiscences,* 36.
106. Hunter, *A High Private's Account,* Vol. X, 511.
107. Dugan letter.
108. Warfield, *Confederate Soldier's Memoirs,* 127.
109. Von Borcke, *Memoirs,* 186, regarding a stop in Poolesville.
110. Quoted in Murfin, *Gleam of Bayonets,* 163.
111. Polley, *A Soldier's Letters,* 82.
112. Bartlett, *A Soldier's Story,* 131.
113. Quoted in Priest, *Antietam,* 4.
114. Markell diary, 13–14 September 1862. According to Virginia O. Bardsley, who edited portions of Markell's diary (see "Frederick Diary: September 5–14, 1862," *Maryland Magazine of History,* June 1965), Maj. Henry Schley, who convinced the Federal troopers to abandon their search, had known the Markells all his life.
115. Thompson letter.
116. The Survivors' Association, *History of the Corn Exchange Regiment,* 35.

## CHAPTER 4: "I'll Die First"

1. John Castle, "Letters from the People: Says There was Cannonading at Braddock Heights," *Valley Register*(?), 24 May 1932, clipping in George Brigham Jr. Library.
2. George William Beale, *A Lieutenant of Cavalry in Lee's Army* (Boston: Gorham Press, 1918), 44. Accounts differ regarding the exact location of Hamburg. Contextual clues in Beale's account (and others) place Hamburg on or near the crest of Catoctin Mountain. Other accounts refer to "Hamburg Pass" on South Mountain.
3. Von Borcke, *Memoirs,* 210–211.
4. A. C. Koogle, "The Fiftieth Anniversary of South Mountain Battle," *The Valley Register,* 13 September 1912. According to the Eighth Federal Population Census, Adam Koogle Sr. was a wheelwright. He and his wife, Catherine, had six children at home in

1860, including eighteen-year-old Christian (who may have been A. C.). Their household also included a twenty-one-year-old wheelwright (who may have been an apprentice), a thirty-five-year-old paid laborer, and three female slaves, ages twenty-four, fourteen, and twelve; the identity of the seven-year-old in Koogle's account is unclear. When Koogle was wounded at Antietam a week later, he was brought home and shared quarters with the wounded Confederate. "It was the mingling of the blue and the gray," he wrote. "I must say we became quite chummy."

5. Quoted in Murfin, *Gleam of Bayonets,* 170; and Bailey, *Bloodiest Day,* 38.
6. E. M. Woodward, *Our Campaigns* (Philadelphia: John E. Potter and Company, 1865), 195.
7. H. W. Burlingame, *Personal Reminiscences of the Civil War, 1861–1865* (1904), copy in George Brigham Jr. Library.
8. Calvin Leach diary (Leach Diary, #1875), in the Southern Historical Collection, University of North Carolina Library, Chapel Hill, typed copy in George Brigham Jr. Library.
9. Quoted in Bailey, *Bloodiest Day,* 47.
10. Transcript of interview with Edna May Dayton, courtesy Steven Stotelmyer. Edna May Dayton's great-great-grandparents were Daniel and Mary Wise; her maternal grandmother was Cecilia, five years old during the battle. Cecilia's future husband, seven in 1862, refused to leave his home and watched the battle from the roof of his family's barn.
11. Daniel H. Hill, "The Battle of South Mountain, or Boonsboro; Fighting for Time at Turner's and Fox's Gaps," *Battles and Leaders of the Civil War,* Vol. II (New York: Century Company, 1884–1887), 562.
12. Otis D. Smith reminiscence (Thatch Papers, #1102), in the Southern Historical Collection, University of North Carolina Library, Chapel Hill, copy in George Brigham Jr. Library.
13. Garland was embalmed and sent home by J. C. Brining, former militia captain, of Boonsboro.
14. Quoted in Bailey, *Bloodiest Day,* 47.
15. Smith reminiscence.
16. NAT letter, camp near Winchester, Virginia, 6 October 1862; courtesy Al Fiedler Jr. collection.
17. John Dooley, *John Dooley: His War Journal,* ed. Joseph T. Durkin (Washington, D.C.: Georgetown University Press, 1945), 35.
18. Sparrow diary.
19. Charles S. Adams, *The Civil War in Frederick County, Maryland: A Guide to Forty-Nine Historic Points of Interest* (self-published, 1995), 24. This church is now known as the Christ Reformed Church.
20. Isaac Hall, *History of the 97th Regiment of New York Volunteers (Conkling Rifles) in the War for the Union* (Utica, N.Y.: Press of L. C. Childs and Sons, 1890), 86.
21. Clifton Johnson, *Battlefield Adventures,* 96. According to the Eighth Federal Population Census, 1860, Jacob Nicodemus employed Alexander Root, age twenty-one, as a farmhand. However, some discrepancy exists regarding Alexander's name (see Chapter 7, note 40). Nicodemus also owned one female slave, thirteen years old.
22. C. C. Kaufman, "Tells of Experiences During the Civil War," *Valley Register,* 25 January and 1 February 1929.
23. Thompson letter.
24. Quoted in Sears, *Landscape Turned Red,* 151.
25. Clipping from the North Carolina State Archives, written by an officer of the Second North Carolina, copy in George Brigham Jr. Library.
26. Col. Alfred Iverson letter to General Hill, 23 August 1895, copy in George Brigham Jr. Library.

27. Thomas Ellis, M.D., *Leaves from the Diary of an Army Surgeon* (New York: John Bradburn, 1863), 248.
28. Burkittsville District Heritage Society, Inc., *Burkittsville, Maryland: A Nineteenth Century Townscape,* 1979.
29. Neese, *Three Years in the Confederate Horse Artillery,* 119.
30. Quoted in Bailey, *Bloodiest Day,* 53. It is likely that most Unionists had either fled or retreated to their cellars by this time.
31. Neese, *Three Years in the Confederate Horse Artillery,* 122.
32. Member of 96th Pennsylvania, quoted in Timothy J. Reese, *Sealed with Their Lives: The Battle for Crampton's Gap, Burkittsville, Maryland, September 14, 1862* (Baltimore: Butternut and Blue, 1998), 102.
33. Quoted in Reese, *Sealed with Their Lives,* 98–99.
34. Thomas Roger Johnson, "War Reminiscences," *Valley Register(?),* clipping in Frederick County Historical Society Archives.
35. Benjamin Crowninshield, *A History of the First Regiment of Massachusetts Cavalry Volunteer,* (Boston and New York: Houghton, Mifflin and Company, 1891), 75.
36. Healey journal, 28.
37. Dooley, *War Journal,* 38.
38. Woodward, *Our Campaigns,* 200.
39. NAT letter, 6 October 1862.
40. Dooley, *War Journal,* 38.
41. Reilly, *Battlefield of Antietam,* 19.
42. Edward O. Lord, ed., *History of the Ninth Regiment New Hampshire Volunteers in the War of the Rebellion* (Concord, N.H.: Republican Press Association, 1895), 90.
43. Matthew H. Hurlenger diary, 15 September 1862, copy in George Brigham Jr. Library.
44. Cole, *Under Five Commanders,* 81.
45. Quoted in Murfin, *Gleam of Bayonets,* 197.
46. R. B. Wilson account, 22 July 1899, Library of Congress, copy in George Brigham Jr. Library.
47. Steven R. Stotelmyer, "The Truth About Wise's Well: Setting the Record Straight on South Mountain," *Blue and Gray,* Vol. VII, No. 1, 30.
48. Quoted in Stotelmyer, *Wise's Well,* 34.
49. Gould, *Story of the Forth-Eighth,* 78.
50. Walcott, *History of the Twenty-First Regiment,* 193.
51. Dayton interview transcript. Cecilia told of staying in a church or school, but she didn't identify where it was or exactly how long the Wises stayed there.
52. Healey journal, 29.
53. Quoted in Stotelmyer, 33.
54. Otho Nesbitt diary, 16 September 1862.
55. John W. M. Long, "South Mountain Battle Events," *Valley Register,* 7 July 1922.
56. Ellis, *Diary of an Army Surgeon,* 259.
57. Doug Bast Collection, The Boonsborough Museum of History.
58. J. Hoke, *Historical Reminiscences of the War* (Chambersburg, Pa. M. A. Foltz, 1884), 24.
59. Thompson letter.
60. Doug Bast, 7 January 1994.
61. Samuel Compton account, Manuscript Department, Duke University, copy in George Brigham Jr. Library.
62. R. B. Wilson account, Library of Congress, copy in George Brigham Jr. Library. Gould of the 48th Pennsylvania also reported the crude burial: "A detail was made to bury the dead, as the hot weather tended to make the bodies unfit to handle in a few hours. Trenches were dug along the side of a hill bordering the road, and the earth pulled down upon the bodies after they had been laid therein. A well close to the house was filled with the bodies of those that lay in the lane in front of our line. At Sharpsburg,

MD, in 1895, the writer was informed by one who was an eye-witness, that forty bodies were taken out of the well, and carried south for burial." (Gould, *Story of the Forty-Eighth*, 78.) Cecilia told her granddaughter that the well was not in use or even abandoned, as some accounts indicate, but rather that the family was in the process of digging it when the troops arrived. (Dayton interview transcript.)

63. Hall, *History of the 97th Regiment*, 86.
64. Hartzler, *Marylanders in the Confederacy*, 50; Gary, *Answering the Call*, 9. One Dr. Jacob Baer is listed as a local physician in Middletown (Rhoderick, *Early History of Middletown*, 67); another is listed in Frederick (C. W. Williams, *Williams' Frederick Directory, City Guide, and Business Mirror*, Frederick: 1859, 27).
65. Anecdotal records list the children as noted. The Eighth Federal Census, 1860, lists the family as follows: Jacob Rudy, forty-five; Eliza Rudy, forty-six; Mary(?), twenty-one; Daniel, nineteen; Cordelia, sixteen; Rebecca, fourteen; Sarah, eleven; Laura, six; and Charlie, six. Their eldest daughter might have left home by 1862, and the use of middle names might account for some of the discrepancies.
66. "Hayes at Middletown," *Valley Register*, 27 April, 1877.
67. Hayes, *Diary and Letters*, 353–354.
68. William Jobe, *Recollections and Reminiscences of a Soldier of the Union in the War of the Rebellion of 1861 to 1865*, Adams County Historical Society, copy in George Brigham Jr. Library.
69. H. N. Minnigh, *History of Company K, 1st Pennsylvania Reserves: The Boys who Fought at Home* (Duncansville, Pa.: Home Point Publisher, n.d.), 38–39.
70. Tim Reese, 28 April 1997. Although Henry McDuell was a vocal Southern sympathizer, there is no record of Magdalena's personal opinions.
71. Ellis, *Diary of an Army Surgeon*, 248.
72. Burkittsville District Heritage Society, *Burkittsville, Maryland*.
73. Ellis, *Diary of an Army Surgeon*, 253.
74. Tim Reese, 28 April 1997. Mell died of pneumonia. The Lees buried him at St. Mark's Episcopal Church near their home. Unlike the remains of other Confederate veterans, which were ultimately moved to Hagerstown, Mell's grave remains undisturbed.
75. Thomas Roger Johnson, *War Reminiscences*.
76. B. F. Blakeslee, *History of the 16th Connecticutt Volunteers* (Hartford: Case, Lockwood & Brainard Company, 1875), 10–11.
77. Sparrow diary.

## CHAPTER 5: "It Was an Awful Time"

1. Von Borcke, *Memoirs*, 219.
2. Warfield, *Confederate Soldier's Memoirs*, 112.
3. Beale, *Lieutenant of Cavalry*, 45.
4. The Survivors' Association, *History of the Corn Exchange Regiment*, 36.
5. Rufus Dawes, *Service with the Sixth Wisconsin Volunteers* (Madison: State Historical Society of Wisconsin, 1962), 79.
6. The Survivors' Association, *History of the Corn Exchange Regiment*, 36–37.
7. Murfin, *Gleam of Bayonets*, 100–101. The ploy may have been somewhat successful, but Wyand's store was too enticing: Hungry Confederates used their bayonets to pry open the shutters and stole his entire stock of goods. (Reilly, *Battlefield of Antietam*, 19–20.) See also Chapter 3 for note of damage done to another Keedysville store earlier in the campaign.
8. "Tilghmanton Man was Another 'Good Samaritan of Antietam,'" *The (Hagerstown) Daily Mail*, 29 April 1961.

9. Henry, *History of the Brethren*, 370.
10. Clifton Johnson, *Battlefield Adventures*, 118.
11. Ellis, *Diary of an Army Surgeon*, 262.
12. W. H. Andres, 1901, quoted in Hildebrand Collection.
13. Hunter, *A High Private's Account*, Vol. X, 511.
14. Clifton Johnson, *Battlefield Adventures*, 114. Similar accounts identify the boatman as Joseph McGraw.
15. John N. Opie, *A Rebel Cavalryman with Lee, Stuart, and Johnson* (Chicago: W. B. Conkey Company, 1899), 78.
16. Clifton Johnson, *Battlefield Adventures*, 119, 104.
17. Hunter, *A High Private's Account*, Vol. X, 512.
18. Quoted in Sears, *Landscape Turned Red*, 179.
19. Clifton Johnson, *Battlefield Adventures*, 109. Johnson does not identify by name any of the people he interviewed. The slave refers to her "boss" as Mr. Delaney and identifies herself as "cook at Delaney's Tavern." The only Delaney listed in the Eighth Federal Population Census, 1860, is a tailor; no "Delaney" is listed as an owner in the slave census. However, the identity and story of every other Sharpsburg resident in Johnson's book has been verified by other sources. Because the woman was a slave, it is especially difficult to find even rudimentary information about her identity.
20. Clifton Johnson, *Battlefield Adventures*, 81.
21. Reilly, *Battlefield of Antietam*, 15.
22. Hildebrand Collection. Landis may have been her married name. This story was told to a granddaughter.
23. Reilly, *Battlefield of Antietam*, 19; Williams, *History and Biographical Record*, 796–797.
24. Reilly, *Battlefield of Antietam*, 20.
25. Reilly, *Battlefield of Antietam*, 22.
26. Virginia Mumma Hildebrand, "A Rival for Barbara Fritchie," Antietam National Battlefield Archives.
27. Clifton Johnson, *Battlefield Adventures*, 118–119. The story told in "A Rival for Barbara Fritchie" is more belabored. It relates how family members and neighbors argued with Theresa, wanting her to remove the flag in the interest of public safety; she is described as "a stubborn, unreasonable, head-strong, spoiled child." See also "Story of Flag at Antietam," by Fred Cross, *The Daily Mail*, 30 January 1934. Other accounts indicate that Theresa didn't remove the flag until threatened and that Confederates searched the house.
28. Margaret Beltemacchi letter to Rep. Goodloe Byron, 3 June 1971, Antietam National Battlefield Archives. The letter relates a story told by a woman known as "Grandma Siepel" in the 1940s, who identified herself as a cousin to Robert E. Lee. The story refers to the minister as "circuit-riding"; rather than literally riding a traditional traveling circuit, it was likely by the 1860s that the minister had a charge of several rural churches.
29. Quoted in Bailey, *Bloodiest Day*, 60.
30. NAT letter, 6 October 1862.
31. Samuel Mumma Sr. (b. 1801, d. 1876) had five children with his first wife, Barbara Hertzler (b. 1807, d. 1833). He married Elizabeth Miller (b. 1815, d. 1898), a sister of D. R. Miller, in 1843 and had eleven more children. Genealogy courtesy Wilmer Mumma.
32. E. Russell Hicks, "The Church on the Battlefield," *Morning Herald*, 23 April 1952.
33. Reilly, *Battlefield of Antietam*, 20; Hildebrand Collection.
34. Reilly, *Battlefield of Antietam*, 21; Frassanito, *Antietam*, 197; John W. Schildt, *Antietam Hospitals* (Chewsville, Md.: Antietam Publications, 1987), 16–17.
35. Favill, *Diary of a Young Officer*, 184.
36. Woodward, *Our Campaigns*, 201.

37. Schildt, *Antietam Hospitals,* 19–20.
38. Crowninshield, *History of the First Regiment,* 76.
39. Williams, *History and Biographical Record,* 369. Although not specified, the passage evidently referred to the Union occupation.
40. James I. Robertson Jr., "A Federal Surgeon at Sharpsburg," *Civil War History,* Vol. VI, No. 2, 136.
41. Schildt, *Antietam Hospitals,* 29.
42. Schildt, *Roads to Antietam* (Hagerstown, Md., 1985), 101.
43. Clifton Johnson, *Battlefield Adventures,* 109.
44. Bast, *History of Boonsboro.* The service records of these two men are not clear. Private Jacob Heck of Boonsboro is listed on the roster of Company G, Second Maryland Infantry, CSA; however, this unit did not form until after the battle of Antietam. Possibly Jacob Heck served in a Virginia unit during the first portion of the war. Federal rosters list two John Hecks: John L. Heck, of Company I, 13th Maryland Infantry (transferred from the First Maryland Infantry Regiment, Potomac Home Brigade); and John R. Heck, Company I, First Maryland Cavalry. This unit participated in the escape through Confederate lines just prior to the surrender of the Harpers Ferry garrison during the 1862 campaign.
45. Charles H. Kirk, ed. and comp., *History of the Fifteenth Pennsylvania Volunteer Cavalry* (Philadelphia: Society of the Fifteenth Pennsylvania Cavalry, 1906), 642.
46. Fred W. Cross, "Joseph McGraw at Antietam," Antietam National Battlefield Archives.
47. Douglas, *I Rode with Stonewall,* 168.
48. Douglas, *I Rode with Stonewall,* 167–168. Jackson's note was carefully saved. Wrote Douglas, "I have seen it spread upon satin and nicely framed, doing duty at bazaars and fairs for 'Confederate Homes,' since the war. During the war it was lithographed in Baltimore, and five hundred dollars were realized from the sale of those lithographs for the use of Confederate hospitals."
49. Von Borcke, *Memoirs,* 227–228.
50. Clifton Johnson, *Battlefield Adventures,* 110. There is no secondary source to corroborate this source. (See Chapter 5, note 19.) The woman clearly dated this incident the seventeenth; from what historians know of Robert E. Lee's movements, it is likely that it actually happened on the sixteenth.
51. Bartlett, *A Soldier's Story,* 136–137.
52. Reilly, *Battlefield of Antietam,* 22.
53. Reilly, *Battlefield of Antietam,* 23; and Hildebrand Collection. Some confusion exists about the family name, but the story was evidently related by Maggie Grice Hoffmaster.
54. Reilly, *Battlefield of Antietam,* 23. There is discrepancy among sources regarding the date of this visit; some authors note 15 September, others 16 September.
55. Appendix A, 141, Claim of Henry Piper vs. the United States, No. 445 Congressional Case December Term, 1886–87, Testimony of Mary Ellen Smith, 17 November 1886, copy at Antietam National Battlefield.
56. Untitled manuscript in Antietam Vertical File, Western Maryland Room, Washington County Public Library.
57. Reilly, *Battlefield of Antietam,* 19. The date of this incident is unclear.
58. Reilly, *Battlefield of Antietam,* 16. It is not clear whether her husband accompanied the family at this time.
59. Nisbet, *Four Years on the Firing Line,* 102.
60. Quoted in Murfin, *Gleam of Bayonets,* 208.
61. Reilly, *Battlefield of Antietam,* 17.

## CHAPTER 6: "Too Afraid to Cry"

1. Blackford, *War Years,* 151.
2. J. Polk Racine, *Recollections of a Veteran, or, Four Years in Dixie* (Elkton, Md.: The Appeal Printing Office, 1894; reprinted by the Cecil County Bicentennial Committee, 1987), 32.
3. James F. Clark letter to Samuel Mumma, 19 March 1906, and Samuel Mumma letter to James F. Clark, 22 March 1906, quoted in Hildebrand Collection. Clark was writing to claim responsibility; Mumma wrote that in 1863 he had talked to another soldier who was also involved and who had described the quilt and shape of the bed to Mumma.
4. Quoted in Sears, *Landscape Turned Red,* 208.
5. Paula S. Reed, *History Report: The D. R. Miller Farm,* September 1991, Antietam National Battlefield; Fred W. Cross, "Alexander W. Davis, of Sharpsburg," *Daily Mail,* 13 March 1934. Unfortunately, very little is known about D. R. Miller. Some historians have speculated that even his name was a local moniker—short for "doctor"—awarded Miller for an affinity with folk medicine.
6. Quoted in Bailey, *Bloodiest Day,* 70.
7. Quoted in Sears, *Landscape Turned Red,* 234.
8. Priest, *Antietam,* 77.
9. A. C. Koogle, *Fiftieth Anniversary.*
10. Clifton Johnson, *Battlefield Adventures,* 114; Cross, "Joseph McGraw at Antietam"; Fred W. Cross, "The Strong House," *Daily Mail,* 22 March 1934. These accounts contain minor discrepancies.
11. NAT letter, 6 October 1862.
12. Reilly, *Battlefield of Antietam,* 10.
13. Samuel Michael letter, 27 November 1862, Antietam National Battlefield Archives.
14. Clifton Johnson, *Battlefield Adventures,* 120. Accounts vary, estimating the number of refugees in the Kretzer cellar from sixty to two hundred.
15. Reilly, *Battlefield of Antietam,* 23, story attributed to Anne Kretzer; *The Obstetrical Records of Dr. Augustus [sic] Biggs, of Sharpsburg, Washington County, Maryland, 1836–1888,* transcribed by Rosamund Ann Ball, Western Maryland Room, Washington County Free Library. Biggs recorded births only in the fathers' names.
16. Reilly, *Battlefield of Antietam,* 14–16; John P. Smith, "Accounts of Damage," *Antietam Valley Record,* 3 October 1895.
17. Reilly, *Battlefield of Antietam,* 20.
18. Interview with Mrs. Stella Lyne, 24 January 1934, transcript at Antietam National Battlefield Archives; Paula Stoner (Reed), *Household Property of the Biggs Family,* 1980, and Jeffrey A. Wyand, *The William Chapline House,* 1974, courtesy Marian and Sid Gale.
19. Clifton Johnson, *Battlefield Adventures,* 111. See Chapter 5, notes 19 and 50.
20. Elizabeth Miller letter, 8 February 1863. The letter is signed "your fond Sister Elisabeth" and, after a postscript, "your Sister ERM." Jacob's oldest daughter was named Elizabeth (b. 1812), but she had married Franklin Blackford; it is not clear why she didn't sign her initials with a B.
21. Reilly, *Battlefield of Antietam,* 18; Douglas, *I Rode with Stonewall,* 170–171; John P. Smith, "Reminiscences of Sharpsburg, Maryland," *Antietam Valley Record,* 26 September 1895.
22. Smith, *Reminiscences of Sharpsburg.* The girls were apparently staying with Savilla Miller at the time. Although Savilla and Jeanette were close in age, Jeanette was evidently Savilla's niece, Elizabeth's daughter. An undated wartime letter from "Milly" Miller (possibly Savilla) complains, "I have only one girl living with me now and could get along very well if Jenett would be more willing to help, but she had an idea in her head that she knows how to do everything and it is no use for her to learn. . . ." (Miller Letter

Collection, Antietam National Battlefield Archives.) Clara Brining was daughter of cabinetmaker and one-time militia captain John C. Brining of Boonsboro.

23. Alexander Hunter, *Johnny Reb and Billy Yank* (New York: Neal Publishing Company, 1905), 286–287.

24. Estimates range from seventy-five to three hundred people.

25. Elizabeth Miller letter, 8 February 1863. She was quoting several family friends who weathered the battle there.

26. Interview with Bud Shackelford, 24 January 1934, transcript at Antietam National Battlefield Archives.

27. Reilly, *Battlefield of Antietam*, 22.

28. Nesbitt diary.

29. Angela Davis, *War Reminiscences*, 43.

30. Untitled narrative, "Civil War—Personal Recollections," Vertical File, Enoch Pratt Public Library, Baltimore, Maryland.

31. Murfin, *Gleam of Bayonets*, 22.

32. Hoke, *Historical Reminiscences*, 26–27.

33. Reilly, *Battlefield of Antietam*, 19.

34. Sears, *Landscape Turned Red*, 297–298.

35. Quoted in Bailey, *Bloodiest Day*, 87.

36. Some records indicate that the Roulettes had five children at the time of the battle, but their youngest child was probably born after the 1860 census was taken; she died in October 1862 and therefore does not appear on later records.

37. Quoted in Sears, *Landscape Turned Red*, 263.

38. Quoted in Murfin, *Gleam of Bayonets*, 257, referenced to Connecticut troops; see also Reilly, *Battlefield of Antietam*, 20: "Captain Samuel Wright of a Company of the 29th Mass. saw Mr. Roulette come out of the cellar and for a short while stand and look at them." The Confederates earlier chased in the Roulette cellar had evidently left by this time, or perhaps they had been chased into the cellar of an outbuilding.

39. Quoted in Bailey, *Bloodiest Day*, 102.

40. McClellan, *Civil War Papers*, 468; the telegram was sent from Middletown at 1:45 P.M. on 17 September.

41. Shackelford Interview.

42. Frassanito, *Antietam*, 267; Judy Farris letter, 6 June 1996, Antietam National Battlefield Archives. Census records from 1860 list David Reel, six young children, and two women who have not been identified by family genealogists, Sarah (age fifty) and Barbara (age twenty-seven). Barbara may have been at the farm on 17 September .

43. Untitled manuscript, Antietam Vertical File, Western Maryland Room, Washington County Free Library.

44. "Tilghmanton Man was Another 'Good Samaritan of Antietam,'" *The Daily Mail*, 29 April 1961.

45. "Report of Captain William M. Graham, Battery K., First US Artillery," *Official Reports of the War of the Rebellion. . . .*, copy at Antietam National Battlefield Archives; Sears, *Landscape Turned Red*, 298; Reilly, *Battlefield of Antietam*, 16; "Martin Eakle at Antietam." Graham attributed the errand of mercy to "Mr. Piper"; perhaps he was too astonished to ask Eakle's name. Reilly described a man who brought bread, ham, cakes, and pies "that had been sent by some good ladies" during the hardest fighting at Bloody Lane, "but no one today knows who he was or where he came from." There was confusion about the Samaritan's identification for years, although today the man is generally believed to have been Eakle. There is no record of where Eakle's wife Kate and their six children, one black female servant, and three slaves weathered the battle.

46. Williams, *History and Biographical Record*, 339.

47. Clifton Johnson, *Battlefield Adventures*, 120–121; Hildebrand Collection.

48. Reilly, *Battlefield of Antietam*, 45.

49. NAT letter, 6 October 1862.
50. Laura Elizabeth (Lee) Battle, *Forget-Me-Nots of the Civil War: A Romance, Containing Reminiscences and Original Letters of Two Confederate Soldiers* (St. Louis, Mo.: A. R. Fleming, 1909), 76–77. Confederate surgeons were working in the Piper barn but probably retreated when the Union line took possession of the farm after driving the Confederates out of the Sunken Road. Since the house today shows no sign of such extensive damage, this episode may have taken place in a summer kitchen.
51. Reilly, *Battlefield of Antietam*, 16.
52. Beale, *Lieutenant of Cavalry*, 48–49.
53. Priest, *Antietam*, 127.
54. Murfin, *Gleam of Bayonets*, 231.
55. Recollections of Ada Mumma Thomas, June 1934, in Hildebrand Collection. According to the Piper Family History compiled by S. Webster Piper, Martha Ada Mumma was born on 1 July 1859, making her only three years old at the time of the battle.
56. Quoted in Bailey, *Bloodiest Day*, 120.
57. Earl Roulette, 30 May 1997. Earl's grandfather Joseph Snavely was twelve in 1862.
58. Quoted in Sears, *Landscape Turned Red*, 294.
59. Fred W. Cross, "A Visit and Reflections at Antietam," 1930, Antietam National Battlefield Archives.
60. Clifton Johnson, *Battlefield Adventures*, 121.
61. Edward A. Moore, *The Story of a Canoneer Under Stonewall Jackson* (New York and Washington: Neale Publishing Company, 1907), 154–155.
62. Elizabeth Miller letter, 8 February 1863. She added, "The shels were all from the yankies that made all this distruction and distress. . . ."
63. Clifton Johnson, *Battlefield Adventures*, 122.
64. Quoted in Bailey, *Bloodiest Day*, 137.
65. Quoted in Bailey, *Bloodiest Day*, 138.
66. Clifton Johnson, *Battlefield Adventures*, 111.
67. Neese, *Three Years in the Confederate Horse Artillery*, 126.
68. Beltemacchi letter.
69. Clifton Johnson, *Battlefield Adventures*, 122.
70. Frye and Schildt, *Antietam Remembered*, 33.

## CHAPTER 7: "A Smell of Death in the Air"

1. Theodore J. Vanneman letter, 18 September 1862, Antietam National Battlefield Archives.
2. Clifton Johnson, *Battlefield Adventures*, 123.
3. Von Borcke, *Memoirs*, 236–237. In marked contrast, Surgeon Ellis noted that the Federal boys had been well fed the night before. "There was beef cooking on the fire. All about the camp, kettles stood in rows on blazing rails; and while the battle raged furiously at but a mile distant, rations were being prepared as quietly as if all were in camp. Thus our tired boys were sure of a supper ere they slept, while if the rebel soldiers had any thing at all to eat that night, it must have been a scanty bite all around." (Ellis, *Diary of an Army Surgeon*, 269–270.)
4. McClellan, *Civil War Papers*, 469.
5. Quoted in Bailey, *Bloodiest Day*, 150.
6. Clifton Johnson, *Battlefield Adventures*, 112.
7. Williams, *History and Biographical Record*, 1115.

8. Maxine Campbell, 1 May 1997. The child was the daughter of Jenny Bragounier Lumm and Solomon Lumm. Solomon Lumm (thirty) was a miller; he and his wife Jenny (twenty-seven) had a three-year-old and a five-year-old daughter in 1862.

9. Reilly, *Battlefield of Antietam*, 23; Hildebrand Collection.

10. Appendix A, Claim of Henry Piper vs. The United States, Testimony of Mary Ellen Smith, 7 November 1886, 141, copy in Antietam National Battlefield Archives.

11. Untitled manuscript, Antietam Vertical File, Western Maryland Room, Washington County Public Library.

12. Appendix A. . . . Testimony of Jeremiah Summers.

13. Reilly, *Battlefield of Antietam*, 19. The date of this incident is unclear.

14. Reilly, *Battlefield of Antietam*, 23.

15. NAT letter, 6 October 1862.

16. Royal W. Figg, *Where Men Only Dare to Go* (Richmond: Whittet and Shepperson, 1885), 47.

17. Wightman, *From Antietam to Fort Fisher*, 57. Private Wightman made this observation in October.

18. Nesbitt diary, 19 September 1862.

19. Scharf, *History of Western Maryland*, 251–252; Ellis, *Diary of an Army Surgeon*, 297.

20. Elizabeth Miller letter, 8 February 1863.

21. Beltemacchi letter.

22. Reilly, *Battlefield of Antietam*, 14.

23. Hildebrand Collection; Fred W. Cross, "A Sharpsburg Boy at Antietam," *Daily Mail*, 16 January 1934.

24. Clifton Johnson, *Battlefield Adventures*, 97.

25. Reilly, *Battlefield of Antietam*, 17.

26. Reilly, *Battlefield of Antietam*, 21.

27. Quoted in Sears, *Landscape Turned Red*, 337.

28. William Child letter, 22 September 1862, Antietam National Battlefield Archives.

29. Hildebrand Collection.

30. Fred W. Cross, "Three Gallant Officers of Ninth Corps at Antietam," *Daily Mail*, 16 February 1934.

31. Barston, *Angels of the Battlefield*, 78.

32. Angela Davis, *War Reminiscences*, 44–46.

33. Murfin, *Gleam of Bayonets*, 262.

34. Reilly, *Battlefield of Antietam*, 17.

35. Samuel Michael letter, 27 November 1862.

36. Clifton Johnson, *Battlefield Adventures*, 117.

37. Clifton Johnson, *Battlefield Adventures*, 101.

38. Reilly, *Battlefield of Antietam*, 23.

39. Favill, *Diary of a Young Officer*, 190.

40. Cross, "Alexander W. Davis, of Sharpsburg," Antietam National Battlefield Archives. This article contains information about "Uncle Aleck" Davis, who worked for the Nicodemus family. Other sources identify the Nicodemuses' hired hand as Alexander Root, mentioned earlier. The Eighth Federal Population Census, 1860, lists Elizabeth Root, fifty, and Alexander Root, twenty-one-year-old farmhand, in the Nicodemus household. Possibly Elizabeth Root married more than once, accounting for two names given to her son at different times.

41. Angela Davis, *War Reminiscences*, 52.

42. Quoted in Sears, *Landscape Turned Red*, 347.

43. Clifton Johnson, *Battlefield Adventures*, 117.

44. Frassanito, *Antietam*, 105; Reilly, *Battlefield of Antietam*, 22.

45. Clifton Johnson, *Battlefield Adventures*, 101.

46. NAT letter, 6 October 1862.

47. Davidson, *Diary and Letters*, 49.
48. Clifton Johnson, *Battlefield Adventures*, 123–124; Fred W. Cross, "Story of Flag at Antietam," *The Daily Mail*, 30 January 1934.
49. *My Diary in Which are Recorded the Movement of the Ninth Massachusetts Volunteers in the War of the Rebellion in the United States*, 19 September 1862.
50. Member of the 13th New York State Volunteers letter, 19 September 1862, printed in the *Rochester Daily Democrat and American*, 1 October 1862.
51. Goss, *Recollections of a Private*, 117.
52. Letter, Charles Curtis Brown Papers, University of Rochester Library, 22 September 1862.
53. Koogle diary, 18 September 1862.
54. Favill, *Diary of a Young Officer*, 190.
55. Galwey, *The Valiant Hours*, 46.
56. Nesbitt diary, 18–20 September 1862.
57. Laura Lee Davidson, "The Services of the Women of Maryland to the Confederate States," Civil War—Personal Narratives Vertical File, Enoch Pratt Public Library. Miss Macgill (spelling varies) was the sister of Dr. Charles Macgill of Hagerstown. In 1861, when a squad of Federal soldiers came to the house to arrest Dr. Macgill, who had Confederate sympathies, she tried to beat the soldiers away with a riding whip. The soldiers drew pistols and only interference by the cool-headed captain precluded an ugly incident. Miss Macgill's brother and father were both arrested. (Scharf, *History of Western Maryland*, 1139.)
58. Angela Davis, *War Reminiscences*, 43.
59. Reilly, *Battlefield of Antietam*, 21.
60. *Rochester Daily Democrat and American*, 30 September 1862.
61. W. W. S. letter, 3 December 1862, printed in the *Rochester Daily Democrat and American*, 9 December 1862. The "Mrs. Lee" in question may have been Mrs. Mary W. Lee of Pennsylvania, who had been quite active in relief work during the first two years of war. "When the battle at Sharpsburg became imminent, she procured transportation and, during the battle, stationed herself along the Sharpsburg road with medical supplies and two large tubs of water. With several other volunteers from Baltimore, she stayed at the Smoketown hospital for nearly three months. (L[inus] P. Brockett, *Women's Work in the Civil War: A Record of Heroism, Patriotism, and Patience* [Boston: R. H. Curran, 1867], 480–485.)
62. Stephen B. Oates, *A Woman of Valor: Clara Barton and the Civil War* (New York: Free Press, 1994), 91–93.
63. George Templeton Strong, *The Diary of George Templeton Strong: The Civil War, 1860–1865*, ed. Allan Nevins and Milton H. Thomas (New York: Macmillan, 1952), 24 September 1862, 260.
64. Quoted in Schildt, *Antietam Hospitals*, 11.
65. H(olstein), *Three Years in Field Hospitals*, 14.
66. Reilly, *Battlefield of Antietam*, 17, 20.
67. William H. Harries, "In the Ranks at Antietam," *Glimpses of the Nation's Struggle, Fourth Series* (St. Paul: H. L. Collins Company, 1898), 558.
68. *Union and Advertiser* (Rochester, N.Y.), 28 November 1862.
69. Jonathan Letterman, M.D., *Medical Recollections of the Army of the Potomac* (New York: Appleton & Company, 1866); and *Memoir of Jonathan Letterman, M.D.* (New York: G. P. Putnam's Sons, 1883); reprint of both volumes, Knoxville: Bohemian Brigade Publishers, 1994, 44–45.
70. Child letters to his wife, one undated and one dated 20 October 1862.
71. Sparrow diary.
72. Sears, *Landscape Turned Red*, 349; Williams, *History and Biographical Record*, 340.
73. Strong, *Diary*, 24 September 1862, 261.

74. Hayes, *Diary and Letters,* 358–359. Several weeks after the Hayes left Rudy household, the family learned that son Daniel, who had shared a bedroom with Hayes, was ill not with scarlet fever but with smallpox. The disease spread through the family, and young son Charlie died. On receiving a worried letter from the Rudys, Lucy Hayes responded that she, her husband, and their servants were all well and that they "felt small–pox proof." *(Valley Register,* 27 April 1877.)

75. Letterman, *Medical Recollections and Memoir,* 99.

76. Quoted at the National Museum of Civil War Medicine.

77. Reilly, *Battlefield of Antietam,* 17. Richardson's wife wrote a poignant letter from the Pry home in October and assigned other reasons for his poor recovery: "He has grown very thin and is very weak yet. . . . If he would only try and think that he was improving I think he would get better much faster. He is very much depressed. . . . Tell poor mother please that she never in her life saw so dirty a place, or such poor food as we have here." (Fannie Richardson letter, October 1862, Israel B. Richardson Papers, Archives, U.S. Army Military Institute, Carlisle Barracks, Pennsylvania; copy in Antietam National Battlefield Archives.)

78. Both are quoted in Smith, "The Battle of Antietam—Hospitals," *Antietam Valley Record,* 31 October 1895; the second originated in H(olstein), *Three Years in Field Hospitals,* 13.

79. H(olstein), *Three Years in Field Hospitals,* 17.

80. Richard Lebherz, "Visiting Aunt Vinnie: Glimpses of Frederick from the Past," *Frederick Gazette,* 24 October 1996.

81. Hayes, *Diary and Letters,* 359. He was referring to Frederick County.

82. Charles F. Johnson, *The Long Roll* (East Aurora, N.Y.: The Roycrofters, 1911), 2, 9 October 1862, 30 November 1862, 203–206.

83. Oates, *A Woman of Valor,* 97–98. This happened in mid-October.

84. This building now houses the National Museum of Civil War Medicine.

85. *The Examiner,* 1 October 1862.

86. Steiner, *Report,* 36–37.

87. Hayes, *Diary and Letters,* 360.

88. Quoted in Sears, *Landscape Turned Red,* 350.

89. Otis Smith. Smith spent three days waiting in a field hospital identified only as being "at the base of the mountain" before being moved to the unidentified schoolhouse.

90. Untitled manuscript, Antietam National Battlefield Archives.

91. Benjamin Prather, letter to his wife in Columbia County, Georgia, 21 September 1862, quoted in *Military Images,* March–April 1991. Prather was probably a member of Cobb's Georgia Brigade. He died on 10 October 1862.

92. Robert Goldthwaite Carter, *Four Brothers in Blue, or, Sunshine and Shadows of the War of the Rebellion* (Austin: University of Texas Press, 1978), 123.

93. H(olstein), *Three Years in Field Hospitals,* 15.

94. Isabella Morrison Fogg, *Records of the Maine Soldier's Relief Agency;* Thomas A. Desjardin, *Self-Imposed Work of Mercy: Civil War Women of the Maine Camp and Hospital Association, 1861–1865* (unpublished); both in the Maine State Archives, Augusta, Maine.

95. Williams, *History and Biographical Record,* 361–362. The farm is not identified.

96. William Roulette, letter to Mary A. Hubbard, 31 December 1862. Roulette was writing to confirm that he had made arrangements to have the remains of Hubbard's brother shipped home, then went on to introduce his family and speak of the destruction the battle had caused. Letter courtesy Earl Roulette/Al Fiedler Jr.

97. Hildebrand Collection; Piper.

98. Clifton Johnson, *Battlefield Adventures,* 117.

99. Samuel Michael, letter to his brother in Indiana, 27 November 1862, Antietam National Battlefield Archives. In the Eighth Federal Population Census, 1860, the Michael family consisted of Adam, sixty-three, a farmer worth $8,000 in real estate and

$1,850 in personal property; Nancy, fifty-nine; Elizabeth, thirty-nine; Samuel, thirty-eight, a "Farm Hand"; Caleb, twenty-five, a "Farm Hand"; and Kate, thirty-six.

100. Williams, *History and Biographical Record,* 764–765.
101. Jacob Miller letter, 7 December 1862. The scourge of illness also swept through Frederick and other communities where sick and wounded soldiers were convalescing. For example, Lewis and Eleanor Main lost three children in September 1862. According to oral tradition, the children died of cholera, and several Union soldiers were sitting on the front steps of the family's home on West Patrick Street, drinking and laughing, while two of the bodies were carried from the house. (Galen Hahn letters, 1 and 14 April 1997.)
102. Nesbitt diary, 25 January 1863.
103. Sister M. letter to Dr. Edward Kershner, 27 January 1862, Clear Spring District Historical Association.
104. Reilly, *Battlefield of Antietam,* 19.
105. Clifton Johnson, *Battlefield Adventures,* 98.
106. Reilly, *Battlefield of Antietam,* 22.
107. Hildebrand Collection.
108. *Valley Register,* 1862, copy in George Brigham Jr. Library.
109. Reilly, *Battlefield of Antietam,* 19–22; John Philemon Smith, "Reminiscences of Sharpsburg," Western Maryland Room, Washington County Free Library, 1912, 76.
110. Hildebrand Collection.
111. Most accounts mention only one "child" being killed (Ellis, *Diary of an Army Surgeon,* 297; Strother, *A Virginia Yankee,* 114); Stephen Sears identifies the child as "a young girl" (Sears, *Landscape Turned Red,* 315). The child's name is not known.

## CHAPTER 8: "Broken Hearts Can't Be Photographed"

1. Schildt, *Antietam Hospitals,* 36; Hildebrand Collection. By some accounts, Stephen and Maria kept one young son at home as well.
2. Frassanito, *Antietam,* 286.
3. Daniel Mowen, *Memoirs of the Civil War,* Kay Ten Eyck Mowen, comp., 13 October 1862, Middletown Historical Society.
4. Strother, *A Virginia Yankee,* 114. ·
5. Crowninshield, *History of the First Regiment,* 76.
6. Appendix A, Claim of Henry Piper vs. the United States, 141.
7. Koogle diary, 17 October 1862.
8. Duncan, *The Social and Economic Impact of the Civil War in Maryland,* 240–214; Austin Stearns, *Three Years with Company K,* ed. Arthur A. Kent (Cranbury, N.J.: Fairleigh Dickinson University Press, 1976), 137–138.
9. Carter, *Four Brothers in Blue,* 122.
10. Sparrow diary.
11. Stearns, *Three Years with Company K,* 137–138.
12. Hanna Marion Johnson interview, 11 January 1934, transcript in Antietam National Battlefield Archives.
13. Henry B. James, *Memories of the Civil War* (New Bedford, Mass.: Franklin E. James, 1898), 117–118.
14. Williams, *History and Biographical Record,* 361.
15. Goss, *Recollections of a Private,* 117–118.
16. *Valley Register,* 9 January 1863.
17. *New York Times,* 15–16 September 1862, quoted in Duncan, *Social and Economic Impact,* 244.
18. Duncan, *Social and Economic Impact,* 244–245.

19. Clifton Johnson, *Battlefield Adventures,* 103.
20. Quoted in Sears, *Landscape Turned Red,* 34.
21. Reilly, *Battlefield of Antietam,* 15.
22. Untitled manuscript in Antietam Vertical File, Western Maryland Room, Washington County Free Library.
23. Samuel Mumma letter, 13(?) March 1867, National Archives.
24. Untitled manuscript, Antietam Vertical File, Western Maryland Room, Washington County Free Library; damage claim filed 6 October 1862, copy in Antietam National Battlefield Archives.
25. Reilly, *Battlefield of Antietam,* 22.
26. Carter, *Four Brothers in Blue,* 116.
27. A detailed inventory is found in Claim No. 334, Congressional Case submitted by Samuel Mumma, Jr., Executors of Samuel Mumma Deceased vs. The United States, filed 29 May 1885, copy in Antietam National Battlefield Archives.
28. Schildt, *Antietam Hospitals,* 23.
29. Clifton Johnson, *Battlefield Adventures,* 116.
30. John Sanderson, "The Decline of the Agricultural Economy of Washington County as a Result of the Ravages Caused by the Civil War," Piper Farm Historical Research Report, 1973, Antietam National Battlefield Archives; Duncan, *Social and Economic Impact;* Williams, *History and Biographical Record,* 367.
31. Steiner, *Report.*
32. Strong diary, 24 September 1862, 260.
33. Barston, *Angels of the Battlefield,* 76.
34. A. W. Wiseman, Assistant Surgeon, Seventh North Carolina Regiment, letter to Mr. Grove, Antietam National Battlefield Archives.
35. Cross, "Joseph McGraw at Antietam."
36. Reilly, *Battlefield of Antietam,* 20.
37. Reilly, *Battlefield of Antietam,* 23. The final ransom demand was for thirty dollars; after that the family hid Logan in an old building, putting down carpeting to muffle his hooves.
38. Reilly, *Battlefield of Antietam,* 22.
39. Reilly, *Battlefield of Antietam,* 19.
40. Letter, quoted in "Life in Frederick During the Civil War."
41. Markell diary, 27 November 1862 and 19 December 1862; *The Examiner,* 15 October 1862 and 4 February 1863. Markell never referred to the arrest of her husband, instead indicating that she didn't know his whereabouts.
42. Engelbrecht diary, 25 October 1862.
43. Brown Family Papers, Frederick County Historical Society Archives. The collection includes the original correspondence requesting and receiving safe passage to Lynchburg in 1861, letters between Benjamin and Dorcas, correspondence from others involved in the case, certification of Brown's status as a loyal citizen, and an oath of allegiance taken by Brown in September 1864. There is a gap in correspondence from 11 November 1862 to 3 May 1864, suggesting that Brown might have been temporarily released. Jacob Engelbrecht noted Brown's first arrest in 1862 and wrote on 27 April 1864, "Benjamin F. Brown & Henry C. Reich . . . were arrested to day by the military authority & taken to Baltimore . . .," with a note added later: "Brown returned home June 16, 1864." However, the charges Brown confronted in 1864 related back to his 1861 trip to Lynchburg and the 1862 care given to Confederate soldiers in his home. The exact sequence of events isn't clear.
44. Douglas, *I Rode with Stonewall,* 180–182.
45. Interview with Hanna Marion Johnson.
46. Reilly, *Battlefield of Antietam,* 22.

47. Samuel Michael letter to his brother, 27 November 1862, Antietam National Battle-field Archives.
48. Sparrow diary.


CHAPTER 9: "Deliver Us From This Terrible War"
1. Engelbrecht diary, 27 April 1863.
2. Engelbrecht diary, 11 and 25 October 1862.
3. Untitled manuscript, Antietam Vertical File, Western Maryland Room, Washington County Free Library; and Piper. Piper's substitute was killed.
4. Williams, *History and Biographical Record*, 761–762.
5. Williams, *History and Biographical Record*, 935.
6. Williams, *History and Biographical Record*, 360.
7. Roulette damage claim, in the possession of Earl Roulette.
8. Nesbitt diary, 25 June 1863.
9. Engelbrecht diary, 18 June 1863.
10. "Life in Frederick During the Civil War." The reminiscence places this event during the 1864 campaign, but it seems more likely that it happened in 1863.
11. Engelbrecht diary, 22 June 1863.
12. William Ballentine, letter, St. Joseph College *Alumnae Quarterly*, Spring 1965.
13. General de Trobriand, *Four Years with the Army of the Potomac*, quoted in "Some Emmitsburg Incidents of the Civil War," *Emmitsburg Times*, 21 October 1933.
14. Lutie Kealhofer diary, 4 and 5 July 1863, quoted in Green, "A People at War," 257–258.
15. Nesbitt diary, 8 July 1863.
16. Daniel Carroll Toomey, *The Civil War in Maryland* (Baltimore: Toomey Press, 1983), 82.
17. Annette Tapert, ed., *The Brothers War: Civil War Letters to Their Loved Ones from the Blue and Gray* (New York: Times Books, Random House, 1988), 152. Letter from Florence McCarthy, serving as chaplain for the Seventh Virginia Volunteer Infantry.
18. Kealhofer diary, 6 July 1863, quoted in Green, "A People at War," 258.
19. W. W. Jacobs, "Custer's Charge: Little Hagerstown the Scene of Bloody Strife," *National Tribune*, 27 August 1896, copy in Western Maryland Room, Washington County Free Library.
20. Toomey, *The Civil War in Maryland*, 81.
21. T. J. C. Williams, *The Civil War in Washington County*, 2, Antietam Vertical File, Western Maryland Room, Washington County Free Library; Roger Keller, *Events of the Civil War in Washington County* (Shippensburg, Pa.: Burd Street Press, 1995), 176.
22. "Smith's Diary Recalls Day Civil War Spy was Hung," *The News*, 23 March 1961, clipping in Frederick County Historical Society Archives. The anecdote from Smith's reminiscence was not dated, but it occurred at the same time that the spy was hanged. (See notes 31, 32.)
23. Riley, *Grandfather's Journal*, 146–147.
24. John Schildt, *September Echoes* (Middletown, Md.: Valley Register, 1960), 201.
25. "Martin Eakle at Antietam."
26. Galwey, *The Valiant Hours*, 27–28.
27. Nesbitt diary, 15 July 1863.
28. Dixon, "What We Saw in the Civil War."
29. Hildebrand Collection; Chris Yeager, "War Exacts Ultimate Price from Rohrbach Family, *Maryland Cracker Barrel*, August/September 1992, 8. Hildebrand dates this incident as 1863, but it evidently happened in 1864.
30. Marian Gouveneur, *As I Remember: Recollections of American Society during the Nineteenth Century* (New York: D. Appleton and Company, 1911), 319.

31. Mowen memoirs, 6 July 1863. Another Federal soldier, John Ryno of the 126th New York Infantry, also passed the spy and noted that Richardson's son and another man were to be hanged the following day. (John L. Ryno, *The Private Diary of Sergeant John L. Ryno,* ed. Norman M. Covert, 1988, typed copy in Maryland Room, C. Burr Artz Public Library, Frederick, Md.)

32. Engelbrecht diary, 11 July 1863.

33. *The Examiner,* 18 February 1863; "Spies, Smugglers and Guerrillas Were Among Those Reported as Operating Here During the Civil War," *Valley News Echo Special,* 17 April 1963. McAleer operated a store on the south side of Patrick Street specializing in liquors, groceries, and teas, although he also sold everything from window glass to plaster.

34. *The Examiner,* 1 April 1863.

35. *The Examiner,* 8 April 1863. In August 1864, Mrs. Jamison was back at her boardinghouse; the newspaper gleefully printed a suggestive story about a search undertaken for a spy rumored to be staying there. The guard found "a man, snuggily ensconced in bed, but not the suspicious character of the Rebel. . . . The scene that ensued is said to have been quite amusing." *(The Examiner,* 31 August 1864.)

36. "Life in Frederick During the Civil War"; *The Examiner,* 9 September 1863. The account does not provide the girls' names, but *The Examiner* article identifies the girls as "three daughters of Mrs. Pettit," and both sources refer to East Second Street.

37. Jacob Miller letter, 19 February 1864.

38. Douglas, *I Rode with Stonewall,* 290.

39. Sparrow diary.

40. Douglas, *I Rode with Stonewall,* 171.

41. Jacob Miller letter, 6 September 1864. It is important to note that these hasty flights happened with every rumor of an approaching column. Many times, during the war's final two years, farmers camped for a night or two with their livestock and valuables in some hidden thicket, then returned home when the expected troops did not arrive. For a good overview of the constant state of anxiety under which the civilians lived, see the Otho Nesbitt diary.

42. Mason Whiting Tyler, *Recollections of the Civil War* (New York: G. P. Putnam's Sons, 1912), 261. Prices had increased since the 1862 campaign.

43. Jacob Miller letter, 6 September 1864.

44. Koogle diary, 6 July 1864.

45. Walter Sanderlin, "A House Divided—The Conflict of Loyalties on the Chesapeake and Ohio Canal, 1861–1865," *Maryland Historical Magazine* (September 1947), 211–213. An official report noted that the Confederates "entered the house boat for the purpose of setting it on fire and but for the resolute and determined manner in which Mrs. Niell [*sic*] the cook in charge of the boat defended the boat it would have been burnt. . . ."

46. Richard Ray Duncan, "Maryland's Reaction to Early's Raid in 1864: A Summer of Bitterness," *Maryland Historical Magazine,* Fall 1969.

47. Sparrow diary.

48. George Blessing, *Valley Register,* 1874, quoted in Virginia Kuhn Draper, *The Smoke Still Rises: Tales Collected in the Hill Country of North-Western Frederick County, Maryland* (Hagerstown, Md.: Copy-Quick Printing and Graphics, 1996), 58–59; Harbaugh, "The Hero of Highland," *Middletown Valley in Song and Story,* 121–124. Local maps note the site as a battlefield.

49. *The Examiner,* 29 July 1864.

50. Engelbrecht diary, 5 July 1864.

51. Gouveneur, *As I Remember,* 320–321.

52. Markell diary, 7 July 1864.

53. "Life in Frederick During the Civil War."

54. For notice of the sheriff's sale, see *The Examiner*, 21 February 1863.
55. Engelbrecht diary, 8 July 1864.
56. *Lew Wallace: An Autobiography*, Vol. 2 (New York: Harper and Brothers, 1906), 743.
57. Engelbrecht diary, 11 July 1864.
58. Glenn Worthington, *Fighting for Time* (Baltimore: Press of the Day Printing Company, 1932), 102.
59. Dixon, "What We Saw in the Civil War."
60. Worthington, *Fighting for Time*, 168–173.
61. Worthington, *Fighting for Time*, 158.
62. Douglas, *I Rode with Stonewall*, 296.
63. Nesbitt diary, 30 July 1864.
64. Engelbrecht diary, 29 July 1864.
65. James Montgomery diary, July 1864, Carlisle Barracks, Pa., U.S. Army Military Institute Archives; copy Western Maryland Room, Washington County Free Library.
66. Jacob Miller letter, 6 September 1864.
67. Gouveneur, *As I Remember*, 325.
68. Scharf, *History of Maryland*, 641.
69. Engelbrecht diary, 3 August 1864; *The Examiner*, 3 August 1864. Engelbrecht listed the people arrested, noting that their families were to be sent south; *The Examiner*, however, notes only the confiscation of Clara's slippers.
70. Laura Lee Davidson; *The Examiner*, 8 April 1863.
71. Gouveneur, *As I Remember*, 326.
72. *The Examiner*, 2 November 1864.
73. Engelbrecht diary, 2 January 1865.

## CHAPTER 10: "When That Time Comes, All Hearts and Hands Will Unite"

1. Clifton Johnson, *Battlefield Adventures*, 104–105.
2. Draper, *The Smoke Still Rises*, 59. The story refers only to '[Smith's] darky,' so it is not clear if the man was a slave or free.
3. (Moore), *Odds and Ends*, 15 August 1861 and 27 February 1862.
4. Kealhofer diary, 25 August 1863, quoted in Green, "A People at War," 259–260. A third slave, Sukey, "remained faithful." Nancy and Harriet stayed in Pennsylvania a short time, then returned to the Kealhofers and remained until set free by Maryland law.
5. Nesbitt diary, 9 September 1862, 1 July 1863, 24 June 1864, and 5 August 1864.
6. Untitled manuscript, Antietam Vertical File, Western Maryland Room, Washington County Public Library. Ironically, while the armies were reportedly absconding with Maryland blacks, a few Confederate soldiers who brought black slaves or servants with them worried about the same problem. John Dooley of Virginia, who traveled with a black servant named Ned, often sent the young man foraging on the soldiers' behalf. During a trip to Hagerstown, a woman "tried to induce him to desert the service and accept his freedom"—which, Dooley noted, Uncle Sam was depriving his white progeny of. Ned returned to his master bearing grapes and the tale of his escape from the crafty "abolishunists." (Dooley, *War Journal*, 31.)
7. Ludolph Longhenry diary, 14 July 1863; quoted in Lance Herdegen, *The Men Stood Like Iron: How the Iron Brigade Won Its Name* (Bloomington and Indianapolis: Indiana University Press, 1997), 13.
8. See *The Examiner*, 1 April 1863: "Wanted, For a term of years, a slave child, either male or female, from 9 to 12 years of age. Apply to H. Winchester, Frederick Female Seminary."

9. Editorial, *The Examiner,* 1 October 1862, quoted in Williams and McKinsey, *History of Frederick County,* 392.

10. *The Examiner,* 19 August 1863.

11. Robert I. Cottom Jr. and Mary Ellen Hayward, *Maryland in the Civil War: A House Divided* (Baltimore: Maryland Historical Society, 1994), 83.

12. Engelbrecht diary, 5 April 1864; *The Examiner,* 6 April 1864.

13. Engelbrecht diary, 31 October 1864.

14. Michael L. Spaur, "What's in a Name?" *The (Frederick) News,* 2 May 1979. This story survived in oral family tradition, and the dates are unclear. Another interpretation is that the original exchange took place after Lincoln issued his Emancipation Proclamation, and the slave worked until Maryland law changed—almost two years.

15. Untitled manuscript, Antietam Vertical File, Western Maryland Room, Washington County Free Library; Schildt, *September Echoes,* 201–202. Other accounts indicate that Emory Summers and a sister were owned and freed by the Sherman family. An untitled manuscript in the files at Antietam National Battlefield, written by a woman who knew the Summerses in 1920, wrote of stopping to warm up on the way to school on winter mornings with Jerry and Susan Summers in their cabin near Bloody Lane; at that time Jerry was still hiring out as a farm laborer to local families. She also indicated that Emory Summers was at that time living in a small log home "off East Chapline street."

16. Mary Giles Blunt, quoted in Green, "A People at War," 259–260.

17. Nesbitt, 1–2 November 1864, 25 December 1865. In 1868, three of Nesbitt's former slaves returned "and asked to move into my little house at the north end of Mill Street and work for us. Nance cooked my victuals for many a long year but she had probably left the old kitchen forever as she's getting old. Mary, Liz, Ellen and Charles often come back to see me" [27 October 1868]." In 1869 he got word that "Morris is sick and would love to come back as he's sorry he ever left. Has done nothing for over a year. Lives with his son who gets $11.00 a month as a livery stable hand and they give him something to eat [January 21, 1869]." And in 1872, "Old Nance came today making peach preserves for all of us. She likes to come back when she is able to make a little money. Came last week and baked six loaves of bread [September 14, 1872]." In a reminiscence written in 1885, when Nesbitt was eighty-one, he noted that Morris and his wife, Sidney, had recently sent word offering to work for "vittuals and clothes as long as I wanted them. I thought I couldn't feed them. I have two children and their mother is sickly, weakly, debeletated." (Reminiscence quoted in a report by David Wiles, Clear Spring District Historical Association.)

18. Dixon, "Slave Days on the Farm."

19. Samuel Michael letter, 7 August 1865, Antietam National Battlefield Archives.

20. Samuel Michael letter, 7 August 1865, Antietam National Battlefield Archives.

21. Hundreds of claims records are on file at the National Archives, Washington, D.C.

22. Frye and Schildt, *Antietam Remembered,* 25.

23. Frassanito, *Antietam,* 267.

24. Williams, *History and Biographical Record,* 367–368.

25. Mowen memoir, 1865.

26. Daniel Hartzler, *Medical Doctors of Maryland,* 91; Engelbrecht diary, 17 May 1865.

27. Engelbrecht diary, 19 July 1865.

28. Williams, *History and Biographical Record,* 914. Gaines was captured again in 1863 while tending wounded men in Williamsport. Helen Smith was the daughter of Dr. Otho J. Smith, a local physician. She died childless in 1868, and Gaines ultimately married a daughter of the Rench family of Sharpsburg; he practiced in Boonsboro until 1893.

29. Mowen memoirs, 25 October 1862, December 1863.

30. Robert J. Trout, *They Followed the Plume: The Story of J.E.B. Stuart and His Staff* (Harrisburg: Stackpole Books, 1993), 72–75. Brien was born in Urbana and raised in Bal-

timore. He had brought his wife to a farm north of Hagerstown in the 1850s, and while commanding the First Virginia Cavalry during the 1862 campaign, camped on the property. After being paroled at Appomattox, he spent some time away from home but in 1882 returned to Urbana, where he purchased the property known as Tyrone.

31. Worthington, *Fighting for Time*, 162–163.

32. Bradley T. Johnson, *Address Before the Association of Confederate Soldiers and Sailors of Maryland*, 10 June 1874 (Baltimore: Kelly, Piet & Company, 1874), 4–8.

33. "Life in Frederick During the Civil War."

34. This area deserves more study; however, several poignant and detailed memoirs of the first Maryland campaign were written by people who had been only four or five years old in 1862.

35. Smith, *Reminiscences of Sharpsburg*, 65.

36. Margaret Burtner Moats, *A History of Keedsyville to 1890* (Boonsboro, Md.: n.p., 1989), 61.

37. Fred W. Cross, "Recollections of Another Sharpsburg Boy," *Hagerstown Daily Mail*, 12 March 1934.

38. Miss "Teet" Kretzer never married and lived in her parents' home until her death, at age ninety-two. Her sister Margaret's daughter, Miss Catherine Adams, served as the village librarian for many years, fascinating patrons with stories of her famous aunt and other tales of the battle. Hildebrand Collection; Maxine Campbell, 1 May 1997.

39. John P. Smith, "The Battle of Antietam—Hospitals," *Antietam Valley Record*, 6 November 1895. Five years after the battle, Elizabeth, Mary, Augusta, and Jane Rohrback were thrilled to receive a handsome framed certificate: "At a stated meeting of E. Company, 1st Regt., Gray Reserves, held at their Armory on Thursday evening, Oct. 31st, 1867, it was unanimously Resolved, that the thanks of this Company be tendered to the Misses Rohrback of Sharpsburg, Maryland, for their kindness and hospitality to one of our members, Mr. Allen Rorke while on the march from Keedysville to Antietam. Resolved that the names of these Good Samaritans be honorably enrolled among our archives and the memory of their Christian Actions be sacredly cherished in our hearts."

40. Frye and Schildt, *Antietam Remembered*, 33–34; Schildt, *September Echoes*, 124. In the latter, Schildt refers to the congregation as the United Church of Christ. The 16th Connecticut Regiment had been formed only three weeks before the battle of Antietam and lost 226 of its members in the Sherrick cornfield.

41. Reilly, *Battlefield of Antietam*, 18.

42. Schildt, *Antietam Hospitals*, 17.

43. Reilly, *Battlefield of Antietam*, 20.

44. Untitled manuscript, Antietam National Battlefield Archives.

45. *Valley Register*, 8 October 1897.

46. *Valley Register*, 27 April 1877. The Rudy and Hayes families remained in touch for years. When Hayes ran for president Mr. Rudy "was very unwell," wrote Mrs. Rudy later, "still he went up town and voted for Hayes."

47. Reilly, *Battlefield of Antietam*, 16; Wilmer M. Mumma, "O. T. Reilly Remembered," *Out of the Past* (Sharpsburg, 1993), 10–12; Ann K. Kretzer "Nostalgic Moments: Pop Reilly 'Mastered' Battle He Witnessed as a Youngster," *Maryland Cracker Barrel*, August/September 1992, 12; Reminiscence of O. T. "Pop" Reilly, written 21 September 1991, courtesy Ann K. Kretzer. Reilly was not the only souvenir dealer and guide; Martin L. Burgan also published postcards and a guidebook about the area.

48. Sparrow diary.

49. Hoke, *Historical Reminiscences*, 27.

50. Hall, *History of the 97th Regiment*, 82–83.

51. H(olstein), *Three Years in Field Hospitals*, 24.

52. Blackford, *War Years*, 140. He was specifically referring to the Urbana ball.

53. Scharf, *Personal Memoirs*, 48–50.

54. Williams and McKinsey, *History of Frederick County,* 369–370.
55. Dooley, *War Journal,* 27.
56. Sparrow diary.
57. Sister M. letter to Dr. Edward Kerschner, 1 March 1863.
58. Worthington, *Fighting for Time,* 206–207.
59. Sears, *Landscape Turned Red,* 341.
60. Clifton Johnson, *Battlefield Adventures,* 113.

# SELECTED BIBLIOGRAPHY

## I. UNPUBLISHED MATERIALS

### Private Collections

Dayton, Edna Mae. Interview transcript, courtesy Steven Stotelmyer.

Kretzer, Ann K. "Reminiscence of O.T. 'Pop' Reilly" 21 September 1991, Courtesy Ann Kretzer.

Kretzer Family Genealogical Material, courtesy Linda Irvin-Craig.

Mumma Geneaological Material, courtesy Wilmer Mumma.

NAT Letter (unidentified Confederate soldier), 6 October 1862; and miscellaneous papers, courtesy Al Fiedler Jr.

Piper, S. Webster, Piper Family History, courtesy Lou and Regina Clark.

(Reed), Paula Stoner, "Household Property of the Biggs Family," 1980, courtesy Marian and Sid Gale.

Roulette Family Papers, courtesy Earl and Annabelle Roulette.

Wyand, Jeffrey A. *The William Chapline House,* 1974, courtesy Marian and Sid Gale.

### Augusta, Maine, Maine State Archives

Records of the Maine Soldier's Relief Agency

Thomas A. Desjardin. *Self-Imposed Work of Mercy: Civil War Women of the Maine Camp and Hospital Association, 1861–1865.*

### Baltimore, Maryland, Maryland Room, Enoch Pratt Public Library

"Civil War—Personal Narratives/Recollections" Collection.

Davidson, Laura Lee. "Service of the Women of Maryland to the Confederate States." *Confederate Veteran,* n.d.

**Boonsboro, Maryland, Boonsborough Museum of History**
This private museum contains a number of local collections.

**Carlisle Barracks, Pennsylvania, U.S. Army Military Institute Archives**
Richardson, Israel B. Papers.
Montgomery, James. Diary.

**Chapel Hill, North Carolina, Southern Historical Collection, University of North Carolina Library**
Leach, Calvin. Diary. (#1875)
Smith, Otis. Reminiscence. (Thatch Family Papers, #1102)

**Clear Spring, Maryland, Clear Spring District Historical Association**
Nesbitt, Otho. Diary and Papers.
Kerschner, Edward. Letters.

**Durham, North Carolina, Manuscript Department, Duke University**
Compton, Samuel. Autobiography.

**Frederick, Maryland, Historical Society of Frederick County, Inc.**
Brown Family. Letters and Papers, 1861–1864.
"The Civil War in the Poolesville Area."
Cramer, Jeremiah. Letter to Colonel Dennis, 24 November 1861.
Dixon, J(esse). Clippings.
Engelbrecht, Jacob. Diary. William R. Quynn, ed., 1976.
Fleming, A. Thomas. Account.
Johnson, Thomas Roger. "War Reminiscences."
"Life in Frederick During the Civil War."

**Frederick, Maryland, Maryland Room, C. Burr Artz Public Library**
*The Examiner.* Microfilm.
Markell, Catherine. Diary. Microfilm.

Ryno, John L. *The Private Diary of Sergeant John L. Ryno,* Norman M. Covert, ed., typed copy, 1988.

Williams, C. S. *Williams' Frederick Directory, City Guide, and Business Mirror,* Frederick: 1859.

**Gettysburg, Pennsylvania, Adams County Historical Society**

Jobe, William. *Recollections and Reminiscences of a Soldier of the Union in the War of the Rebellion of 1861 to 1865.*

**Gettysburg, Pennsylvania, Gettysburg National Military Park Archives**

Healy, Sam. Journal.

**Hagerstown, Maryland, Western Maryland Room, Washington County Free Library**

Bast, John H., Sr. *The History of Boonsboro.*

Biggs, Augustin. *The Obstetrical Records of Dr. Augustus [sic] Biggs, of Sharpsburg, Washington County, Maryland, 1836–1888.*

Burkittsville District Heritage Society, Inc., *Burkittsville, Maryland: A Nineteenth Century Townscape,* 1979.

Davis, Angela Kirkham. *War Reminiscences: Letter.*

Hildebrand, Virginia Mumma. Collection.

Koogle, John. Diaries for the Years 1861–1868, with notes by Fred S. Palmer.

(Moore, Doyle), *Odds and Ends, by Gum,* typed compilation/summary of *The Odd Fellow* (Boonsboro).

Smith, John Philemon. *Reminiscences of Sharpsburg,* 1912.

Thompson, David L. Letter to Elias, October (?) 1862.

Williams, Thomas J. C. *The Civil War in Washington County.*

**Madison, Wisconsin, State Historical Society of Wisconsin**

Duncan, Richard Ray. *The Social and Economic Impact of the Civil War in Maryland.* The Ohio State University, Ph.D. dissertation, 1963. Microfilm.

Eighth Federal Population Census, 1860, Schedule 1 (Free Inhabitants) and Schedule 2 (Slave Inhabitants). Microfilm.

*My Diary in Which are Recorded the Movement of the Ninth Massachusetts Volunteers in the War of the Rebellion in the United States.*

Ward, David A. *Amidst a Tempest of Shot and Shell: A History of the Ninety-Sixth Pennsylvania Volunteers.* Southern Connecticut State University, master's thesis, 1988. Microfilm.

**Middletown, Maryland, George Brigham Jr. Library**
This private library contains copies of the following:
Castle, John. "Letters from the People: Says There was Cannonading at Braddock Heights," *Valley Register(?),* 24 May 1932.
Dugan, Ivy W., Letter, 1 October 1862.
Hurlenger, Matthew. Diary.
Iverson, Alfred. Letter to General Hill, 23 August 1885.
Jones, William Ellis. Diary.
*The Land We Love,* September 1867.
Sparrow, Allen. Diary.

**Middletown, Maryland, Middletown Valley Historical Society**
Mowen, Daniel. *Memoirs of the Civil War,* Kay Ten Eyck Mowen, comp.

**Sharpsburg, Maryland, Antietam National Battlefield Archives**
Beltemacchi, Margaret. Letter to Rep. Goodloe Byron, 3 June 1971.
Child, William. Letters to his wife, 1862.
Cross, Fred W. *Alexander W. Davis of Sharpsburg.*
Cross, Fred W. *Joseph McGraw at Antietam.*
Cross, Fred W. *Story of Flag Woman Saved at Antietam,* 1929.
Cross, Fred W. *A Visit and Reflections at Antietam,* 1930.
Farris, Judy. Letter to Al Fiedler Jr. and Paul Chiles, 6 June 1996.
Hildebrand, Virginia Mumma. "A Rival for Barbara Fritchie."
Johnson, Hanna Marion. Interview transcript, 11 January 1934.
Lyne, Stella. Interview transcript, 24 January 1934.
Michael, Samuel. Letters to David Michael, 1862–1865.
Miller Family. Letters to Amelia and Christian Houser, 1859–1865.
Reed, Paula S. *History Report: The D. R. Miller Farm,* September 1991.
Sanderson, John. "The Decline of the Agricultural Economy of Washington County as a Result of the Ravages Caused by the Civil War," *Piper Farm Historical Research Report,* 1973.
Shackelford, Bud. Interview transcript, 24 January 1934.
Vanneman, Theodore J. Letter to his wife, 18 September 1862.
Wilshin, Francis F. *Report on the Piper Farm "Slave Quarters,"* 1969.

Wiseman, A. W. Letter.

**Richmond, Virginia, Virginia State Museum**
Boulware, J. R. Diary.

**Rochester, New York, University of Rochester**
Charles Curtis Brown Papers.

**Washington, D.C., Manuscripts Division, Library of Congress**
Claims for Damages Made Against the United States, Manuscripts Division, Library of Congress.
Wilson, R. B. Account, 22 July 1899.

**II. BOOKS AND ARTICLES**
Adams, Charles S. *The Civil War in Frederick County, Maryland: A Guide to Forty-Nine Historic Points of Interest.* Self-published, 1995.
_____. *The Civil War in Washington County, Maryland: A Guide to Sixty-Six Points of Interest.* Self-published, 1996.
Ankrum, Reverend Freeman. *Maryland and Pennsylvania Historical Sketches.* Masontown, Pa.: *The Times-Sun,* 1947.
Bailey, Ronald H., and the editors of Time-Life Books. *The Bloodiest Day: The Battle of Antietam.* Alexandria: Time-Life Books, 1984.
Ballentine, William. "Letter." St. Joseph College: *Alumnae Quarterly* (Spring 1965).
(Bartlett, Napier). *A Soldier's Story of the War, Including the Marches and Battles of the Washington Artillery and of Other Louisiana Troops.* New Orleans: Clark and Hafeline, 1874.
Barston, George. *Angels of the Battlefield: A History of the Catholic Sisterhoods in the Late Civil War.* Philadelphia: Catholic Art Publishing Company, 1879.
Battle, Laura Elizabeth (Lee). *Forget-Me-Nots of the Civil War: A Romance, Containing Reminiscences and Original Letters of Two Confederate Soldiers.* St. Louis, Mo.: A. R. Fleming, Printers, 1909.
Beale, George William. *A Lieutenant of Cavalry in Lee's Army.* Boston: Gorham Press, 1918.
Blackford, W(illiam) W. *War Years with Jeb Stuart.* New York: Charles Scribners' Sons, 1945.

Blakeslee, B. F. *History of the Sixteenth Connecticut Volunteers.* Hartford: Case, Lockwood and Brainard Company, 1875.

Blassingame, John W., ed. *Slave Testimony: Two Centuries of Letters, Speeches, Interviews, and Autobiographies.* Baton Rouge: Louisiana State University Press, 1977.

Bowman, Carl F. *Brethren Society: The Cultural Transformation of a "Peculiar People."* Baltimore: Johns Hopkins University Press, 1995.

Brockett, L(inus) P. *Woman's Work in the Civil War: A Record of Heroism, Patriotism, and Patience.* Boston: R. H. Curran, 1867.

Brown, George William. *Baltimore and the Nineteenth of April, 1861.* Baltimore: Johns Hopkins University Press, 1887.

Brugger, Robert J. *Maryland: A Middle Temperament.* Baltimore: Johns Hopkins University Press in association with the Maryland Historical Society, 1988.

Burlingame, H. W. *Personal Reminiscences of the Civil War, 1861–1865.* (1904).

Camper, Charles, and J. W. Kirley, comp. *Historical Record of the First Maryland Infantry.* Washington: Gibson Brothers, 1871.

Carter, Robert Goldthwaite. *Four Brothers in Blue, or Sunshine and Shadows of the War of the Rebellion.* Austin: University of Texas Press, 1978.

Chamberlayne, Ham. *Ham Chamberlayne—A Virginian: Letters and Papers of an Artillery Officer in the War for Southern Independence, 1861–1865.* Richmond: Dietz Printing Company, 1932.

Clark, Charles Branch. *Politics in Maryland During the Civil War.* Chestertown, Md.: n.p., 1952.

Cole, Jacob H. *Under Five Commanders, or A Boy's Experience with the Army of the Potomac.* Paterson, N.J.: News Printing Company, 1906.

A Confederate. *The Grayjackets: And How They Lived, Fought and Died, for Dixie.* Richmond: Jones Brothers and Company, 1867.

Conrad, W. P., and Ted Alexander. *When War Passed This Way.* Greencastle, Pa.: A Greencastle Bicentennial Publication, 1982.

Cooling, B(enjamin) F(ranklin). *Jubal Early's Raid on Washington, 1864.* Baltimore: The Nautical & Aviation Publishing Company of America, 1989.

Cottom, Robert I., Jr., and Mary Ellen Hayward. *Maryland in the Civil War: A House Divided.* Baltimore: The Maryland Historical Society, 1994.

Cross, Fred W. "Recollections of Another Sharpsburg Boy." *The Daily Mail.* 12 March 1934.

_____. "A Sharpsburg Boy at Antietam." *The Daily Mail*. 16 January 1934.

_____. "Story of Flag at Antietam." *The Daily Mail*. 30 January 1934.

_____. "The Strong House." *The Daily Mail*. 22 March 1934.

_____. "Three Gallant Officers of Ninth Corps at Antietam." *The Daily Mail*. 16 February 1934.

Crowninshield, Benjamin. *A History of the First Regiment of Massachusetts Cavalry Volunteers*. Boston and New York: Houghton, Mifflin and Company, 1891.

Dall, Caroline H. *Barbara Fritchie*. Boston: Roberts Brothers, 1892.

Davidson, Greenlee. *Diary and Letters, 1851–1865*. Verona, Va.: Virginia McClure Press, 1975, c. Charles W. Turner.

Davis, William C., and the editors of Time-Life Books. *Brother Against Brother: The War Begins*. Alexandria: Time-Life Books, 1983.

Dawson, Francis. *Reminiscences of Confederate Service, 1861–1865*. Ed. Bell I. Wiley. Baton Rouge: Louisiana State University Press, 1980.

De Trobriand, Regis. *Four Years with the Army of the Potomac*. Boston: Ticknor and Company, 1989; quoted in "Some Emmitsburg Incidents of the Civil War," *Emmitsburg Times*, 21 October 1933.

Doleman, Marguerite. *We the Blacks of Washington County*. Hagerstown(?): Washington County Bicentennial Committee, 1976.

Dooley, John. *John Dooley: His War Journal*. Ed. Joseph T. Durkin. Washington, D.C.: Georgetown University Press, 1945.

Douglas, Henry Kyd. *I Rode with Stonewall*. Ed. Fletcher M. Green. Chapel Hill: University of North Carolina Press, 1940.

Draper, Virginia Kuhn. *The Smoke Still Rises; Tales Collected in the Hill Country of North-Western Frederick County, Maryland*. Hagerstown, Md.: Copy-Quick Printing and Graphics, 1996.

Duncan, Richard Ray. "Maryland's Reaction to Early's Raid in 1864: A Summer of Bitterness." *Maryland Historical Magazine* (Fall 1969).

Ellis, Thomas, M.D. *Leaves from the Diary of an Army Surgeon*. New York: John Bradburn, 1863.

An English Combatant. *Battle-fields of the South, From Bull Run to Fredericksburgh*. New York: John Bradburn, 1864; reprint, Time-Life Books, 1984.

Ernst, Ora. "Slaves Passed Through Here on Way to Freedom." *Morning Herald*. 18 December 1978.

Favill, Josiah Marshall. *Diary of a Young Officer Serving with the Armies of the United States During the War of the Rebellion.* Chicago: R. R. Donnelly and Sons Company, 1909.

Figg, Royal W. *Where Men Only Dare to Go.* Richmond: Whittet and Shepperson, 1885.

Forbes, Edwin. *Thirty Years After: An Artist's Memoir of the Civil War.* Baton Rouge: Louisiana State University Press, 1993.

Frassanito, William. *Antietam: The Photographic Legacy of America's Bloodiest Day.* New York: Charles Scribner's Sons, 1978.

French, S. Bassett. *Centennial Tales: Memoirs of Colonel "Chester" S. Bassett French, Extra Aide-de-Camp to Generals Lee and Jackson, The Army of Northern Virginia, 1861–1865.* Comp. Glen Oldaker. New York: A Reflection Book, 1962.

Frye, Dennis, and John W. Schildt. *Antietam Remembered: A Guide to Selected Historic Sites in the Antietam Valley.* Hagerstown, Md.: Tri-State Printing, 1987.

Fuller, Marsha Lynne. *African American Manumissions of Washington County, Maryland.* Hagerstown, Md.: Desert Sheik Press, 1997.

Galwey, Thomas Francis. *The Valiant Hours.* Ed. W. S. Nye. Harrisburg, Pa.: Stackpole Company, 1961.

Gary, Keith O. *Answering the Call: The Organization and Recruiting of the Potomac Home Brigade Maryland Volunteers.* Bowie, Md.: Heritage Books, 1996.

*General Jesse Lee Reno at Frederick: Barbara Fritchie and Her Flag.* Civil War Papers Read before the Commandery of the State of Massachusetts, Military Order of the Loyal Legion and of the US, Vol. 2. Boston: Printed for the Commandery, 1900.

Gibbon, John. *Personal Recollections of the Civil War.* New York: G. P. Putnam's Sons, 1928.

Gordon, Paul, and Rita Gordon. *Frederick County, Maryland: A Playground of the Civil War.* Frederick, Md.: M&B Printing, 1994.

Goss, Warren Lee. *Recollections of a Private: A Story of the Army of the Potomac.* New York: Thomas Y. Crowell and Company, 1890.

Gould, Joseph. *The Story of the Forty-Eighth.* Philadelphia: A. M. Slocum Company, 1908.

Gouveneur, Marian. *As I Remember: Recollections of American Society during the Nineteenth Century.* New York: D. Appleton and Company, 1911.

Green, Fletcher M. "A People at War: Hagerstown, Maryland, June 15–August 31, 1863." *Maryland Historical Magazine* (December 1945).

Hall, Isaac. *History of the Ninety-Seventh Regiment of New York Volunteers (Conkling Rifles) in the War for the Union.* Utica: Press of L. C. Childs and Sons, 1890.

Harbaugh, T. C. *Middletown Valley in Song and Story.* Self-published, 1910.

Harries, William H. "In the Ranks at Antietam." *Glimpses of the Nation's Struggle, Fourth Series.* St. Paul: H. L. Collins Company, 1898.

Hartzler, Daniel D. *Marylanders in the Confederacy.* Westminster, Md.: Family Line Publications, 1986.

_____. *Medical Doctors of Maryland in the Confederate States Army.* Hagerstown, Md.: Tri-State Printing. 1979.

"Hayes at Middletown." *The Valley Register,* 27 April 1877.

Hayes, Rutherford B. *Diary and Letters of Rutherford Birchard Hayes, Nineteenth President of the United States, Vol. II: 1861–1865.* Ed. Charles Richard Williams. The Ohio State Archaeological and Historical Society, 1922.

Helfenstein, Ernest. *A History of the All Saints' Parish in Frederick County, Maryland,* Frederick, Md.: n.p., 1932.

Helman, James A. *History of Emmitsburg, Maryland.* Frederick, Md.: Citizen Press, 1906.

Henry, J. Maurice. *History of the Brethren in Maryland.* Elgin, Ill.: Brethren Publishing House, 1936.

Herdegen, Lance. *The Men Stood Like Iron: How the Iron Brigade Won Its Name.* Bloomington and Indianapolis: Indiana University Press, 1997.

Hicks, E. Russell. "The Church on the Battlefield." *Morning Herald.* 23 April 1952.

Hicks, E. Russell, and Reverend Freeman Ankrum. "The Church on the Battlefield: The Brethren Congregation." *Morning Herald.* 21 April 1959.

Hill, Daniel H. "The Battle of South Mountain, or Boonsboro: Fighting for Time at Turner's and Fox's Gaps." *Battles and Leaders of the Civil War,* Volume II. Ed. R. U. Johnson and C. C. Buel. New York: Century Company, 1884–87.

Hinkley, Julian Wisner. *Service with the Third Wisconsin Infantry.* Madison(?): Wisconsin History Commission, Original Papers #7, 1912.

Hoke, J(acob). *Historical Reminiscences of the War.* Chambersburg, Pa.: M. A. Foltz, 1884.

H(olstein), Mrs. (Anna). *Three Years in Field Hospitals of the Army of the Potomac.* Philadelphia: J. B. Lippincott Company, 1867.

Hunter, Alexander. "A High Private's Account of the Battle of Sharpsburg." *Southern Historical Society Papers,* Part 1 (Volume X, Richmond, Va.: 1882) and Part 2 (Volume XI, Richmond, Va.: 1883).

_____. *Johnny Reb and Billy Yank.* New York: Neal Publishing Company, 1905.

Jackson, Mrs. Mary Anna. *Memoirs of Stonewall Jackson.* Louisville, 1895.

Jacobs, W. W. "Custer's Charge: Little Hagerstown the Scene of Bloody Strife." *National Tribune.* 27 August 1896.

James, Henry B. *Memories of the Civil War.* New Bedford, Mass.: Franklin E. James, 1898.

Johnson, Bradley T. *Address Before the Association of Confederate Soldiers and Sailors of Maryland, June 10, 1874.* Baltimore: Kelly, Piet and Company, 1874.

_____. "Address on the First Maryland Campaign." *Southern Historical Society Papers,* Vol. XII. Richmond, Va.: 1884.

_____. "Memoir of Jane Claudia Johnson." *Southern Historical Society Papers,* Vol. XXIX. Richmond, Va.: 1901.

Johnson, Charles F. *The Long Roll.* East Aurora, N.Y.: The Roycrofters, 1911.

Johnson, Clifton. *Battlefield Adventures: The Stories of Dwellers on the Scenes of Conflict in Some of the Most Notable Battles of the Civil War.* Boston: Houghton Mifflin, 1915.

Johnston, David E. *The Story of a Confederate Boy in the Civil War.* Portland, Ore.: Prudhomme Company, 1914.

Jones, Mollie Hays. "Reminiscences of the Civil War." *The Montgomery County Story,* Vol. IV, No. 2 (February 1961).

Kaufman, C. C. "Tells of Experiences During the Civil War." *The Valley Register,* 25 January and 1 February 1929.

Keller, Roger. *Events of the Civil War in Washington County.* Shippensburg, Pa.: Burd Street Press, 1995.

Kirk, Charles H., ed. and comp. *History of the Fifteenth Pennsylvania Volunteer Cavalry.* Philadelphia: 1906.

Koogle, A. C. "Fiftieth Anniversary of South Mountain Battle." *The Valley Register.* 13 September 1912.

Kretzer, Ann K. "Nostalgic Moments: Pop Reilly 'Mastered' Battle He Witnessed as a Youngster." *Maryland Cracker Barrel* (August/September 1992).

Lebherz, Richard. "Visiting Aunt Vinnie: Glimpses of Frederick from the Past." *Frederick Gazette.* 24 October 1996.

Letterman, Jonathan, M.D. *Medical Recollections of the Army of the Potomac.* Appleton and Company, 1866; *Memoir of Jonathan Letterman, M.D.* New York: G. P. Putnam's Sons, 1883; reprint of both volumes, Knoxville: Bohemian Brigade Publishers, 1994.

Long, John W. M. "South Mountain Battle Events." *The Valley Register.* 7 July 1922.

Lord, Edward O., ed. *History of the Ninth Regiment New Hampshire Volunteers in the War of the Rebellion.* Concord, N.H.: Republican Press Association, 1895.

Markell, C. Sue. *Short Stories of Life in Frederick in 1830.* Attic Treasures, 1948.

McClellan, George. *The Civil War Papers of George B. McClellan: Selected Correspondence, 1860–1865.* Ed. Stephen Sears. New York: Ticknor and Fields, 1989.

McDaniel, J. J. *Diary of Battles, Marches and Incidents of the Seventh South Carolina Regiment.* 186?.

McKim, Randolph. *A Soldier's Recollections: Leaves from the Diary of a Young Confederate.* New York: Longmans, Green, and Company, 1910.

Minnigh, H. N. *History of Company K, 1st Pennsylvania Reserves: The Boys Who Fought at Home.* Duncansville, Pa.: Home Point Publisher, n.d.

Moats, Margaret Burtner. *A History of Keedysville to 1890.* Boonsboro, 1989.

Moore, Edward A. *The Story of a Canoneer Under Stonewall Jackson.* New York and Washington: Neale Publishing Company, 1907.

Mumma, Wilmer M. "O. T. Remembered." *Out of the Past.* Sharpsburg, 1993.

Murfin, James V. *The Gleam of Bayonets: The Battle of Antietam and the Maryland Campaign of 1862.* New York: Yoseloff, 1965.

Neese, George M. *Three Years in the Confederate Horse Artillery.* New York and Washington: Neale Publishing Company, 1911.

Nisbet, James Cooper. *Four Years on the Firing Line.* Ed. Bell Irvin Wiley. Jackson, Tenn.: McCowat-Mercer Press, 1893.

Oates, Stephen B. *A Woman of Valor: Clara Barton and the Civil War.* New York: Free Press, 1994.

Opie, John N. *A Rebel Cavalryman with Lee, Stuart, and Johnson.* Chicago: W. B. Conkey Company, 1899.

Owen, William Miller. *In Camp Life and Battle with the Washington Artillery of the Potomac.* Philadelphia: J. B. Lippincott Company, 1867.

Poague, William Thomas. *Gunner with Stonewall: Reminiscences of William Thomas Poague.* Ed. Monroe F. Cockrell. Jackson, Tenn.: McCowat-Mercer Press, 1957.

Polley, J. B. *A Soldier's Letters to Charming Nellie.* New York and Washington: Neale Publishing Company, 1908.

Prather, Benjamin. "A Wounded Confederate Soldier Meets Mr. Lincoln (Letter)." *Military Images* (March–April 1991).

Priest, John M. *Antietam: The Soldier's Battle.* Shippensburg, Pa.: White Mane Publishing Company, 1988.

Quynn, Dorothy McKay, and William Rogers Quynn. "Barbara Frietschie." *Maryland Historical Magazine* (September 1942).

Racine, J. Polk. *Recollections of a Veteran, or, Four Years in Dixie.* Elkton, Md.: The Appeal Printing Office, 1894; reprint, Cecil County Bicentennial Committee, 1987.

Ranck, James B., Dorothy S. Ranck, Margaret R. Motter, and Katharine E. Dutrow. *Unto Us: A History of the Evangelical Reformed Church.* Frederick, 1964.

Reese, Timony J. *Sealed With Their Lives: The Battle for Crampton's Gap, Burkittsville, Maryland, September 14, 1862.* Baltimore: Butternut and Blue, 1998.

Reilly, Oliver T. *The Battlefield of Antietam.* Hagerstown, Md.: Self-published, 1906.

Rhoderick, George C., Jr. *The Early History of Middletown, Maryland.* Middletown, Md.: Middletown Valley Historical Society, 1989.

Riley, Franklin Lafayette. *Grandfather's Journal: Company B, Sixteenth Mississippi Infantry Volunteers . . . May 27, 1861–July 15, 1865.* Ed. Austin C. Dobbins. Dayton, Ohio: Morningside Press, 1988.

Robertson, James I., Jr. "A Federal Surgeon at Sharpsburg." *Civil War History* (June 1960).

Robson, John S. *How a One-Legged Rebel Lives: Reminiscences of the Civil War.* 1898.

Sanderlin, Walter. "A House Divided—The Conflict of Loyalties on the C&O Canal, 1861–1865." *Maryland Historical Magazine* (September 1947).

Scammon, E(liakim). P. "The General Reno Story." *Fremont Journal*. 29 March 1889.

Scharf, J. Thomas. *History of Maryland*. Hatboro, Pa.: Tradition Press, 1967.

_____. *History of Western Maryland*. Philadelphia, Pa.: L. H. Evarts, 1882.

_____. *The Personal Memoirs of Jonathan Thomas Scharf of the First Maryland Artillery*. Ed. Tom Kelley. Baltimore, Md.: Butternut and Blue, 1992.

Schildt, John W. *Antietam Hospitals*. Chewsville, Md.: Antietam Publications, 1987.

_____. *Roads to Antietam*. Hagerstown, Md.: Antietam Publications, 1985.

_____. *September Echoes*. Middletown, Md.: Valley Register, 1960.

Sears, Stephen W. *Landscape Turned Red: The Battle of Antietam*. New York: Popular Library Books, 1985.

Small, Abner. *Road to Richmond: The Civil War Memoirs of Major Abner Small of the 16th Maine Volunteers*. Ed. Harold Adamson Small. Berkeley: University of California Press, 1939.

Smith, John P. "Accounts of Damage." *Antietam Valley Record*. 3 October 1895.

_____. "The Battle of Antietam—Hospitals." *Antietam Valley Record*. 31 October 1895.

_____. "The Battle of Antietam—Hospitals." *Antietam Valley Record*. 6 November 1895.

_____. "Reminiscences of Sharpsburg, Maryland." *Antietam Valley Record*. 26 September 1895.

"Smith's Diary Recalls Day Civil War Spy Was Hung." *The News*. 23 March 1961.

Spaur, Michael L. "What's in a Name?" *The News*. 2 May 1979.

"Spies, Smugglers and Guerillas Were Among Those Reported as Operating Here During the Civil War." *Valley News Echo Special*. 17 April 1963.

Spooner, Henry J. *The Maryland Campaign with the Fourth Rhode Island*. Providence: Snow and Farnham, 1903.

Stearns, Austin. *Three Years with Company K*. Ed. Arthur A. Kent. Cranbury, N.J.: Fairleigh Dickinson University Press, 1976.

Steiner, Lewis H., M.D. *Report of Lewis H. Steiner*. New York: Anson D. F. Randolph, 1862.

Stevens, John W. *Reminiscences of the Civil War.* Hillsboro, Tex.: Hillsboro Mirror Printing, 1902.

Stone, James Madison. *Personal Recollections of the Civil War.* Boston, 1918.

Stonebraker, Joseph R. *A Rebel of '61.* New York: Wynkoop Hallenbeck Crawford Company, 1899.

Stotelmyer, Steven R. "The Truth About Wise's Well: Setting the Record Straight on South Mountain." *Blue and Gray* (October 1990).

Strong, George Templeton. *The Diary of George Templeton Strong: The Civil War, 1860–1865.* Ed. Allan Nevins and Milton H. Thomas. New York: Macmillan, 1952.

Strother, David Hunter. *A Virginia Yankee in the Civil War: The Diaries of David Hunter Strother.* Ed. Cecil D. Eby Jr. Chapel Hill: University of North Carolina Press, 1961.

The Survivors' Association. *History of the Corn Exchange Regiment, 118th Pennsylvania Volunteers, from the First Engagement at Antietam to Appomattox.* Philadelphia: 1892.

Tappert, Annette, ed. *The Brothers War: Civil War Letters to Their Loved Ones from the Blue and Gray.* New York: Times Books, Random House, 1988.

"Tilghmanton Man Was Another 'Good Samaritan of Antietam.'" *The Daily Mail.* 29 April 1961.

Toomey, Daniel Carroll. *The Civil War in Maryland.* Baltimore: Toomey Press, 1983.

Trout, Robert J. *They Followed the Plume: The Story of J. E. B. Stuart and His Staff.* Harrisburg: Stackpole Books, 1993.

Tyler, Mason Whiting. *Recollections of the Civil War.* New York: G. P. Putnam's Sons, 1912.

The Urbana Civic Association. *History and Legends of Urbana Election District, Frederick County, Maryland.* Frederick, Md., 1976.

Von Borcke, Heros. *Memoirs of the Confederate War for Independence,* Vol. 1. 1867; reprint ed. New York: Peter Smith, 1938.

Walcott, Charles F. *History of the Twenty-First Regiment Massachusetts Volunteers in the War for the Preservation of the Union, 1861–1865.* Boston: Houghton Mifflin, 1882.

Wallace, Lew. *Lew Wallace: An Autobiography,* Vol. 2. New York: Harper and Brothers, 1906.

Ware, John N. "Sharpsburg." *Confederate Veteran* (April 1821).

Warfield, Edgar. *A Confederate Soldier's Memoirs.* Richmond: Masonic Home Press, 1936.

Warren, Mame, and Marion E. Warren. *Maryland Time Exposures, 1840–1940.* Baltimore: Johns Hopkins University Press, 1984.

Watson, William. *Letters of a Civil War Surgeon.* Ed. Paul Fatout. West Lafayette, Ind.: Purdue Research Foundation, 1961.

White, John Goldsborough. "A Rebel's Memoirs of the Civil War." *The Sun.* 19 May 1929.

Whittier, John Greenleaf. "Barbara Frietchie." *Atlantic Monthly* (October 1863).

Wightman, Edward King. *From Antietam to Fort Fisher: The Civil War Letters of Edward King Wightman, 1862–1865.* Cranbury, N.J.: Associated University Presses, 1985.

Williams, Thomas J. C. *History and Biographical Record of Washington County, Maryland.* John M. Runk and L. R. Titsworth, 1906.

Williams, Thomas J. C., and Folger McKinsey. *History of Frederick County, Maryland.* Frederick, Md.: L. R. Titsworth & Company, 1910.

Woodward, E. M. *Our Campaigns.* Philadelphia: John E. Potter and Company, 1865.

Worthington, Glenn. *Fighting for Time.* Frederick, 1932.

Yeager, Chris. "War Exacts Ultimate Price from Rohrbach Family." *Maryland Cracker Barrel* (August/September 1992).

><+>·O·<+><

## Local Historians/Descendants Cited

Doug Bast, Boonsborough Museum of History, Boonsboro, Md., 7 January 1994.

Carl Brown, Maryland Room, C. Burr Artz Public Library, Frederick, Md., 2 May 1997.

Maxine Campbell, Sharpsburg, Md., 1 May 1997.

Galen Hahn, Winston-Salem, North Carolina, 1 and 14 April, 1997 (correspondence).

Missy Kretzer, Sharpsburg, Md., 18 September 1998.

Wilmer Mumma, Sharpsburg, Md., 14 September 1998.

Mary Anna Munch, Sharpsburg, Md., 27 April 1997.

Tim Reese, Burkittsville, Md., 28 April 1997.

Earl and Annabelle Roulette, Sharpsburg, Md., 30 May 1997.

**Newspapers Cited**
*The Antietam Valley Record* (Keedysville?, Md.)
*The Daily Mail* (Hagerstown, Md.)
*The Examiner* (Frederick, Md.)
*Frederick Gazette* (Frederick, Md.)
*Morning Herald* (Hagerstown, Md.)
*The News* (Frederick, Md.)
*The Odd Fellow* (Boonsboro, Md.)
*Rochester Daily Democrat and American* (Rochester, N.Y.)
*The Sun* (Baltimore, Md.)
*The Valley Register* (Middletown, Md.)

# INDEX